DISCARD

ELFQUEST:
WOLFRIDER
VOLUME ONE

ELFQUEST CREATED BY
**WENDY &
RICHARD PINI**

ELFQUEST:
WOLFRIDER
VOLUME **ONE**

ELFQUEST: WOLFRIDER VOLUME ONE
Published by DC Comics. Cover, compilation,
timeline and character introduction copyright
© 2003 Warp Graphics, Inc. All Rights Reserved.

Originally published in single magazine form in
ELFQUEST VOL. 2, NUMBER 19, 21, 23, 25, 27, 29,
31; ELFQUEST-BLOOD OF TEN CHIEFS #2;
ELFQUEST-HIDDEN YEARS #5; ELFQUEST-NEW
BLOOD SPECIAL #1; ELFQUEST-NEW BLOOD 1993
SPECIAL #1. Copyright © 1992, 1993, 1997, 1998
Warp Graphics, Inc. All Rights Reserved. All
characters, their distinctive likenesses and
related elements featured in this publication are
trademarks of Warp Graphics, Inc. The stories,
characters and incidents featured in this
publication are entirely fictional. DC Comics
does not read or accept unsolicited submissions
of ideas, stories or artwork.

DC Comics, 1700 Broadway, New York, NY 10019
A Warner Bros. Entertainment Company
Printed in Canada. Second Printing.
ISBN: 1-4012-0131-8

Cover illustration by Wendy Pini

QUEST: WOLFRIDER VOLUME ONE

The ElfQuest Saga is an ever-unfolding story spanning countless millennia that follows the adventures of humans, trolls and various elfin tribes. Some of the events that occur prior to the time of this volume are outlined below using the very first published ElfQuest story, "Fire & Flight," as a benchmark. That tale will be released in this format in 2004.

0

1,000

2,000

2,000 - 300 YEARS BEFORE

Goodtree, eighth chief of the Wolfriders, founds a new Holt deep in the woods and creates the Father Tree where the Wolfriders can all live. Her son, *Mantricker*, is the first in several generations to have to deal with nomadic humans again.

Mantricker's son, *Bearclaw*, discovers Greymung's trolls who live in the caverns and tunnels beneath the Holt. Bearclaw becomes the Wolfriders' tenth chief.

In the distant Forbidden Grove near Blue Mountain, *Petalwing* and the preservers tirelessly protect their mysterious wrapstuff bundles.

Among the Wolfriders, *Treestump, Clearbrook, Moonshade, Strongbow, One-Eye, Redlance, Pike, Rainsong* and *Woodlock* are born.

4,000 YEARS BEFORE

Freefoot leads the Wolfriders during a prosperous time. Game is plentiful and life is easy.

Freefoot's son, Oakroot, subsequently becomes chief and later takes the name *Tanner*.

3,000

4,000

5,000

9,000 YEARS BEFORE

Wolfrider chief Timmorn feels the conflict between his elf and wolf sides, and leaves the tribe to find his own destiny. *Rahnee the She-Wolf* takes over as leader, followed by her son *Prey-Pacer*.

6,000

7,000

10,000 YEARS BEFORE

Over time, the early High Ones become too many for their faraway planet to support. Eventually groups of these beings travel into space to seek out possibilities on other worlds, bringing along trolls and preservers as helpers. *Timmain's* group discovers the World of Two Moons, but as the crystalline ship approaches, the trolls revolt. The High Ones lose control and crash-land far in the new world's past. Ape-like primitive humans greet them with brutality, and the elfin High Ones scatter into the surrounding forest.

In order to survive, Timmain magically takes on a wolf's form and hunts for the other elves. In time, the High Ones adapt, making a spartan life for themselves. *Timmorn*, first chief of the Wolfriders, is born to Timmain and a true wolf.

8,000

9,000

10,000 YEARS BEFORE

10,000

0
475
600
1,000
2,000
3,000
4,000
5,000
6,000
7,000
8,000
9,000
10,000

475 YEARS BEFORE

Strongbow, out hunting without permission from his chief, finds himself running for his life from a very angry bear.

OUR STORY BEGINS HERE...

7,000 YEARS BEFORE

A crucial event occurs during the reign of the fourth chief of the Wolfriders: Swift-Spear goes to war for the first time against the humans of a nearby village. The humans are forced to leave, and he earns the name *Two-Spear.*

Two-Spear has strange dreams of the humans returning and believes the elves are no longer safe. He becomes obsessed by the dreams and tries repeatedly to convince the Wolfriders they must wipe out the human threat for all time. When his chieftainship is challenged by his sister *Huntress Skyfire,* the tribe splits. Two-Spear leaves with his followers, and Skyfire becomes chief of the remaining tribe.

600 YEARS BEFORE

Deep in the desert to the south of the Holt, *Rayek* is born to Sun Villagers Jarrah and Ingen. *Leetah* is born to Suntoucher and Toorah twelve years later.

10,000 – 8,000 YEARS BEFORE

In a long diaspora, descendants of the High Ones wander the world. *Savah* and her family settle the Sun Village in the desert at Sorrow's End. Lord Voll and the Gliders move into Blue Mountain and shut themselves away from the world.

Guttlekraw becomes king of the trolls, who have fled to the cold north.

Ekuar and two rock-shaper companions discover the abandoned palace-ship of the High Ones but are enslaved by Guttlekraw. Glaciers force the trolls to move south, tunneling under the future Holt of the Wolfriders.

Greymung rebels against Guttlekraw. Guttlekraw and his cohorts return north, and the three rock-shaper elves escape in the melee. Greymung, now king of the forest trolls, sends a scout to search for the escaped trio.

Winnowill leaves Blue Mountain, finds the troll, seduces him and gives birth to *Two-Edge.* She later kills the troll.

The ElfQuest saga spans thousands of years and to date has introduced readers to hundreds of characters. At the time of the stories in this volume, these are the major characters you will meet and get to know.

THE WOLFRIDERS

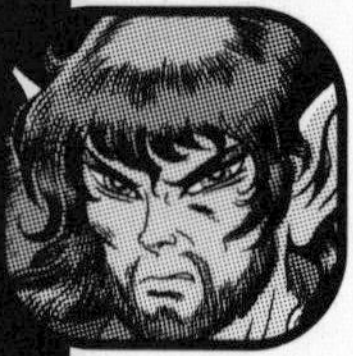

BEARCLAW

Tenth chief of the Wolfriders, Bearclaw leads the tribe in decisive fashion. Still, he prides himself in his ability to track, hunt and fight on his own, often going out solo against the tribe's better judgment. He's quick to action but is also easily tempted by dreamberry wine or gambling with the trolls. Joyleaf is the only one able to persuade him away from a course he's set.

JOYLEAF

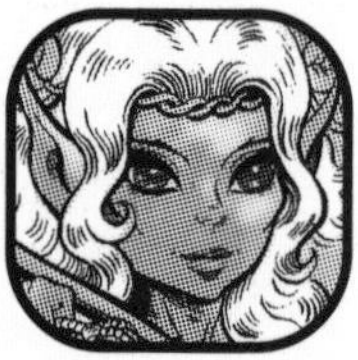

Bearclaw's lifemate is the one elf who can channel his fiery temper and energies into something productive. Joyleaf's wisdom often has prevented the tribe from making a foolish mistake. While she loves her mate, she remains fierce in her own convictions and is a force to reckon with when her tribe or her cub Cutter are threatened.

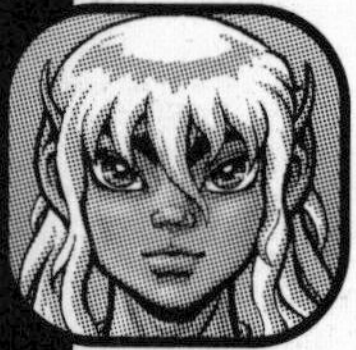

CUTTER

While his name denotes his skill with a sword, Cutter is not a cold and merciless death-dealer. Strong in his beliefs, he will nevertheless bend even the most fundamental of them if the well-being of his tribe is at stake. Skywise believes that what sets Cutter apart from all past Wolfrider chieftains is his imagination and ability to not only accept change, but take advantage of it.

SKYWISE

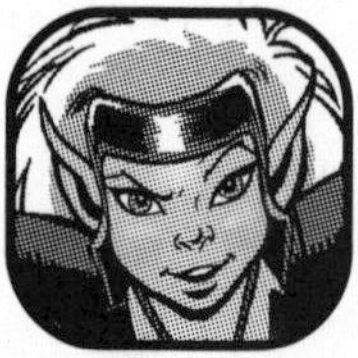

Orphaned at birth, Skywise is the resident stargazer of the Wolfriders, and only his interest in elf maidens rivals his passion for understanding the mysteries of the universe. Skywise is Cutter's counselor, confidant, and closest friend. While he is capable of deep seriousness, nothing can diminish Skywise's jovial and rakish manner.

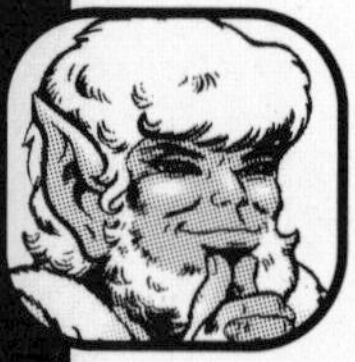

TREESTUMP

Seemingly gruff and no-nonsense, Treestump also has a vulnerable side, especially when it comes to protecting the well-being of his tribemates. More than a thousand years of living with "the Way" has given Treestump a wellspring of wisdom, allowing him to find calm even in the face of great danger. He is something of a father figure to the entire tribe.

STRONGBOW

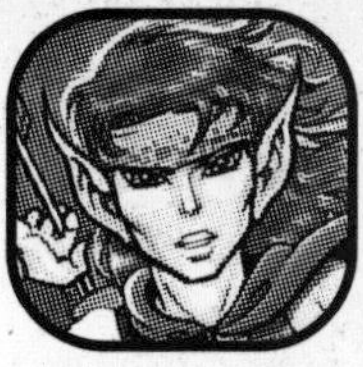

Strongbow is the reserved, silent master archer of the Wolfriders. Ever the devil's advocate, he is often proved right but finds no value in saying "I told you so." Strongbow is extremely serious, rarely smiles, and prefers sending to audible speech. He is completely devoted to his lifemate, Moonshade, and intensely proud of their son Dart.

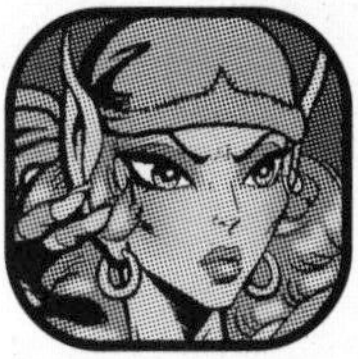

NIGHTFALL

Nightfall is the beautiful counterpoint to her lifemate, Redlance, and one of the most skilled hunters in the tribe. She is cool and calculated, neither vengeful nor violent unless absolutely necessary. The relationship between Nightfall and Redlance is very much one of yin and yang. Nightfall grew up with Cutter and is strongly loyal to the young chief.

REDLANCE

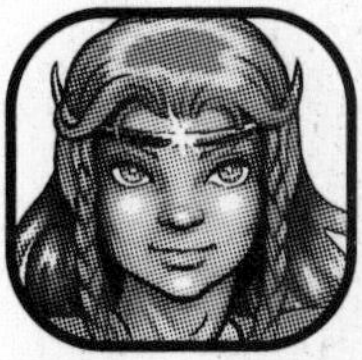

Redlance is the sweet-natured plantshaper of the Wolfriders. Indeed, he will only use his talents defensively to protect the tribe. Redlance is too much a pacifist at heart to do willful harm, and this gentleness makes him a natural to care for the cubs of the tribe. Redlance is a master of the soft counsel, gently prodding other, more headstrong elves in the right direction.

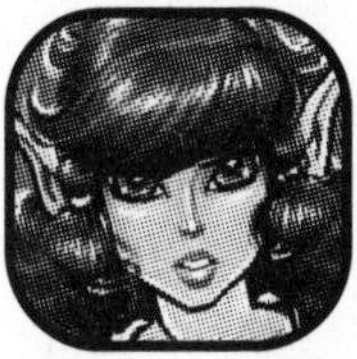

MOONSHADE

Moonshade is the Wolfriders' tanner. Though the process can be lengthy and tedious, she enjoys the quiet hours spent bringing the beauty out of a supple hide. Moonshade, like her lifemate Strongbow, is very much a traditionalist, strong-minded and with unshakable beliefs. Completely devoted to her mate, Moonshade will defend him even when she knows he's wrong.

SCOUTER

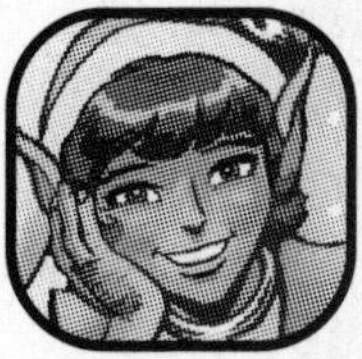

Scouter has the sharpest eyes of all the Wolfriders. He is steadfast, loyal, and often overprotective. He is also extremely intolerant of anyone, tribemates included, whom he perceives as putting his loved ones in jeopardy. Dewshine and Scouter have been lovemates for most of their lives, yet are not Recognized.

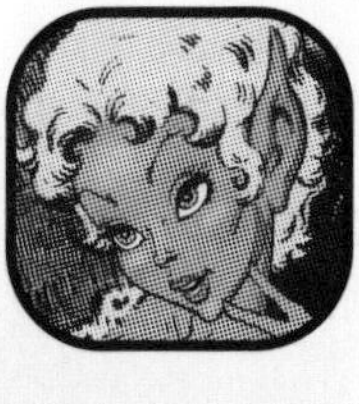

DEWSHINE

Dewshine, swift and graceful as a deer, is the most agile and free-spirited of the Wolfriders – and that takes some doing! She has a beautiful voice, full of melody and laughter. Song and dance are passions with her, and she has a talent for mimicking birdsong.

CLEARBROOK

Calm, dignified and thoughtful, choosing her words carefully, Clearbrook is the eldest female Wolfrider. An elder of the tribe, she advises in a quiet manner that masks the fierceness of an accomplished warrior, but her fury knows no bounds if her loved ones are threatened.

ONE-EYE

Woodhue gained his new sobriquet after his right eye was put out by humans. Needless to say, this seeded a lifelong hatred and distrust of the "five-fingers." Although he still considers Cutter a cub, One-Eye never questions Cutter's judgments; Cutter is chief and that is that. One-Eye is fierce in battle, especially when his cub, Scouter, or his lifemate, Clearbrook, is endangered.

PIKE

Pike is the Wolfriders' resident storyteller, taking his name from his preferred weapon. The most ordinary and happy-go-lucky of the Wolfriders, Pike has no grand ideals or desires for quests – he is a follower and rarely questions his chief's orders. Fully immersed in the "now of wolf thought" he clings through thick and thin to his two greatest loves: dreamberries and taking the easy path.

THE TROLLS

The trolls are the descendants of the ape-like servants of the firstcomers, who, having rebelled at their slave-like status within the palace-ship, caused the cosmic disaster that left them all stranded in the primeval, prehistoric era of the World of Two Moons. Taking to caves and tunnels beneath the land, they adapted over time to grow more massive, uglier and much greedier.

PICKNOSE

His name was inspired by his most prominent facial feature, which resembles the curved business end of a pick. The success of Picknose's interactions with the Wolfriders has been mixed at best, for while he does possess a sort of honor, he is also an opportunist of the first water.

OLD MAGGOTY

Old Maggoty was caught by Bearclaw one night stealing dreamberries near the Wolfriders' Holt. The two then became liaisons for their respective peoples in matters of trade. Old Maggoty is a master of herb lore and is renowned for brewing dreamberry wine, a potent lavender distillation that can set even the strongest-stomached elf on his pointed ear.

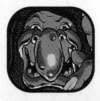

ODDBIT

Oddbit embodies all the troll maidenly virtues: she's greedy, deceptive, manipulative, coy, vain and fickle. She is the ultimate material girl, adorning the footstools of both King Guttlekraw and, later, King Greymung. After Picknose rescued her, Oddbit kept the lovesick troll dangling for years.

KING GUTTLEKRAW

Guttlekraw rules over the ferocious northern trolls who inhabit the caverns and tunnels surrounding the remains of the palace-like starship that brought the High Ones to the World of Two Moons. For thousands of years this merciless tyrant and his warriors have made certain that no elves can ever return to their ancestral vessel.

KING GREYMUNG

Compared to the rigors of life in the frozen north, Greymung and his forest trolls have it easy. While he may have shown some grit when he rebelled against Guttlekraw in the distant past, now Greymung has little to do but sit on his jewel-encrusted throne, mistrusting one and all in his underground kingdom.

TWO-EDGE

Two-Edge is the cunning half-troll, half-elf son of Winnowill and a troll named Smelt. An ingenious mastersmith and inventor, he is a teacher to the trolls. Like Timmorn, Two-Edge is unique on the World of Two Moons. Abused as a child by his mother, Two-Edge was devastated when she killed his father and now walks a fine line between cleverness and insanity.

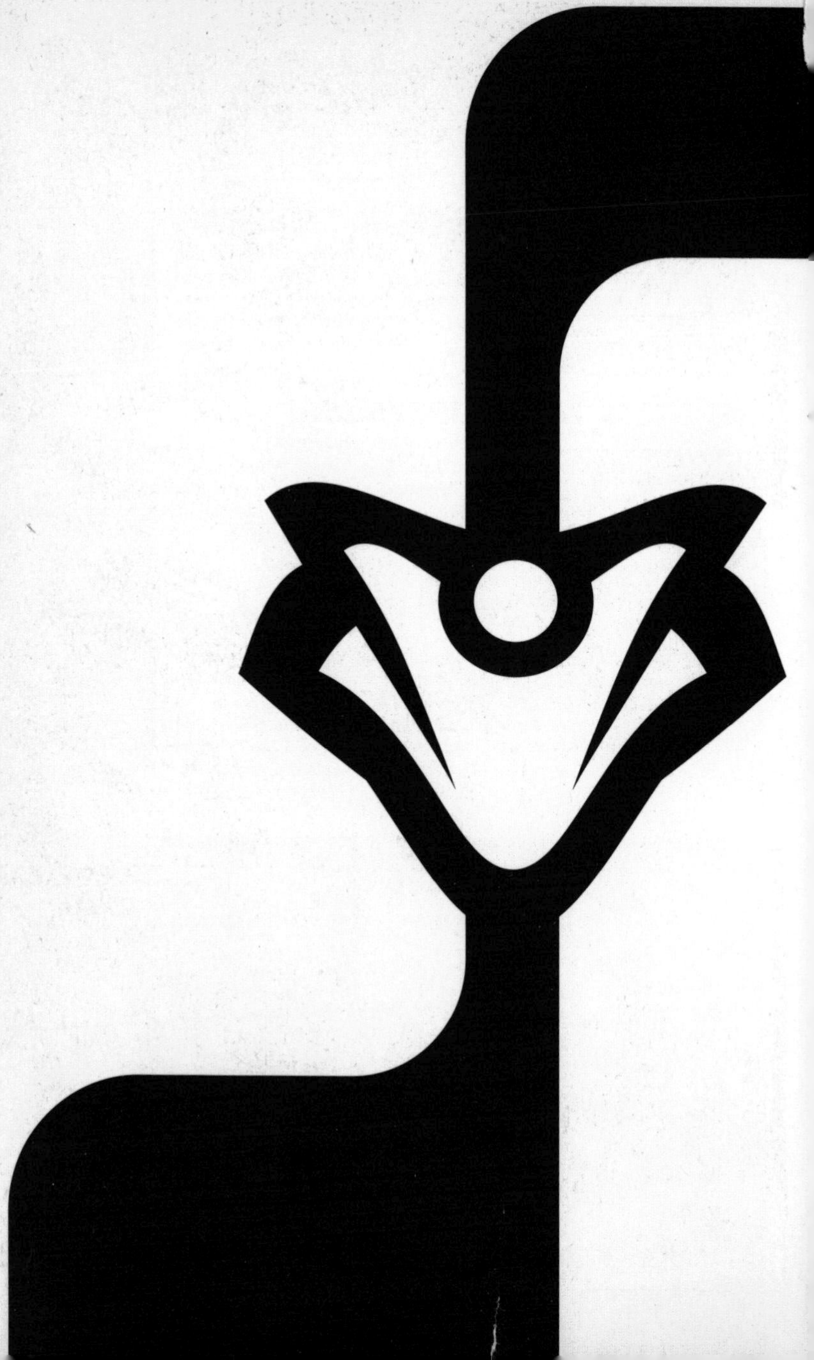

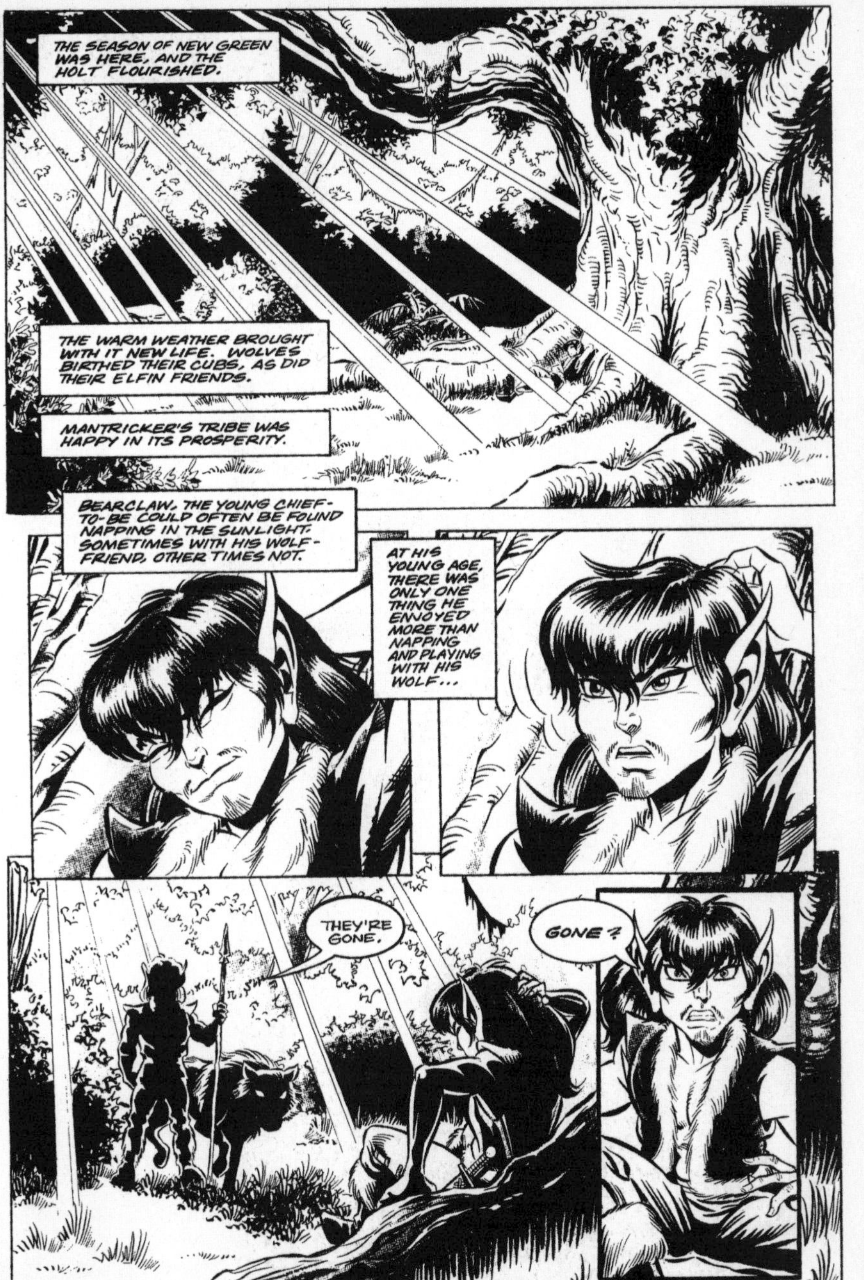
THE SEASON OF NEW GREEN WAS HERE, AND THE HOLT FLOURISHED.
THE WARM WEATHER BROUGHT WITH IT NEW LIFE. WOLVES BIRTHED THEIR CUBS, AS DID THEIR ELFIN FRIENDS.
MANTRICKER'S TRIBE WAS HAPPY IN ITS PROSPERITY.
BEARCLAW, THE YOUNG CHIEF-TO-BE COULD OFTEN BE FOUND NAPPING IN THE SUNLIGHT. SOMETIMES WITH HIS WOLF-FRIEND, OTHER TIMES NOT.
AT HIS YOUNG AGE, THERE WAS ONLY ONE THING HE ENJOYED MORE THAN NAPPING AND PLAYING WITH HIS WOLF...
THEY'RE GONE.
GONE?

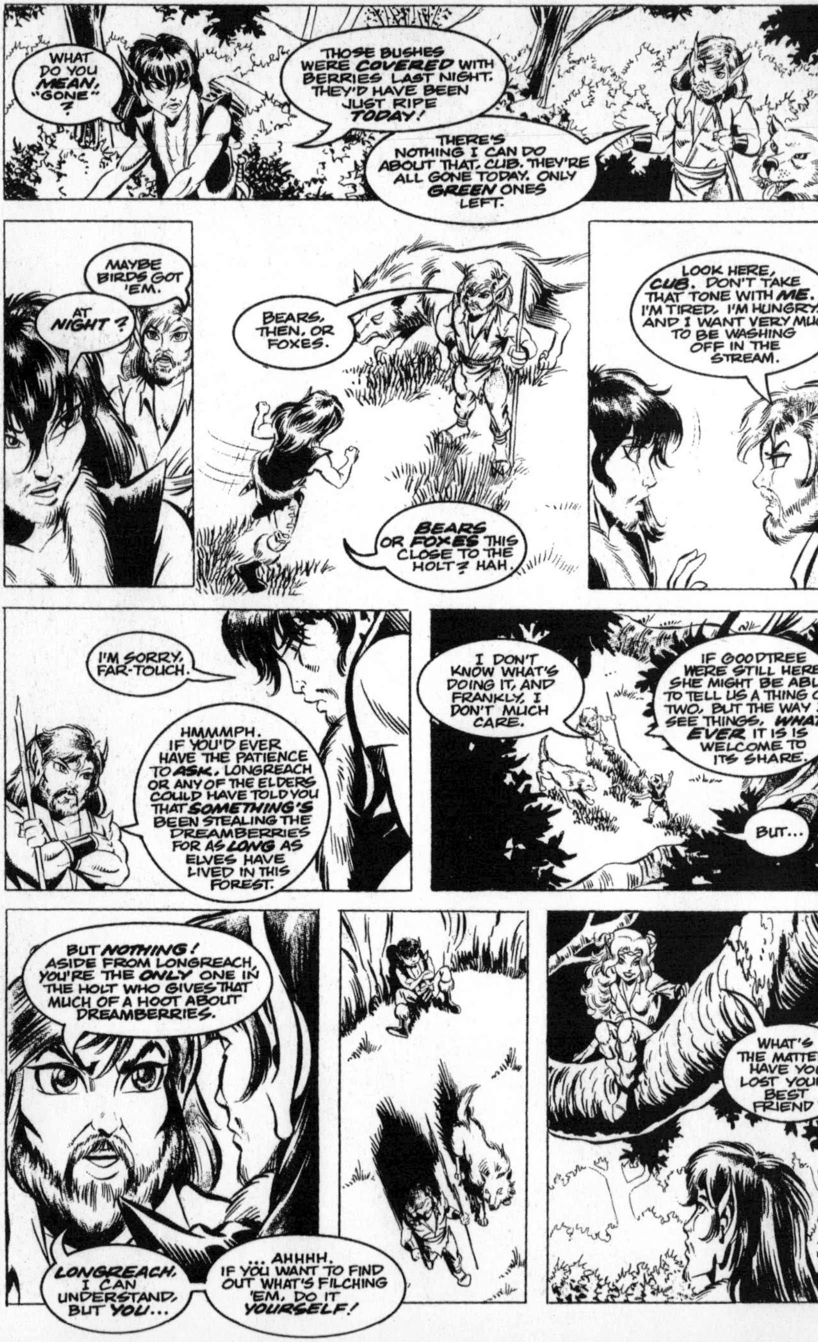
WHAT DO YOU MEAN, "GONE"?
THOSE BUSHES WERE COVERED WITH BERRIES LAST NIGHT. THEY'D HAVE BEEN JUST RIPE TODAY!
THERE'S NOTHING I CAN DO ABOUT THAT, CUB. THEY'RE ALL GONE TODAY. ONLY GREEN ONES LEFT.
MAYBE BIRDS GOT 'EM.
AT NIGHT?
BEARS, THEN, OR FOXES.
BEARS OR FOXES THIS CLOSE TO THE HOLT? HAH.
LOOK HERE, CUB. DON'T TAKE THAT TONE WITH ME. I'M TIRED, I'M HUNGRY, AND I WANT VERY MUCH TO BE WASHING OFF IN THE STREAM.
I'M SORRY, FAR-TOUCH.
HMMMPH. IF YOU'D EVER HAVE THE PATIENCE TO ASK, LONGREACH OR ANY OF THE ELDERS COULD HAVE TOLD YOU THAT SOMETHING'S BEEN STEALING THE DREAMBERRIES FOR AS LONG AS ELVES HAVE LIVED IN THIS FOREST.
I DON'T KNOW WHAT'S DOING IT, AND FRANKLY, I DON'T MUCH CARE.
IF GOODTREE WERE STILL HERE, SHE MIGHT BE ABLE TO TELL US A THING OR TWO, BUT THE WAY I SEE THINGS, WHATEVER IT IS IS WELCOME TO ITS SHARE.
BUT...
BUT NOTHING! ASIDE FROM LONGREACH, YOU'RE THE ONLY ONE IN THE HOLT WHO GIVES THAT MUCH OF A HOOT ABOUT DREAMBERRIES.
LONGREACH, I CAN UNDERSTAND, BUT YOU...
... AHHHH. IF YOU WANT TO FIND OUT WHAT'S FILCHING 'EM, DO IT YOURSELF!
WHAT'S THE MATTER? HAVE YOU LOST YOUR BEST FRIEND?

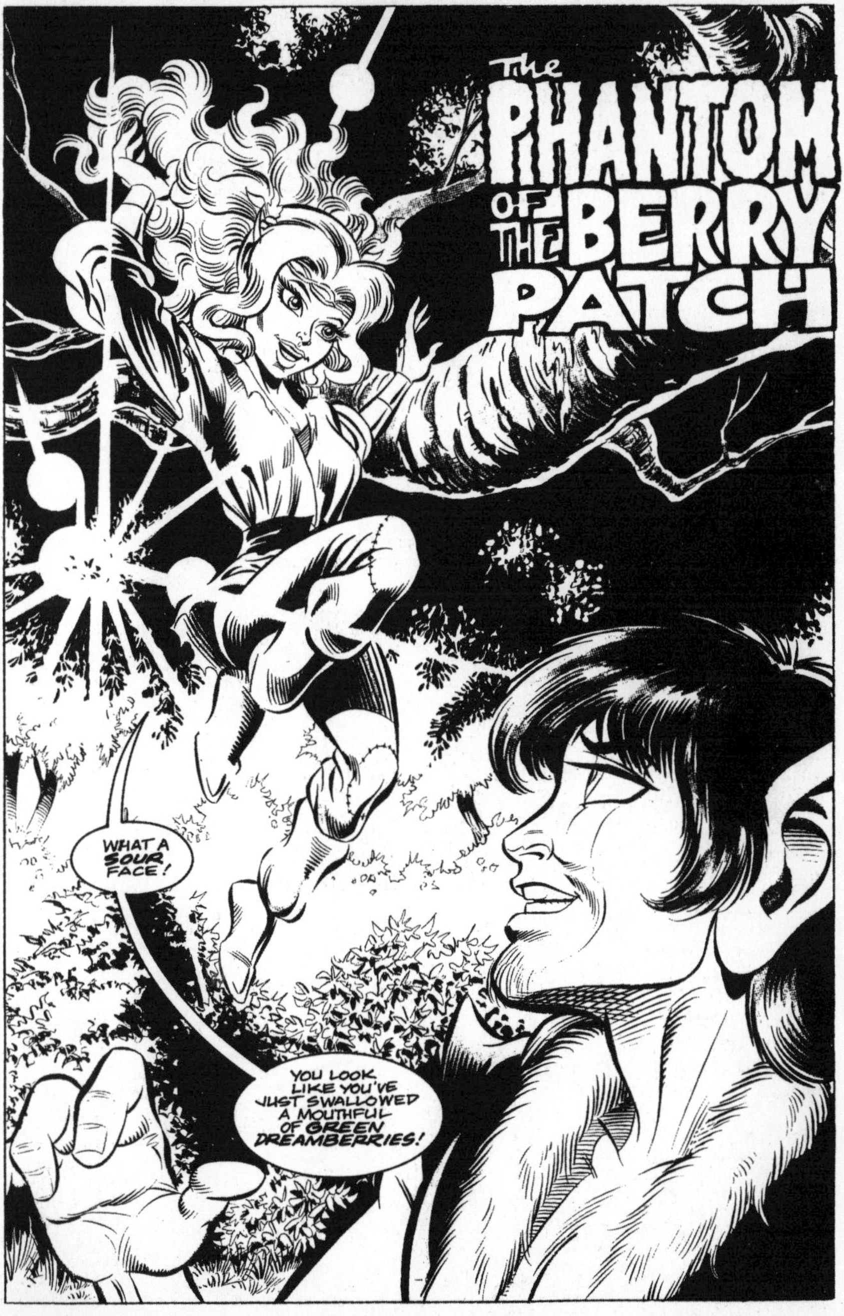
The PHANTOM OF THE BERRY PATCH
WHAT A SOUR FACE!
YOU LOOK LIKE YOU'VE JUST SWALLOWED A MOUTHFUL OF GREEN DREAMBERRIES!

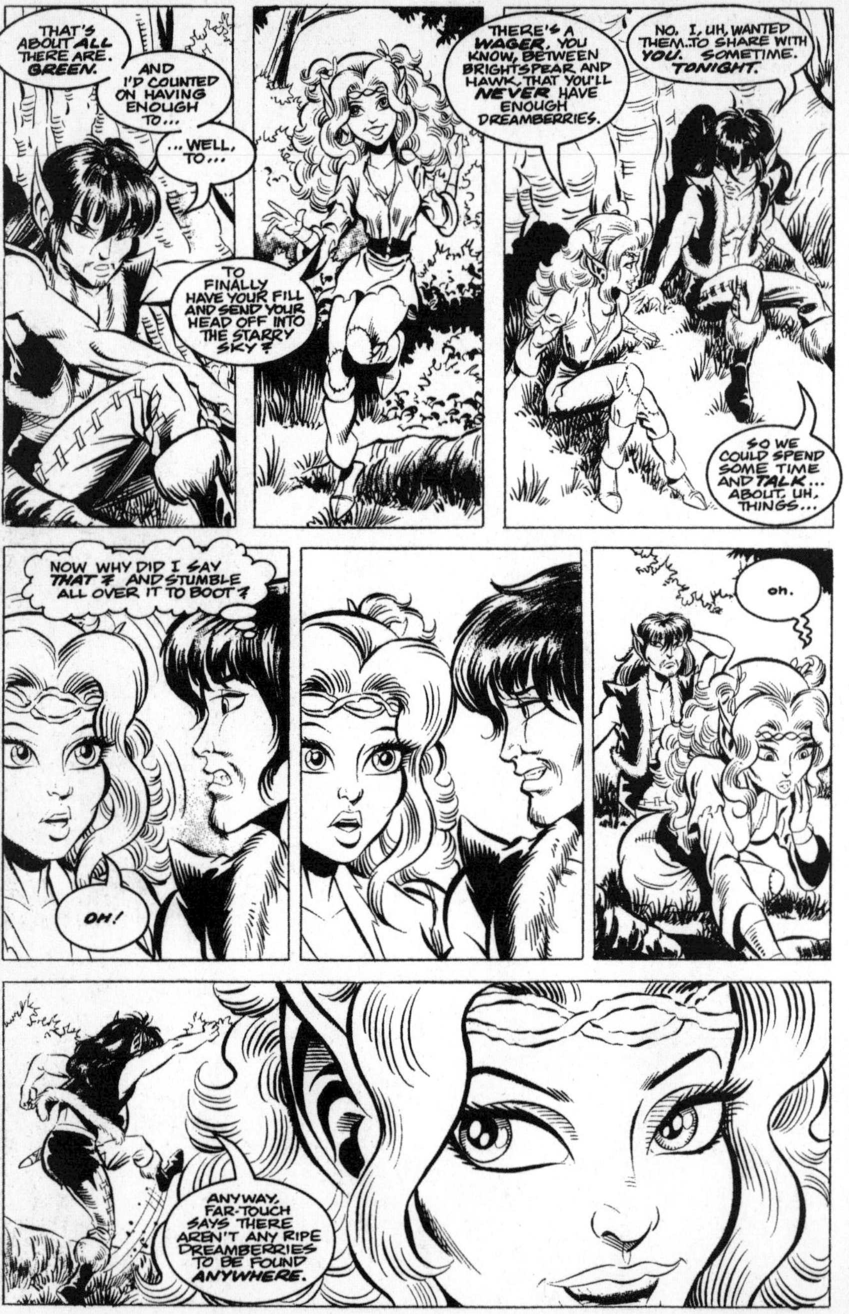

THAT'S ABOUT ALL THERE ARE. GREEN.
AND I'D COUNTED ON HAVING ENOUGH TO...
...WELL, TO...
TO FINALLY HAVE YOUR FILL AND SEND YOUR HEAD OFF INTO THE STARRY SKY?
THERE'S A WAGER, YOU KNOW, BETWEEN BRIGHTSPEAR AND HAWK, THAT YOU'LL NEVER HAVE ENOUGH DREAMBERRIES.
NO. I, UH, WANTED THEM...TO SHARE WITH YOU. SOMETIME. TONIGHT.
SO WE COULD SPEND SOME TIME AND TALK... ABOUT, UH, THINGS...
NOW WHY DID I SAY THAT? AND STUMBLE ALL OVER IT TO BOOT?
OH!
oh.
ANYWAY, FAR-TOUCH SAYS THERE AREN'T ANY RIPE DREAMBERRIES TO BE FOUND ANYWHERE.

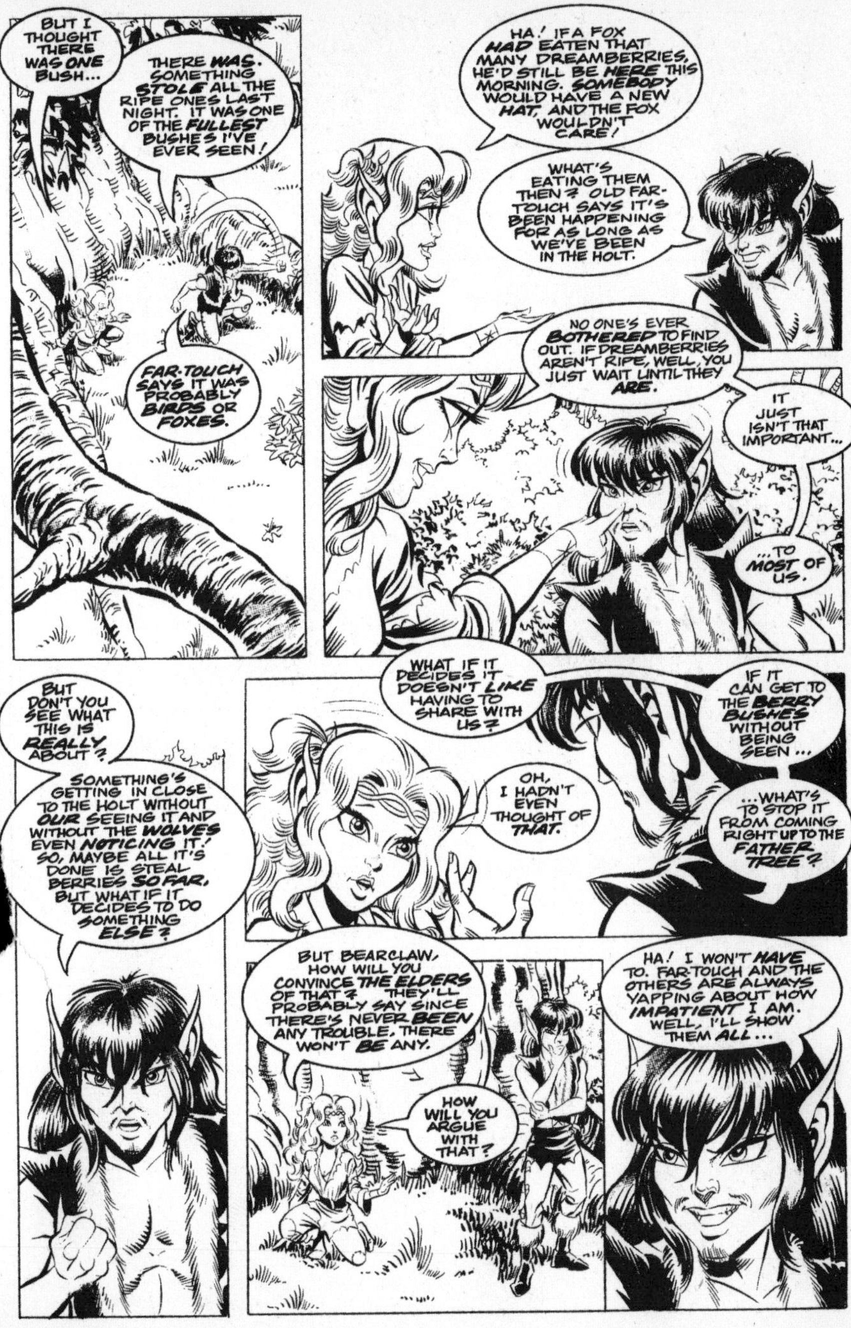
BUT I THOUGHT THERE WAS ONE BUSH...
THERE WAS. SOMETHING STOLE ALL THE RIPE ONES LAST NIGHT. IT WAS ONE OF THE FULLEST BUSHES I'VE EVER SEEN!
FAR-TOUCH SAYS IT WAS PROBABLY BIRDS OR FOXES.
HA! IF A FOX HAD EATEN THAT MANY DREAMBERRIES, HE'D STILL BE HERE THIS MORNING. SOMEBODY WOULD HAVE A NEW HAT, AND THE FOX WOULDN'T CARE!
WHAT'S EATING THEM THEN? OLD FAR-TOUCH SAYS IT'S BEEN HAPPENING FOR AS LONG AS WE'VE BEEN IN THE HOLT.
NO ONE'S EVER BOTHERED TO FIND OUT. IF DREAMBERRIES AREN'T RIPE, WELL, YOU JUST WAIT UNTIL THEY ARE.
IT JUST ISN'T THAT IMPORTANT...
...TO MOST OF US.
BUT DON'T YOU SEE WHAT THIS IS REALLY ABOUT?
SOMETHING'S GETTING IN CLOSE TO THE HOLT WITHOUT OUR SEEING IT AND WITHOUT THE WOLVES EVEN NOTICING IT! SO, MAYBE ALL IT'S DONE IS STEAL BERRIES SO FAR. BUT WHAT IF IT DECIDES TO DO SOMETHING ELSE?
WHAT IF IT DECIDES IT DOESN'T LIKE HAVING TO SHARE WITH US?
IF IT CAN GET TO THE BERRY BUSHES WITHOUT BEING SEEN...
...WHAT'S TO STOP IT FROM COMING RIGHT UP TO THE FATHER TREE?
OH, I HADN'T EVEN THOUGHT OF THAT.
BUT BEARCLAW, HOW WILL YOU CONVINCE THE ELDERS OF THAT? THEY'LL PROBABLY SAY SINCE THERE'S NEVER BEEN ANY TROUBLE, THERE WON'T BE ANY.
HOW WILL YOU ARGUE WITH THAT?
HA! I WON'T HAVE TO. FAR-TOUCH AND THE OTHERS ARE ALWAYS YAPPING ABOUT HOW IMPATIENT I AM. WELL, I'LL SHOW THEM ALL...

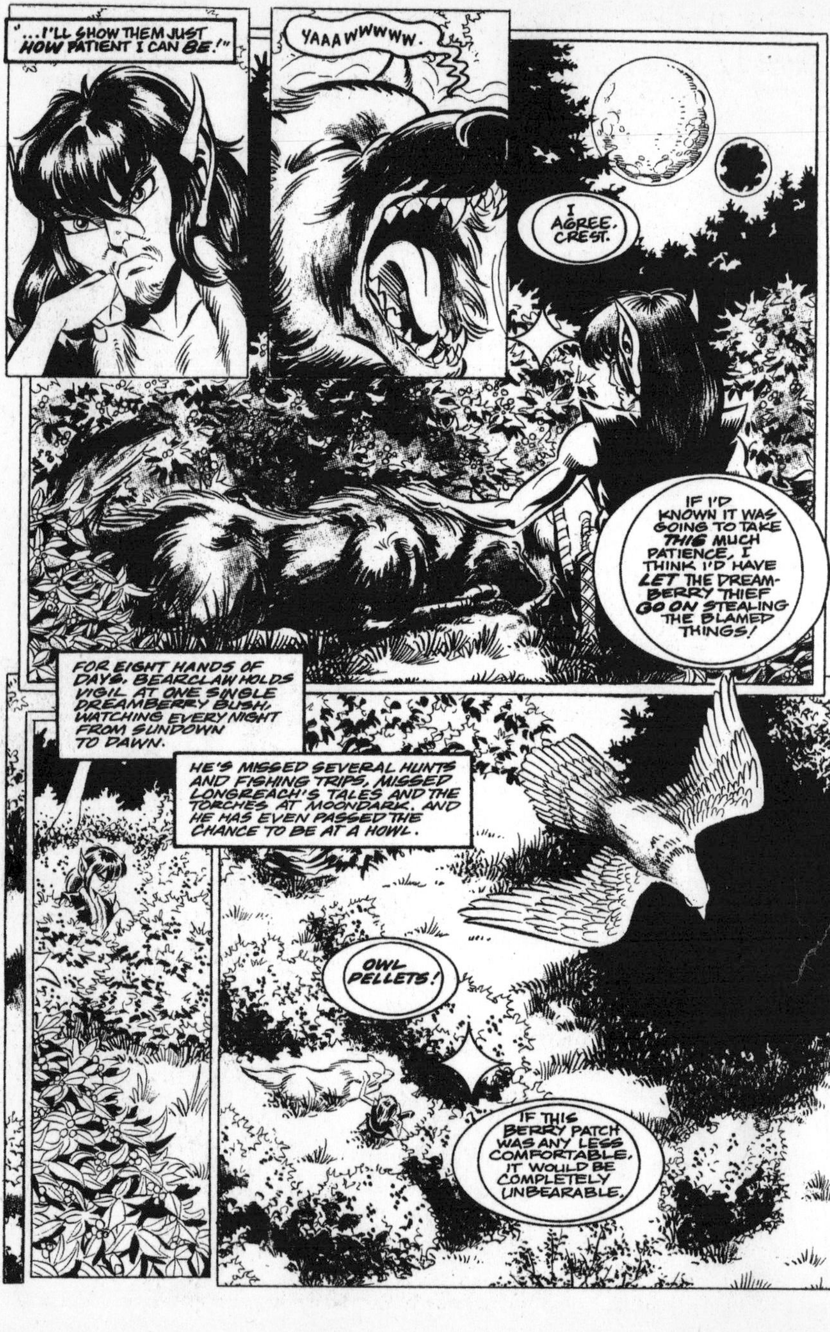
"...I'LL SHOW THEM JUST HOW PATIENT I CAN BE!"
YAAAWWWWW.
I AGREE, CREST.
IF I'D KNOWN IT WAS GOING TO TAKE THIS MUCH PATIENCE, I THINK I'D HAVE LET THE DREAMBERRY THIEF GO ON STEALING THE BLAMED THINGS!
FOR EIGHT HANDS OF DAYS, BEARCLAW HOLDS VIGIL AT ONE SINGLE DREAMBERRY BUSH, WATCHING EVERY NIGHT FROM SUNDOWN TO DAWN.
HE'S MISSED SEVERAL HUNTS AND FISHING TRIPS, MISSED LONGREACH'S TALES AND THE TORCHES AT MOONDARK. AND HE HAS EVEN PASSED THE CHANCE TO BE AT A HOWL.
OWL PELLETS!
IF THIS BERRY PATCH WAS ANY LESS COMFORTABLE, IT WOULD BE COMPLETELY UNBEARABLE.

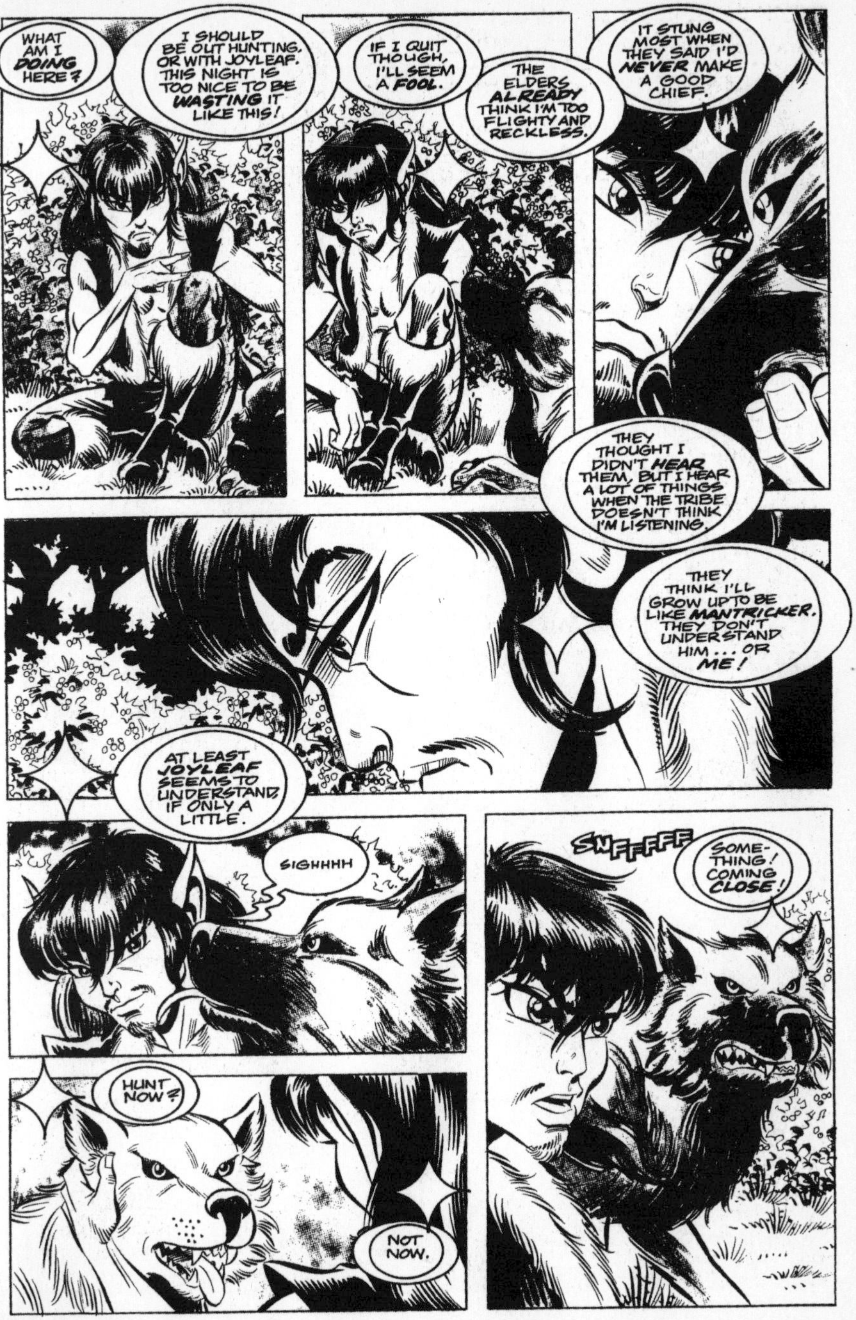
WHAT AM I DOING HERE?
I SHOULD BE OUT HUNTING, OR WITH JOYLEAF. THIS NIGHT IS TOO NICE TO BE WASTING IT LIKE THIS!
IF I QUIT THOUGH, I'LL SEEM A FOOL.
THE ELDERS ALREADY THINK I'M TOO FLIGHTY AND RECKLESS.
IT STUNG MOST WHEN THEY SAID I'D NEVER MAKE A GOOD CHIEF.
THEY THOUGHT I DIDN'T HEAR THEM, BUT I HEAR A LOT OF THINGS WHEN THE TRIBE DOESN'T THINK I'M LISTENING.
THEY THINK I'LL GROW UP TO BE LIKE MANTRICKER. THEY DON'T UNDERSTAND HIM ... OR ME!
AT LEAST JOYLEAF SEEMS TO UNDERSTAND, IF ONLY A LITTLE.
SIGHHHH
HUNT NOW?
NOT NOW.
SNFFFFF
SOME-THING! COMING CLOSE!

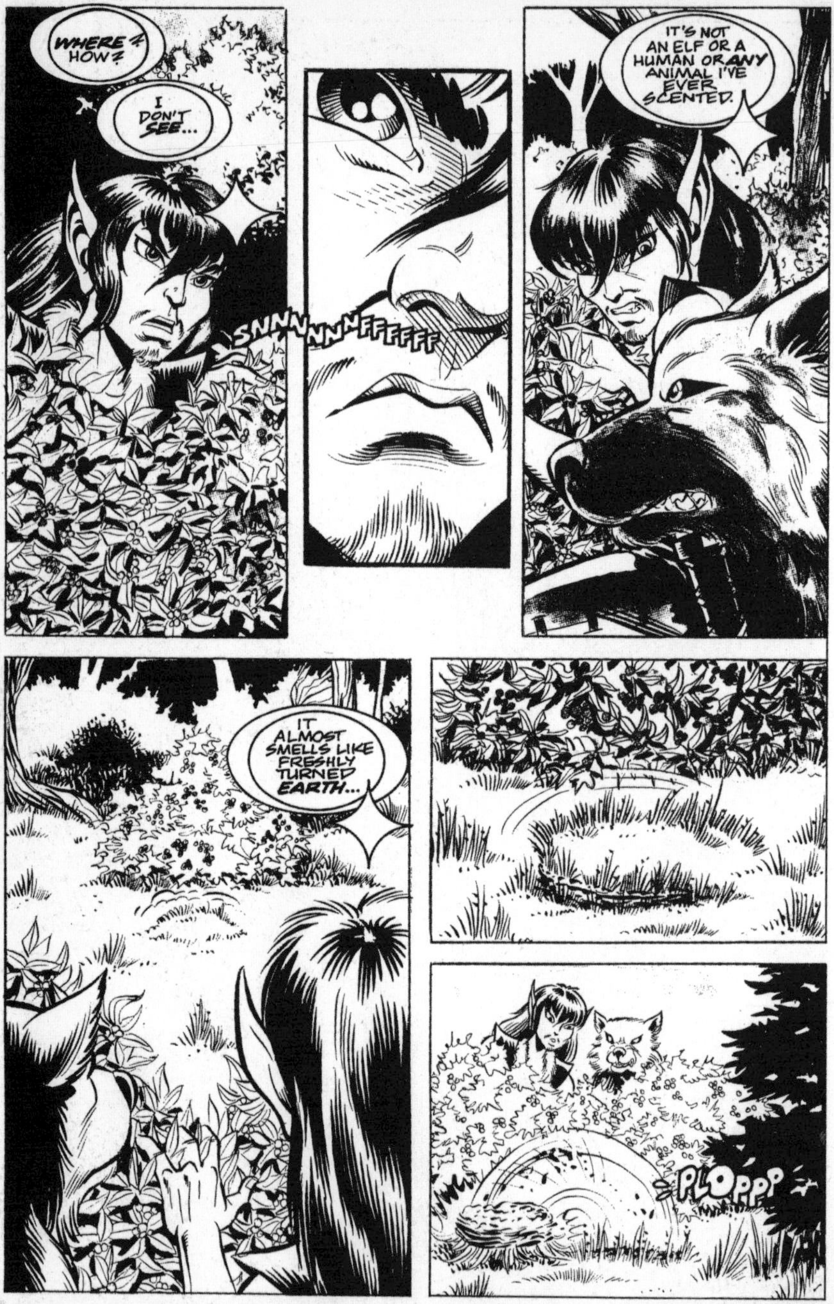
WHERE? HOW?
I DON'T SEE...
SNNNNNNNFFFFFF
IT'S NOT AN ELF OR A HUMAN OR ANY ANIMAL I'VE EVER SCENTED.
IT ALMOST SMELLS LIKE FRESHLY TURNED EARTH...
PLOPPP

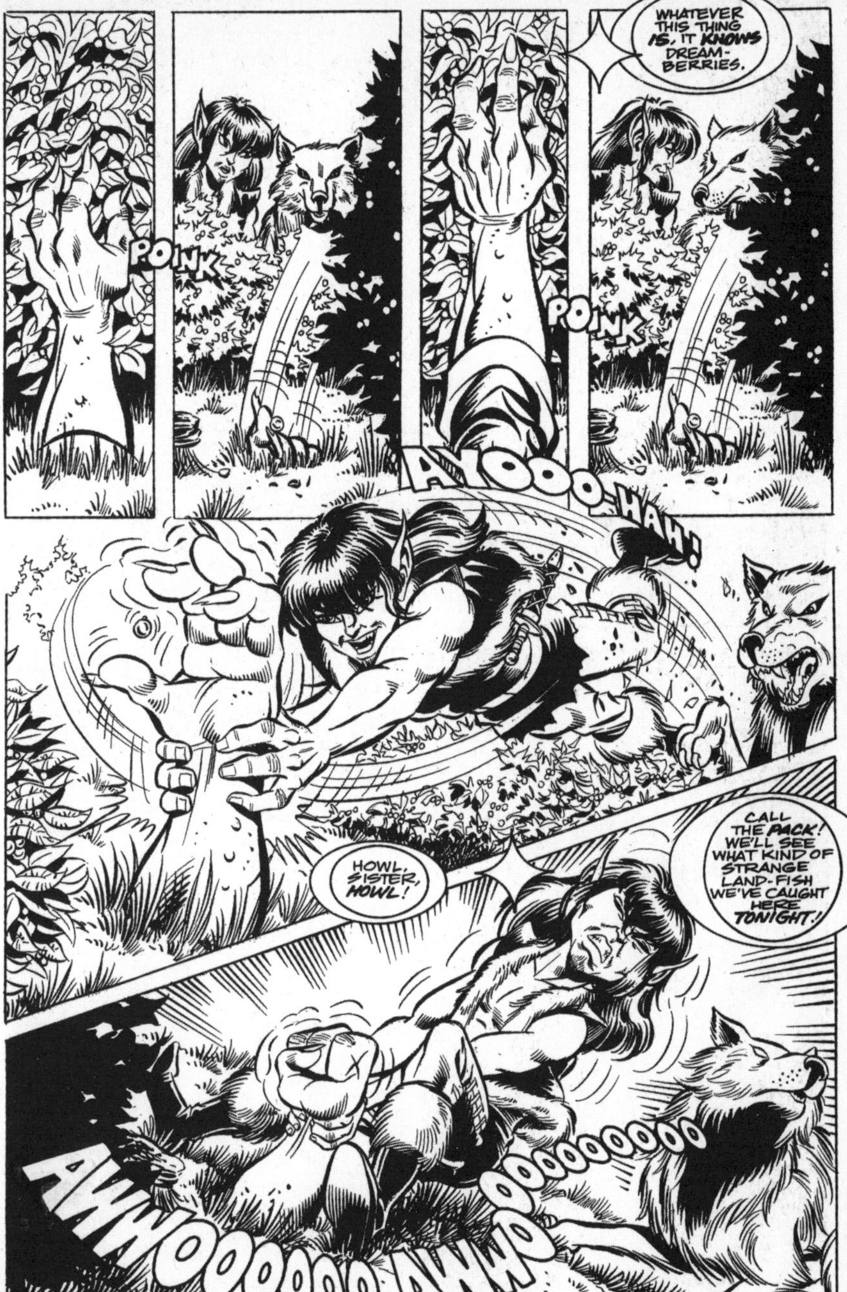
POINK
WHATEVER THIS THING IS, IT KNOWS DREAM-BERRIES.
POINK
AYOOO-HAH!
HOWL, SISTER, HOWL!
CALL THE PACK! WE'LL SEE WHAT KIND OF STRANGE LAND-FISH WE'VE CAUGHT HERE TONIGHT!
AWWOOOOOOO AWWOOOOOOOOOOO

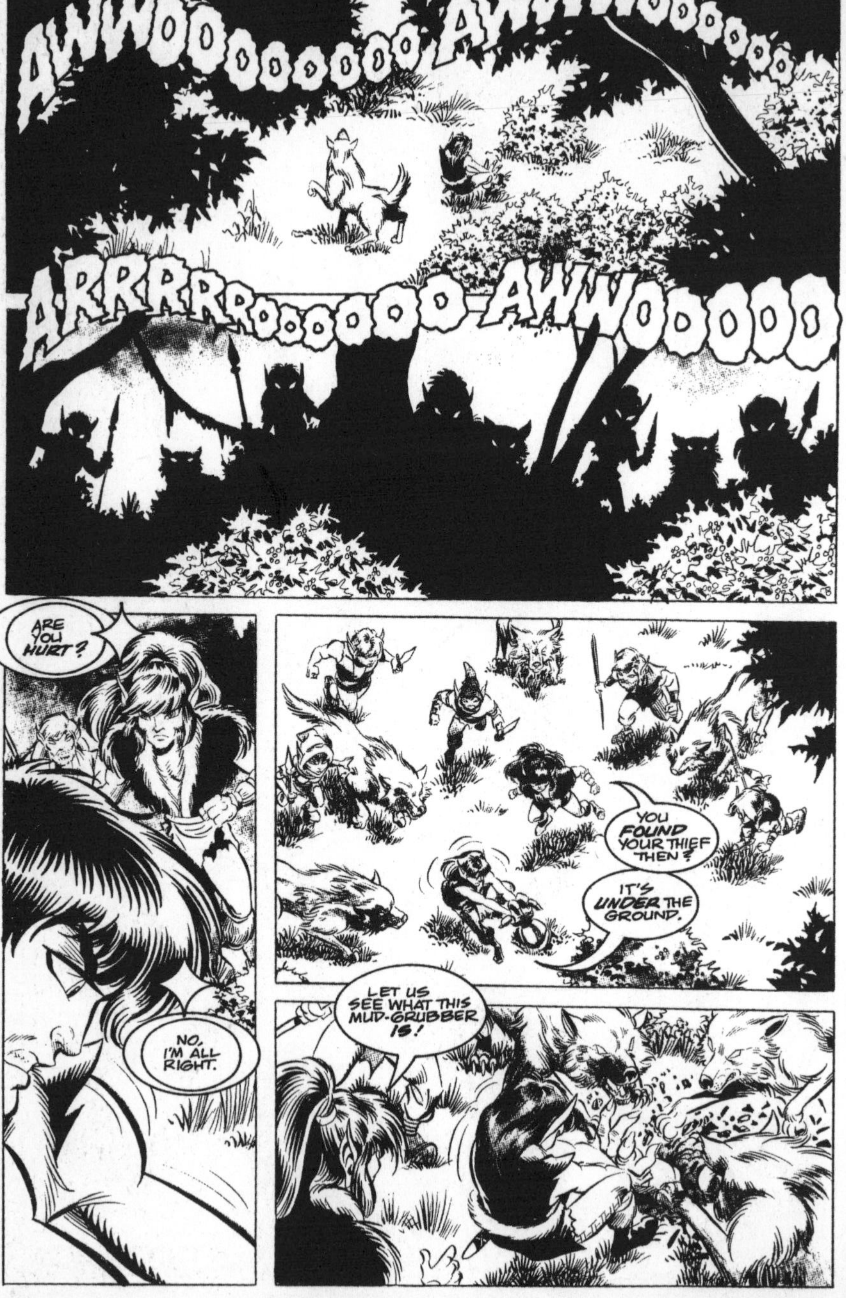
AWWOOOOOOOOO AWWWOOOOOOO
ARRRRROOOOOOO AWWOOOOO
ARE YOU HURT?
NO, I'M ALL RIGHT.
YOU FOUND YOUR THIEF THEN?
IT'S UNDER THE GROUND.
LET US SEE WHAT THIS MUD-GRUBBER IS!

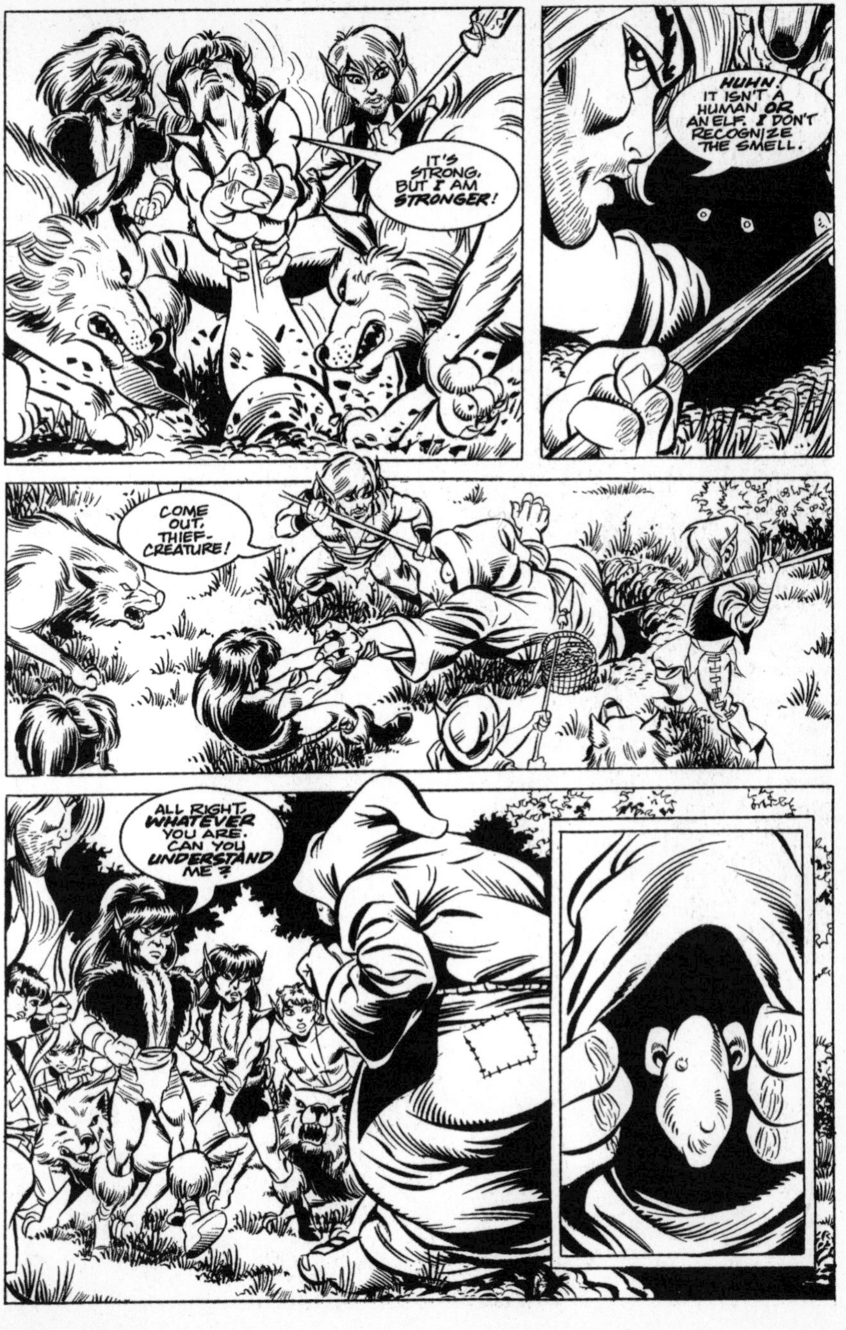
IT'S STRONG, BUT I AM STRONGER!
HUHN! IT ISN'T A HUMAN OR AN ELF. I DON'T RECOGNIZE THE SMELL.
COME OUT, THIEF-CREATURE!
ALL RIGHT, WHATEVER YOU ARE. CAN YOU UNDERSTAND ME?

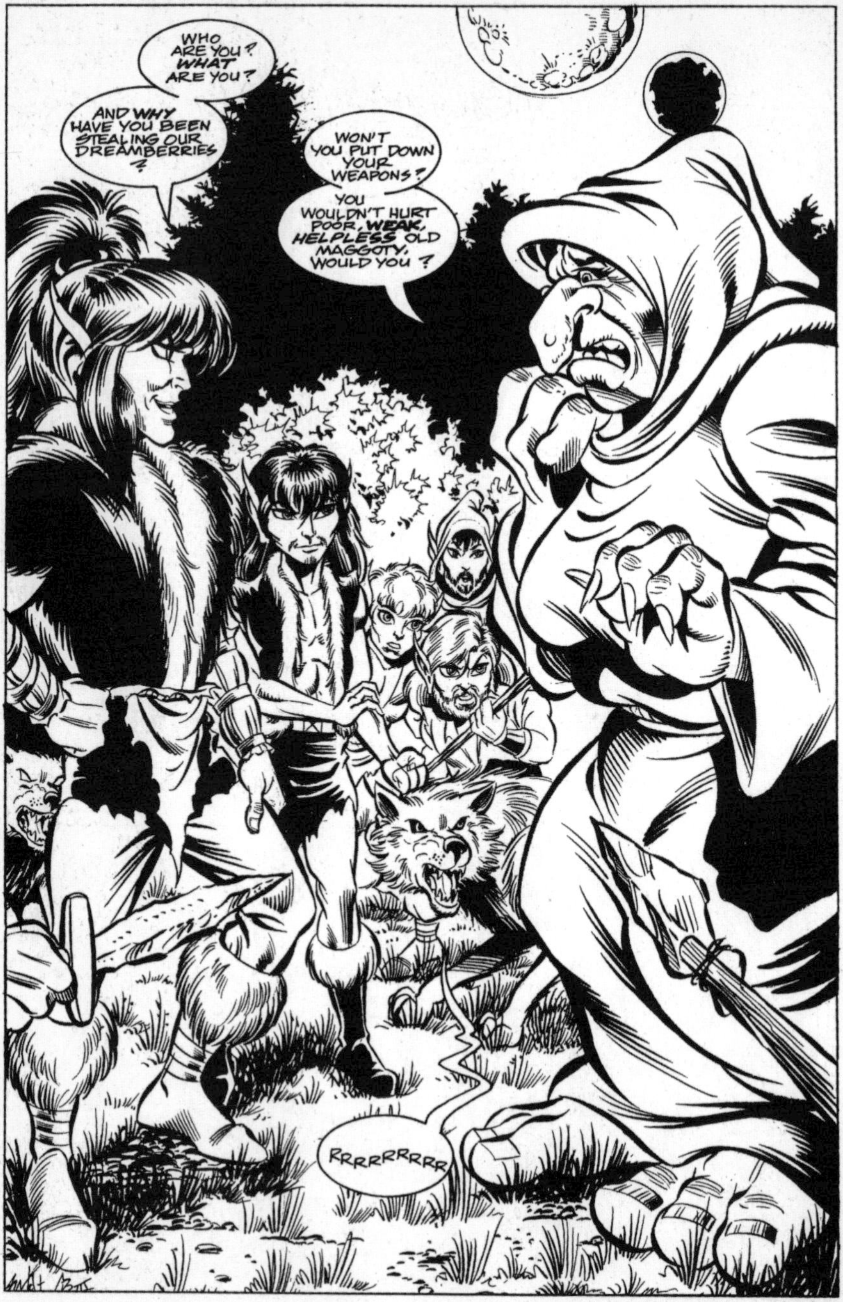
WHO ARE YOU? WHAT ARE YOU?
AND WHY HAVE YOU BEEN STEALING OUR DREAMBERRIES?
WON'T YOU PUT DOWN YOUR WEAPONS?
YOU WOULDN'T HURT POOR, WEAK, HELPLESS OLD MAGGOTY, WOULD YOU?
RRRRRRRRR

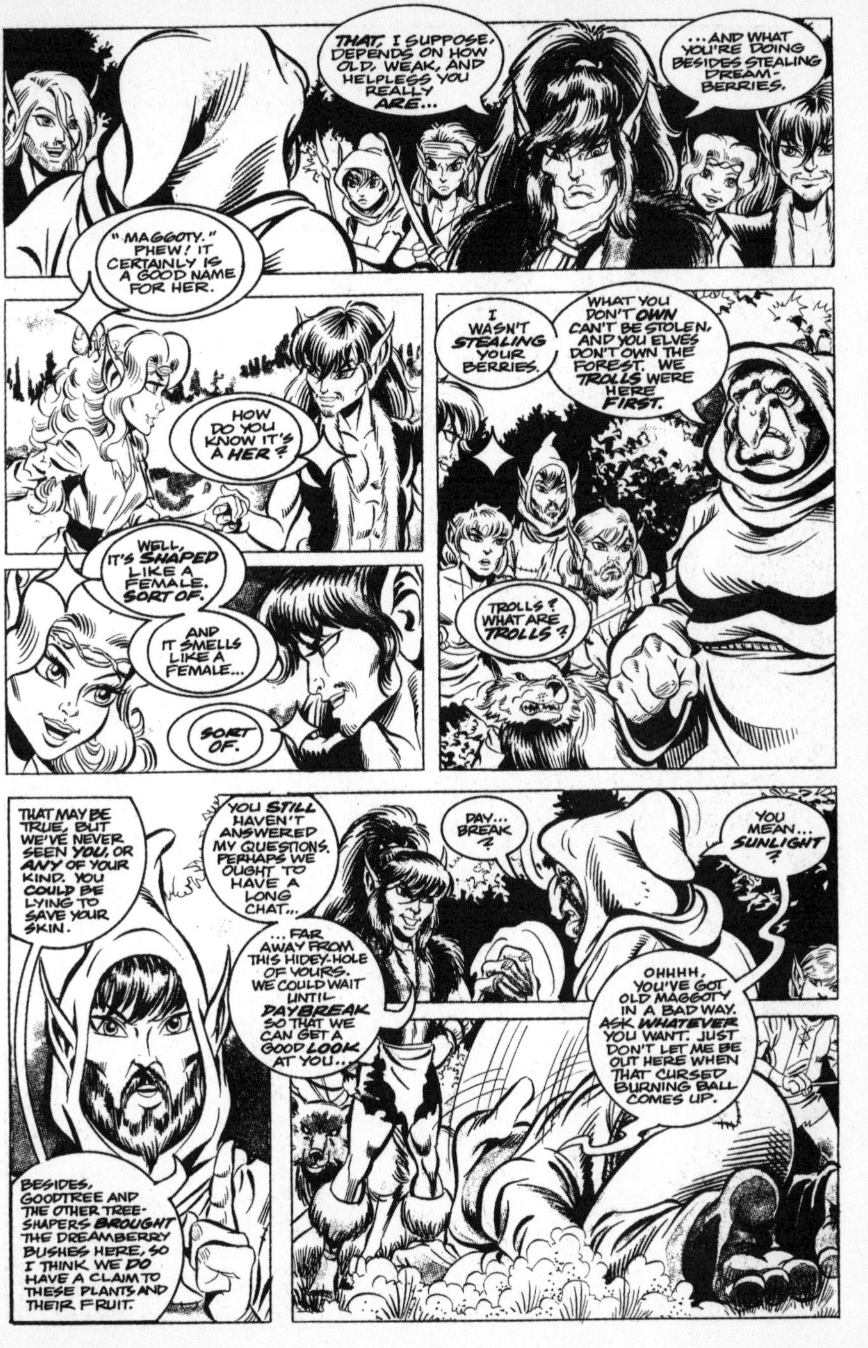
THAT, I SUPPOSE, DEPENDS ON HOW OLD, WEAK, AND HELPLESS YOU REALLY ARE...
...AND WHAT YOU'RE DOING BESIDES STEALING DREAM-BERRIES.
"MAGGOTY." PHEW! IT CERTAINLY IS A GOOD NAME FOR HER.
HOW DO YOU KNOW IT'S A HER?
WELL, IT'S SHAPED LIKE A FEMALE. SORT OF.
AND IT SMELLS LIKE A FEMALE...
SORT OF.
I WASN'T STEALING YOUR BERRIES.
WHAT YOU DON'T OWN CAN'T BE STOLEN, AND YOU ELVES DON'T OWN THE FOREST. WE TROLLS WERE HERE FIRST.
TROLLS? WHAT ARE TROLLS?
THAT MAY BE TRUE, BUT WE'VE NEVER SEEN YOU, OR ANY OF YOUR KIND. YOU COULD BE LYING TO SAVE YOUR SKIN.
BESIDES, GOODTREE AND THE OTHER TREE-SHAPERS BROUGHT THE DREAMBERRY BUSHES HERE, SO I THINK WE DO HAVE A CLAIM TO THESE PLANTS AND THEIR FRUIT.
YOU STILL HAVEN'T ANSWERED MY QUESTIONS. PERHAPS WE OUGHT TO HAVE A LONG CHAT...
...FAR AWAY FROM THIS HIDEY-HOLE OF YOURS. WE COULD WAIT UNTIL DAYBREAK SO THAT WE CAN GET A GOOD LOOK AT YOU...
DAY... BREAK?
YOU MEAN... SUNLIGHT?
OHHHH, YOU'VE GOT OLD MAGGOTY IN A BAD WAY. ASK WHATEVER YOU WANT. JUST DON'T LET ME BE OUT HERE WHEN THAT CURSED BURNING BALL COMES UP.

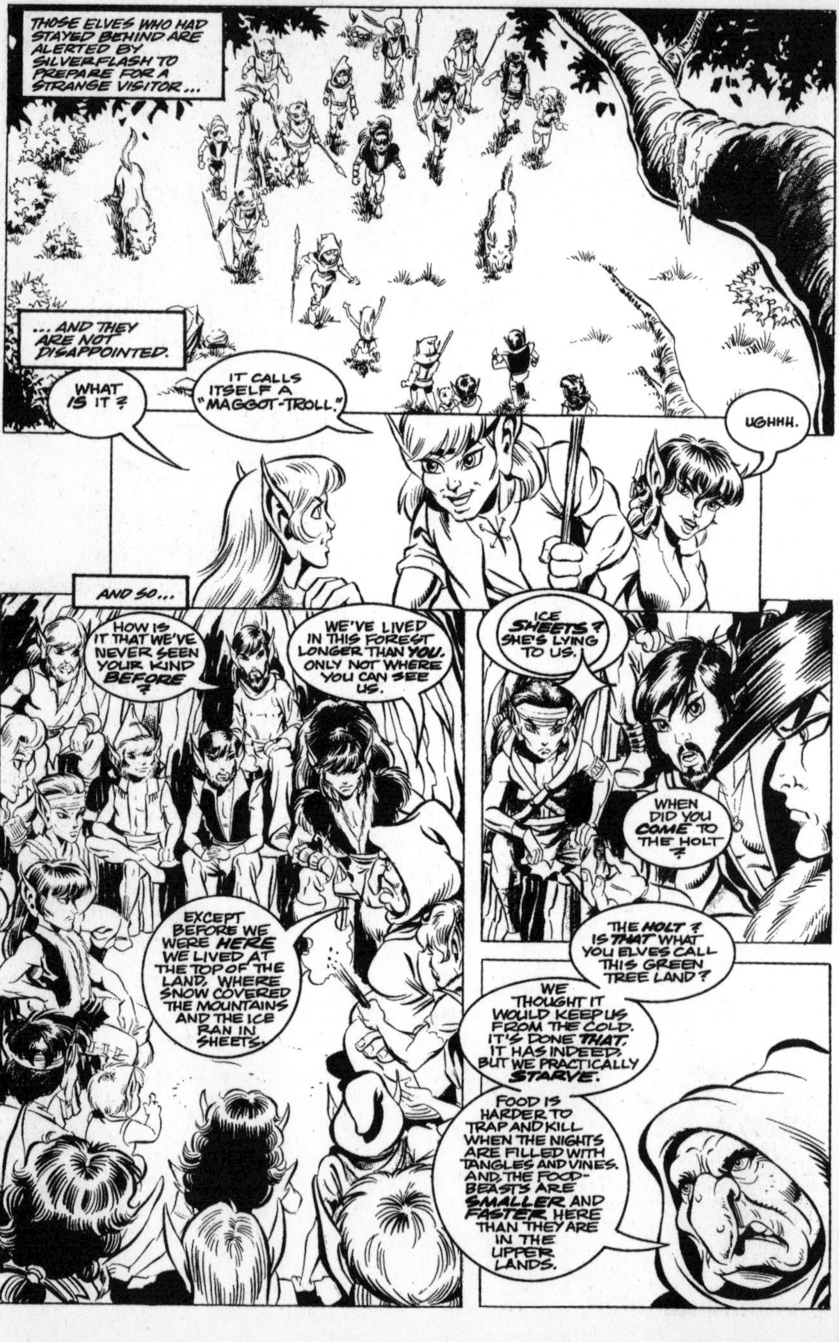
THOSE ELVES WHO HAD STAYED BEHIND ARE ALERTED BY SILVERFLASH TO PREPARE FOR A STRANGE VISITOR...
... AND THEY ARE NOT DISAPPOINTED.
WHAT IS IT ?
IT CALLS ITSELF A "MAGGOT-TROLL."
UGHHH
AND SO...
HOW IS IT THAT WE'VE NEVER SEEN YOUR KIND BEFORE ?
WE'VE LIVED IN THIS FOREST LONGER THAN YOU. ONLY NOT WHERE YOU CAN SEE US.
EXCEPT BEFORE WE WERE HERE WE LIVED AT THE TOP OF THE LAND, WHERE SNOW COVERED THE MOUNTAINS AND THE ICE RAN IN SHEETS.
ICE SHEETS ? SHE'S LYING TO US.
WHEN DID YOU COME TO THE HOLT ?
THE HOLT ? IS THAT WHAT YOU ELVES CALL THIS GREEN TREE LAND ?
WE THOUGHT IT WOULD KEEP US FROM THE COLD. IT'S DONE THAT, IT HAS INDEED, BUT WE PRACTICALLY STARVE.
FOOD IS HARDER TO TRAP AND KILL WHEN THE NIGHTS ARE FILLED WITH TANGLES AND VINES. AND THE FOOD-BEASTS ARE SMALLER AND FASTER HERE THAN THEY ARE IN THE UPPER LANDS.

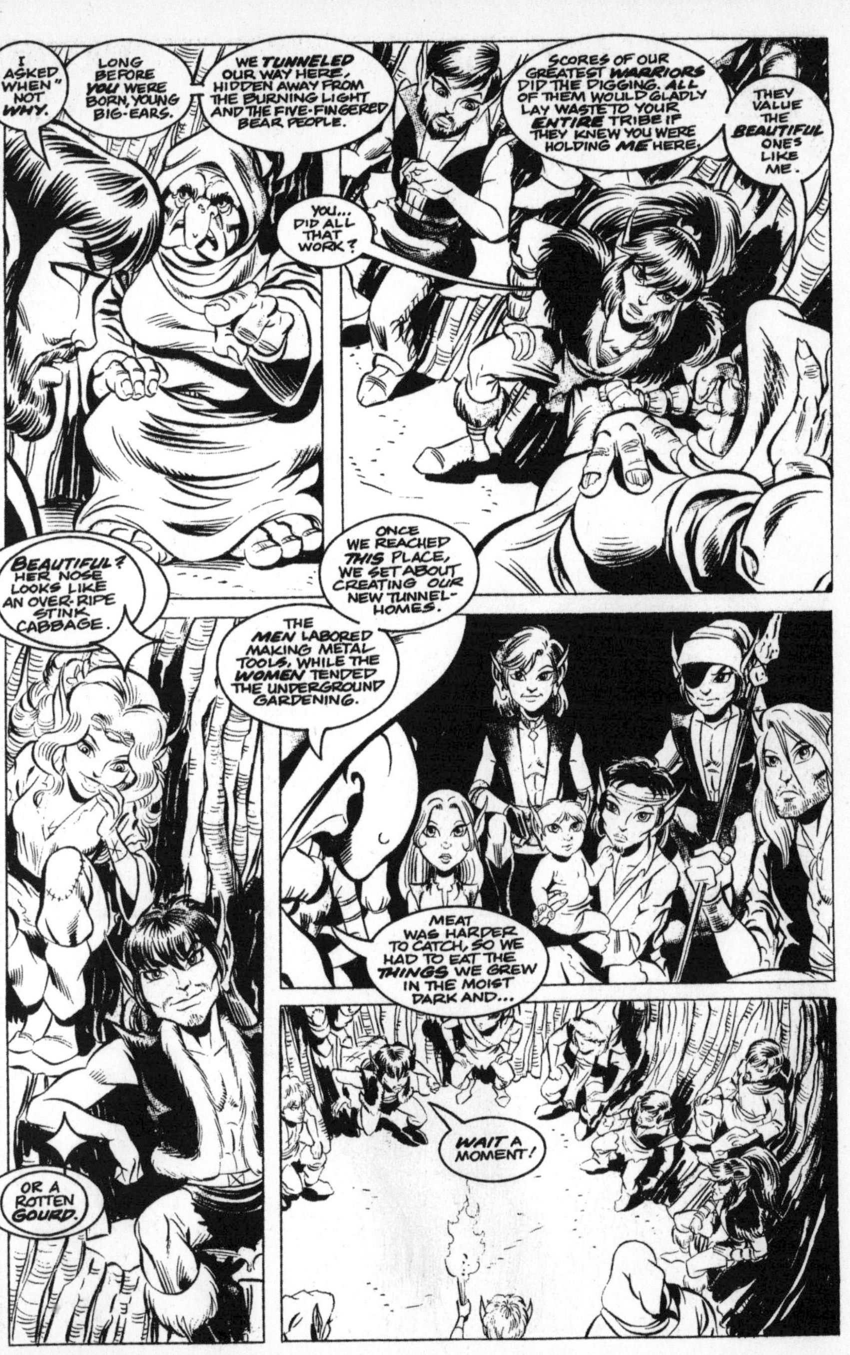
I ASKED "WHEN" NOT WHY.
LONG BEFORE YOU WERE BORN, YOUNG BIG-EARS.
WE TUNNELED OUR WAY HERE, HIDDEN AWAY FROM THE BURNING LIGHT AND THE FIVE-FINGERED BEAR PEOPLE.
YOU... DID ALL THAT WORK?
SCORES OF OUR GREATEST WARRIORS DID THE DIGGING. ALL OF THEM WOULD GLADLY LAY WASTE TO YOUR ENTIRE TRIBE IF THEY KNEW YOU WERE HOLDING ME HERE.
THEY VALUE THE BEAUTIFUL ONES LIKE ME.
BEAUTIFUL? HER NOSE LOOKS LIKE AN OVER-RIPE STINK CABBAGE.
OR A ROTTEN GOURD.
ONCE WE REACHED THIS PLACE, WE SET ABOUT CREATING OUR NEW TUNNEL-HOMES.
THE MEN LABORED MAKING METAL TOOLS, WHILE THE WOMEN TENDED THE UNDERGROUND GARDENING.
MEAT WAS HARDER TO CATCH, SO WE HAD TO EAT THE THINGS WE GREW IN THE MOIST DARK AND...
WAIT A MOMENT!

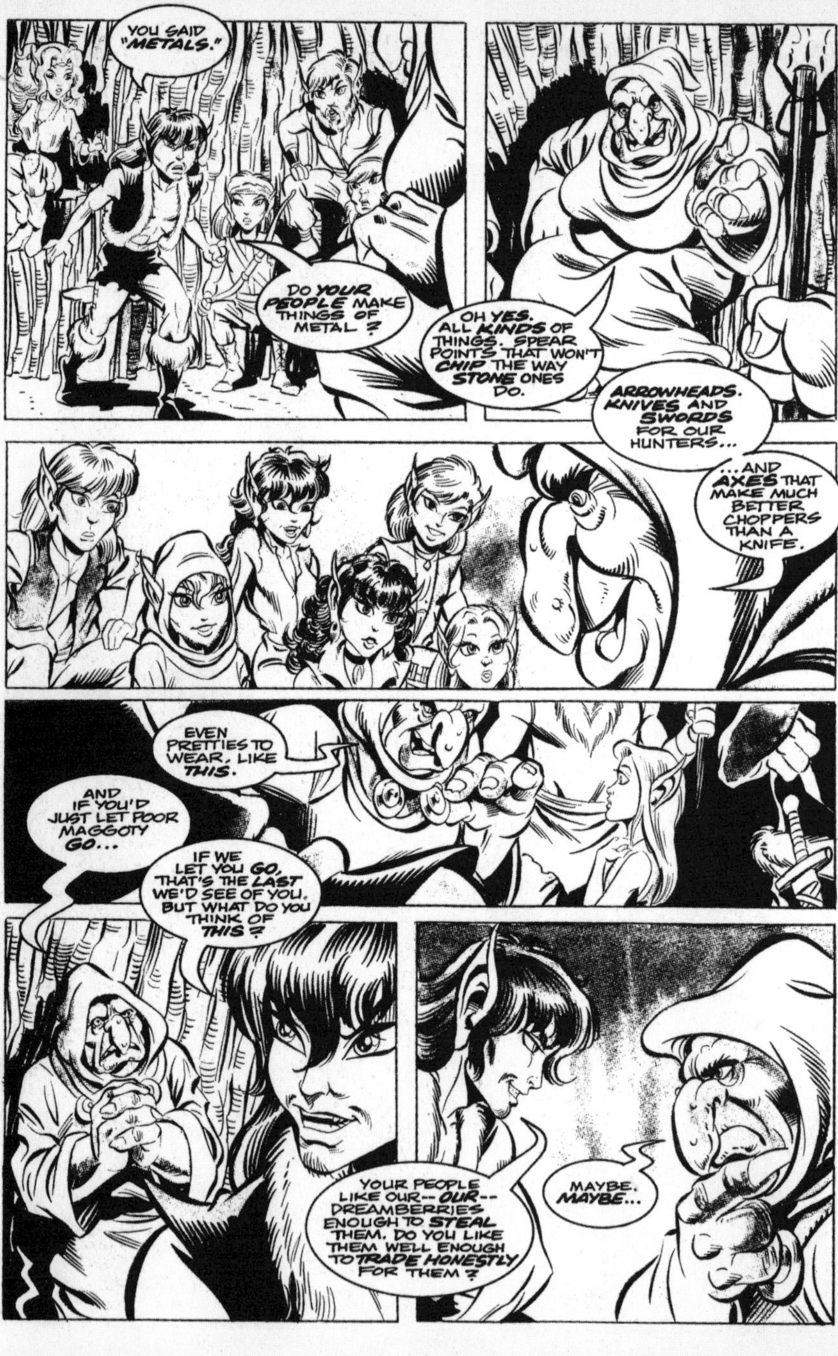

YOU SAID "METALS."
DO YOUR PEOPLE MAKE THINGS OF METAL?
OH YES. ALL KINDS OF THINGS. SPEAR POINTS THAT WON'T CHIP THE WAY STONE ONES DO.
ARROWHEADS. KNIVES AND SWORDS FOR OUR HUNTERS...
...AND AXES THAT MAKE MUCH BETTER CHOPPERS THAN A KNIFE.
EVEN PRETTIES TO WEAR, LIKE THIS.
AND IF YOU'D JUST LET POOR MAGGOTY GO...
IF WE LET YOU GO, THAT'S THE LAST WE'D SEE OF YOU. BUT WHAT DO YOU THINK OF THIS?
YOUR PEOPLE LIKE OUR-- OUR-- DREAMBERRIES ENOUGH TO STEAL THEM. DO YOU LIKE THEM WELL ENOUGH TO TRADE HONESTLY FOR THEM?
MAYBE. MAYBE...

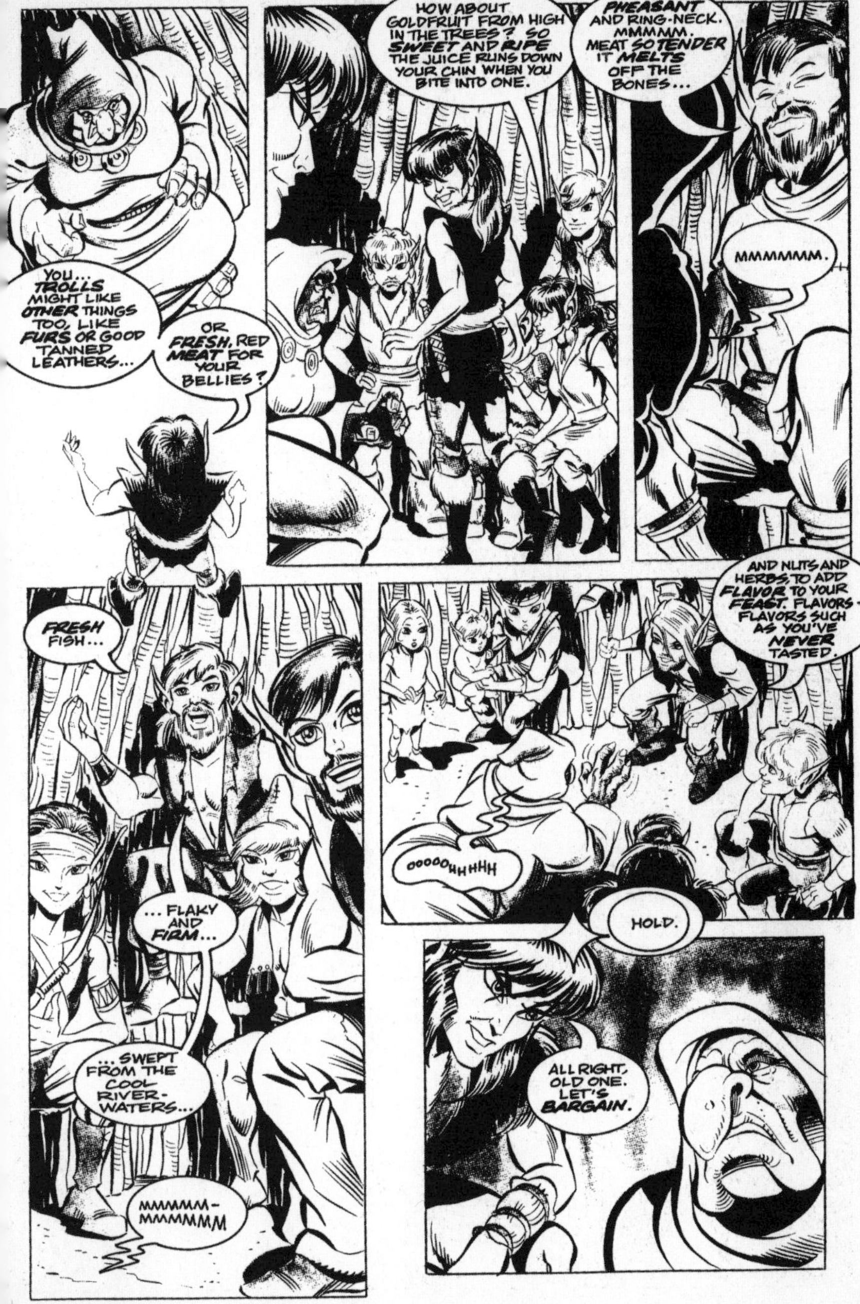
YOU... TROLLS MIGHT LIKE OTHER THINGS TOO, LIKE FURS OR GOOD TANNED LEATHERS...
OR FRESH, RED MEAT FOR YOUR BELLIES?
HOW ABOUT GOLDFRUIT FROM HIGH IN THE TREES? SO SWEET AND RIPE THE JUICE RUNS DOWN YOUR CHIN WHEN YOU BITE INTO ONE.
PHEASANT AND RING-NECK. MMMMM. MEAT SO TENDER IT MELTS OFF THE BONES...
MMMMMM.
FRESH FISH...
...FLAKY AND FIRM...
...SWEPT FROM THE COOL RIVER-WATERS...
MMMMM-MMMMMM
AND NUTS AND HERBS, TO ADD FLAVOR TO YOUR FEAST. FLAVORS—FLAVORS SUCH AS YOU'VE NEVER TASTED.
OOOOOHHHHH
HOLD.
ALL RIGHT, OLD ONE. LET'S BARGAIN.

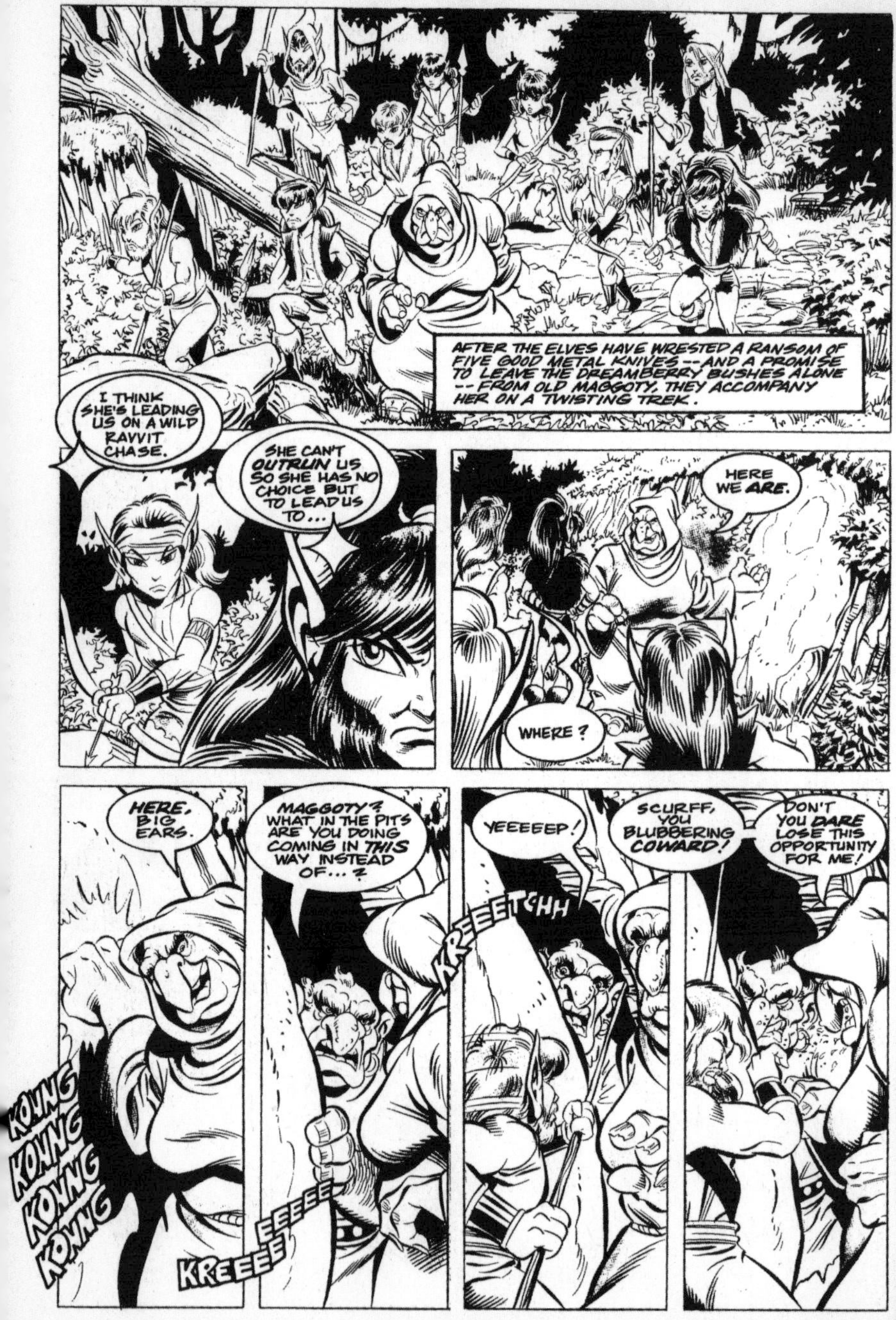
AFTER THE ELVES HAVE WRESTED A RANSOM OF FIVE GOOD METAL KNIVES -- AND A PROMISE TO LEAVE THE DREAMBERRY BUSHES ALONE -- FROM OLD MAGGOTY, THEY ACCOMPANY HER ON A TWISTING TREK.
I THINK SHE'S LEADING US ON A WILD RAVVIT CHASE.
SHE CAN'T OUTRUN US SO SHE HAS NO CHOICE BUT TO LEAD US TO...
HERE WE ARE.
WHERE?
HERE, BIG EARS.
KONNG KONNG KONNG KONNG
MAGGOTY? WHAT IN THE PITS ARE YOU DOING COMING IN THIS WAY INSTEAD OF...?
KREEEEEEEEE
KREEEETCHH
YEEEEEP!
SCURFF, YOU BLUBBERING COWARD!
DON'T YOU DARE LOSE THIS OPPORTUNITY FOR ME!

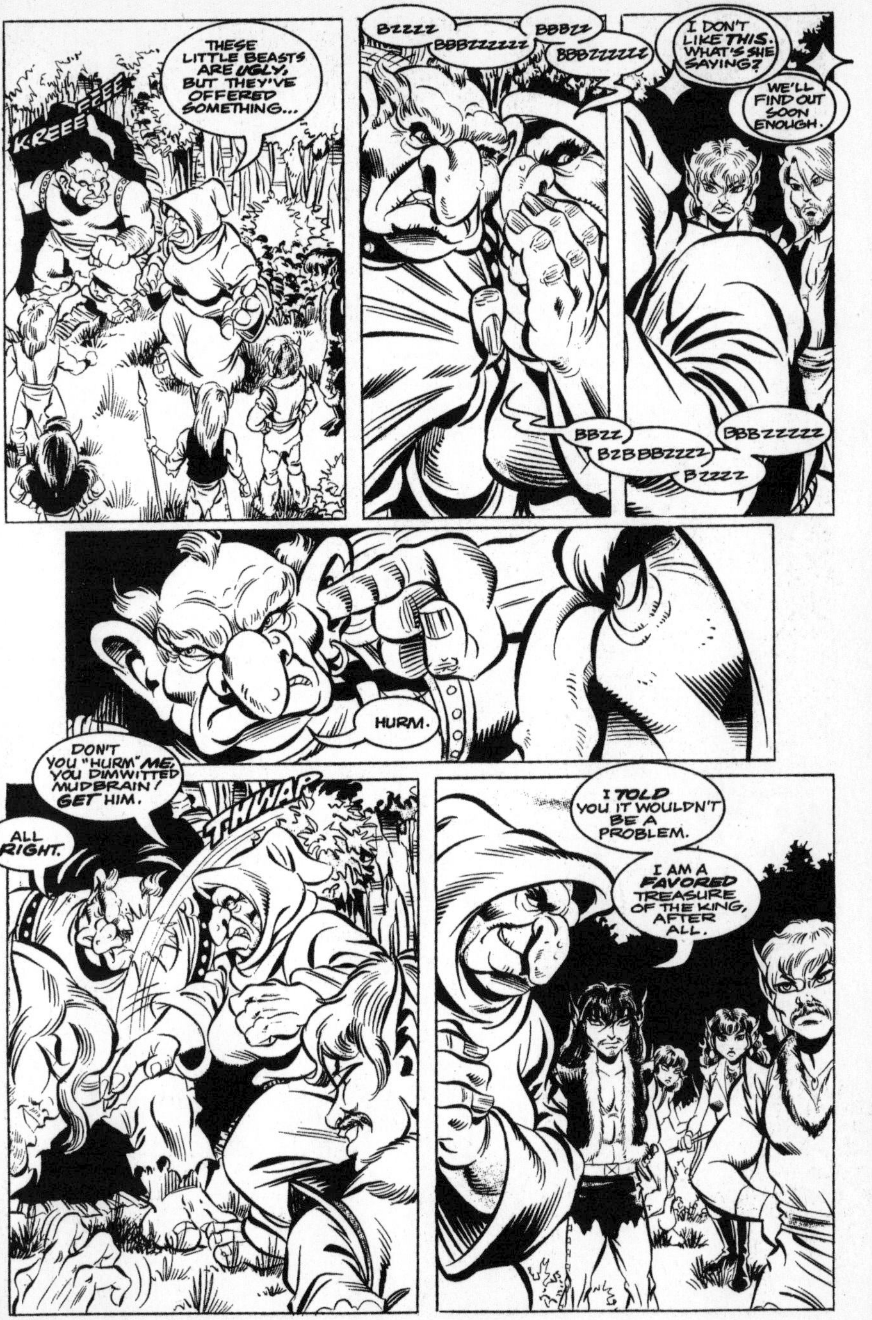

KREEEEEEE
THESE LITTLE BEASTS ARE UGLY, BUT THEY'VE OFFERED SOMETHING...
BZZZZ
BBBZZZZZZZZ
BBBZZ
BBBZZZZZZZ
I DON'T LIKE THIS. WHAT'S SHE SAYING?
WE'LL FIND OUT SOON ENOUGH.
BBZZ
BZBBBZZZZ
BZZZZ
BBBZZZZZZ
HURM.
DON'T YOU "HURM" ME, YOU DIMWITTED MUDBRAIN! GET HIM.
ALL RIGHT.
THWAP
I TOLD YOU IT WOULDN'T BE A PROBLEM.
I AM A FAVORED TREASURE OF THE KING, AFTER ALL.

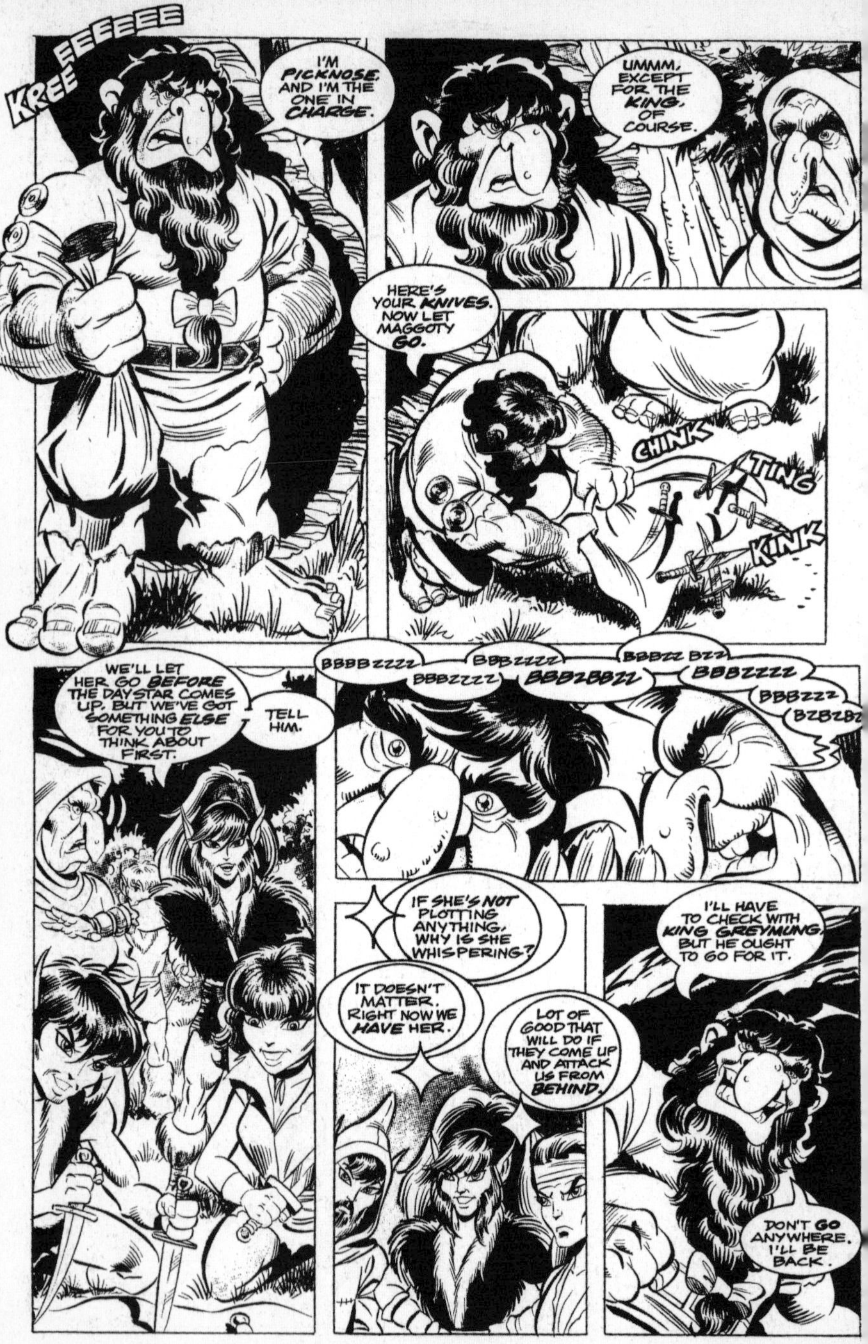
KREEEEEEEEEE
I'M PICKNOSE, AND I'M THE ONE IN CHARGE.
UMMM, EXCEPT FOR THE KING, OF COURSE.
HERE'S YOUR KNIVES. NOW LET MAGGOTY GO.
CHINK
TING
KINK
WE'LL LET HER GO BEFORE THE DAYSTAR COMES UP. BUT WE'VE GOT SOMETHING ELSE FOR YOU TO THINK ABOUT FIRST.
TELL HIM.
BBBBzzzz
BBBzzzz
BBBzzzz
BBBzBBzz
BBBzz Bzz
BBBzzzz
BBBzzz
BzBzBz
IF SHE'S NOT PLOTTING ANYTHING, WHY IS SHE WHISPERING?
IT DOESN'T MATTER. RIGHT NOW WE HAVE HER.
LOT OF GOOD THAT WILL DO IF THEY COME UP AND ATTACK US FROM BEHIND.
I'LL HAVE TO CHECK WITH KING GREYMUNG, BUT HE OUGHT TO GO FOR IT.
DON'T GO ANYWHERE. I'LL BE BACK.

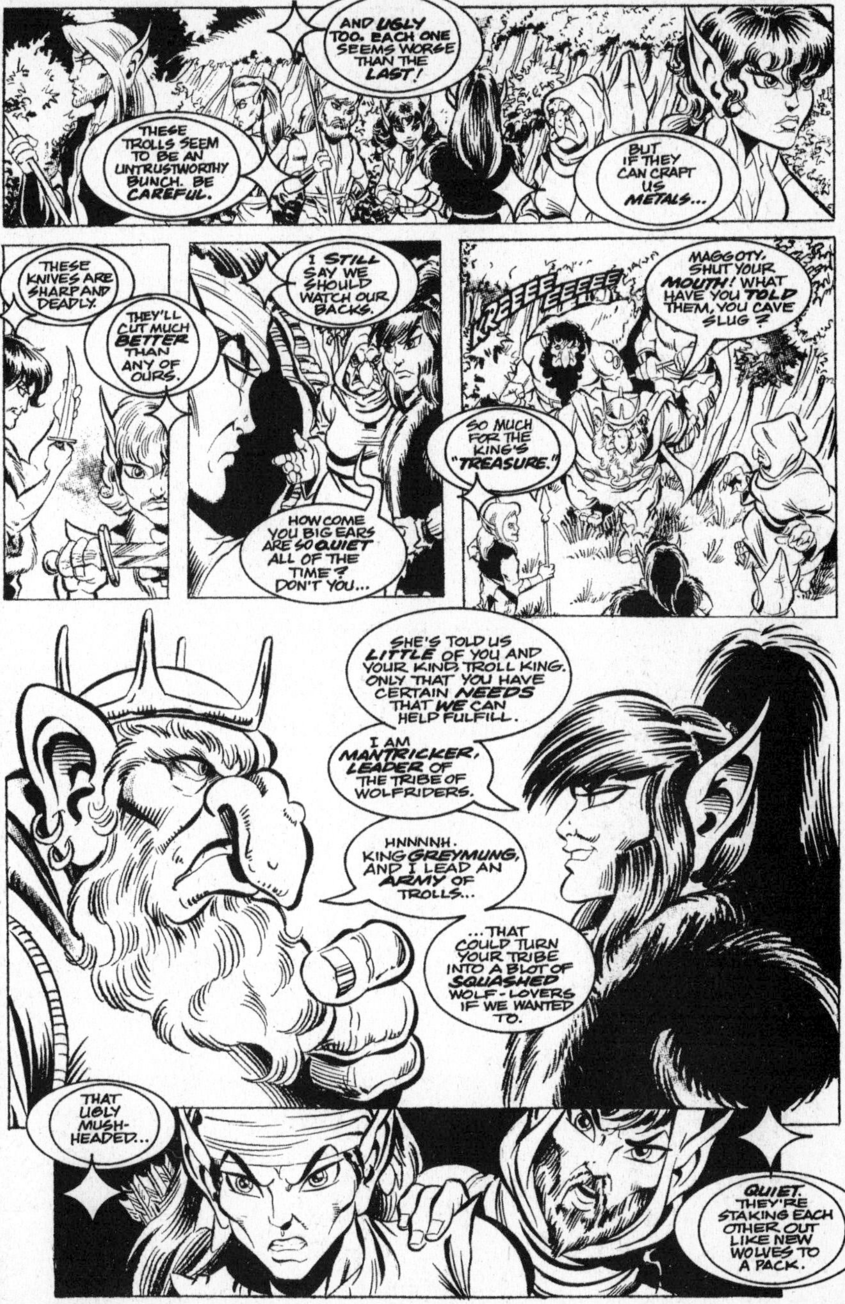
AND UGLY TOO. EACH ONE SEEMS WORSE THAN THE LAST!
THESE TROLLS SEEM TO BE AN UNTRUSTWORTHY BUNCH. BE CAREFUL.
BUT IF THEY CAN CRAFT US METALS...
THESE KNIVES ARE SHARP AND DEADLY.
THEY'LL CUT MUCH BETTER THAN ANY OF OURS.
I STILL SAY WE SHOULD WATCH OUR BACKS.
HOW COME YOU BIG EARS ARE SO QUIET ALL OF THE TIME? DON'T YOU...
KREEEEEEEEEEE
MAGGOTY. SHUT YOUR MOUTH! WHAT HAVE YOU TOLD THEM, YOU CAVE SLUG?
SO MUCH FOR THE KING'S "TREASURE."
SHE'S TOLD US LITTLE OF YOU AND YOUR KIND, TROLL KING. ONLY THAT YOU HAVE CERTAIN NEEDS THAT WE CAN HELP FULFILL.
I AM MANTRICKER, LEADER OF THE TRIBE OF WOLFRIDERS.
HNNNNH. KING GREYMUNG, AND I LEAD AN ARMY OF TROLLS...
...THAT COULD TURN YOUR TRIBE INTO A BLOT OF SQUASHED WOLF-LOVERS IF WE WANTED TO.
THAT UGLY MUSH-HEADED...
QUIET. THEY'RE STAKING EACH OTHER OUT LIKE NEW WOLVES TO A PACK.

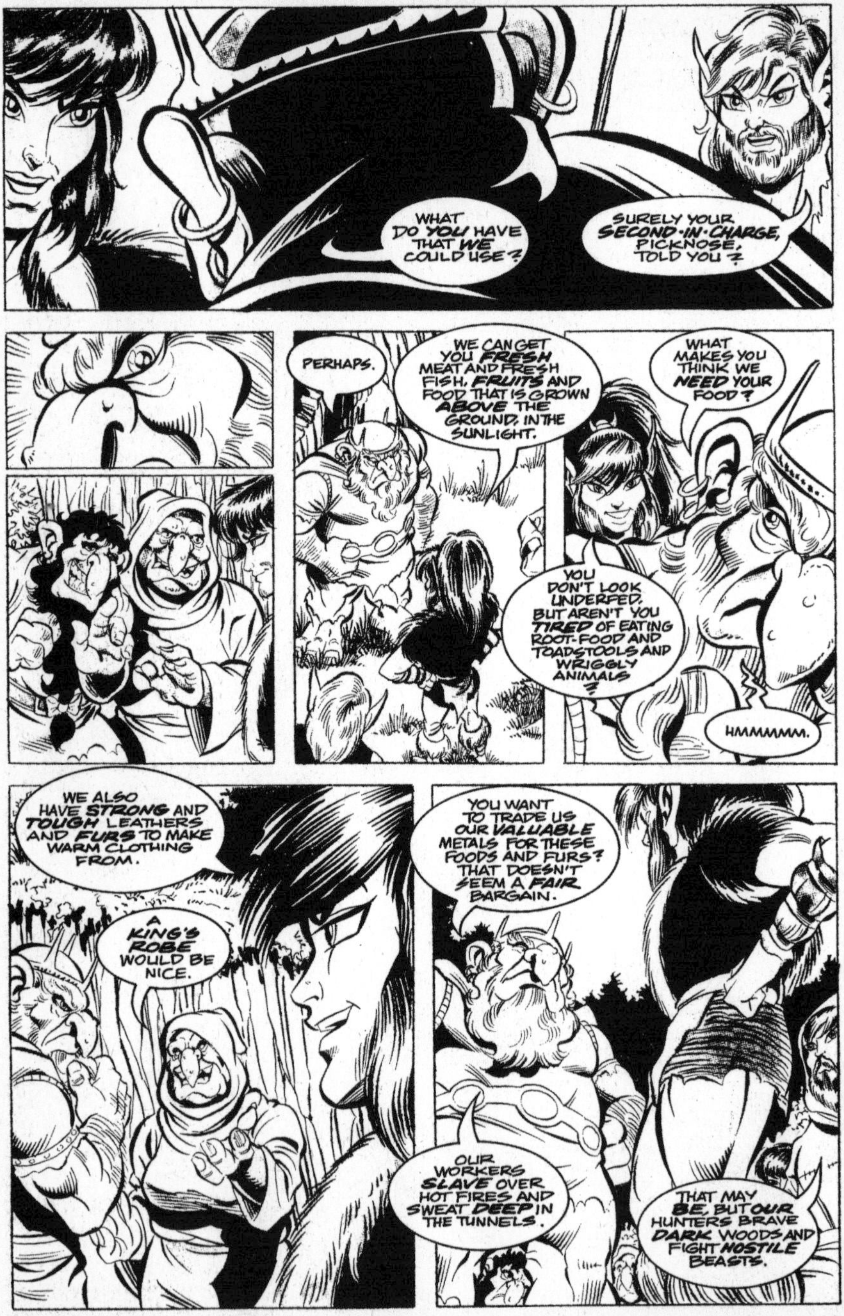
WHAT DO YOU HAVE THAT WE COULD USE?
SURELY YOUR SECOND-IN-CHARGE, PICKNOSE, TOLD YOU?
PERHAPS.
WE CAN GET YOU FRESH MEAT AND FRESH FISH, FRUITS AND FOOD THAT IS GROWN ABOVE THE GROUND, IN THE SUNLIGHT.
WHAT MAKES YOU THINK WE NEED YOUR FOOD?
YOU DON'T LOOK UNDERFED, BUT AREN'T YOU TIRED OF EATING ROOT-FOOD AND TOADSTOOLS AND WRIGGLY ANIMALS?
HMMMMM.
WE ALSO HAVE STRONG AND TOUGH LEATHERS AND FURS TO MAKE WARM CLOTHING FROM.
A KING'S ROBE WOULD BE NICE.
YOU WANT TO TRADE US OUR VALUABLE METALS FOR THESE FOODS AND FURS? THAT DOESN'T SEEM A FAIR BARGAIN.
OUR WORKERS SLAVE OVER HOT FIRES AND SWEAT DEEP IN THE TUNNELS.
THAT MAY BE, BUT OUR HUNTERS BRAVE DARK WOODS AND FIGHT HOSTILE BEASTS.

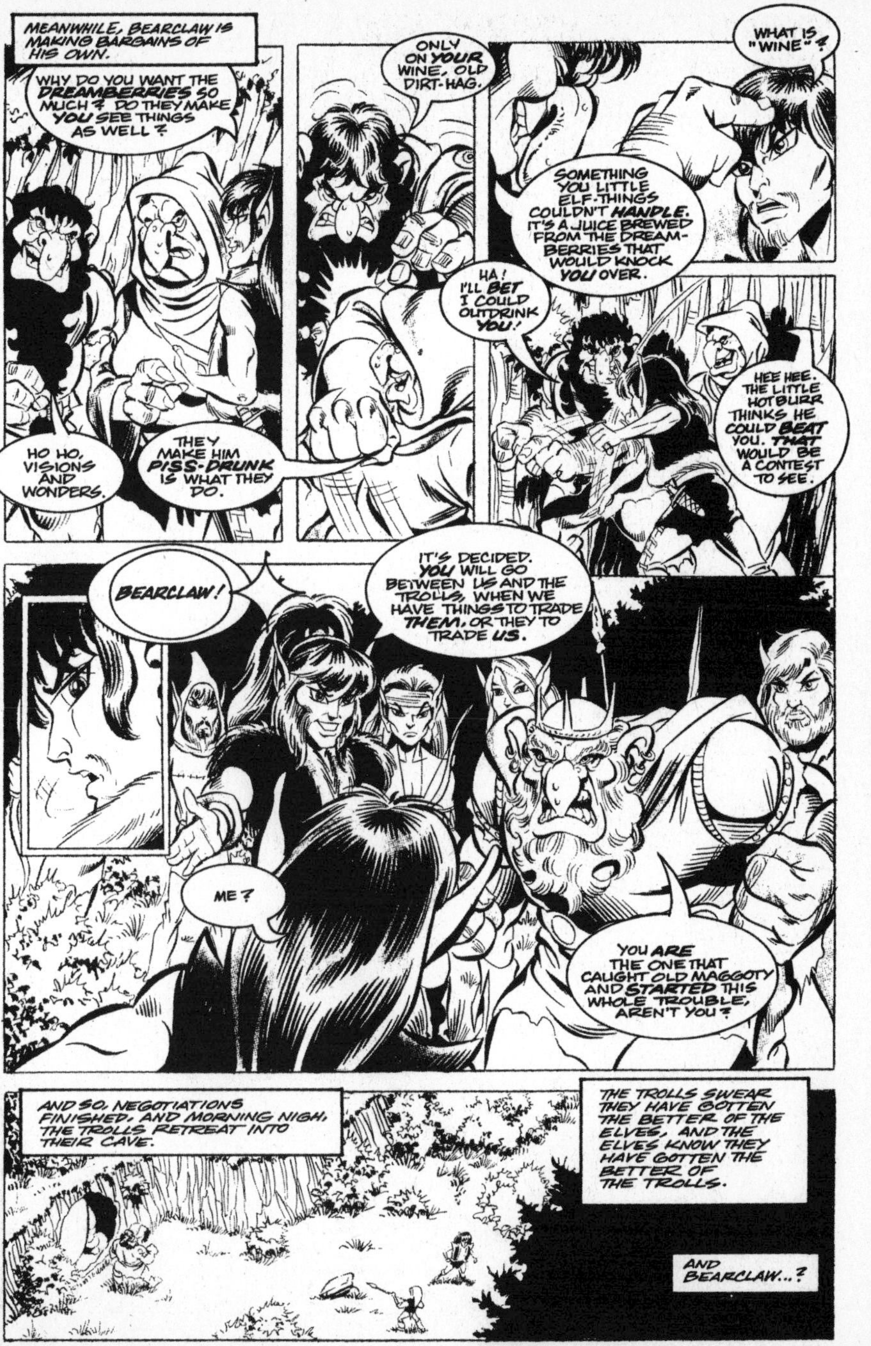
MEANWHILE, BEARCLAW IS MAKING BARGAINS OF HIS OWN.
WHY DO YOU WANT THE DREAMBERRIES SO MUCH? DO THEY MAKE YOU SEE THINGS AS WELL?
HO HO, VISIONS AND WONDERS.
THEY MAKE HIM PISS-DRUNK IS WHAT THEY DO.
ONLY ON YOUR WINE, OLD DIRT-HAG.
WHAT IS "WINE"?
SOMETHING YOU LITTLE ELF-THINGS COULDN'T HANDLE. IT'S A JUICE BREWED FROM THE DREAMBERRIES THAT WOULD KNOCK YOU OVER.
HA! I'LL BET I COULD OUTDRINK YOU!
HEE HEE. THE LITTLE HOTBURR THINKS HE COULD BEAT YOU. THAT WOULD BE A CONTEST TO SEE.
BEARCLAW!
IT'S DECIDED. YOU WILL GO BETWEEN US AND THE TROLLS, WHEN WE HAVE THINGS TO TRADE THEM, OR THEY TO TRADE US.
ME?
YOU ARE THE ONE THAT CAUGHT OLD MAGGOTY AND STARTED THIS WHOLE TROUBLE, AREN'T YOU?
AND SO, NEGOTIATIONS FINISHED, AND MORNING NIGH, THE TROLLS RETREAT INTO THEIR CAVE.
THE TROLLS SWEAR THEY HAVE GOTTEN THE BETTER OF THE ELVES, AND THE ELVES KNOW THEY HAVE GOTTEN THE BETTER OF THE TROLLS.
AND BEARCLAW...?

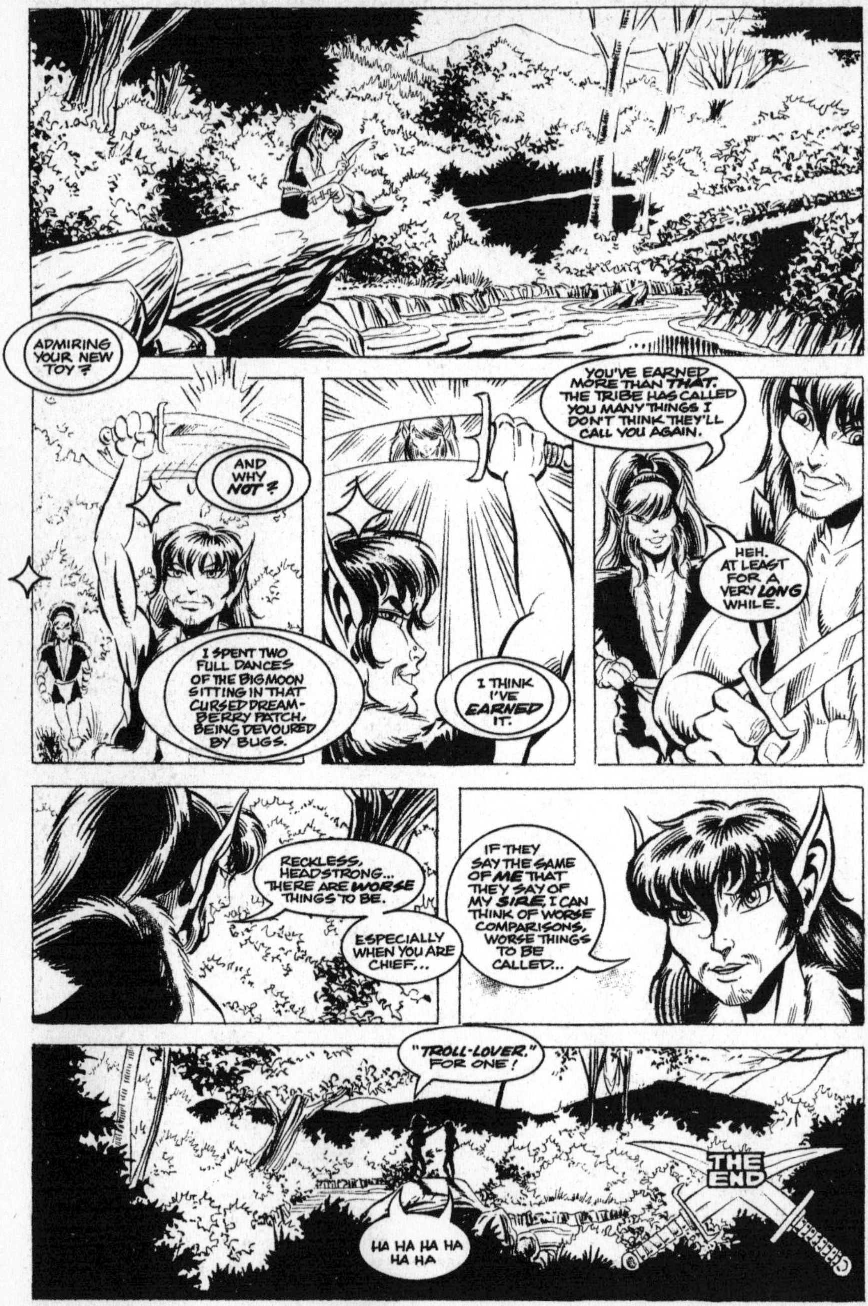
ADMIRING YOUR NEW TOY?
AND WHY NOT?
I SPENT TWO FULL DANCES OF THE BIG MOON SITTING IN THAT CURSED DREAM-BERRY PATCH, BEING DEVOURED BY BUGS.
I THINK I'VE EARNED IT.
YOU'VE EARNED MORE THAN THAT. THE TRIBE HAS CALLED YOU MANY THINGS I DON'T THINK THEY'LL CALL YOU AGAIN.
HEH. AT LEAST FOR A VERY LONG WHILE.
RECKLESS, HEADSTRONG... THERE ARE WORSE THINGS TO BE.
ESPECIALLY WHEN YOU ARE CHIEF...
IF THEY SAY THE SAME OF ME THAT THEY SAY OF MY SIRE, I CAN THINK OF WORSE COMPARISONS, WORSE THINGS TO BE CALLED...
"TROLL-LOVER," FOR ONE!
HA HA HA HA HA HA
THE END

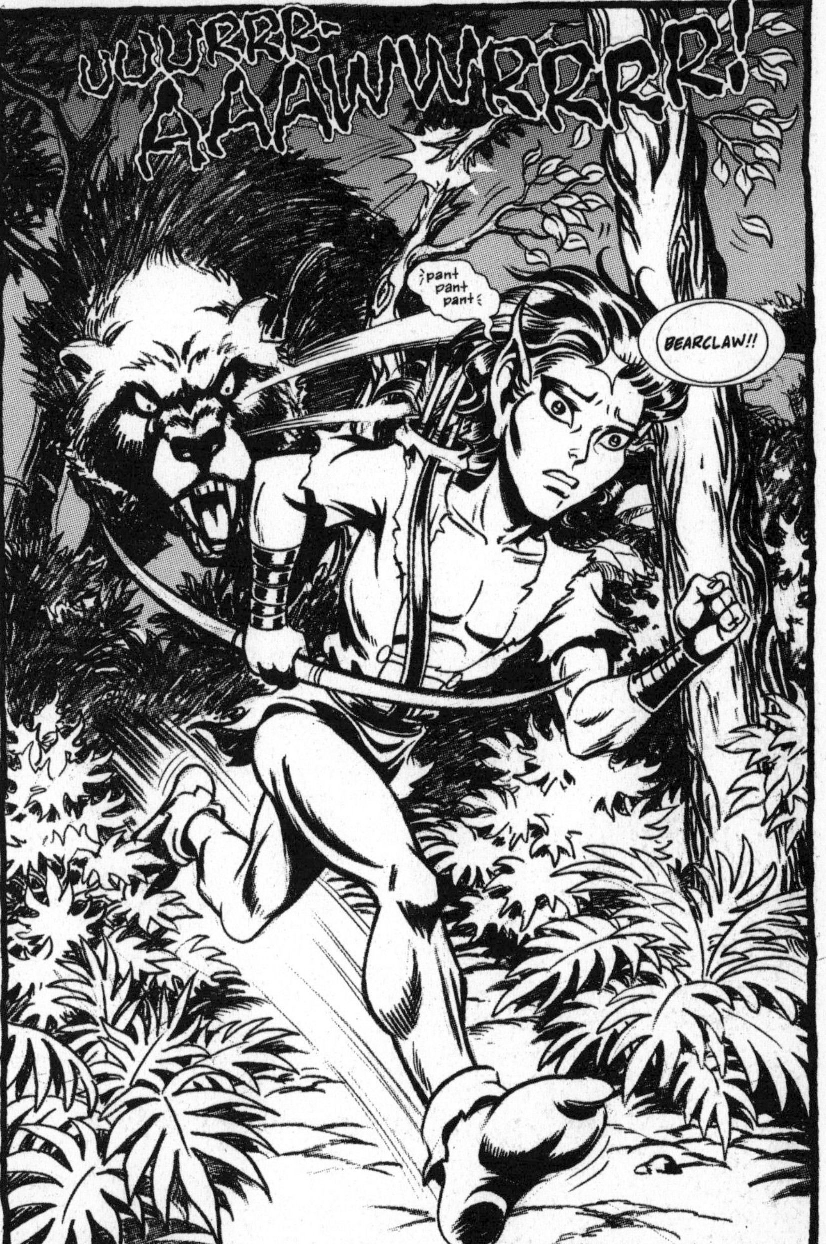
UUURRR-
AAAWWRRRR!
pant pant pant
BEARCLAW!!

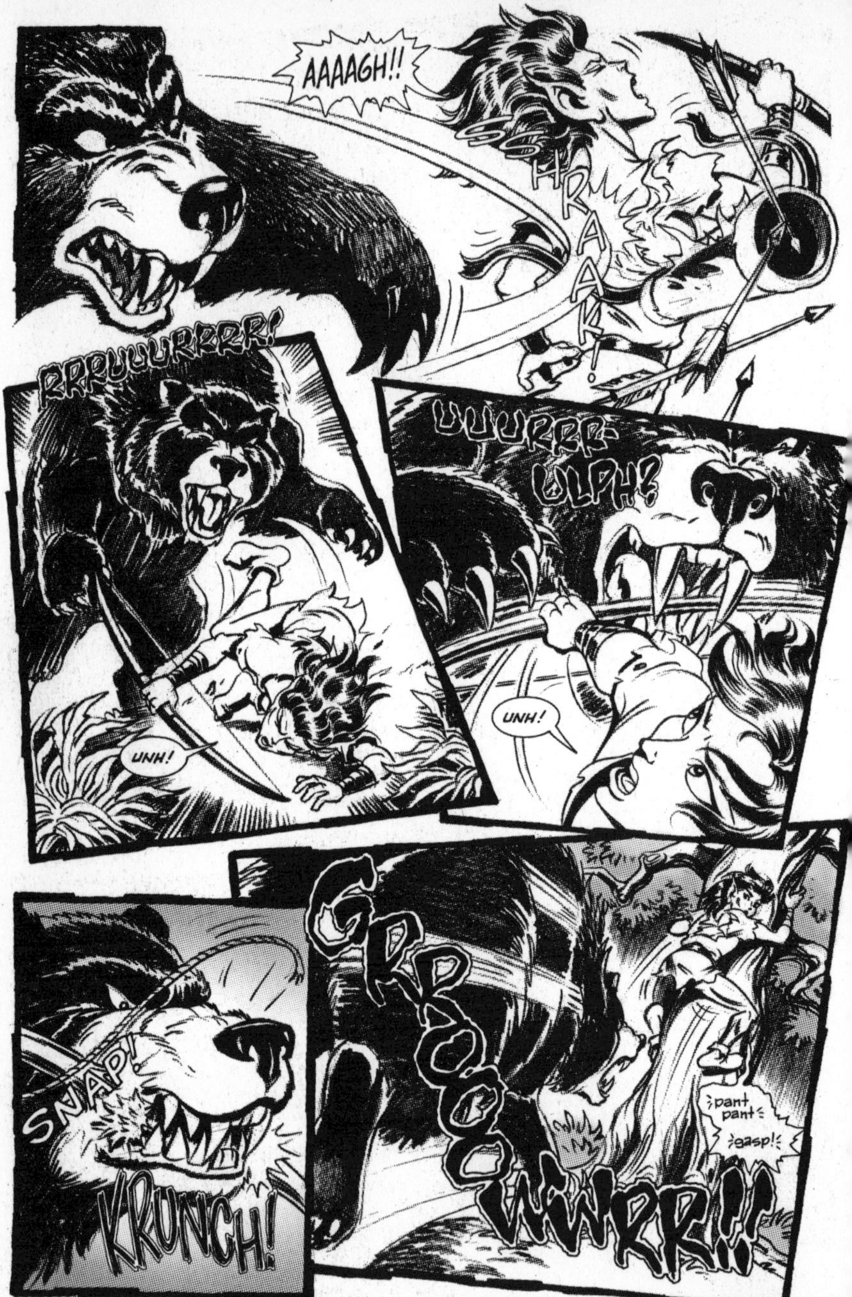
AAAAGH!!
SSHRAAAK!
RRRUUURRRR!
UNH!
UUURRR-ULPH?
UNH!
SNAP!
KRUNCH!
GRRROOOOWWRR!!
pant pant
gasp!

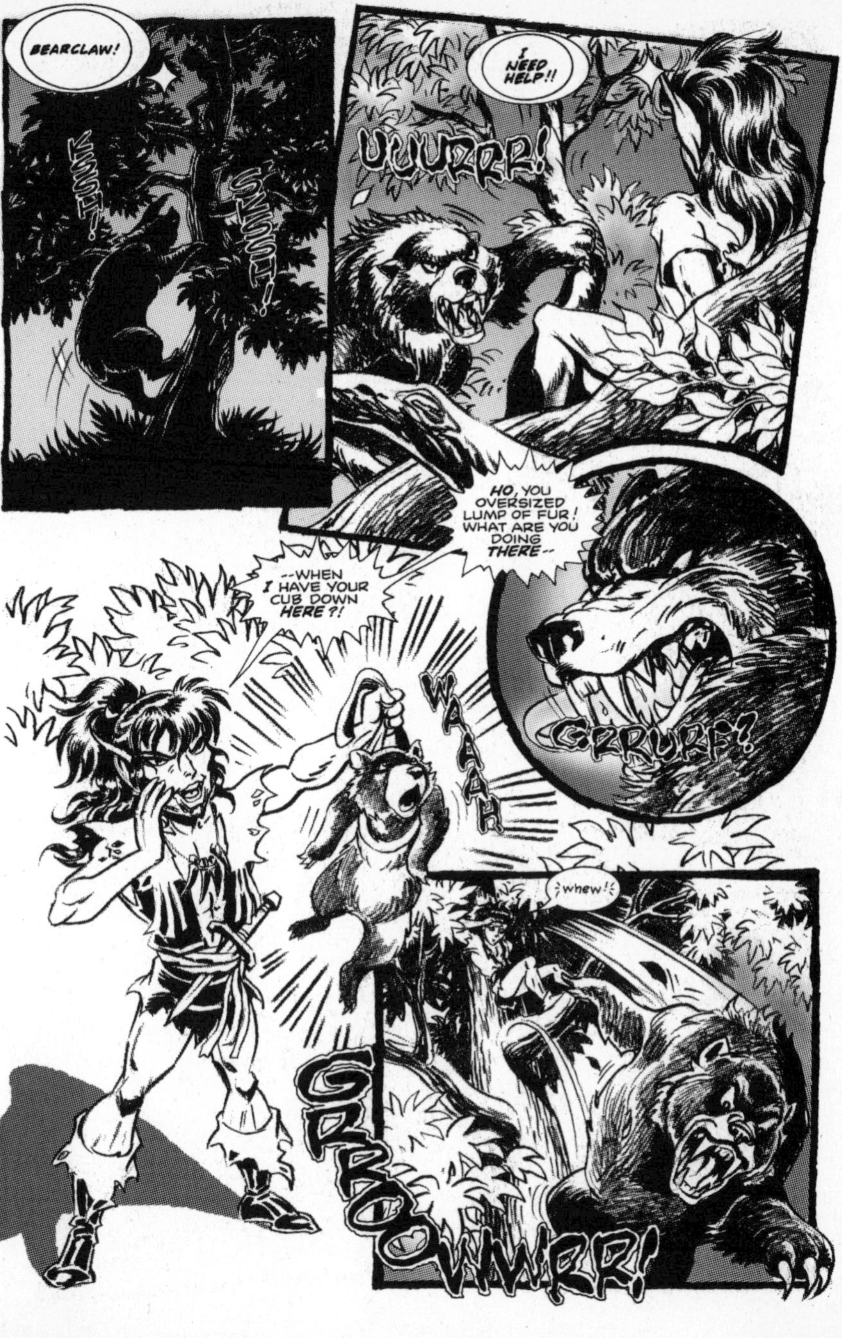
BEARCLAW!
VISSH!
SWISSH!
I NEED HELP!!
UUURRR!
HO, YOU OVERSIZED LUMP OF FUR! WHAT ARE YOU DOING THERE--
--WHEN I HAVE YOUR CUB DOWN HERE?!
WAAAAH
GRRURF?
whew!
GRROOWWRR!

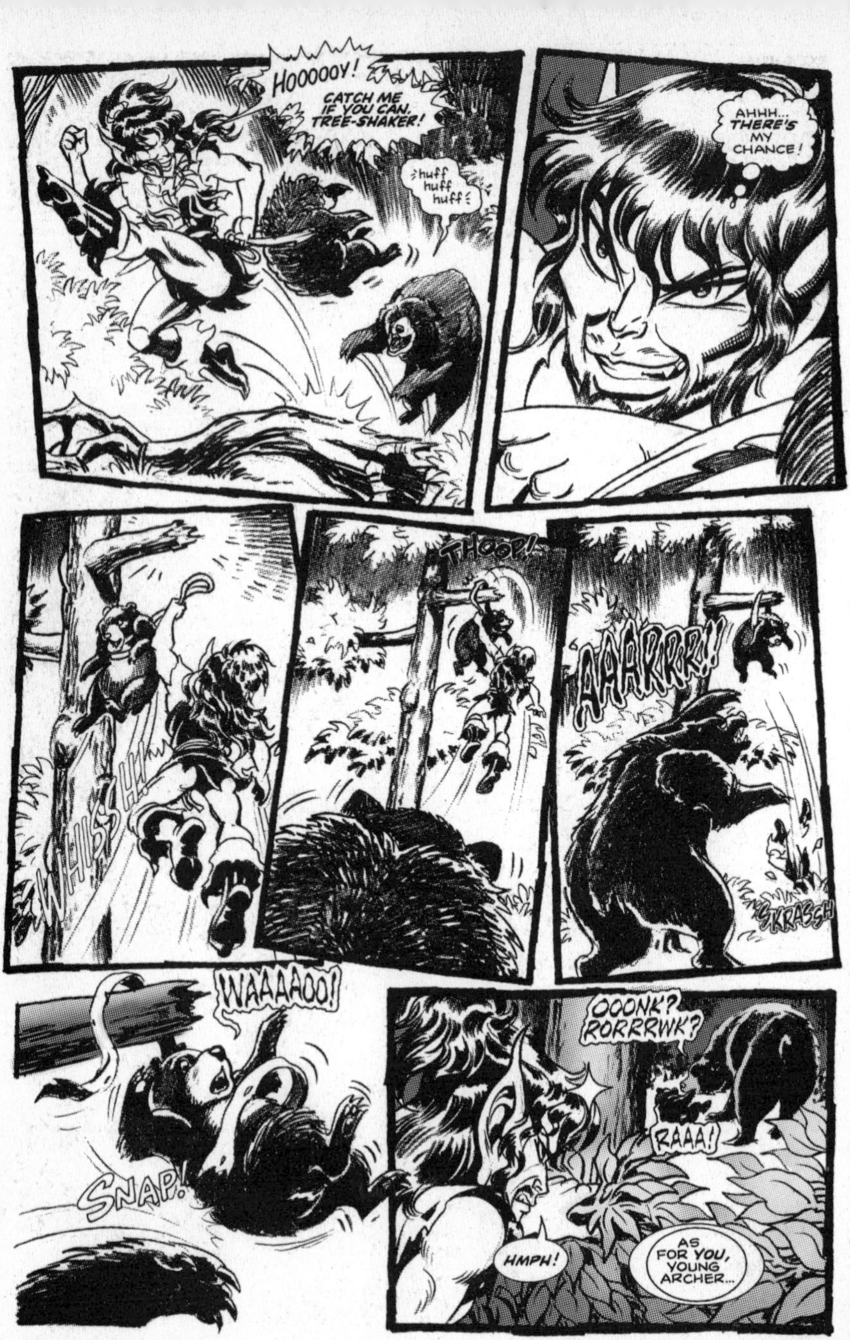
HOOOOOY!
CATCH ME IF YOU CAN, TREE-SHAKER!
huff huff huff
AHHH... THERE'S MY CHANCE!
WHISSH!
THOOP!
AAARRR!
SKRASSH
WAAAAOO!
SNAP.
OOONK? RORRRWK?
RAAA!
HMPH!
AS FOR YOU, YOUNG ARCHER...

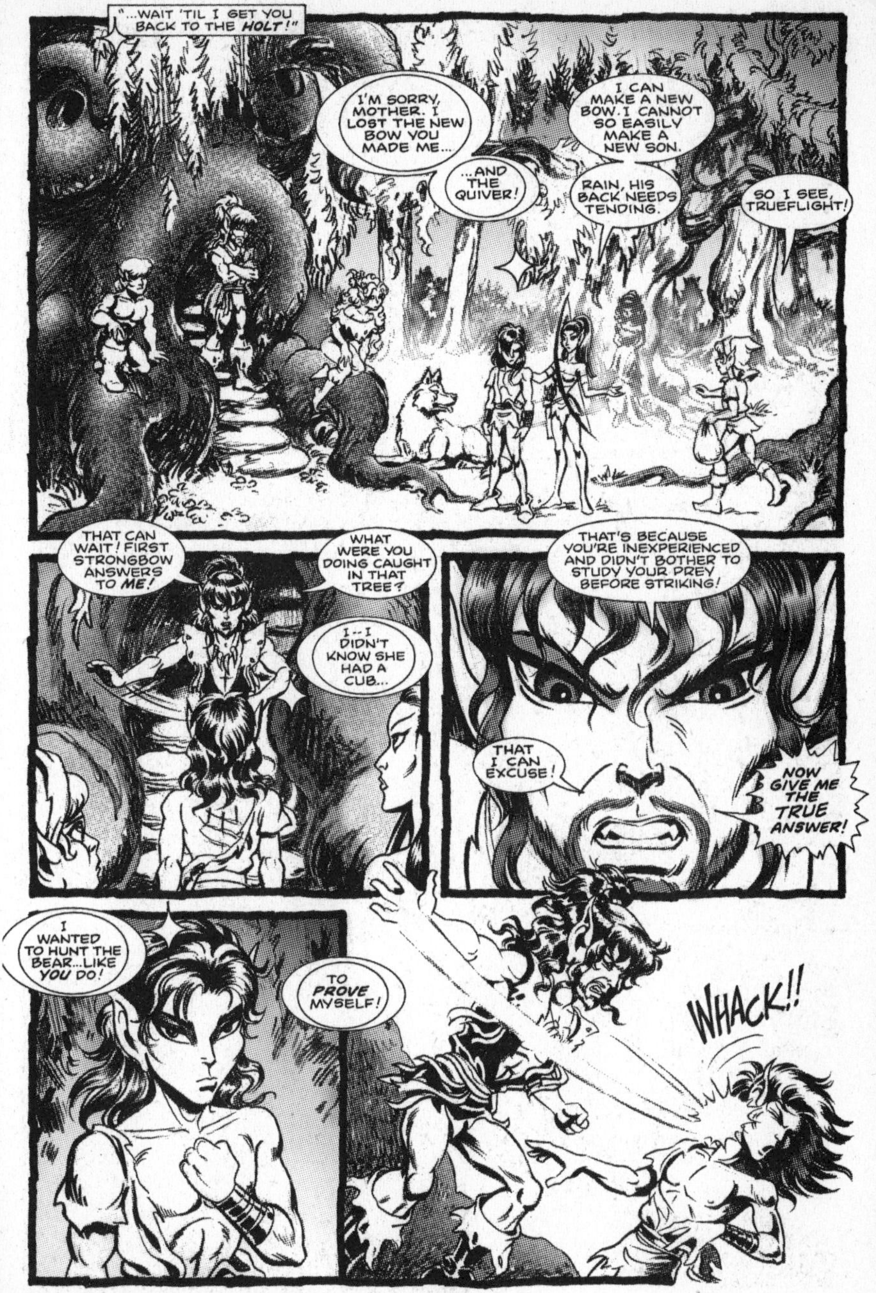
"...WAIT 'TIL I GET YOU BACK TO THE HOLT!"
I'M SORRY, MOTHER. I LOST THE NEW BOW YOU MADE ME...
...AND THE QUIVER!
I CAN MAKE A NEW BOW. I CANNOT SO EASILY MAKE A NEW SON.
RAIN, HIS BACK NEEDS TENDING.
SO I SEE, TRUEFLIGHT!
THAT CAN WAIT! FIRST STRONGBOW ANSWERS TO ME!
WHAT WERE YOU DOING CAUGHT IN THAT TREE?
I--I DIDN'T KNOW SHE HAD A CUB...
THAT'S BECAUSE YOU'RE INEXPERIENCED AND DIDN'T BOTHER TO STUDY YOUR PREY BEFORE STRIKING!
THAT I CAN EXCUSE!
NOW GIVE ME THE TRUE ANSWER!
I WANTED TO HUNT THE BEAR...LIKE YOU DO!
TO PROVE MYSELF!
WHACK!!

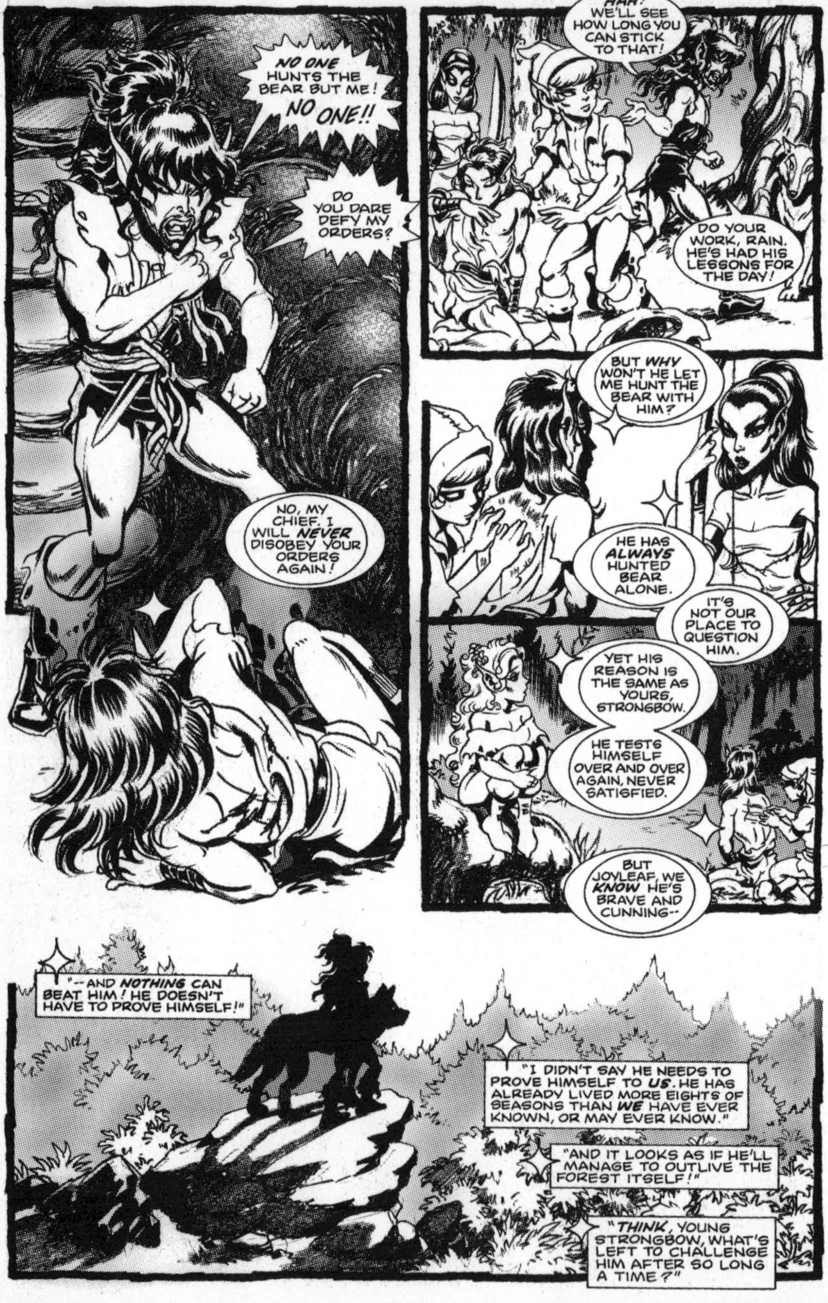
NO ONE HUNTS THE BEAR BUT ME! NO ONE!!
DO YOU DARE DEFY MY ORDERS?
NO, MY CHIEF. I WILL NEVER DISOBEY YOUR ORDERS AGAIN!
HAH! WE'LL SEE HOW LONG YOU CAN STICK TO THAT!
DO YOUR WORK, RAIN. HE'S HAD HIS LESSONS FOR THE DAY!
BUT WHY WON'T HE LET ME HUNT THE BEAR WITH HIM?
HE HAS ALWAYS HUNTED BEAR ALONE.
IT'S NOT OUR PLACE TO QUESTION HIM.
YET HIS REASON IS THE SAME AS YOURS, STRONGBOW.
HE TESTS HIMSELF OVER AND OVER AGAIN, NEVER SATISFIED.
BUT JOYLEAF, WE KNOW HE'S BRAVE AND CUNNING--
"--AND NOTHING CAN BEAT HIM! HE DOESN'T HAVE TO PROVE HIMSELF!"
"I DIDN'T SAY HE NEEDS TO PROVE HIMSELF TO US. HE HAS ALREADY LIVED MORE EIGHTS OF SEASONS THAN WE HAVE EVER KNOWN, OR MAY EVER KNOW."
"AND IT LOOKS AS IF HE'LL MANAGE TO OUTLIVE THE FOREST ITSELF!"
"THINK, YOUNG STRONGBOW, WHAT'S LEFT TO CHALLENGE HIM AFTER SO LONG A TIME?"

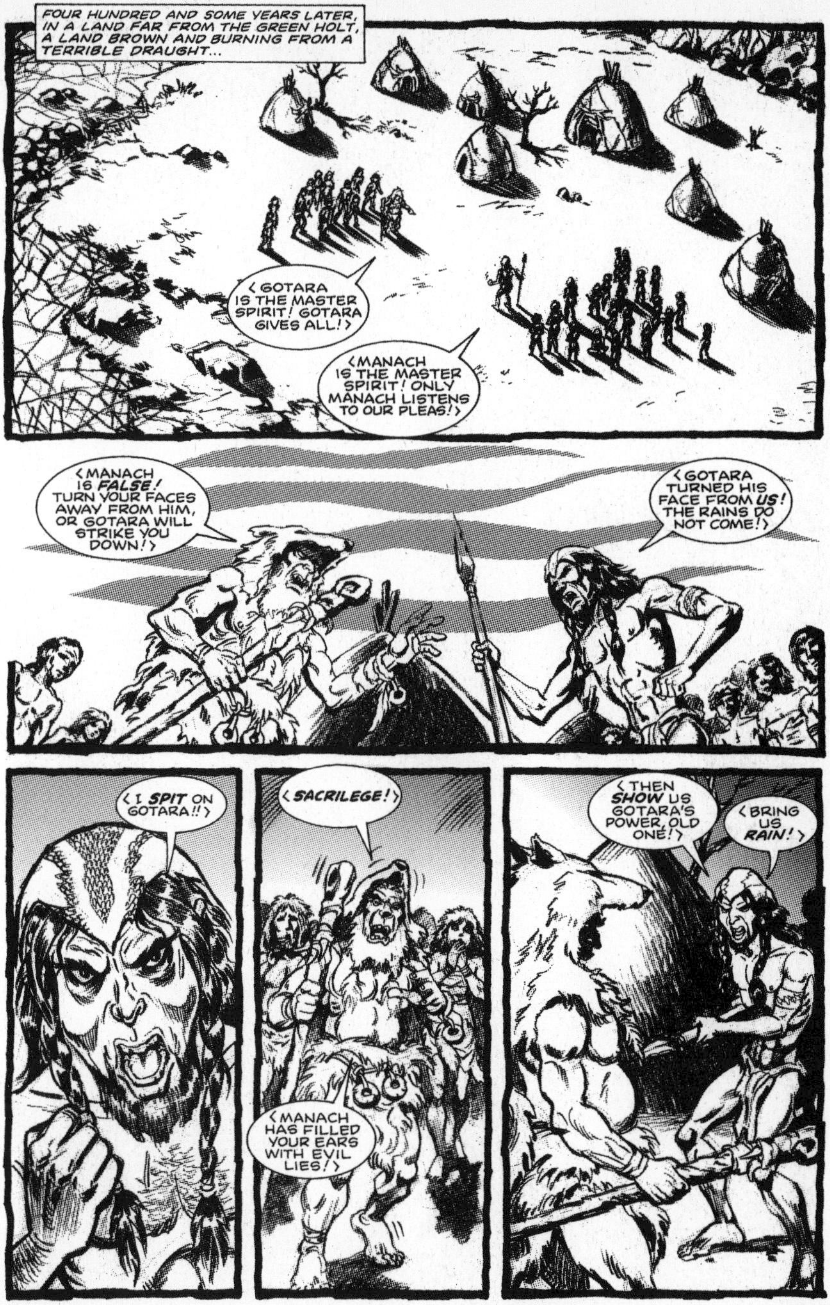

FOUR HUNDRED AND SOME YEARS LATER, IN A LAND FAR FROM THE GREEN HOLT, A LAND BROWN AND BURNING FROM A TERRIBLE DRAUGHT...
<GOTARA IS THE MASTER SPIRIT! GOTARA GIVES ALL!>
<MANACH IS THE MASTER SPIRIT! ONLY MANACH LISTENS TO OUR PLEAS!>
<MANACH IS FALSE! TURN YOUR FACES AWAY FROM HIM, OR GOTARA WILL STRIKE YOU DOWN!>
<GOTARA TURNED HIS FACE FROM US! THE RAINS DO NOT COME!>
<I SPIT ON GOTARA!!>
<SACRILEGE!>
<MANACH HAS FILLED YOUR EARS WITH EVIL LIES!>
<THEN SHOW US GOTARA'S POWER, OLD ONE!>
<BRING US RAIN!>

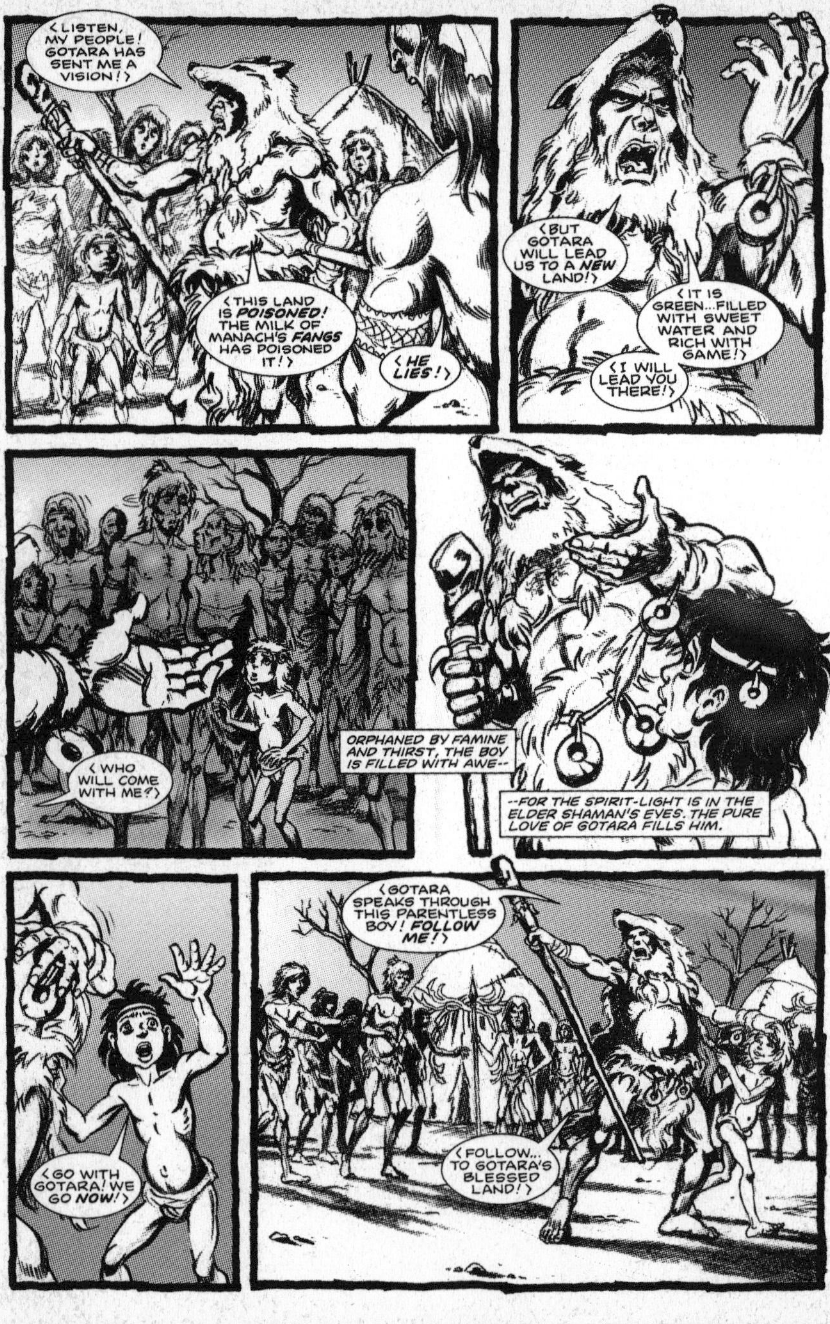

‹LISTEN, MY PEOPLE! GOTARA HAS SENT ME A VISION!›
‹THIS LAND IS POISONED! THE MILK OF MANACH'S FANGS HAS POISONED IT!›
‹HE LIES!›
‹BUT GOTARA WILL LEAD US TO A NEW LAND!›
‹IT IS GREEN... FILLED WITH SWEET WATER AND RICH WITH GAME!›
‹I WILL LEAD YOU THERE!›
‹WHO WILL COME WITH ME?›
ORPHANED BY FAMINE AND THIRST, THE BOY IS FILLED WITH AWE--
--FOR THE SPIRIT-LIGHT IS IN THE ELDER SHAMAN'S EYES. THE PURE LOVE OF GOTARA FILLS HIM.
‹GO WITH GOTARA! WE GO NOW!›
‹GOTARA SPEAKS THROUGH THIS PARENTLESS BOY! FOLLOW ME!›
‹FOLLOW... TO GOTARA'S BLESSED LAND!›

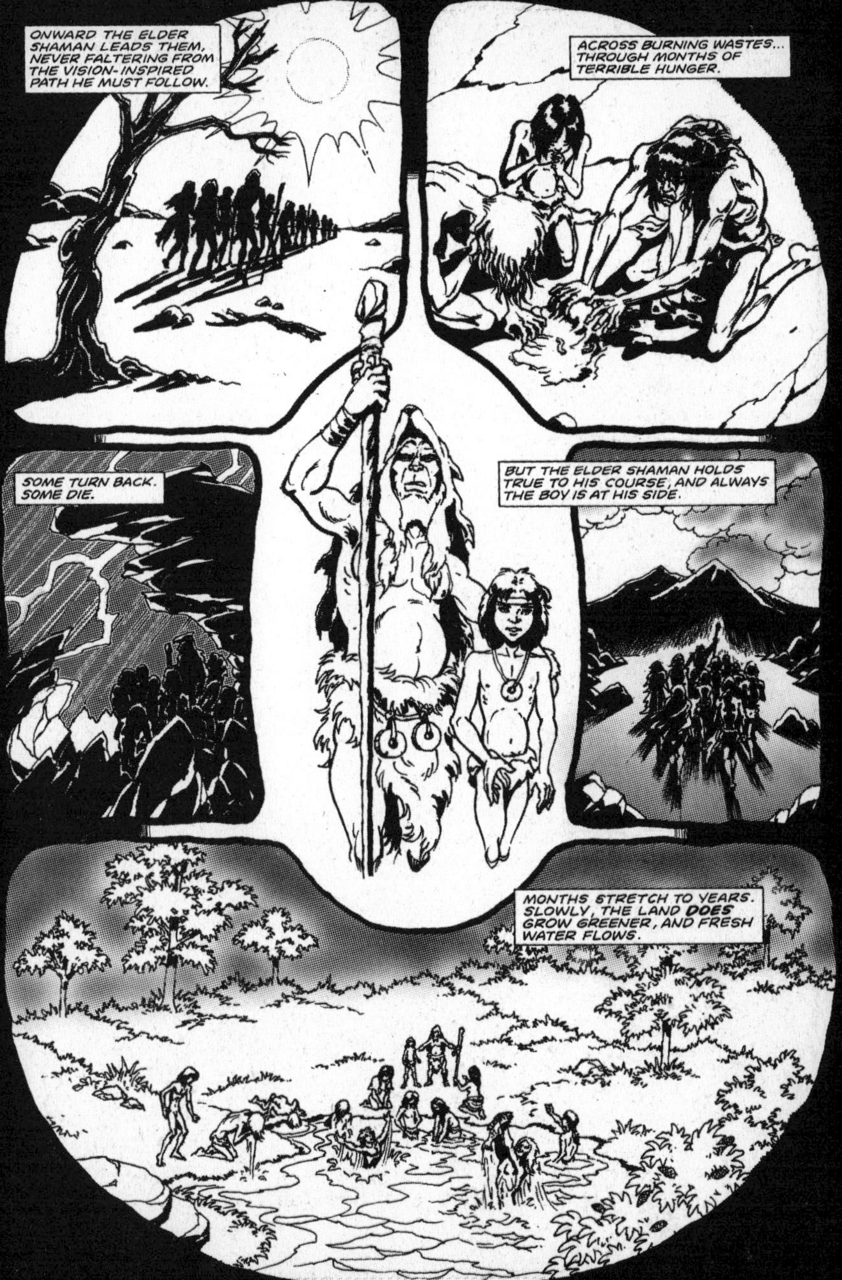
ONWARD THE ELDER SHAMAN LEADS THEM, NEVER FALTERING FROM THE VISION-INSPIRED PATH HE MUST FOLLOW.
ACROSS BURNING WASTES... THROUGH MONTHS OF TERRIBLE HUNGER.
SOME TURN BACK. SOME DIE.
BUT THE ELDER SHAMAN HOLDS TRUE TO HIS COURSE, AND ALWAYS THE BOY IS AT HIS SIDE.
MONTHS STRETCH TO YEARS. SLOWLY, THE LAND DOES GROW GREENER, AND FRESH WATER FLOWS.

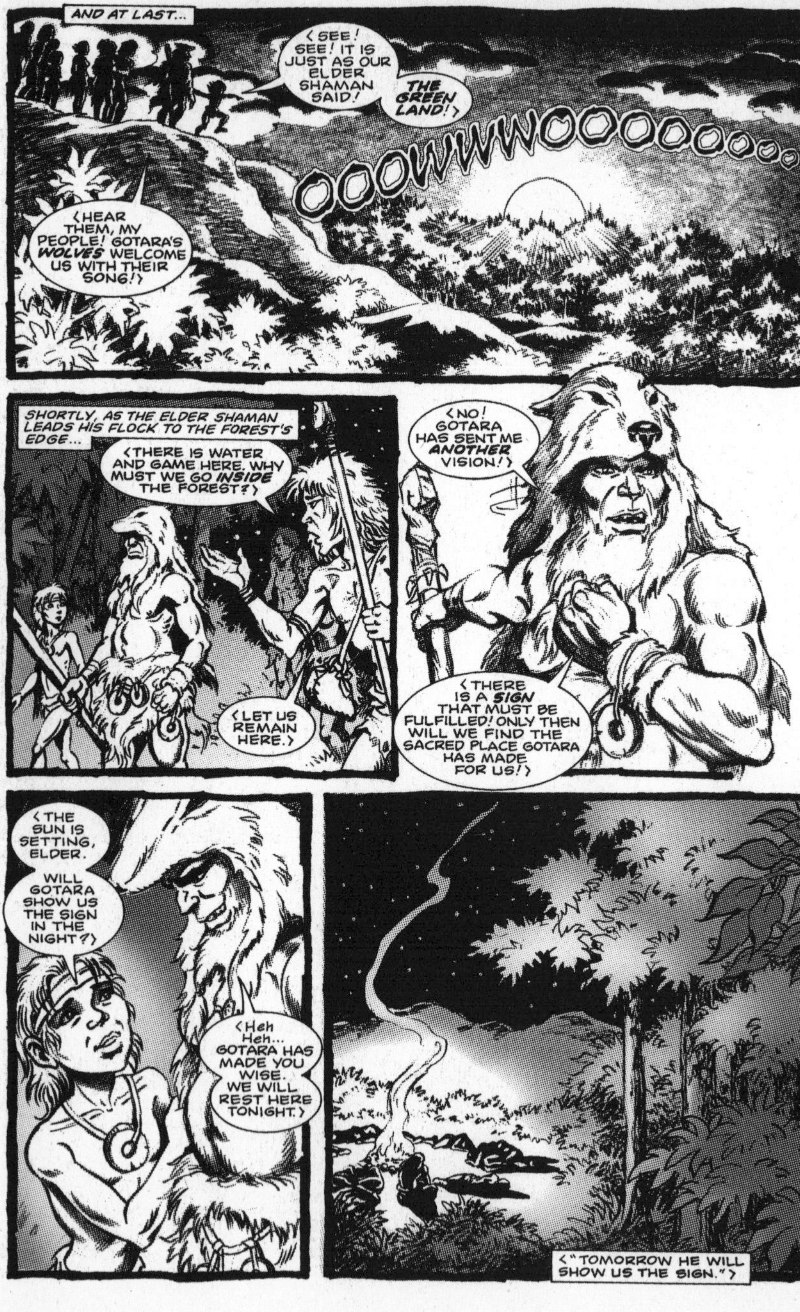
AND AT LAST...
<SEE! SEE! IT IS JUST AS OUR ELDER SHAMAN SAID!
THE GREEN LAND!>
OOOWWWOOOOOOOOoo
<HEAR THEM, MY PEOPLE! GOTARA'S WOLVES WELCOME US WITH THEIR SONG!>
SHORTLY, AS THE ELDER SHAMAN LEADS HIS FLOCK TO THE FOREST'S EDGE...
<THERE IS WATER AND GAME HERE. WHY MUST WE GO INSIDE THE FOREST?>
<LET US REMAIN HERE.>
<NO! GOTARA HAS SENT ME ANOTHER VISION!>
<THERE IS A SIGN THAT MUST BE FULFILLED! ONLY THEN WILL WE FIND THE SACRED PLACE GOTARA HAS MADE FOR US!>
<THE SUN IS SETTING, ELDER.
WILL GOTARA SHOW US THE SIGN IN THE NIGHT?>
<Heh Heh... GOTARA HAS MADE YOU WISE. WE WILL REST HERE TONIGHT.>
<"TOMORROW HE WILL SHOW US THE SIGN.">

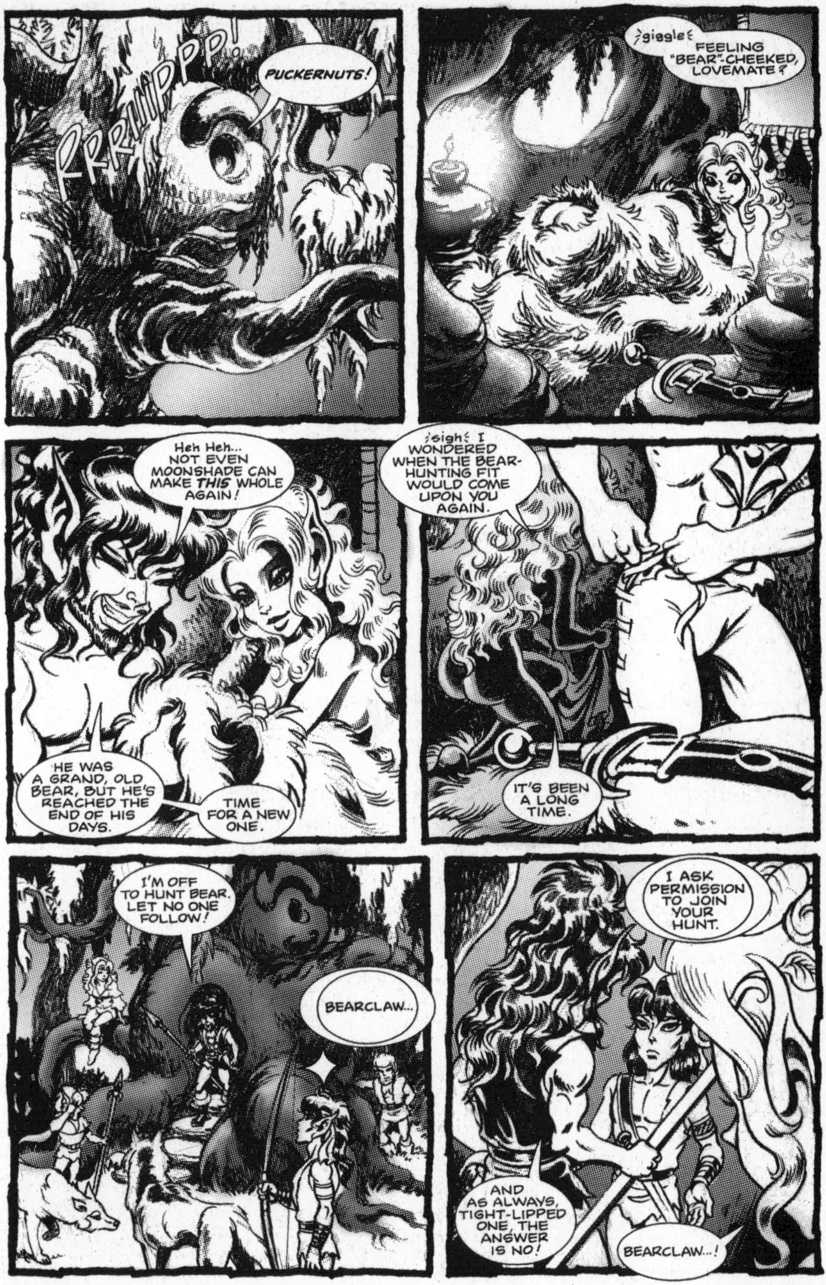
RRRIIIPPP!
PUCKERNUTS!
giggle
FEELING "BEAR"-CHEEKED, LOVEMATE?
Heh Heh... NOT EVEN MOONSHADE CAN MAKE THIS WHOLE AGAIN!
HE WAS A GRAND, OLD BEAR, BUT HE'S REACHED THE END OF HIS DAYS.
TIME FOR A NEW ONE.
sigh I WONDERED WHEN THE BEAR-HUNTING FIT WOULD COME UPON YOU AGAIN.
IT'S BEEN A LONG TIME.
I'M OFF TO HUNT BEAR. LET NO ONE FOLLOW!
BEARCLAW...
I ASK PERMISSION TO JOIN YOUR HUNT.
AND AS ALWAYS, TIGHT-LIPPED ONE, THE ANSWER IS NO!
BEARCLAW...!

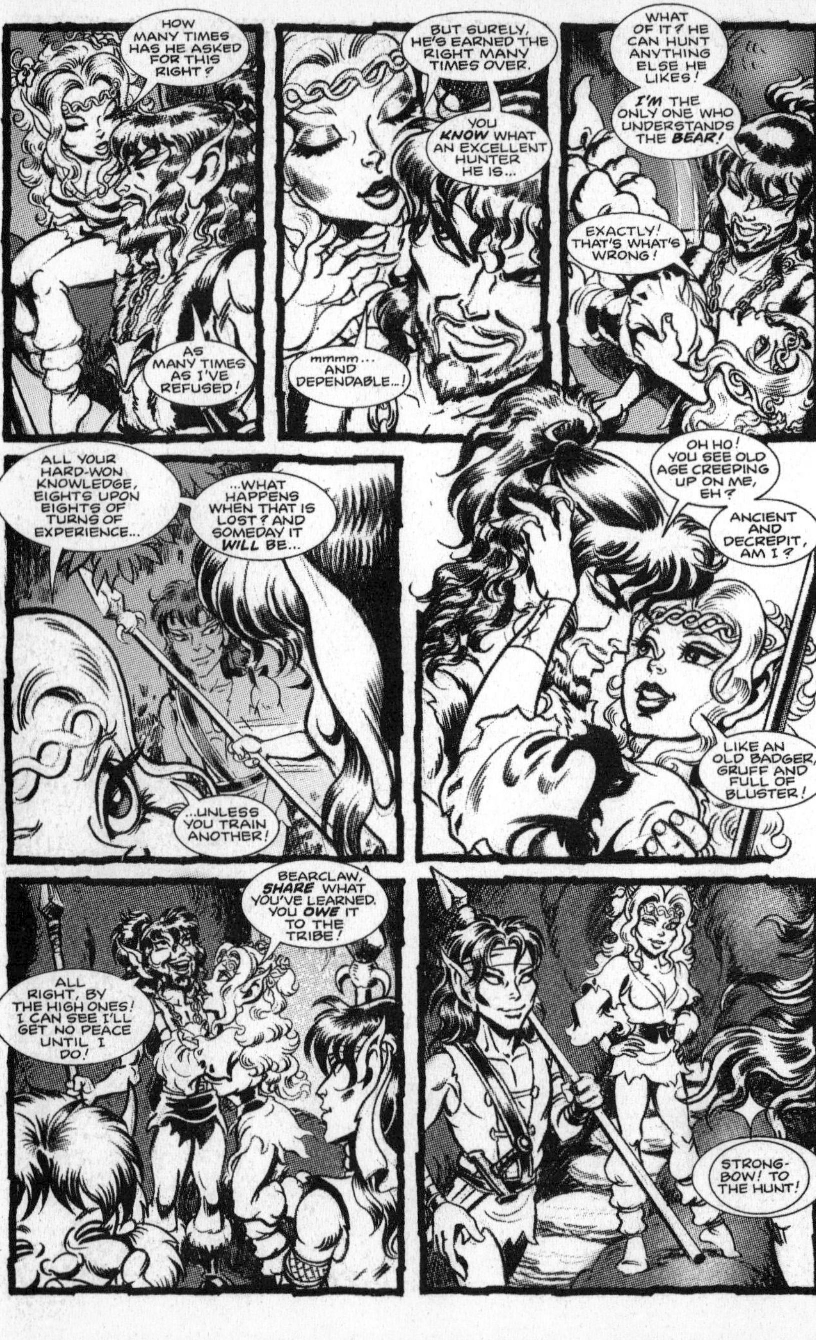
HOW MANY TIMES HAS HE ASKED FOR THIS RIGHT?
AS MANY TIMES AS I'VE REFUSED!
BUT SURELY, HE'S EARNED THE RIGHT MANY TIMES OVER.
YOU KNOW WHAT AN EXCELLENT HUNTER HE IS...
mmmm... AND DEPENDABLE...!
WHAT OF IT? HE CAN HUNT ANYTHING ELSE HE LIKES!
I'M THE ONLY ONE WHO UNDERSTANDS THE BEAR!
EXACTLY! THAT'S WHAT'S WRONG!
ALL YOUR HARD-WON KNOWLEDGE, EIGHTS UPON EIGHTS OF TURNS OF EXPERIENCE...
...WHAT HAPPENS WHEN THAT IS LOST? AND SOMEDAY IT WILL BE...
...UNLESS YOU TRAIN ANOTHER!
OH HO! YOU SEE OLD AGE CREEPING UP ON ME, EH?
ANCIENT AND DECREPIT, AM I?
LIKE AN OLD BADGER, GRUFF AND FULL OF BLUSTER!
BEARCLAW, SHARE WHAT YOU'VE LEARNED. YOU OWE IT TO THE TRIBE!
ALL RIGHT, BY THE HIGH ONES! I CAN SEE I'LL GET NO PEACE UNTIL I DO!
STRONG-BOW! TO THE HUNT!

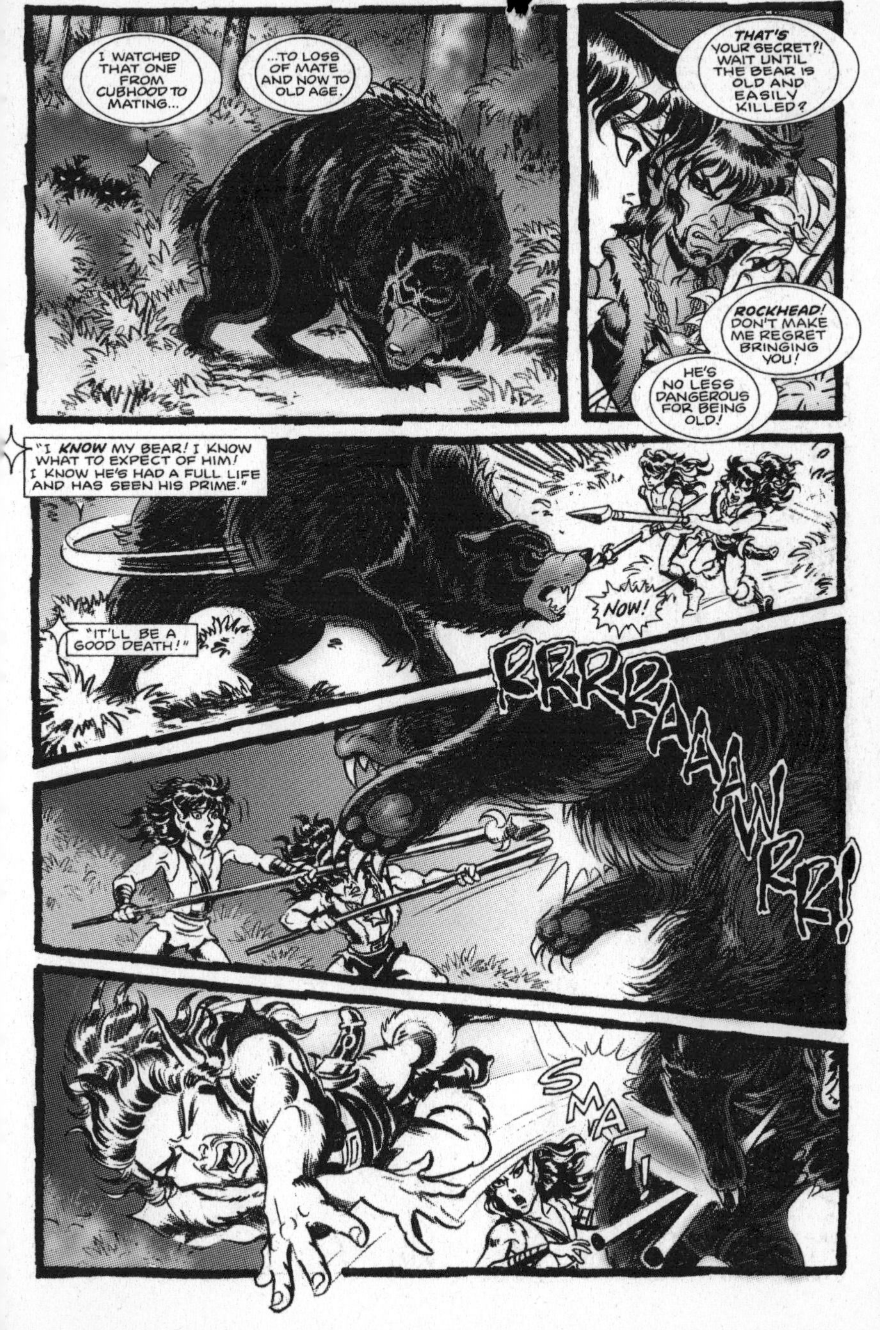
I WATCHED THAT ONE FROM CUBHOOD TO MATING...
...TO LOSS OF MATE AND NOW TO OLD AGE.
THAT'S YOUR SECRET?! WAIT UNTIL THE BEAR IS OLD AND EASILY KILLED?
ROCKHEAD! DON'T MAKE ME REGRET BRINGING YOU!
HE'S NO LESS DANGEROUS FOR BEING OLD!
"I KNOW MY BEAR! I KNOW WHAT TO EXPECT OF HIM! I KNOW HE'S HAD A FULL LIFE AND HAS SEEN HIS PRIME."
NOW!
"IT'LL BE A GOOD DEATH!"
RRRRAAAAWRR!
SMAT!

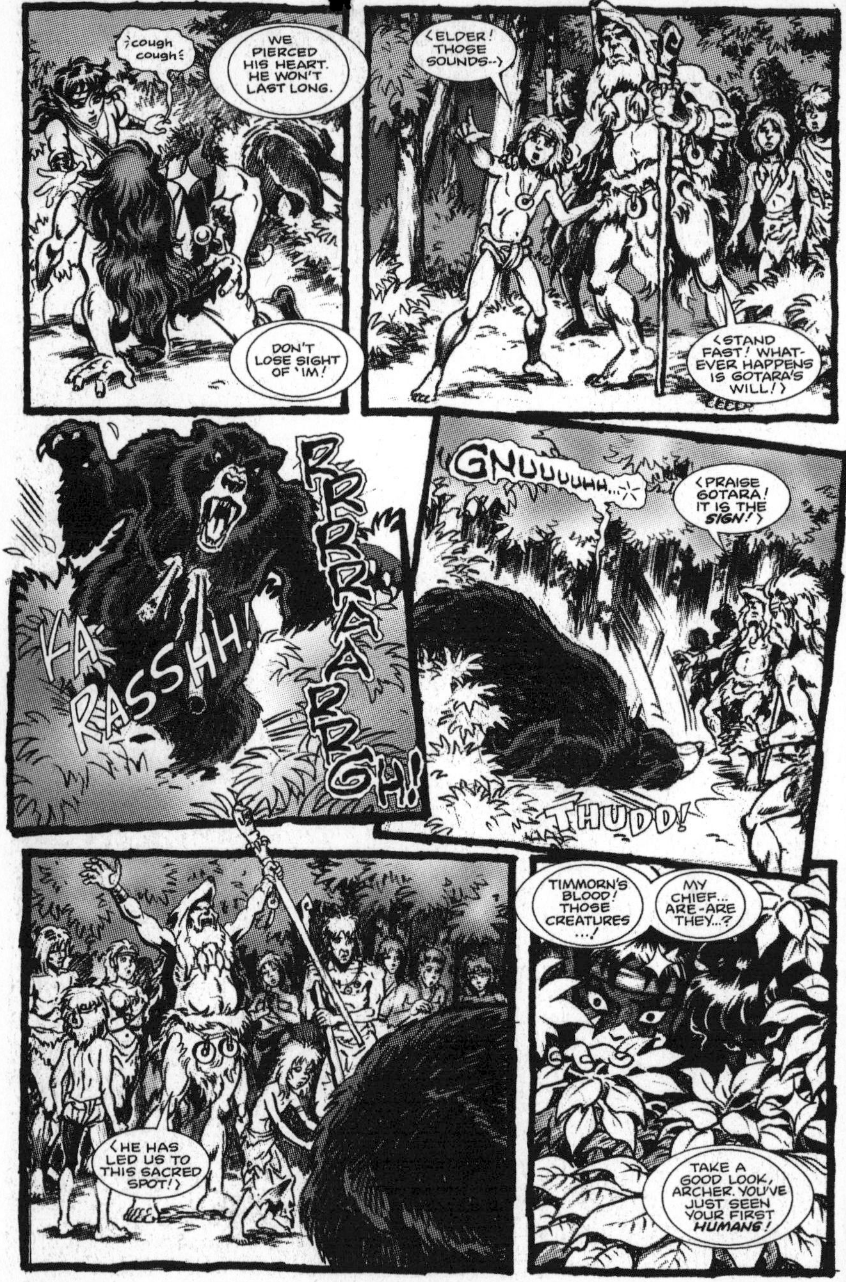

cough cough
WE PIERCED HIS HEART. HE WON'T LAST LONG.
DON'T LOSE SIGHT OF 'IM!
<ELDER! THOSE SOUNDS-->
<STAND FAST! WHATEVER HAPPENS IS GOTARA'S WILL!>
KA-RASSHH!
RRRRAAARRGH!
GNUUUUHH...
<PRAISE GOTARA! IT IS THE SIGN!>
THUDD!
<HE HAS LED US TO THIS SACRED SPOT!>
TIMMORN'S BLOOD! THOSE CREATURES ...!
MY CHIEF... ARE-ARE THEY...?
TAKE A GOOD LOOK, ARCHER. YOU'VE JUST SEEN YOUR FIRST HUMANS!

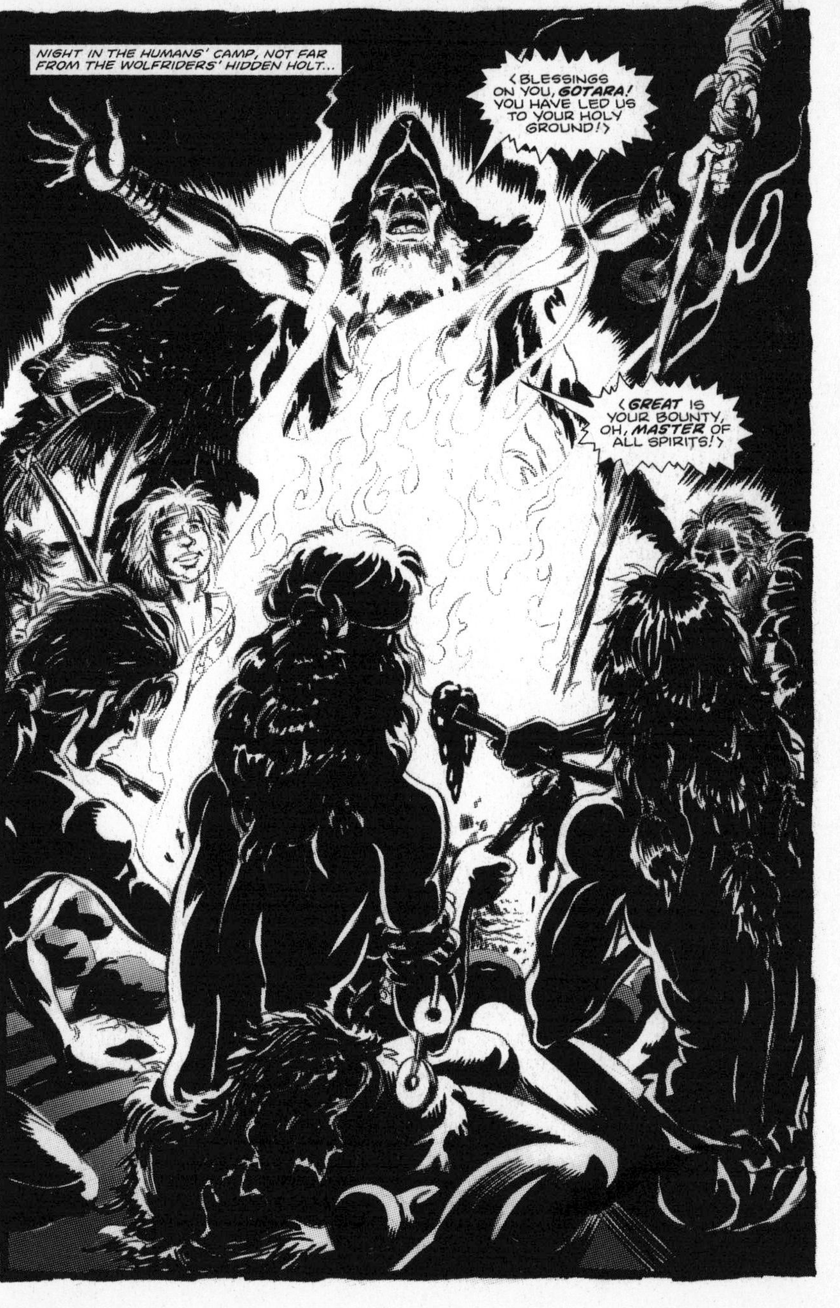
NIGHT IN THE HUMANS' CAMP, NOT FAR FROM THE WOLFRIDERS' HIDDEN HOLT...
〈BLESSINGS ON YOU, **GOTARA!** YOU HAVE LED US TO YOUR HOLY GROUND!〉
〈**GREAT** IS YOUR BOUNTY, OH, **MASTER** OF ALL SPIRITS!〉

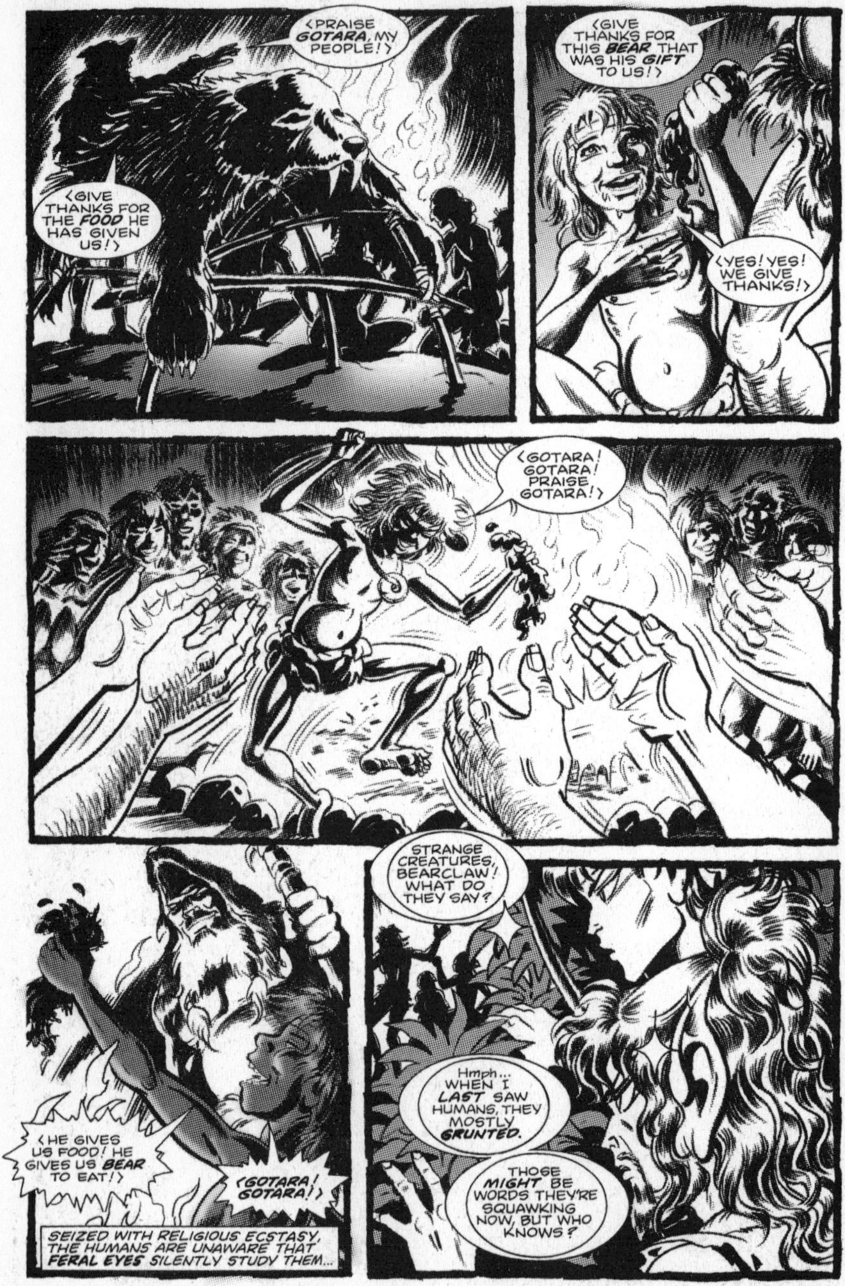

‹PRAISE GOTARA, MY PEOPLE!›
‹GIVE THANKS FOR THE FOOD HE HAS GIVEN US!›
‹GIVE THANKS FOR THIS BEAR THAT WAS HIS GIFT TO US!›
‹YES! YES! WE GIVE THANKS!›
‹GOTARA! GOTARA! PRAISE GOTARA!›
‹HE GIVES US FOOD! HE GIVES US BEAR TO EAT!›
‹GOTARA! GOTARA!›
SEIZED WITH RELIGIOUS ECSTASY, THE HUMANS ARE UNAWARE THAT FERAL EYES SILENTLY STUDY THEM...
STRANGE CREATURES, BEARCLAW! WHAT DO THEY SAY?
Hmph... WHEN I LAST SAW HUMANS, THEY MOSTLY GRUNTED.
THOSE MIGHT BE WORDS THEY'RE SQUAWKING NOW, BUT WHO KNOWS?

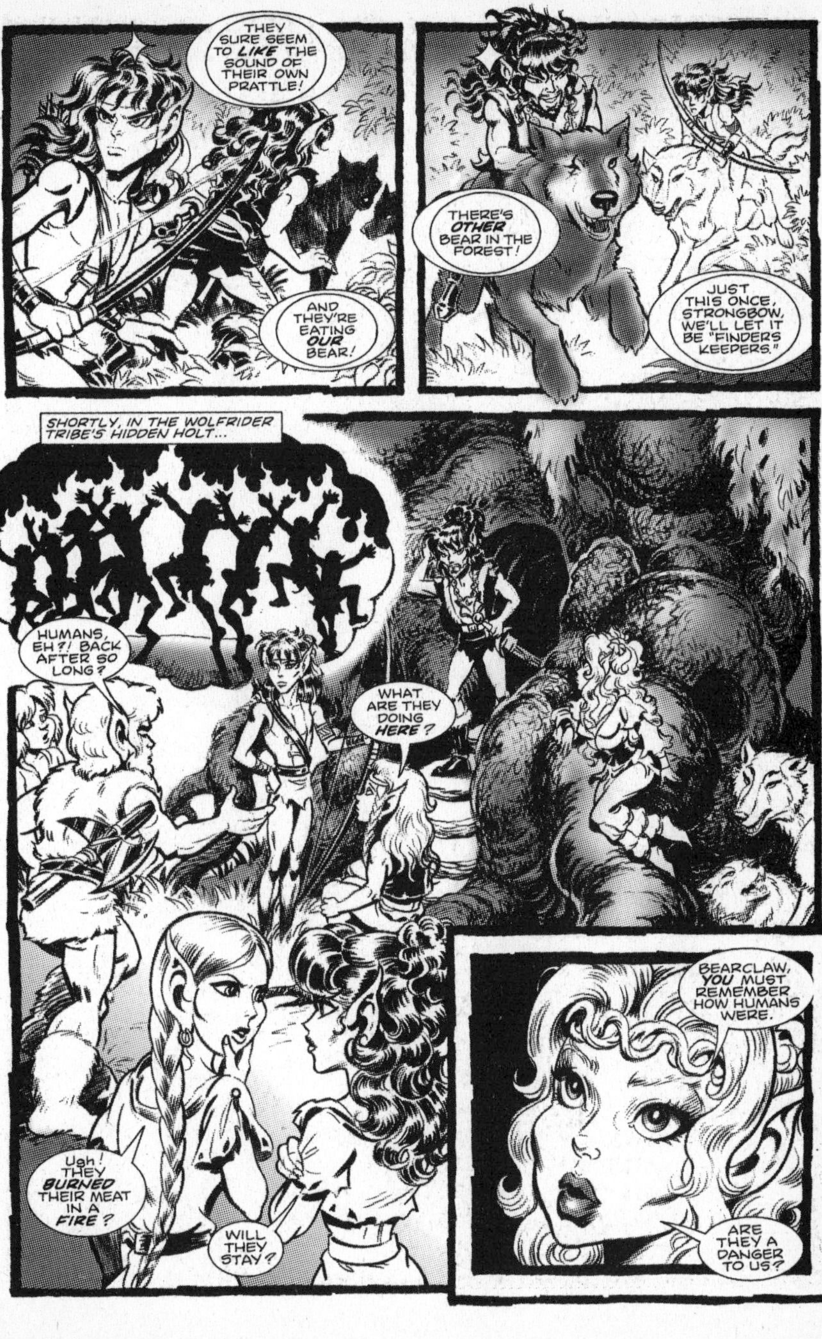
THEY SURE SEEM TO LIKE THE SOUND OF THEIR OWN PRATTLE!
AND THEY'RE EATING OUR BEAR!
THERE'S OTHER BEAR IN THE FOREST!
JUST THIS ONCE, STRONGBOW, WE'LL LET IT BE "FINDERS KEEPERS."
SHORTLY, IN THE WOLFRIDER TRIBE'S HIDDEN HOLT...
HUMANS, EH?! BACK AFTER SO LONG?
WHAT ARE THEY DOING HERE?
Ugh! THEY BURNED THEIR MEAT IN A FIRE?
WILL THEY STAY?
BEARCLAW, YOU MUST REMEMBER HOW HUMANS WERE.
ARE THEY A DANGER TO US?

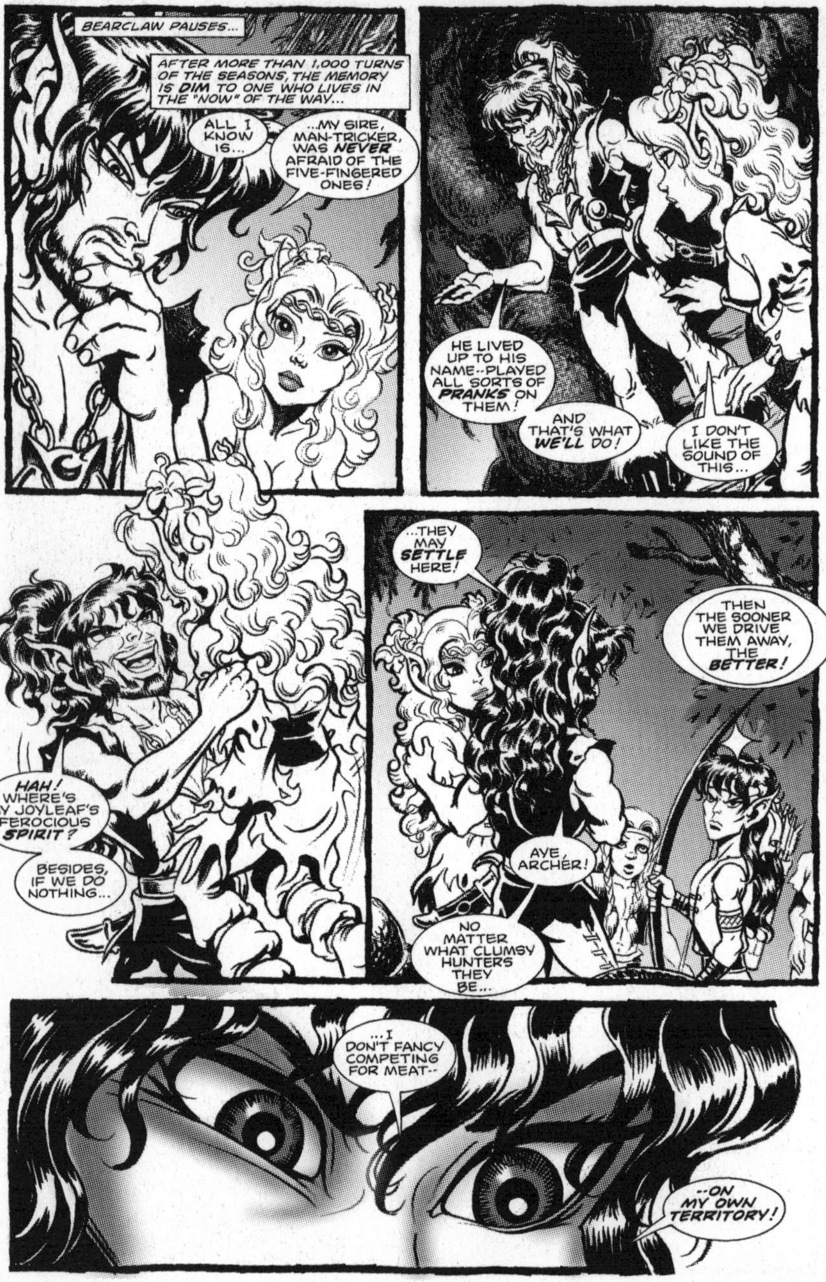
BEARCLAW PAUSES...
AFTER MORE THAN 1,000 TURNS OF THE SEASONS, THE MEMORY IS DIM TO ONE WHO LIVES IN THE "NOW" OF THE WAY...
ALL I KNOW IS...
...MY SIRE, MAN-TRICKER, WAS NEVER AFRAID OF THE FIVE-FINGERED ONES!
HE LIVED UP TO HIS NAME--PLAYED ALL SORTS OF PRANKS ON THEM!
AND THAT'S WHAT WE'LL DO!
I DON'T LIKE THE SOUND OF THIS...
HAH! WHERE'S MY JOYLEAF'S FEROCIOUS SPIRIT?
BESIDES, IF WE DO NOTHING...
...THEY MAY SETTLE HERE!
THEN THE SOONER WE DRIVE THEM AWAY, THE BETTER!
AYE, ARCHER!
NO MATTER WHAT CLUMSY HUNTERS THEY BE...
...I DON'T FANCY COMPETING FOR MEAT--
--ON MY OWN TERRITORY!

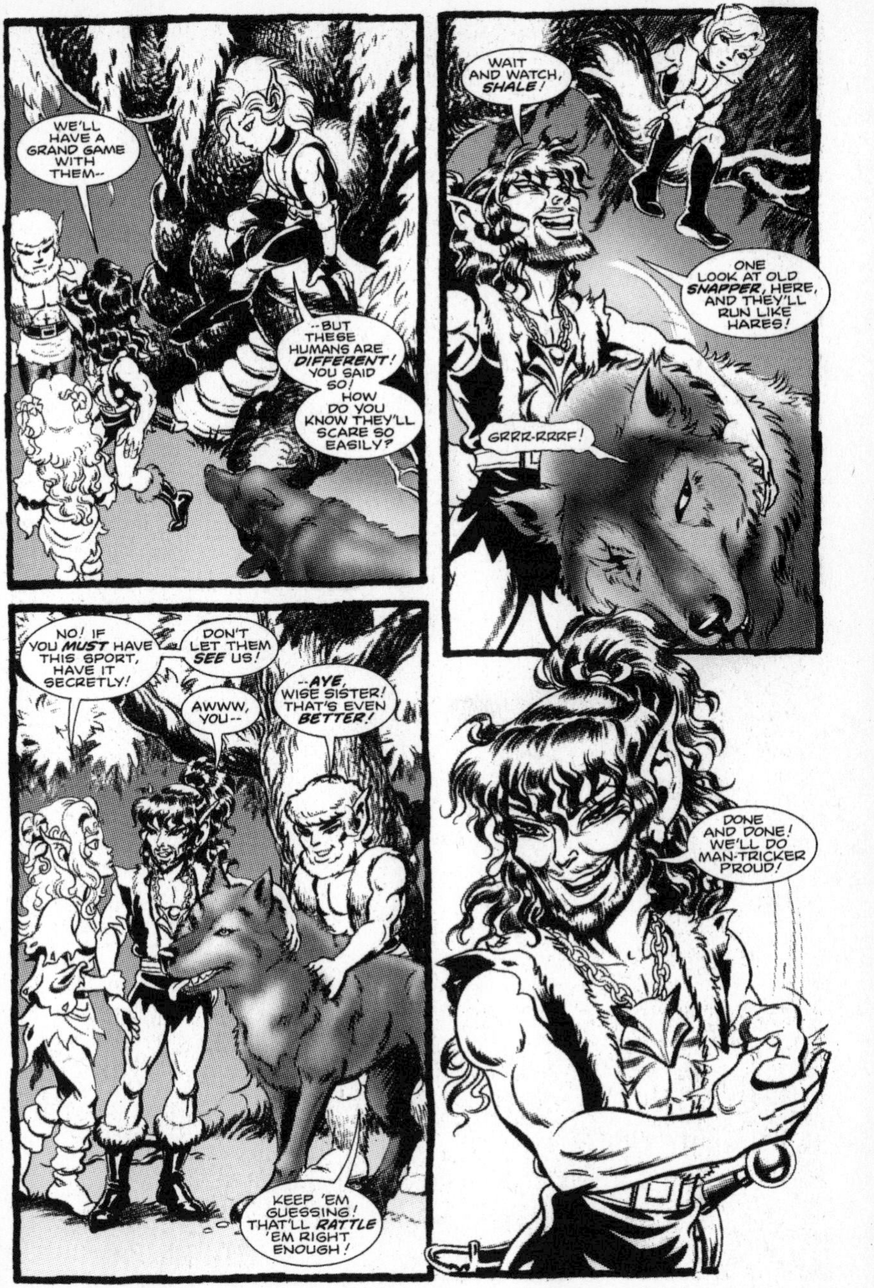
WE'LL HAVE A GRAND GAME WITH THEM--
--BUT THESE HUMANS ARE DIFFERENT! YOU SAID SO! HOW DO YOU KNOW THEY'LL SCARE SO EASILY?
WAIT AND WATCH, SHALE!
ONE LOOK AT OLD SNAPPER, HERE, AND THEY'LL RUN LIKE HARES!
GRRR-RRRF!
NO! IF YOU MUST HAVE THIS SPORT, HAVE IT SECRETLY!
DON'T LET THEM SEE US!
AWWW, YOU--
--AYE, WISE SISTER! THAT'S EVEN BETTER!
KEEP 'EM GUESSING! THAT'LL RATTLE 'EM RIGHT ENOUGH!
DONE AND DONE! WE'LL DO MAN-TRICKER PROUD!

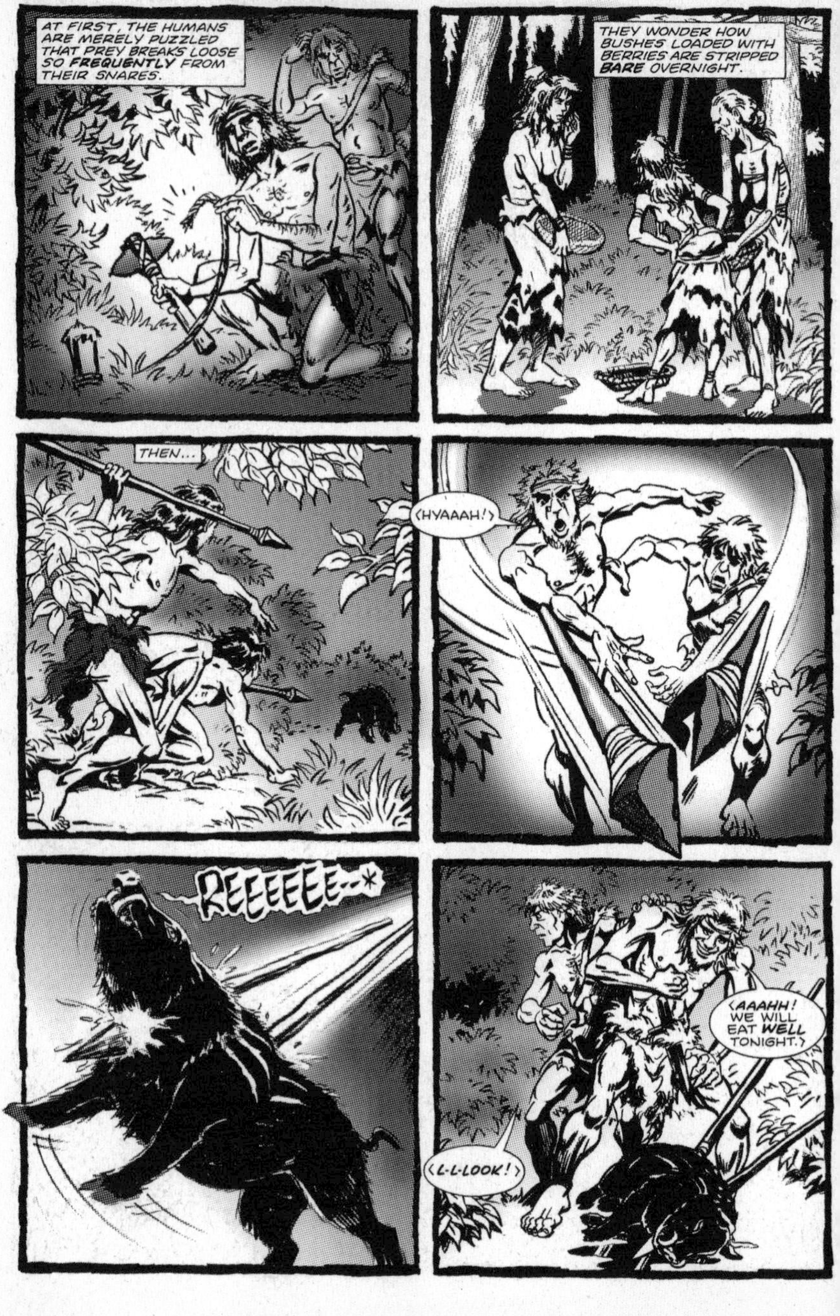
AT FIRST, THE HUMANS ARE MERELY PUZZLED THAT PREY BREAKS LOOSE SO FREQUENTLY FROM THEIR SNARES.
THEY WONDER HOW BUSHES LOADED WITH BERRIES ARE STRIPPED BARE OVERNIGHT.
THEN...
‹HYAAAH!›
REEEEEE--*
‹AAAHH! WE WILL EAT WELL TONIGHT.›
‹L-L-LOOK!›

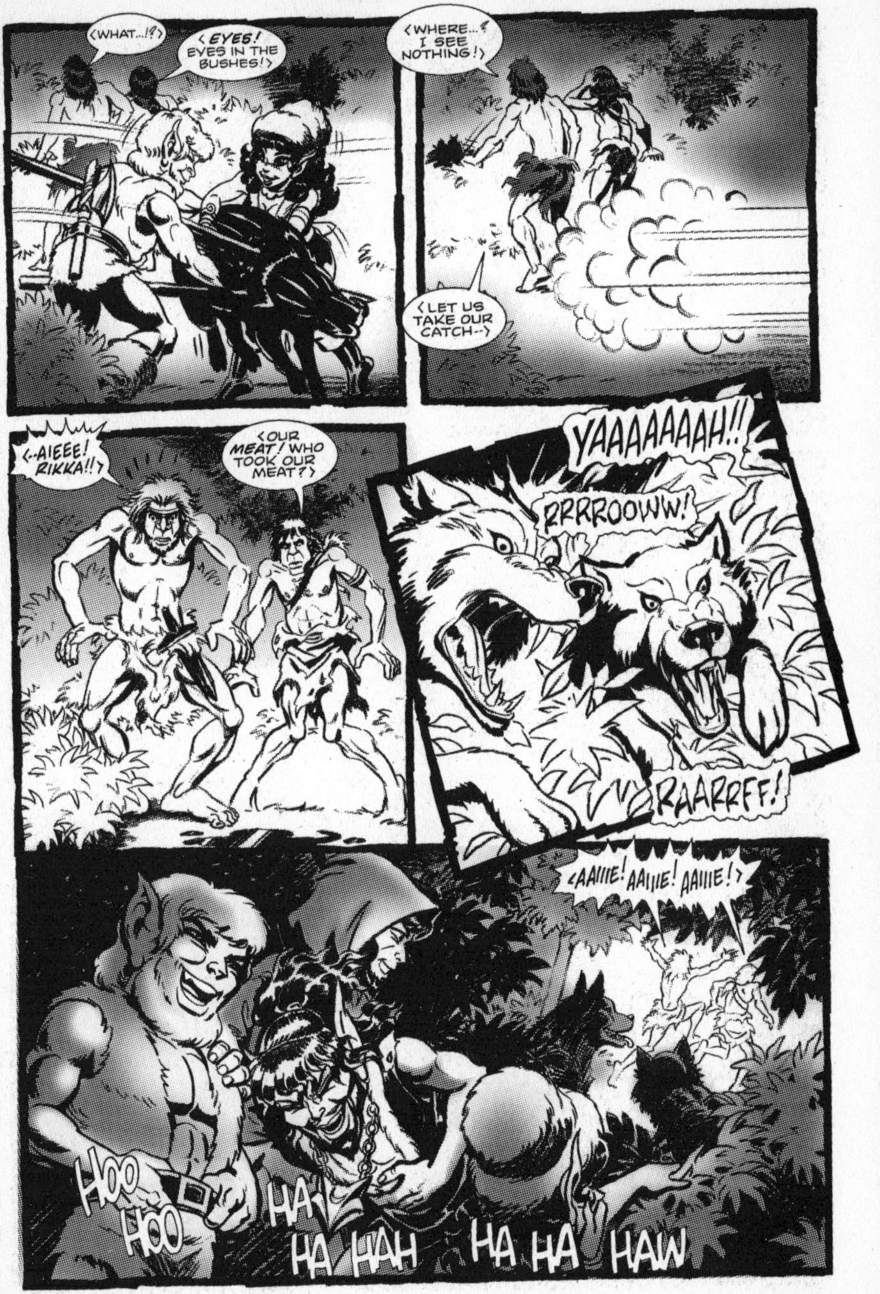

‹WHAT...!?›
‹EYES! EYES IN THE BUSHES!›
‹WHERE...? I SEE NOTHING!›
‹LET US TAKE OUR CATCH--›
‹--AIEEE! RIKKA!!›
‹OUR MEAT! WHO TOOK OUR MEAT?›
YAAAAAAAH!!
RRRROOWW!
RAARRFF!
‹AAIIIE! AAIIIE! AAIIIE!›
HOO HOO
HA HA HAH
HA HA HAW

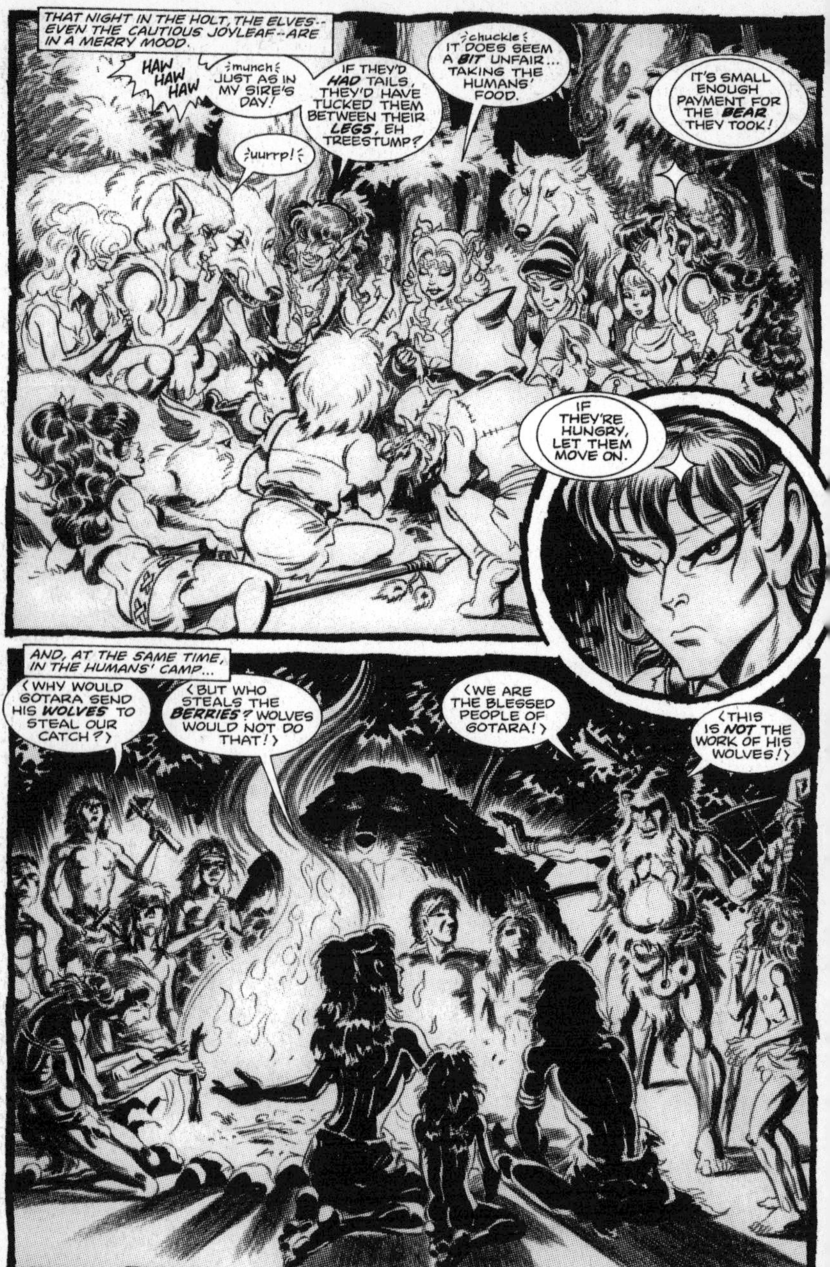
THAT NIGHT IN THE HOLT, THE ELVES--EVEN THE CAUTIOUS JOYLEAF--ARE IN A MERRY MOOD.
HAW HAW HAW
munch JUST AS IN MY SIRE'S DAY!
IF THEY'D HAD TAILS, THEY'D HAVE TUCKED THEM BETWEEN THEIR LEGS, EH TREESTUMP?
uurrp!
chuckle IT DOES SEEM A BIT UNFAIR... TAKING THE HUMANS' FOOD.
IT'S SMALL ENOUGH PAYMENT FOR THE BEAR THEY TOOK!
IF THEY'RE HUNGRY, LET THEM MOVE ON.
AND, AT THE SAME TIME, IN THE HUMANS' CAMP...
<WHY WOULD GOTARA SEND HIS WOLVES TO STEAL OUR CATCH?>
<BUT WHO STEALS THE BERRIES? WOLVES WOULD NOT DO THAT!>
<WE ARE THE BLESSED PEOPLE OF GOTARA!>
<THIS IS NOT THE WORK OF HIS WOLVES!>

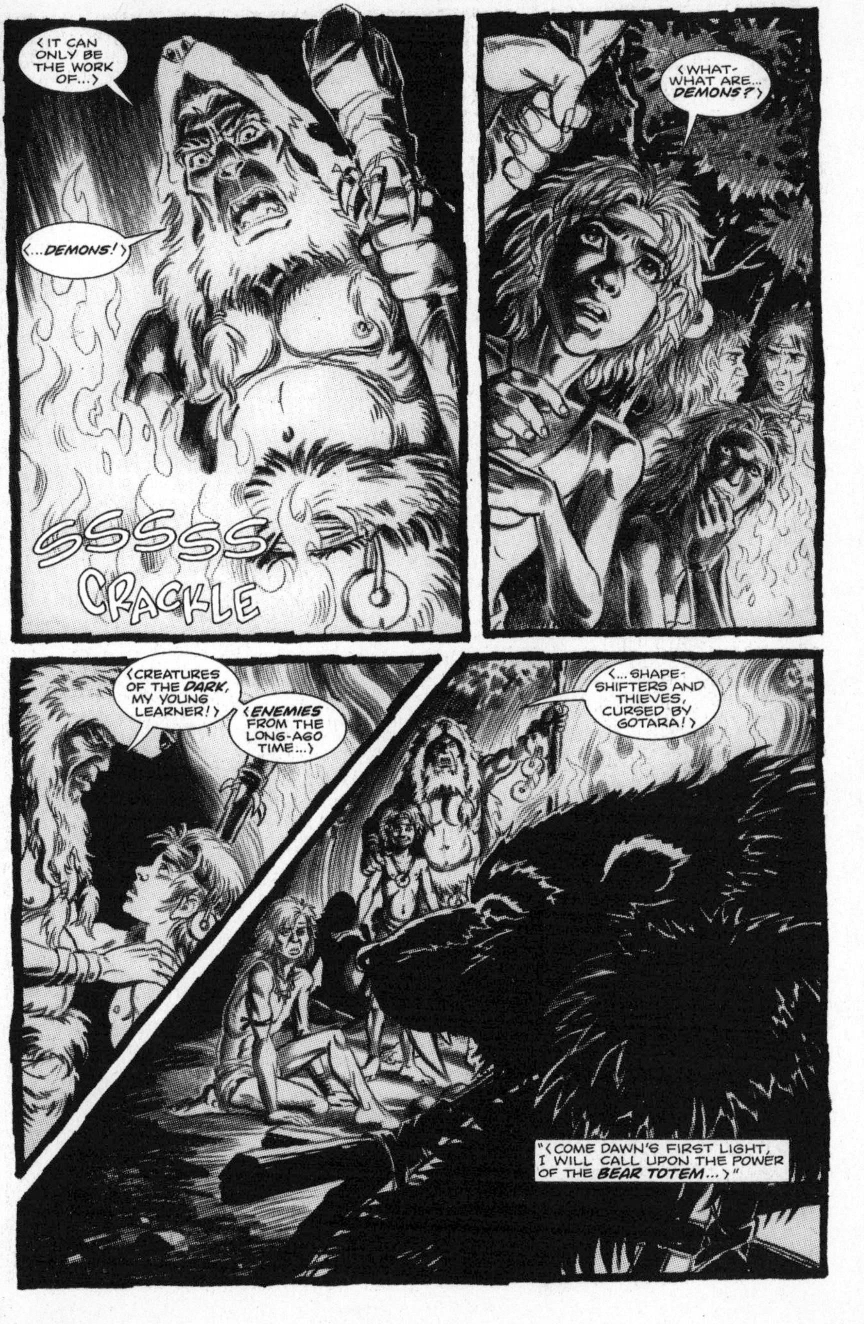

‹IT CAN ONLY BE THE WORK OF...›
‹...DEMONS!›
SSSSSS
CRACKLE
‹WHAT-WHAT ARE... DEMONS?›
‹CREATURES OF THE DARK, MY YOUNG LEARNER!›
‹ENEMIES FROM THE LONG-AGO TIME...›
‹...SHAPE-SHIFTERS AND THIEVES, CURSED BY GOTARA!›
"‹COME DAWN'S FIRST LIGHT, I WILL CALL UPON THE POWER OF THE BEAR TOTEM...›"

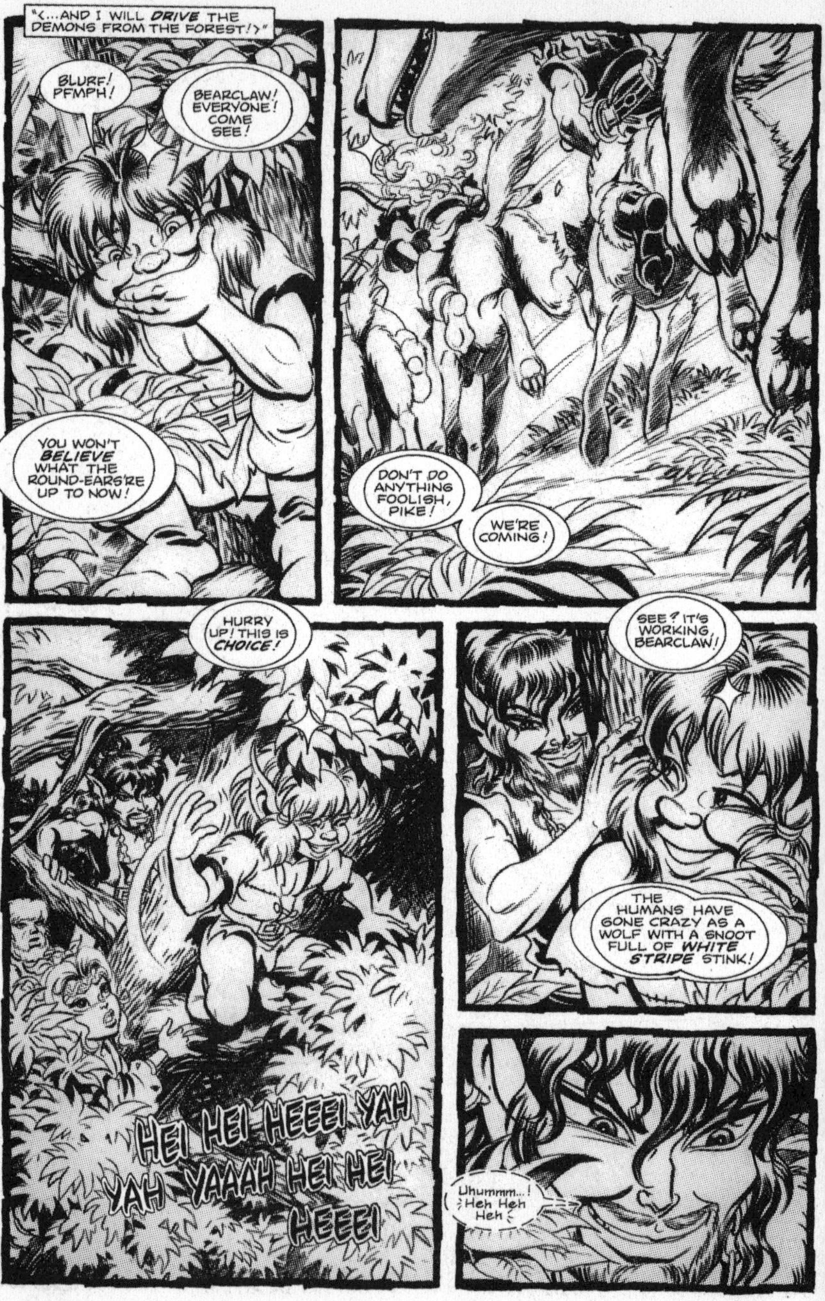
"<...AND I WILL DRIVE THE DEMONS FROM THE FOREST!>"
BLURF! PFMPH!
BEARCLAW! EVERYONE! COME SEE!
YOU WON'T BELIEVE WHAT THE ROUND-EARS'RE UP TO NOW!
DON'T DO ANYTHING FOOLISH, PIKE!
WE'RE COMING!
HURRY UP! THIS IS CHOICE!
HEI HEI HEEEI YAH YAH YAAAH HEI HEI HEEEI
SEE? IT'S WORKING, BEARCLAW!
THE HUMANS HAVE GONE CRAZY AS A WOLF WITH A SNOOT FULL OF WHITE STRIPE STINK!
Uhummm...! Heh Heh Heh

HEI HEI HEEEI YAH YAH YAAAH HEI HEI HEEEI
‹OUT, DEMONS, OUT! BY THE POWER OF GOTARA, I CAST YOU OUT!›
‹BY THE SPIRIT OF GOTARA'S MIGHTIEST CREATION, THE BEAR...›
‹...I CAST YOU OUT!›

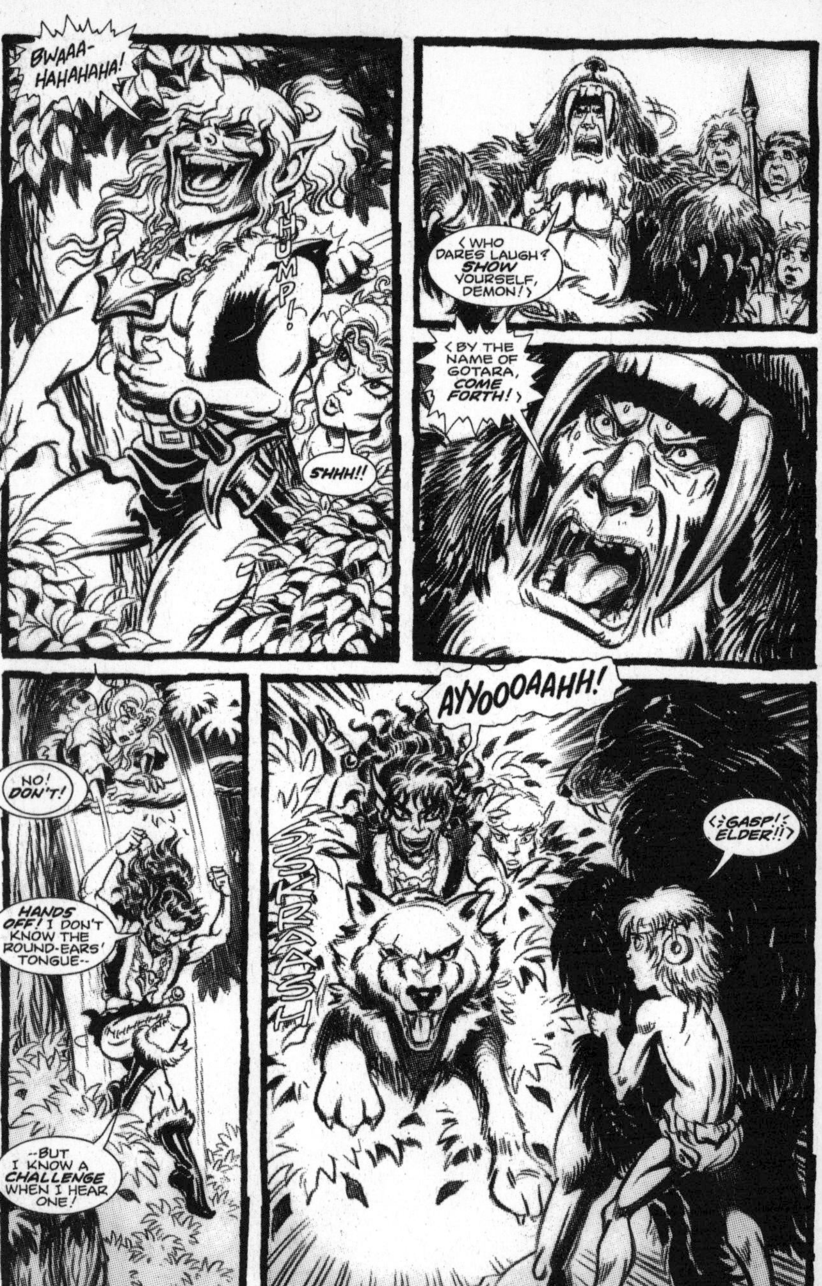

BWAAA-HAHAHAHA!
THUMP!
SHHH!!
⟨WHO DARES LAUGH? SHOW YOURSELF, DEMON!⟩
⟨BY THE NAME OF GOTARA, COME FORTH!⟩
NO! DON'T!
HANDS OFF! I DON'T KNOW THE ROUND-EARS' TONGUE--
--BUT I KNOW A CHALLENGE WHEN I HEAR ONE!
AYYOOOAAHH!
SSHRAASH
⟨GASP! ELDER!!⟩

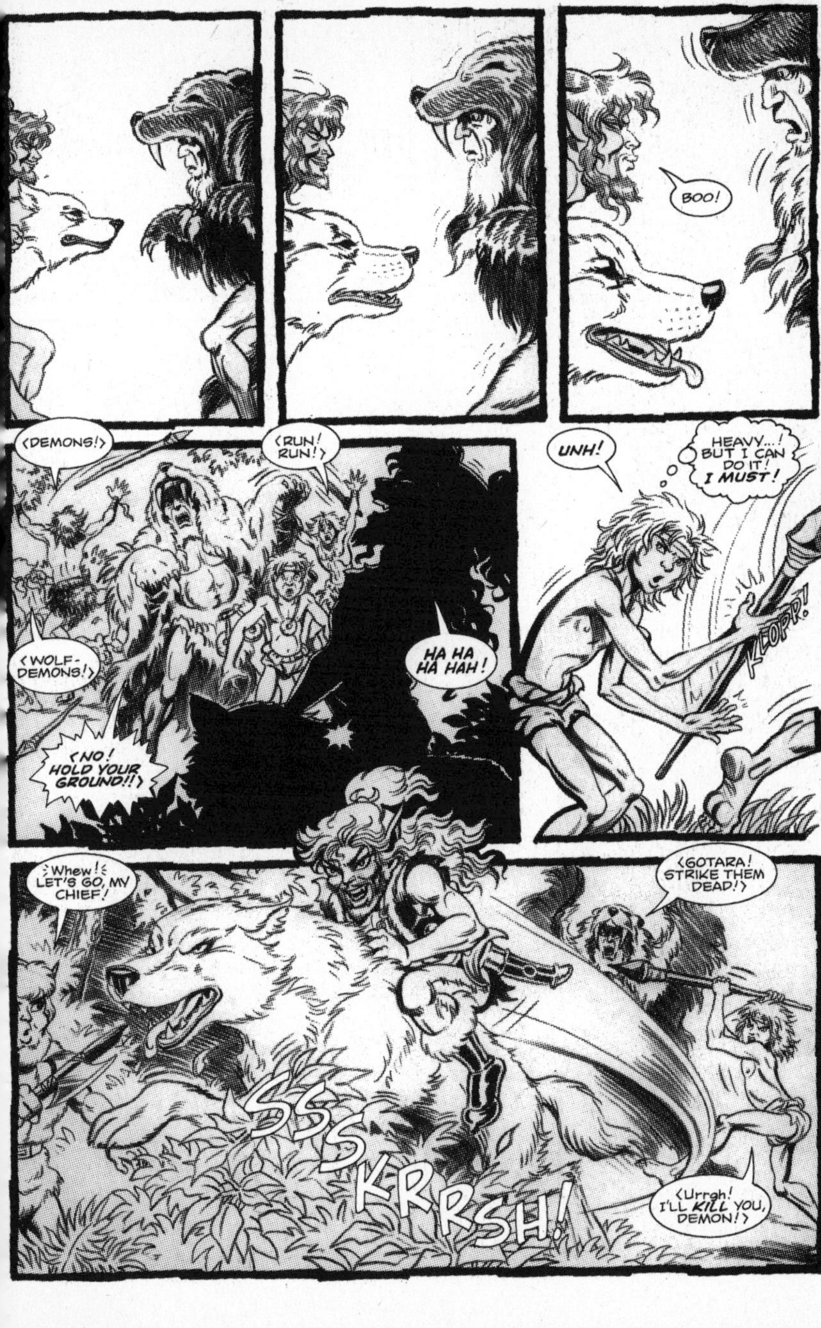
BOO!
⟨DEMONS!⟩
⟨RUN! RUN!⟩
⟨WOLF-DEMONS!⟩
⟨NO! HOLD YOUR GROUND!!⟩
HA HA HA HAH!
UNH!
HEAVY...! BUT I CAN DO IT! I MUST!
KLOPP!
Whew! LET'S GO, MY CHIEF!
⟨GOTARA! STRIKE THEM DEAD!⟩
SSS KRRSH!
⟨Urrgh! I'LL KILL YOU, DEMON!⟩

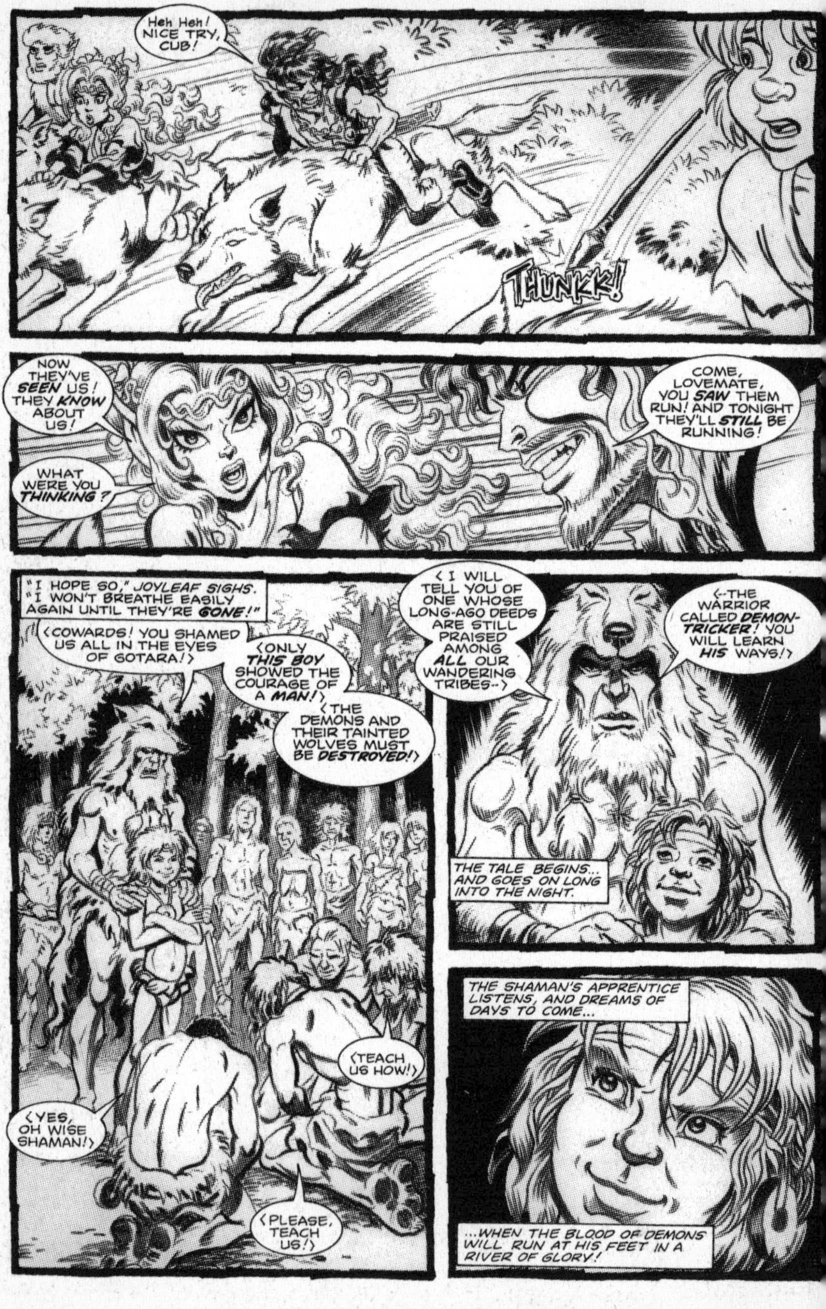

Heh Heh! NICE TRY, CUB!
THUNKK!
NOW THEY'VE SEEN US! THEY KNOW ABOUT US!
WHAT WERE YOU THINKING?
COME, LOVEMATE, YOU SAW THEM RUN! AND TONIGHT THEY'LL STILL BE RUNNING!
"I HOPE SO," JOYLEAF SIGHS. "I WON'T BREATHE EASILY AGAIN UNTIL THEY'RE GONE!"
‹COWARDS! YOU SHAMED US ALL IN THE EYES OF GOTARA!›
‹ONLY THIS BOY SHOWED THE COURAGE OF A MAN!›
‹THE DEMONS AND THEIR TAINTED WOLVES MUST BE DESTROYED!›
‹TEACH US HOW!›
‹YES, OH WISE SHAMAN!›
‹PLEASE, TEACH US!›
‹I WILL TELL YOU OF ONE WHOSE LONG-AGO DEEDS ARE STILL PRAISED AMONG ALL OUR WANDERING TRIBES--›
‹--THE WARRIOR CALLED DEMON-TRICKER! YOU WILL LEARN HIS WAYS!›
THE TALE BEGINS... AND GOES ON LONG INTO THE NIGHT.
THE SHAMAN'S APPRENTICE LISTENS, AND DREAMS OF DAYS TO COME...
...WHEN THE BLOOD OF DEMONS WILL RUN AT HIS FEET IN A RIVER OF GLORY!

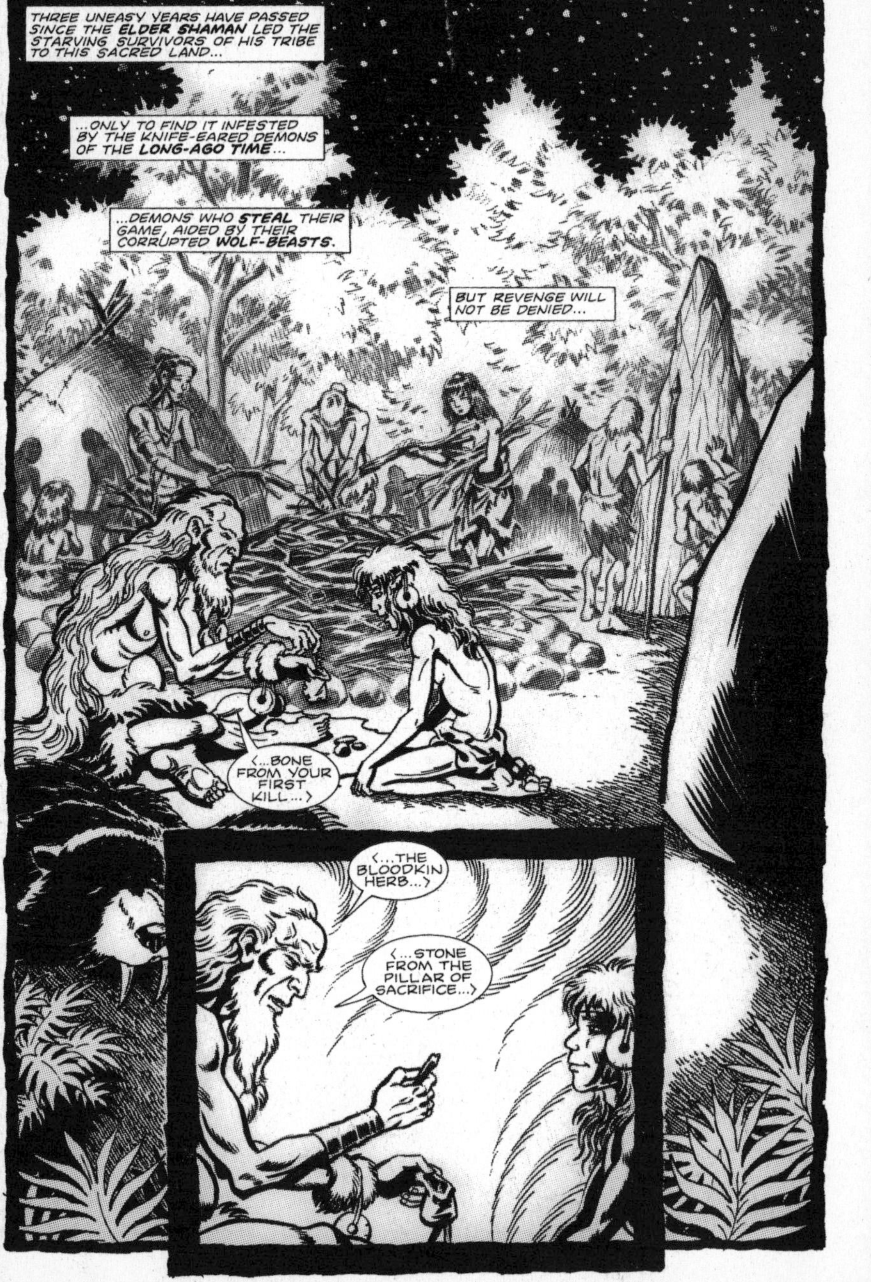

THREE UNEASY YEARS HAVE PASSED SINCE THE ELDER SHAMAN LED THE STARVING SURVIVORS OF HIS TRIBE TO THIS SACRED LAND...
...ONLY TO FIND IT INFESTED BY THE KNIFE-EARED DEMONS OF THE LONG-AGO TIME...
...DEMONS WHO STEAL THEIR GAME, AIDED BY THEIR CORRUPTED WOLF-BEASTS.
BUT REVENGE WILL NOT BE DENIED...
‹...BONE FROM YOUR FIRST KILL...›
‹...THE BLOODKIN HERB...›
‹...STONE FROM THE PILLAR OF SACRIFICE...›

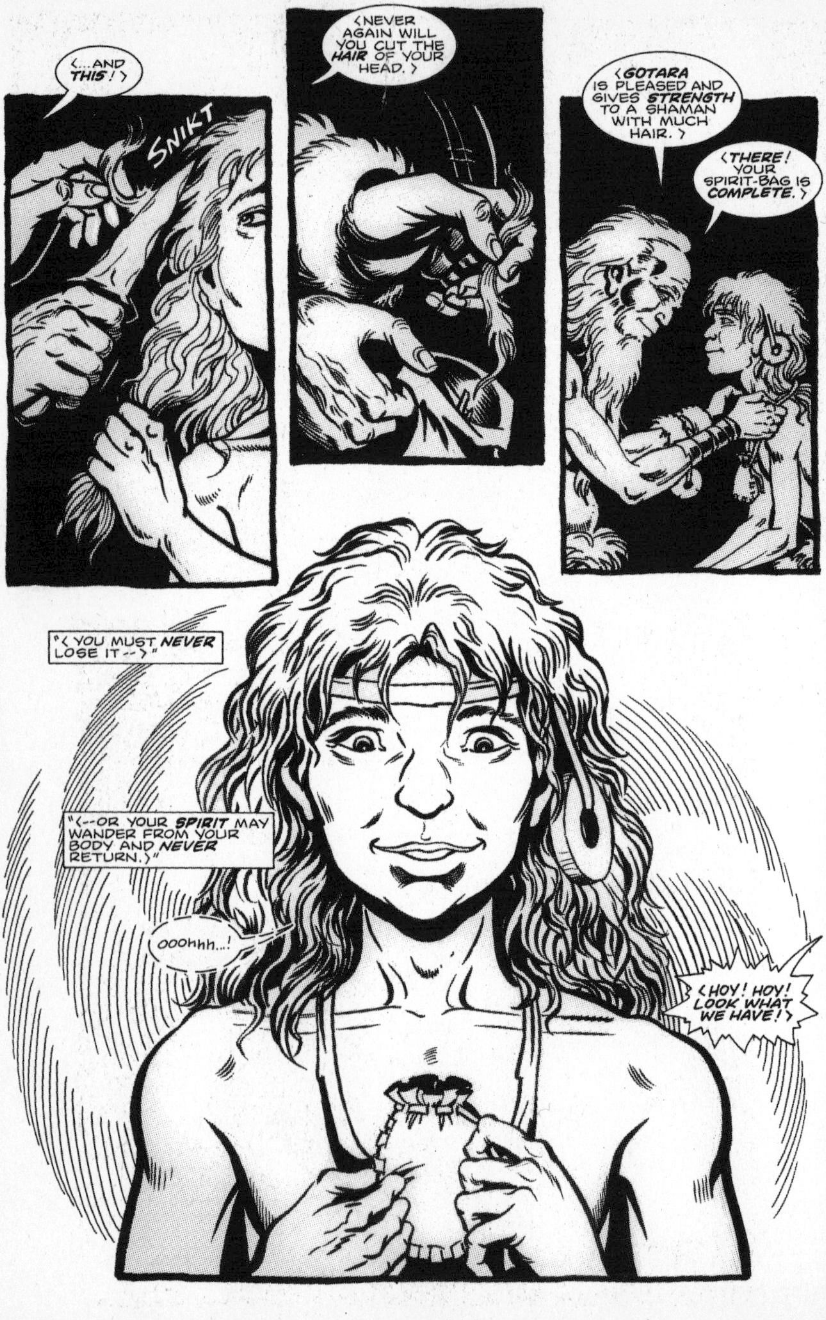

<...AND THIS!>
SNIKT
<NEVER AGAIN WILL YOU CUT THE HAIR OF YOUR HEAD.>
<GOTARA IS PLEASED AND GIVES STRENGTH TO A SHAMAN WITH MUCH HAIR.>
<THERE! YOUR SPIRIT-BAG IS COMPLETE.>
"<YOU MUST NEVER LOSE IT-->"
"<--OR YOUR SPIRIT MAY WANDER FROM YOUR BODY AND NEVER RETURN.>"
OOOHHH...!
<HOY! HOY! LOOK WHAT WE HAVE!>

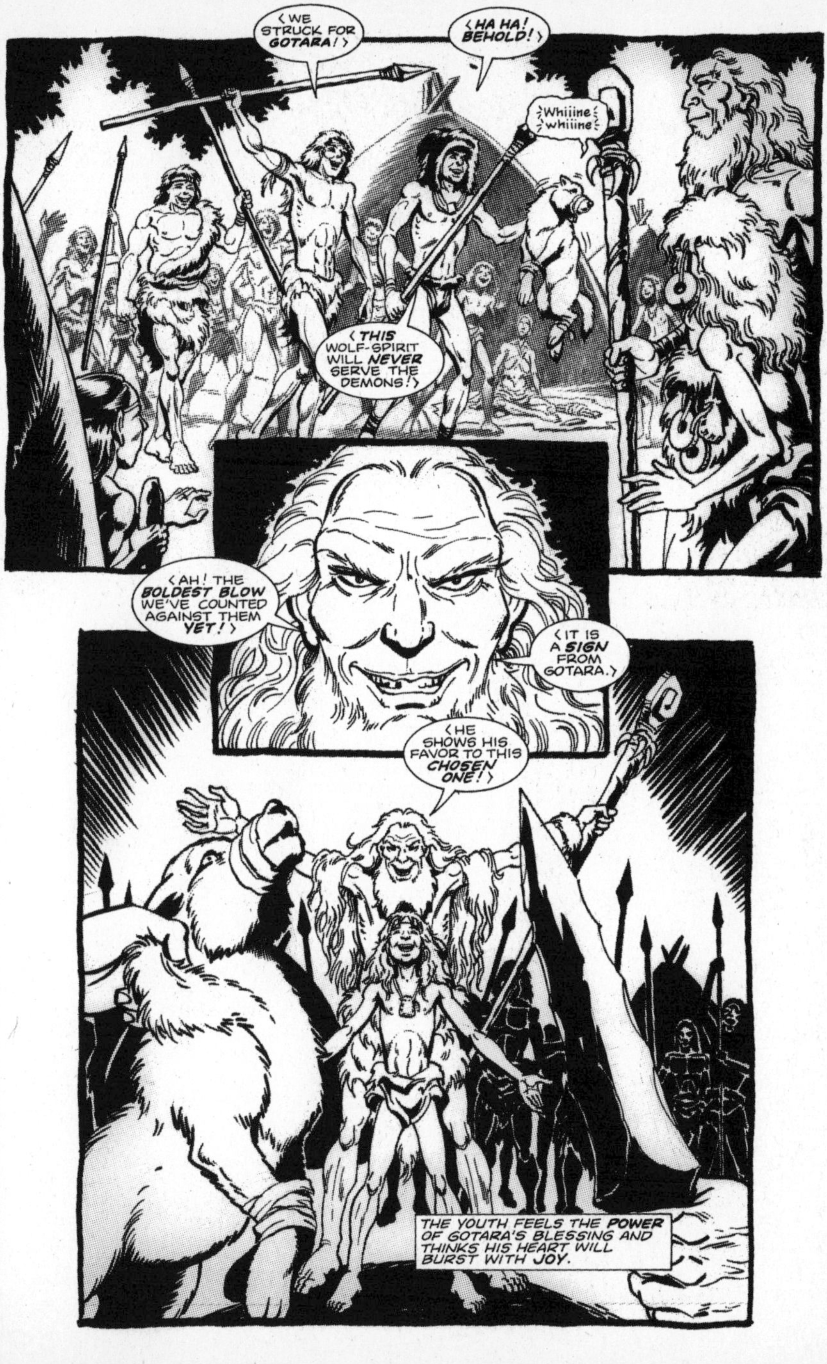

<WE STRUCK FOR GOTARA!>
<HA HA! BEHOLD!>
Whiiine whiiine
<THIS WOLF-SPIRIT WILL NEVER SERVE THE DEMONS!>
<AH! THE BOLDEST BLOW WE'VE COUNTED AGAINST THEM YET!>
<IT IS A SIGN FROM GOTARA.>
<HE SHOWS HIS FAVOR TO THIS CHOSEN ONE!>
THE YOUTH FEELS THE POWER OF GOTARA'S BLESSING AND THINKS HIS HEART WILL BURST WITH JOY.

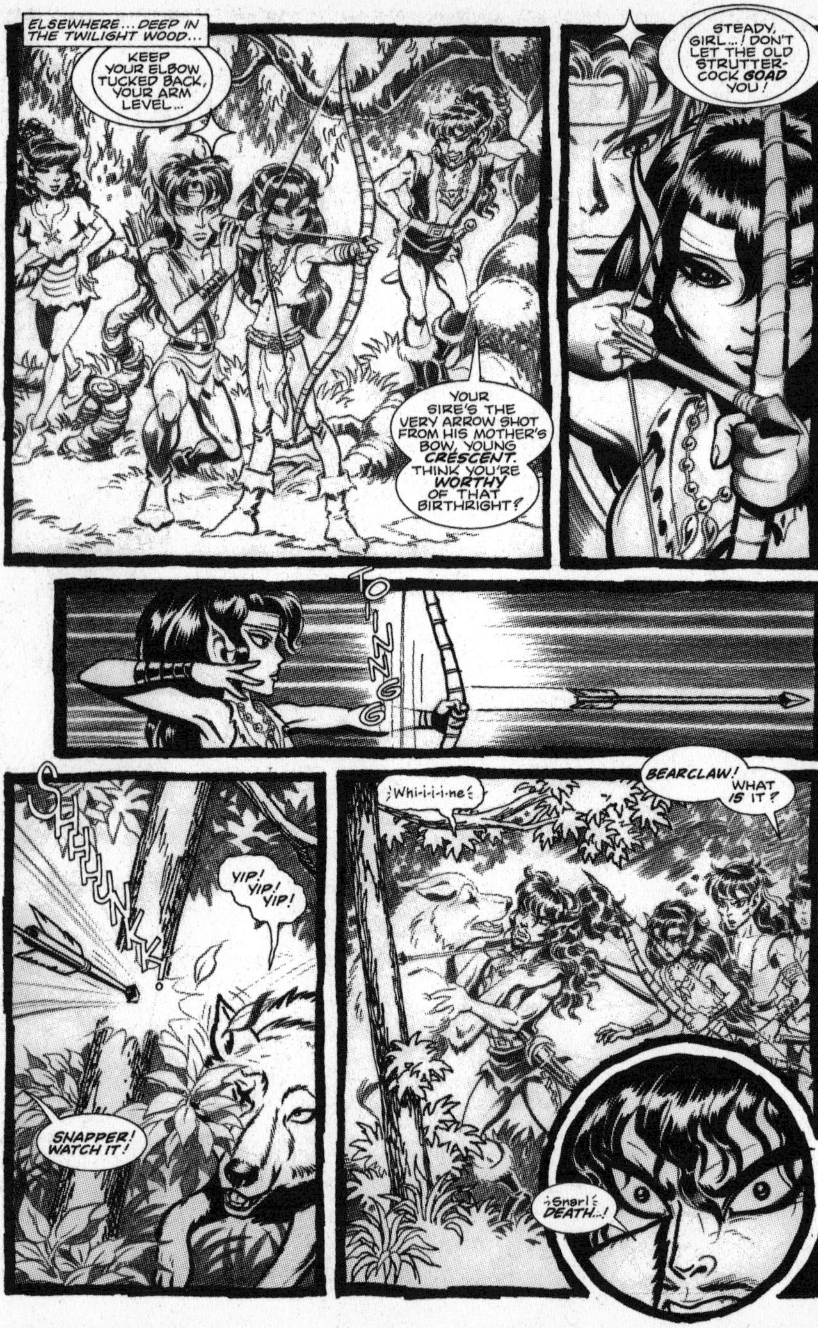

ELSEWHERE... DEEP IN THE TWILIGHT WOOD...
KEEP YOUR ELBOW TUCKED BACK, YOUR ARM LEVEL...
YOUR SIRE'S THE VERY ARROW SHOT FROM HIS MOTHER'S BOW, YOUNG CRESCENT. THINK YOU'RE WORTHY OF THAT BIRTHRIGHT?
STEADY, GIRL...! DON'T LET THE OLD STRUTTER-COCK GOAD YOU!
TO-I-I-NNGG
SHHHUNKK!
YIP! YIP! YIP!
SNAPPER! WATCH IT!
Whi-i-i-i-ne
BEARCLAW! WHAT IS IT?
Snarl DEATH...!

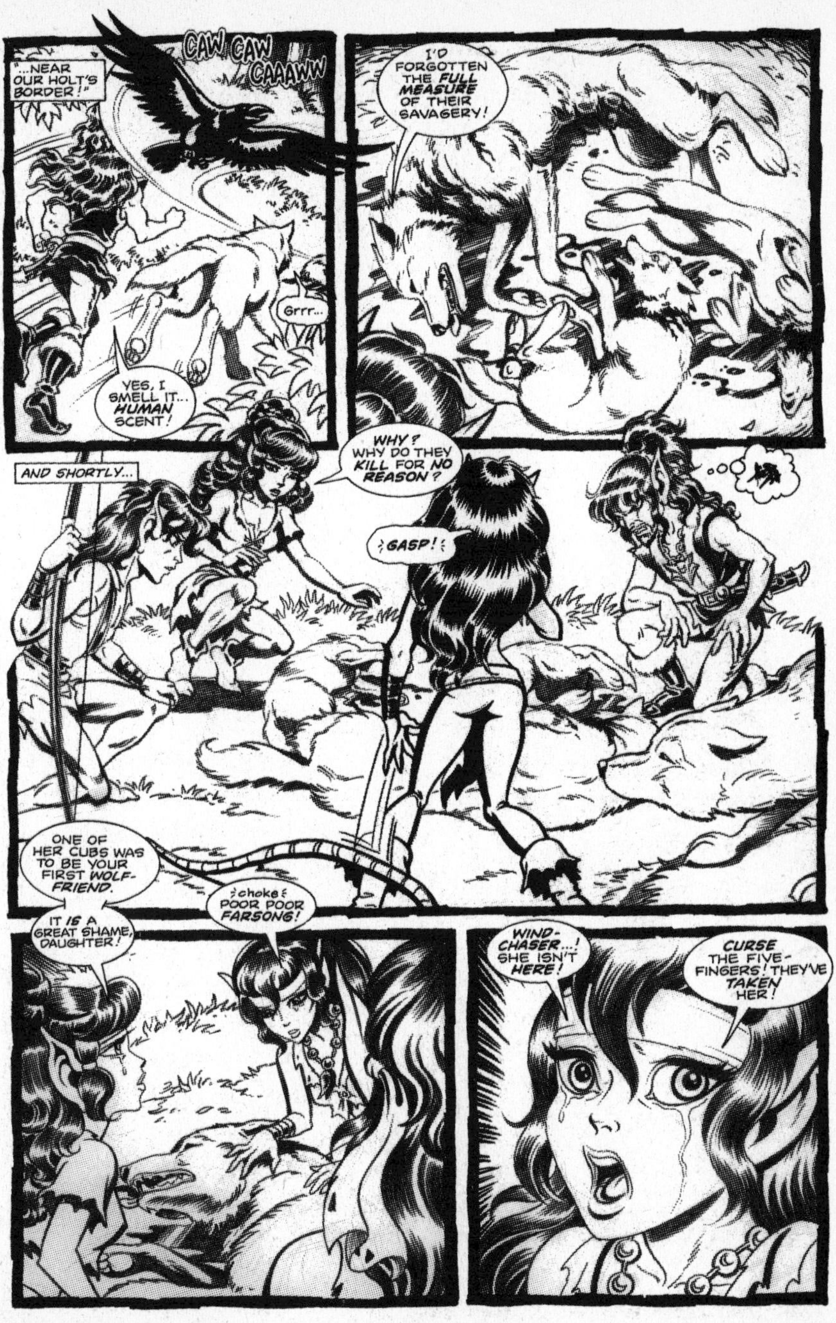

"...NEAR OUR HOLT'S BORDER!"
CAW CAW CAAAWW
Grrr...
YES, I SMELL IT... HUMAN SCENT!
I'D FORGOTTEN THE FULL MEASURE OF THEIR SAVAGERY!
AND SHORTLY...
WHY? WHY DO THEY KILL FOR NO REASON?
GASP!
ONE OF HER CUBS WAS TO BE YOUR FIRST WOLF-FRIEND.
IT IS A GREAT SHAME, DAUGHTER!
choke POOR POOR FARSONG!
WIND-CHASER...! SHE ISN'T HERE!
CURSE THE FIVE-FINGERS! THEY'VE TAKEN HER!

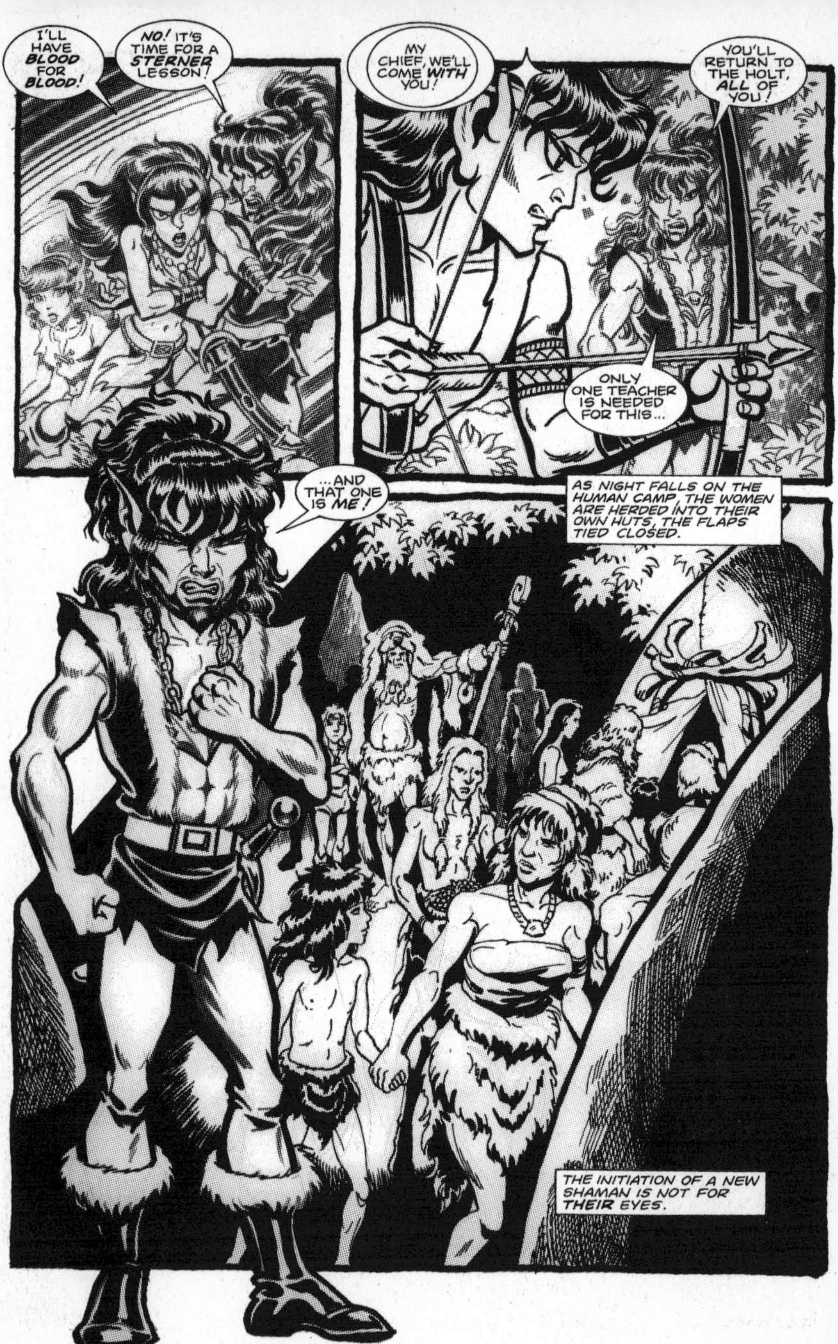
I'LL HAVE BLOOD FOR BLOOD!
NO! IT'S TIME FOR A STERNER LESSON!
MY CHIEF, WE'LL COME WITH YOU!
YOU'LL RETURN TO THE HOLT, ALL OF YOU!
ONLY ONE TEACHER IS NEEDED FOR THIS...
...AND THAT ONE IS ME!
AS NIGHT FALLS ON THE HUMAN CAMP, THE WOMEN ARE HERDED INTO THEIR OWN HUTS, THE FLAPS TIED CLOSED.
THE INITIATION OF A NEW SHAMAN IS NOT FOR THEIR EYES.

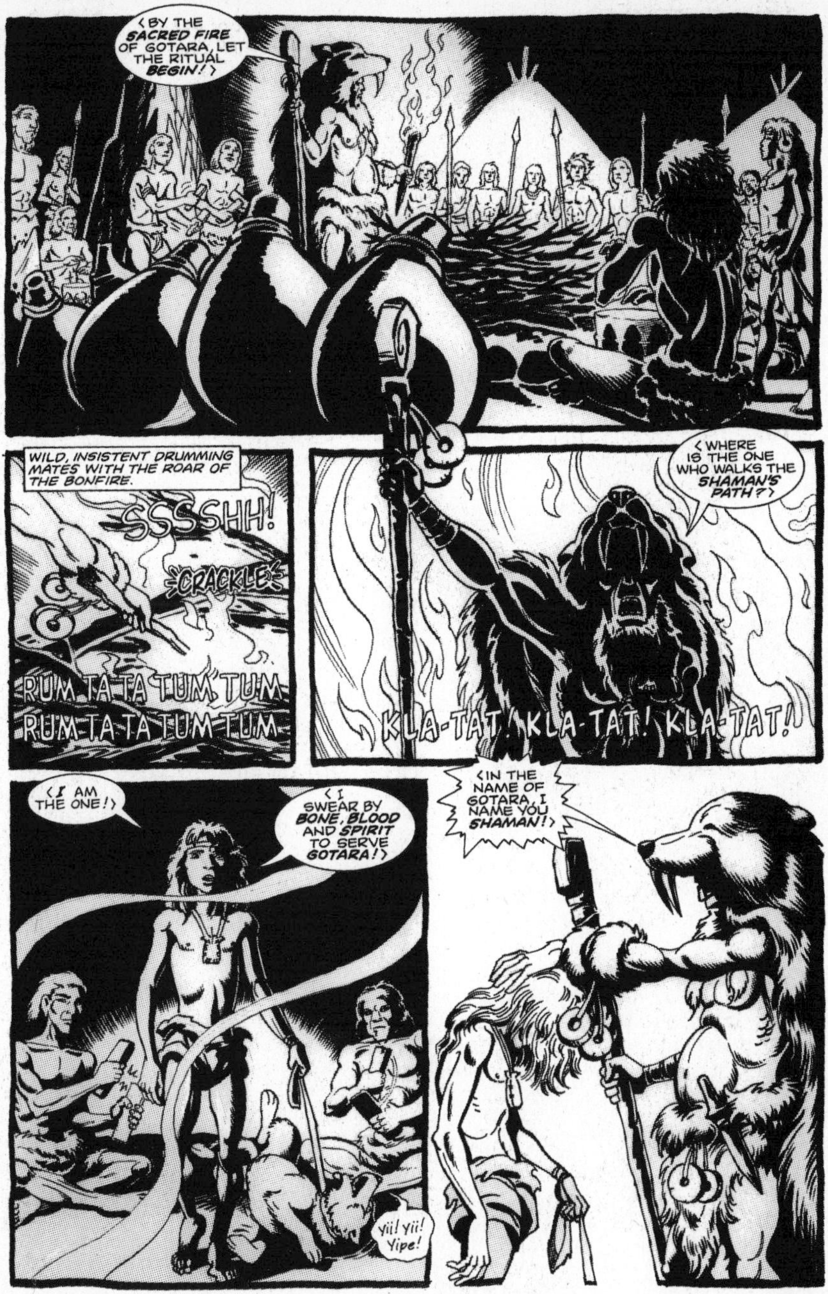

‹BY THE SACRED FIRE OF GOTARA, LET THE RITUAL BEGIN!›
WILD, INSISTENT DRUMMING MATES WITH THE ROAR OF THE BONFIRE.
SSSSHH!
CRACKLE
RUM TA TA TUM TUM
RUM TA TA TUM TUM
‹WHERE IS THE ONE WHO WALKS THE SHAMAN'S PATH?›
KLA-TAT! KLA-TAT! KLA-TAT!
‹I AM THE ONE!›
‹I SWEAR BY BONE, BLOOD AND SPIRIT TO SERVE GOTARA!›
Yii! Yii! Yipe!
‹IN THE NAME OF GOTARA, I NAME YOU SHAMAN!›

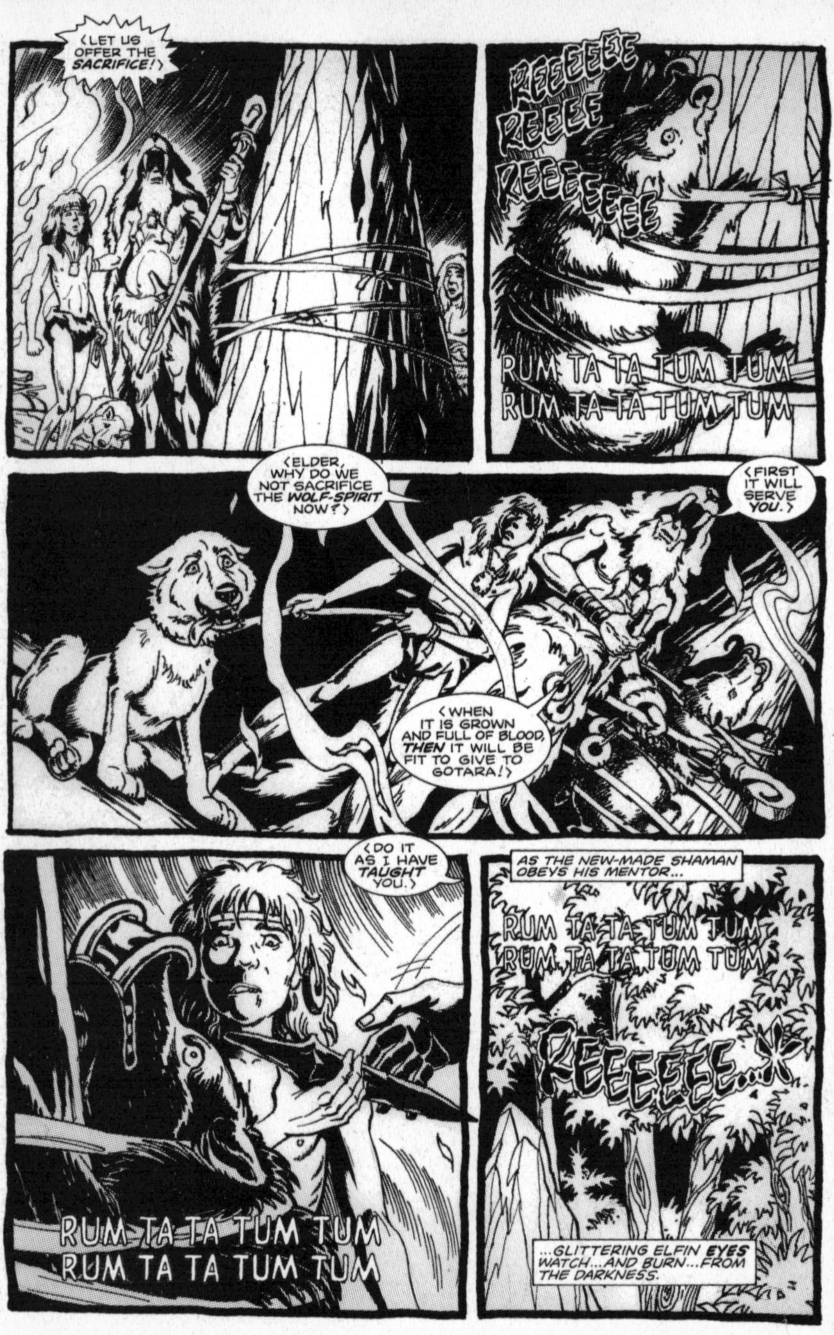

‹LET US OFFER THE SACRIFICE!›
REEEEEE REEEE REEEEEEEE
RUM TA TA TUM TUM RUM TA TA TUM TUM
‹ELDER, WHY DO WE NOT SACRIFICE THE WOLF-SPIRIT NOW?›
‹FIRST IT WILL SERVE YOU.›
‹WHEN IT IS GROWN AND FULL OF BLOOD, THEN IT WILL BE FIT TO GIVE TO GOTARA!›
‹DO IT AS I HAVE TAUGHT YOU.›
AS THE NEW-MADE SHAMAN OBEYS HIS MENTOR...
RUM TA TA TUM TUM RUM TA TA TUM TUM
RUM TA TA TUM TUM RUM TA TA TUM TUM
REEEEEEE...!
...GLITTERING ELFIN EYES WATCH...AND BURN...FROM THE DARKNESS.

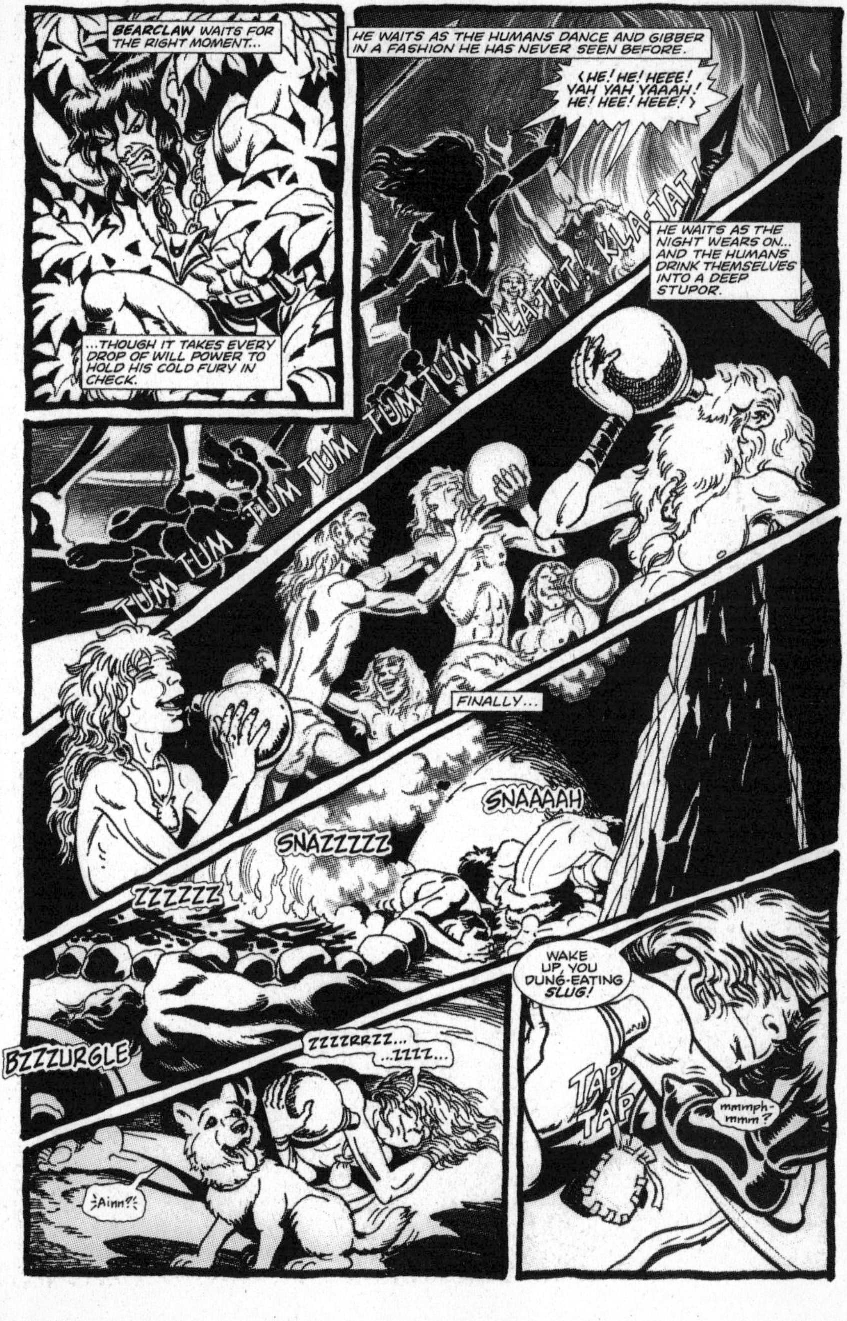
BEARCLAW WAITS FOR THE RIGHT MOMENT...
...THOUGH IT TAKES EVERY DROP OF WILL POWER TO HOLD HIS COLD FURY IN CHECK.
HE WAITS AS THE HUMANS DANCE AND GIBBER IN A FASHION HE HAS NEVER SEEN BEFORE.
‹HE! HE! HEEE! YAH YAH YAAAH! HE! HEE! HEEE!›
TUM TUM TUM TUM TUM TUM KLA-TAT! KLA-TAT!
HE WAITS AS THE NIGHT WEARS ON... AND THE HUMANS DRINK THEMSELVES INTO A DEEP STUPOR.
FINALLY...
SNAAAAAH
SNAZZZZZ
ZZZZZZ
BZZZURGLE
ZZZZRRZZZ... ...ZZZZ...
¡Ainn?!
WAKE UP, YOU DUNG-EATING SLUG!
TAP TAP
mmmph-mmm?

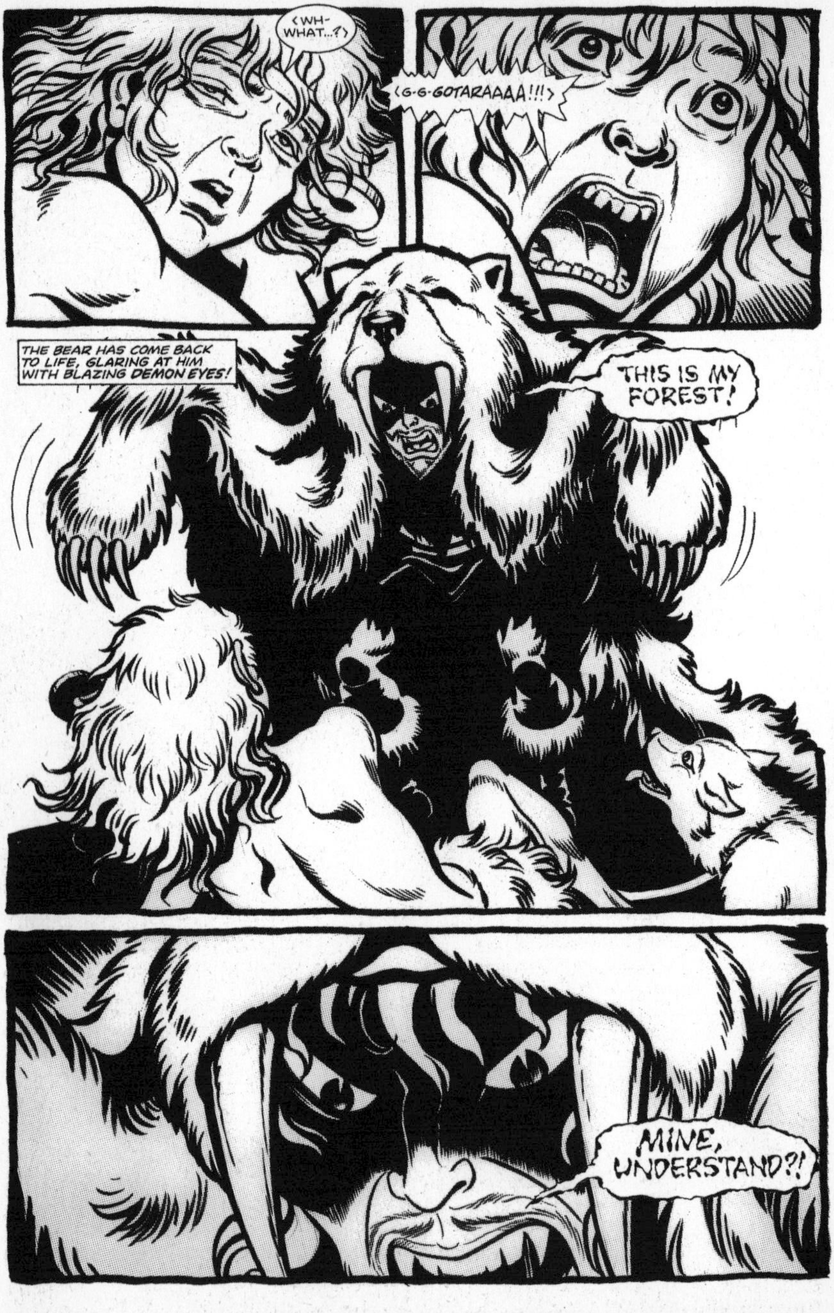
‹WH-WHAT...?›
‹G-G-GOTARAAAA!!!›
THE BEAR HAS COME BACK TO LIFE, GLARING AT HIM WITH BLAZING DEMON EYES!
THIS IS MY FOREST!
MINE, UNDERSTAND?!

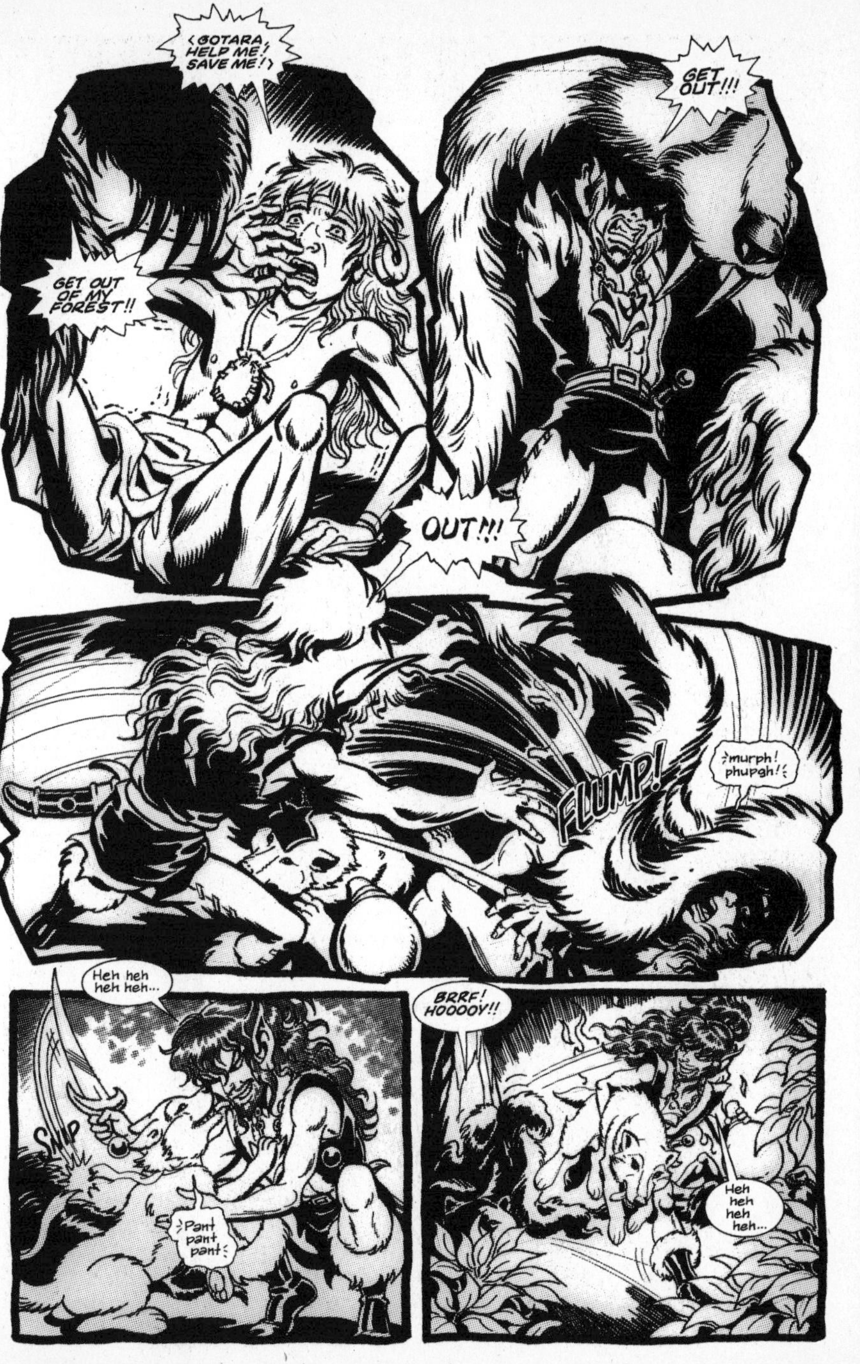
<GOTARA HELP ME! SAVE ME!>
GET OUT OF MY FOREST!!
GET OUT!!!
OUT!!!
FLUMP!
murph! phupgh!
Heh heh heh heh...
SNIP
Pant pant pant
BRRF! HOOOOY!!
Heh heh heh heh...

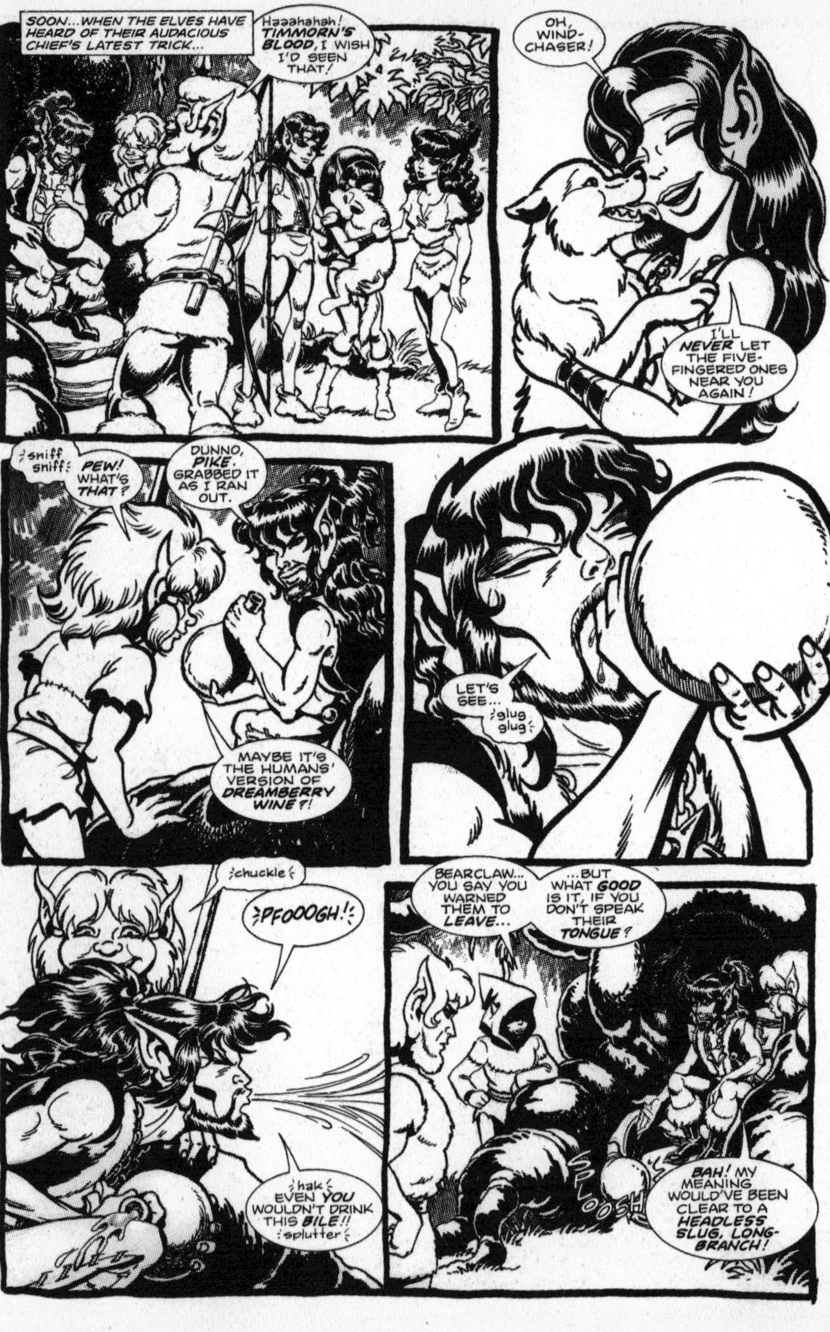
SOON...WHEN THE ELVES HAVE HEARD OF THEIR AUDACIOUS CHIEF'S LATEST TRICK...
Haaahahah! TIMMORN'S BLOOD, I WISH I'D SEEN THAT!
OH, WIND-CHASER!
I'LL NEVER LET THE FIVE-FINGERED ONES NEAR YOU AGAIN!
sniff sniff PEW! WHAT'S THAT?
DUNNO, PIKE. GRABBED IT AS I RAN OUT.
MAYBE IT'S THE HUMANS' VERSION OF DREAMBERRY WINE?!
LET'S SEE... glug glug
chuckle
PFOOOGH!
hak EVEN YOU WOULDN'T DRINK THIS BILE!! splutter
BEARCLAW... YOU SAY YOU WARNED THEM TO LEAVE...
...BUT WHAT GOOD IS IT, IF YOU DON'T SPEAK THEIR TONGUE?
SPLOOSH
BAH! MY MEANING WOULD'VE BEEN CLEAR TO A HEADLESS SLUG, LONG-BRANCH!

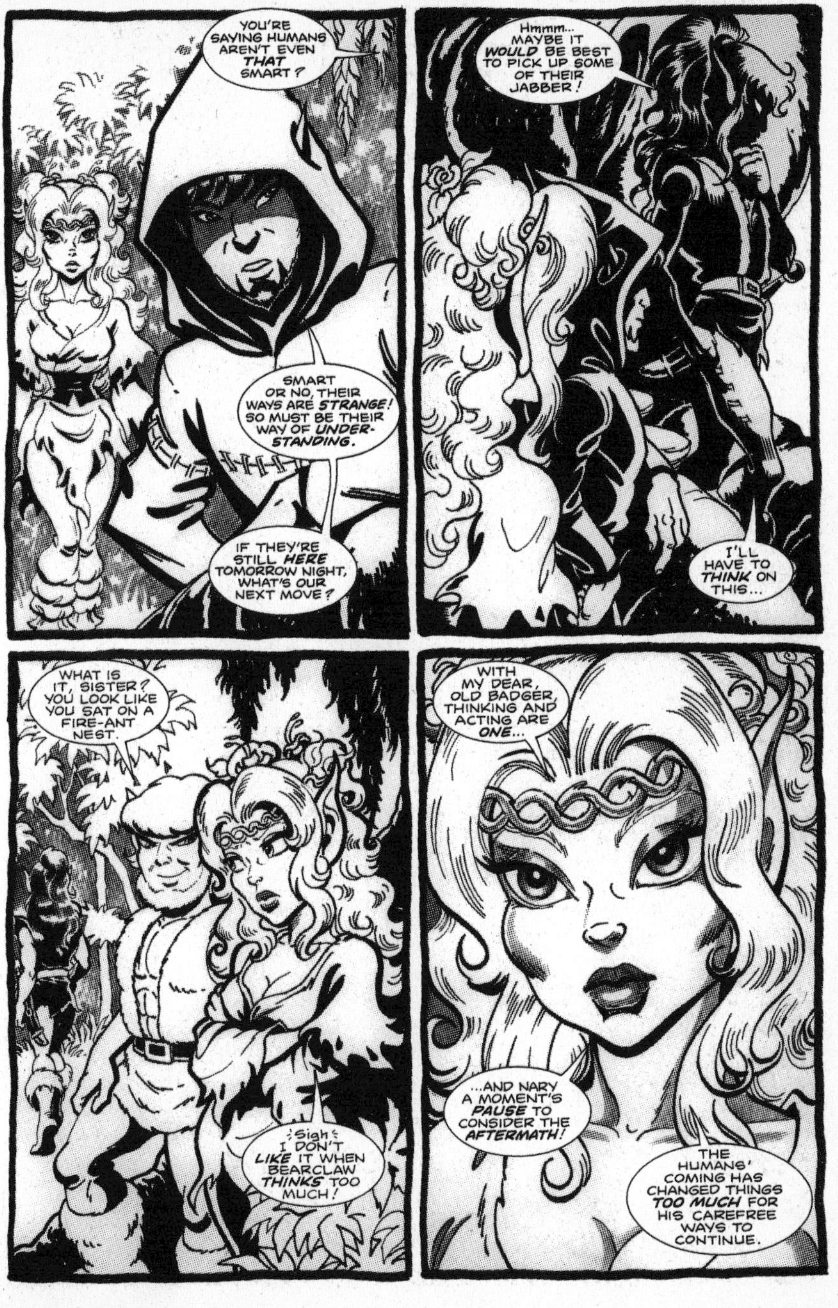
YOU'RE SAYING HUMANS AREN'T EVEN THAT SMART?
SMART OR NO, THEIR WAYS ARE STRANGE! SO MUST BE THEIR WAY OF UNDER-STANDING.
IF THEY'RE STILL HERE TOMORROW NIGHT, WHAT'S OUR NEXT MOVE?
Hmmm... MAYBE IT WOULD BE BEST TO PICK UP SOME OF THEIR JABBER!
I'LL HAVE TO THINK ON THIS...
WHAT IS IT, SISTER? YOU LOOK LIKE YOU SAT ON A FIRE-ANT NEST.
Sigh
I DON'T LIKE IT WHEN BEARCLAW THINKS TOO MUCH!
WITH MY DEAR, OLD BADGER THINKING AND ACTING ARE ONE...
...AND NARY A MOMENT'S PAUSE TO CONSIDER THE AFTERMATH!
THE HUMANS' COMING HAS CHANGED THINGS TOO MUCH FOR HIS CAREFREE WAYS TO CONTINUE.

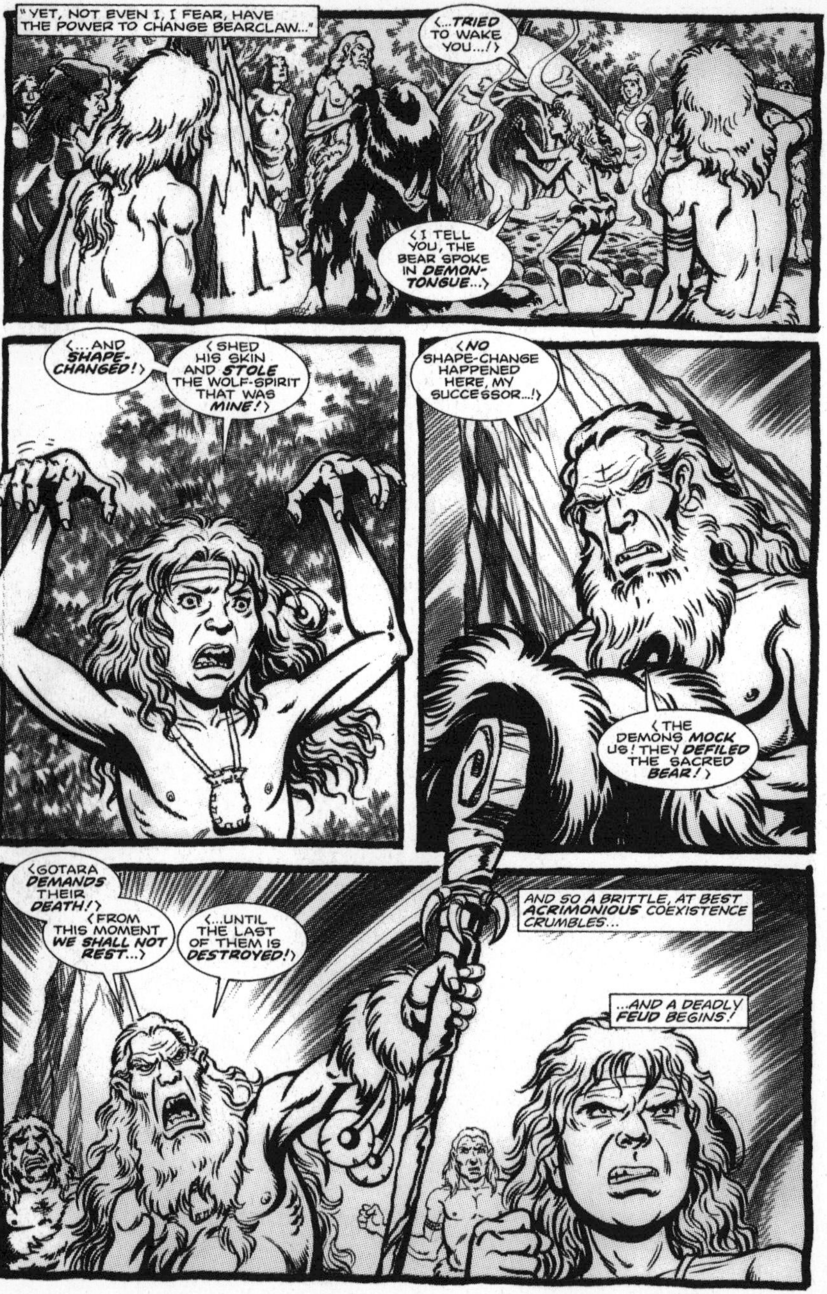
"YET, NOT EVEN I, I FEAR, HAVE THE POWER TO CHANGE BEARCLAW..."
<...TRIED TO WAKE YOU...!>
<I TELL YOU, THE BEAR SPOKE IN DEMON-TONGUE...>
<...AND SHAPE-CHANGED!>
<SHED HIS SKIN AND STOLE THE WOLF-SPIRIT THAT WAS MINE!>
<NO SHAPE-CHANGE HAPPENED HERE, MY SUCCESSOR...!>
<THE DEMONS MOCK US! THEY DEFILED THE SACRED BEAR!>
<GOTARA DEMANDS THEIR DEATH!>
<FROM THIS MOMENT WE SHALL NOT REST...>
<...UNTIL THE LAST OF THEM IS DESTROYED!>
AND SO A BRITTLE, AT BEST ACRIMONIOUS COEXISTENCE CRUMBLES...
...AND A DEADLY FEUD BEGINS!

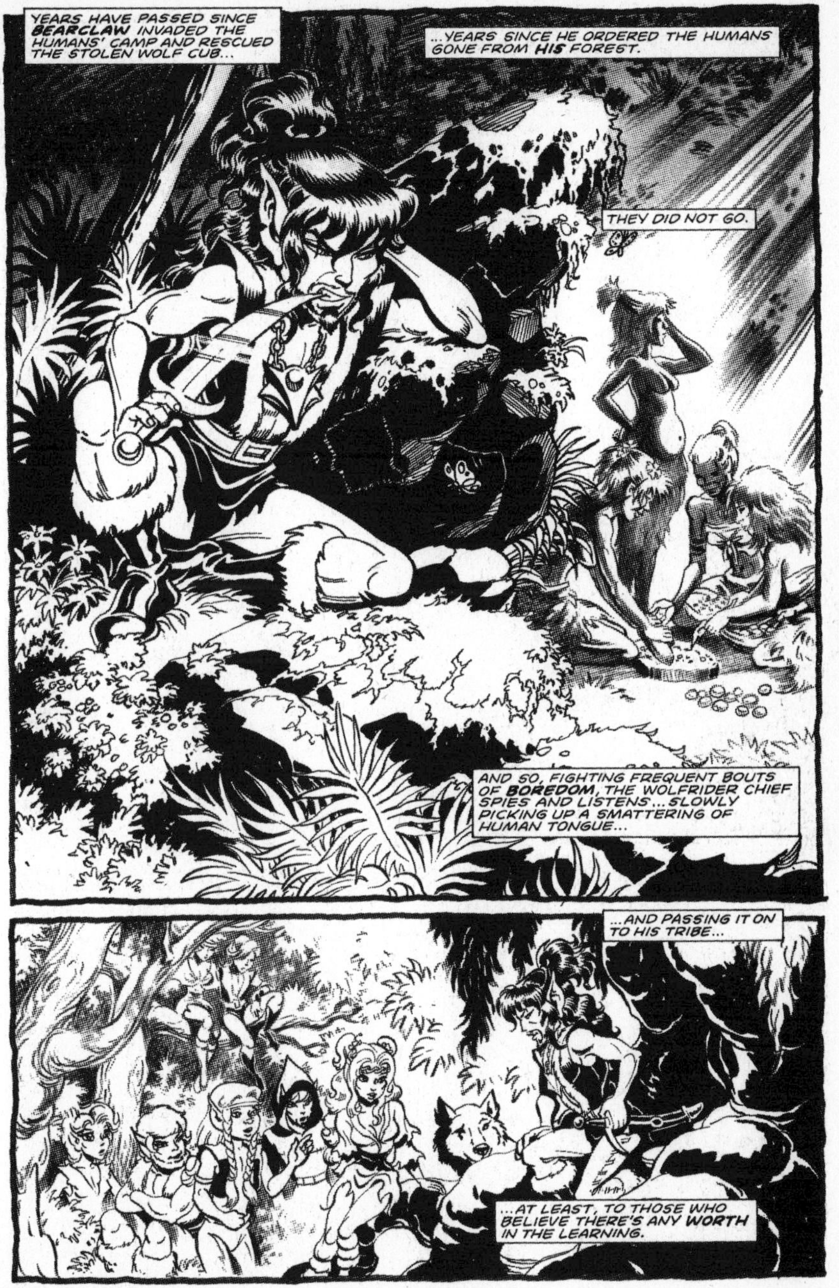
YEARS HAVE PASSED SINCE BEARCLAW INVADED THE HUMANS' CAMP AND RESCUED THE STOLEN WOLF CUB...
...YEARS SINCE HE ORDERED THE HUMANS GONE FROM HIS FOREST.
THEY DID NOT GO.
AND SO, FIGHTING FREQUENT BOUTS OF BOREDOM, THE WOLFRIDER CHIEF SPIES AND LISTENS... SLOWLY PICKING UP A SMATTERING OF HUMAN TONGUE...
...AND PASSING IT ON TO HIS TRIBE...
...AT LEAST, TO THOSE WHO BELIEVE THERE'S ANY WORTH IN THE LEARNING.

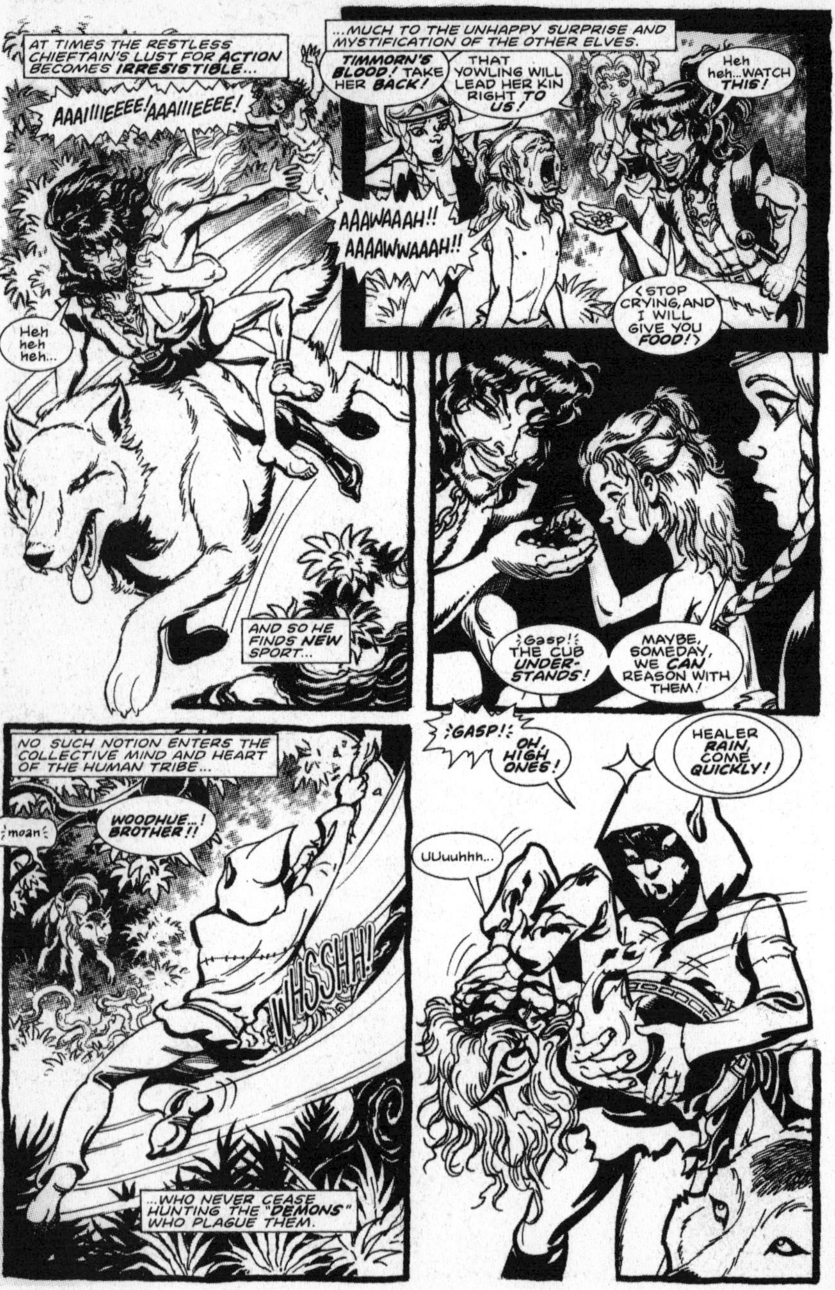
AT TIMES THE RESTLESS CHIEFTAIN'S LUST FOR ACTION BECOMES IRRESISTIBLE...
AAAIIIIEEEE! AAAIIIEEEE!
Heh heh heh...
AND SO HE FINDS NEW SPORT...
...MUCH TO THE UNHAPPY SURPRISE AND MYSTIFICATION OF THE OTHER ELVES.
TIMMORN'S BLOOD! TAKE HER BACK!
THAT YOWLING WILL LEAD HER KIN RIGHT TO US!
Heh heh...WATCH THIS!
AAAWAAAH!! AAAAWWAAAH!!
<STOP CRYING, AND I WILL GIVE YOU FOOD!>
Gasp! THE CUB UNDERSTANDS!
MAYBE, SOMEDAY, WE CAN REASON WITH THEM!
NO SUCH NOTION ENTERS THE COLLECTIVE MIND AND HEART OF THE HUMAN TRIBE...
moan
WOODHUE...! BROTHER!!
WHSSHH!
...WHO NEVER CEASE HUNTING THE "DEMONS" WHO PLAGUE THEM.
GASP! OH, HIGH ONES!
HEALER RAIN, COME QUICKLY!
UUuuhhh...

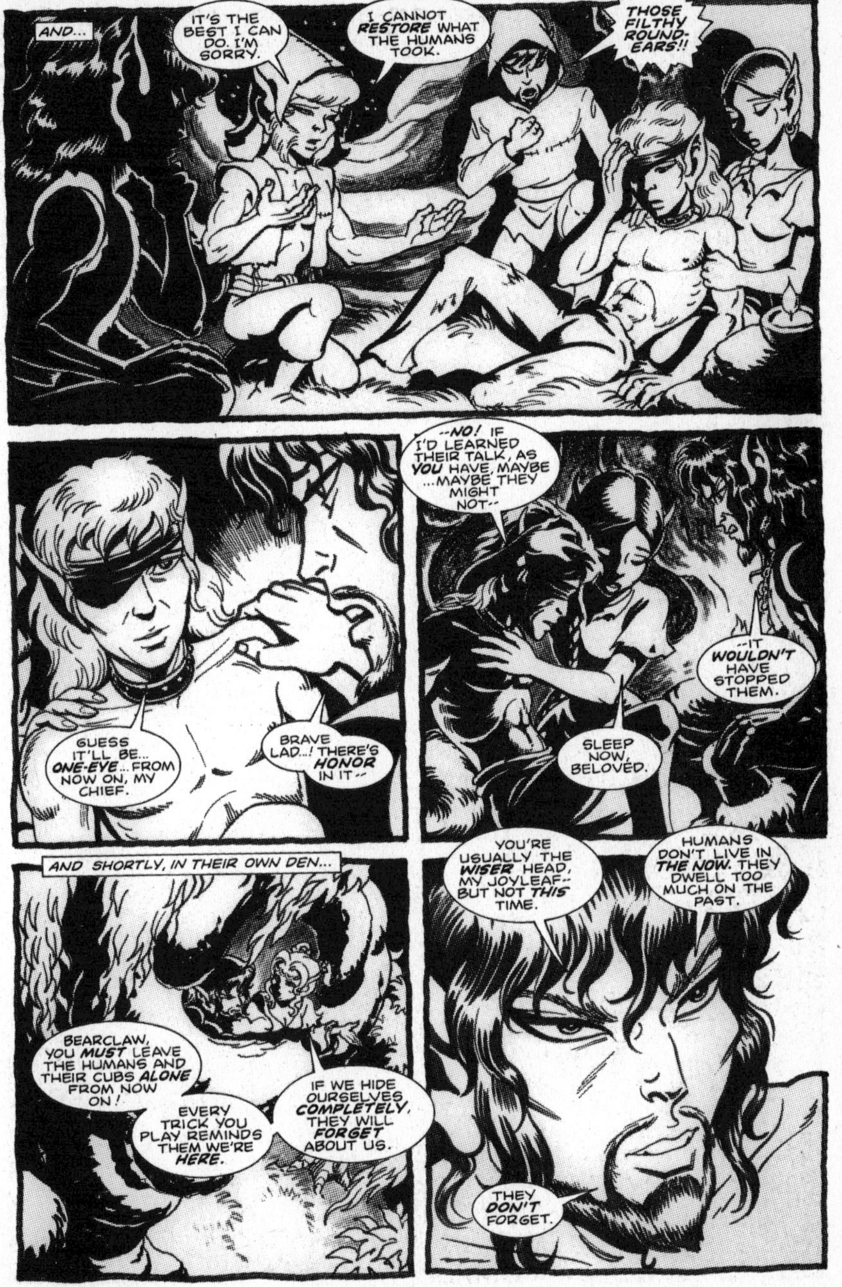
AND...
IT'S THE BEST I CAN DO. I'M SORRY.
I CANNOT RESTORE WHAT THE HUMANS TOOK.
THOSE FILTHY ROUND-EARS!!
GUESS IT'LL BE... ONE-EYE... FROM NOW ON, MY CHIEF.
BRAVE LAD...! THERE'S HONOR IN IT--
--NO! IF I'D LEARNED THEIR TALK, AS YOU HAVE, MAYBE ...MAYBE THEY MIGHT NOT--
--IT WOULDN'T HAVE STOPPED THEM.
SLEEP NOW, BELOVED.
AND SHORTLY, IN THEIR OWN DEN...
BEARCLAW, YOU MUST LEAVE THE HUMANS AND THEIR CUBS ALONE FROM NOW ON!
EVERY TRICK YOU PLAY REMINDS THEM WE'RE HERE.
IF WE HIDE OURSELVES COMPLETELY, THEY WILL FORGET ABOUT US.
YOU'RE USUALLY THE WISER HEAD, MY JOYLEAF-- BUT NOT THIS TIME.
HUMANS DON'T LIVE IN THE NOW. THEY DWELL TOO MUCH ON THE PAST.
THEY DON'T FORGET.

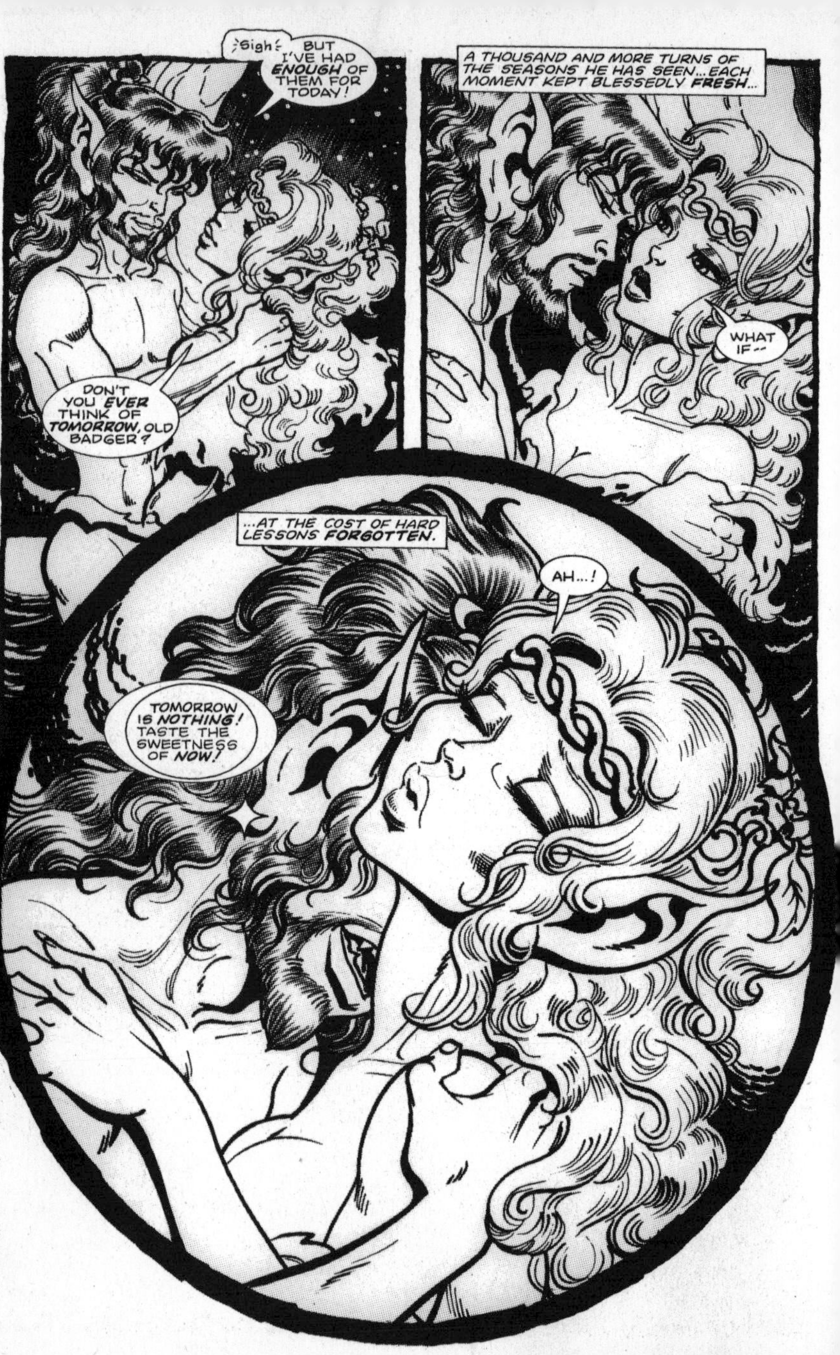

-Sigh- BUT I'VE HAD ENOUGH OF THEM FOR TODAY!
DON'T YOU EVER THINK OF TOMORROW, OLD BADGER?
A THOUSAND AND MORE TURNS OF THE SEASONS HE HAS SEEN... EACH MOMENT KEPT BLESSEDLY FRESH...
WHAT IF--
...AT THE COST OF HARD LESSONS FORGOTTEN.
AH...!
TOMORROW IS NOTHING! TASTE THE SWEETNESS OF NOW!

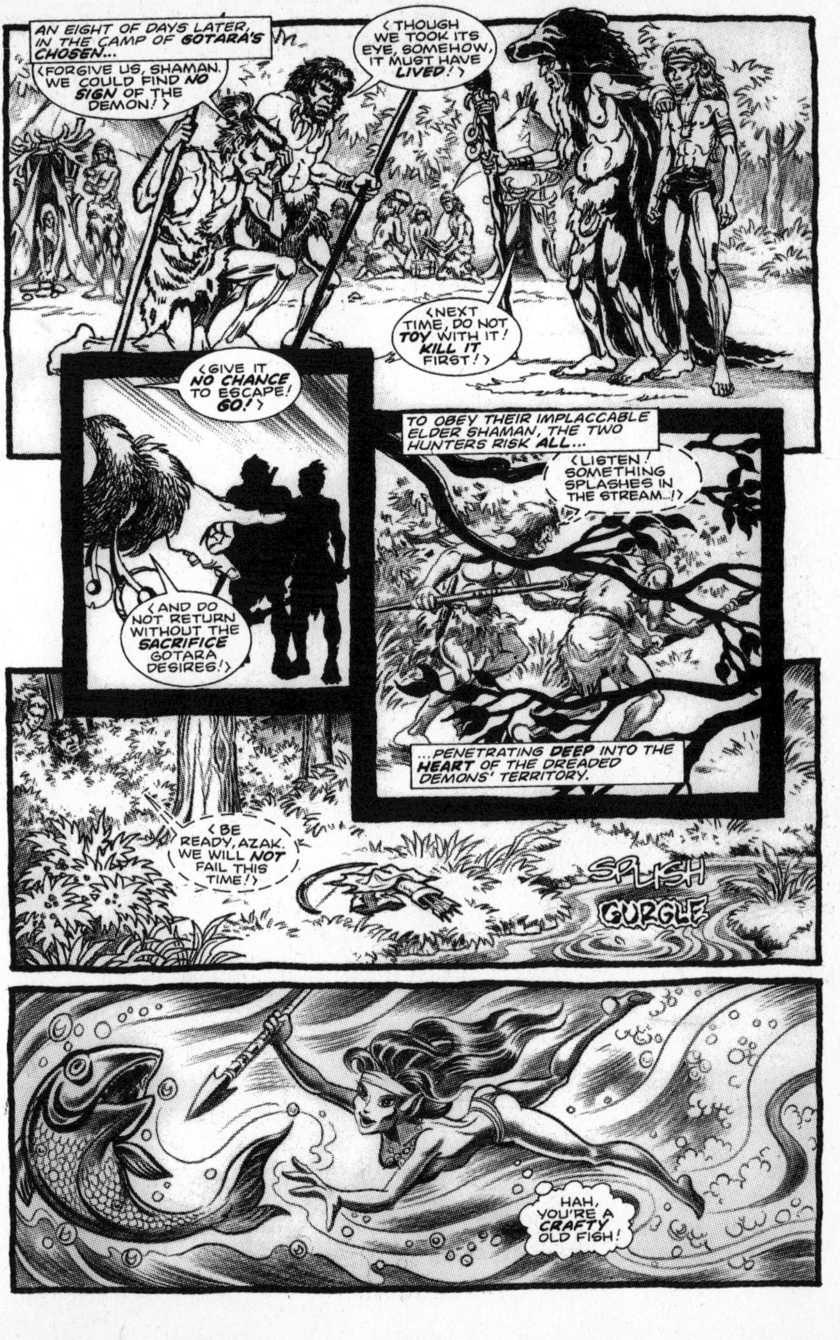
AN EIGHT OF DAYS LATER, IN THE CAMP OF GOTARA'S CHOSEN...
‹FORGIVE US, SHAMAN. WE COULD FIND NO SIGN OF THE DEMON!›
‹THOUGH WE TOOK ITS EYE, SOMEHOW, IT MUST HAVE LIVED!›
‹NEXT TIME, DO NOT TOY WITH IT! KILL IT FIRST!›
‹GIVE IT NO CHANCE TO ESCAPE! GO!›
‹AND DO NOT RETURN WITHOUT THE SACRIFICE GOTARA DESIRES!›
TO OBEY THEIR IMPLACCABLE ELDER SHAMAN, THE TWO HUNTERS RISK ALL...
‹LISTEN! SOMETHING SPLASHES IN THE STREAM...!›
...PENETRATING DEEP INTO THE HEART OF THE DREADED DEMONS' TERRITORY.
‹BE READY, AZAK. WE WILL NOT FAIL THIS TIME!›
SPLISH
GURGLE
HAH, YOU'RE A CRAFTY OLD FISH!

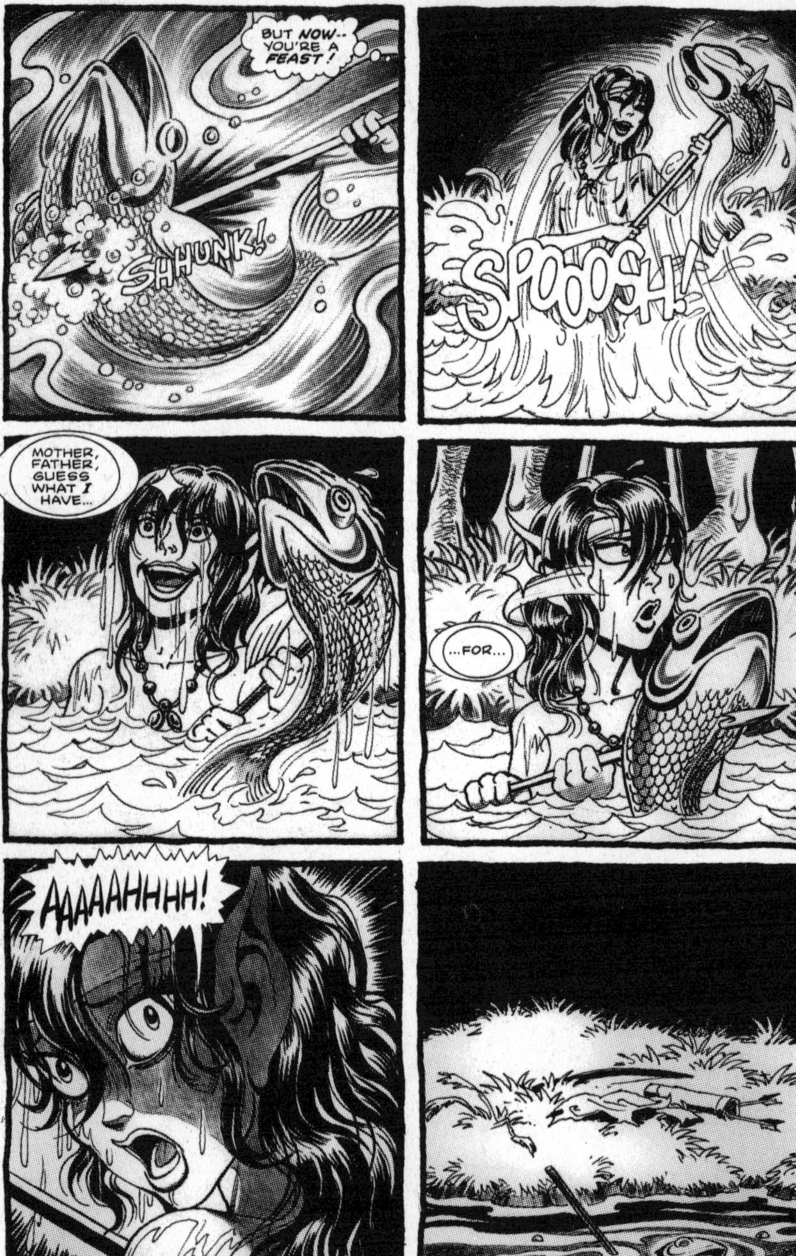
BUT NOW-- YOU'RE A FEAST!
SHHUNK!
SPOOOSH!
MOTHER, FATHER, GUESS WHAT I HAVE...
...FOR...
AAAAHHHH!

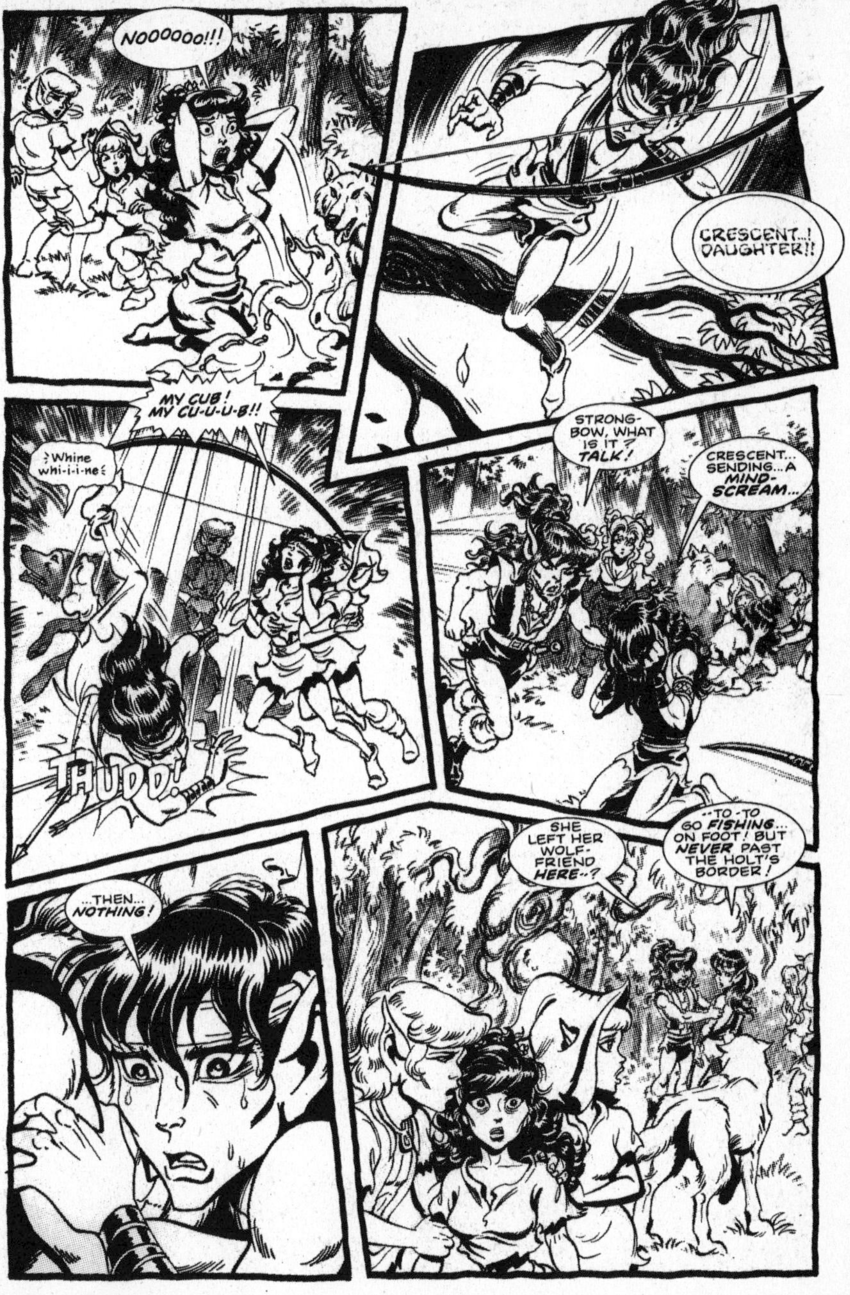
NOOOOOO!!!
CRESCENT...! DAUGHTER!!
MY CUB! MY CU-U-U-B!!
Whine whi-i-i-ne
THUDD!
STRONG-BOW, WHAT IS IT? TALK!
CRESCENT... SENDING... A MIND-SCREAM...
...THEN... NOTHING!
SHE LEFT HER WOLF-FRIEND HERE--?
--TO-TO GO FISHING... ON FOOT! BUT NEVER PAST THE HOLT'S BORDER!

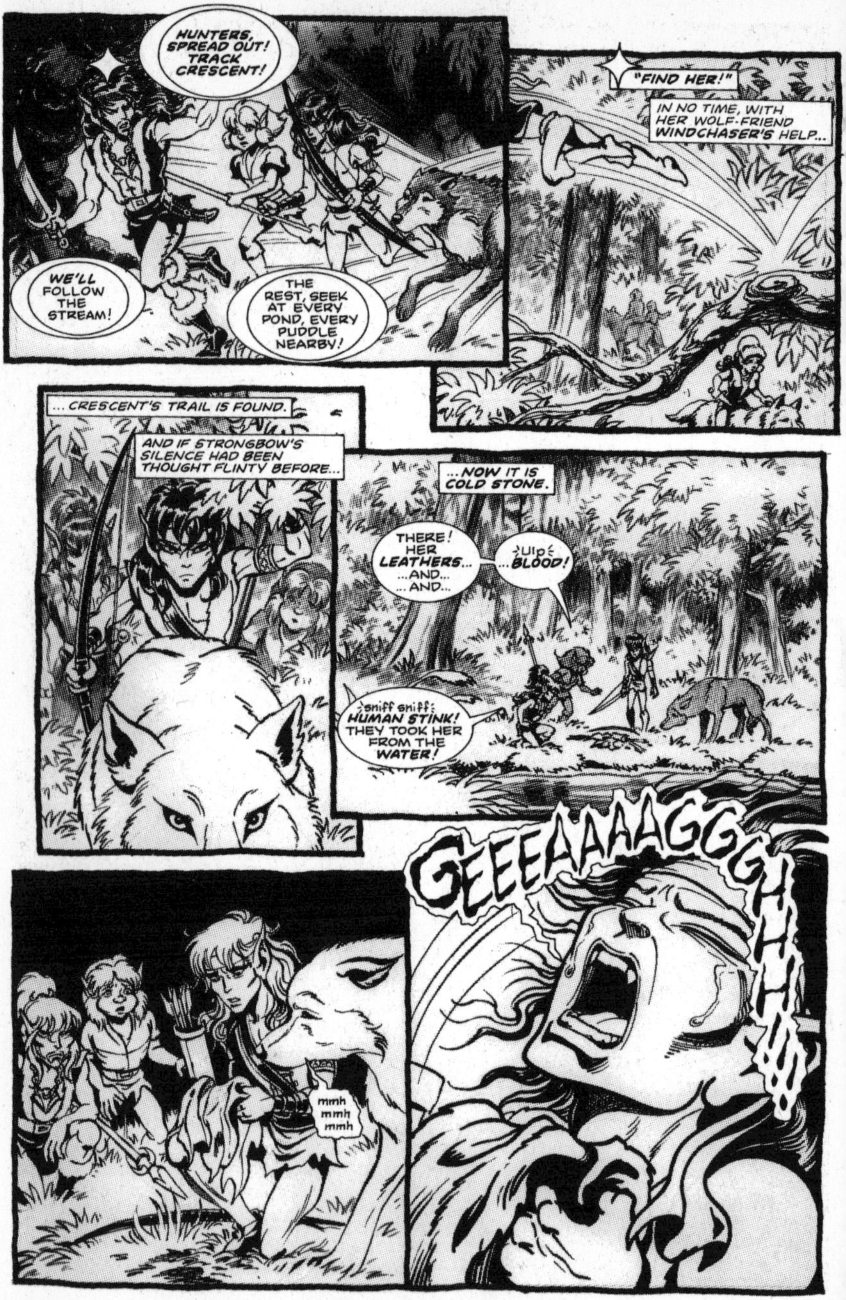
HUNTERS, SPREAD OUT! TRACK CRESCENT!
WE'LL FOLLOW THE STREAM!
THE REST, SEEK AT EVERY POND, EVERY PUDDLE NEARBY!
"FIND HER!"
IN NO TIME, WITH HER WOLF-FRIEND WINDCHASER'S HELP...
...CRESCENT'S TRAIL IS FOUND.
AND IF STRONGBOW'S SILENCE HAD BEEN THOUGHT FLINTY BEFORE...
...NOW IT IS COLD STONE.
THERE! HER LEATHERS... ...AND... ...AND...
ulp ...BLOOD!
sniff sniff HUMAN STINK! THEY TOOK HER FROM THE WATER!
mmh mmh mmh
GEEEAAAAGGGHHH!!

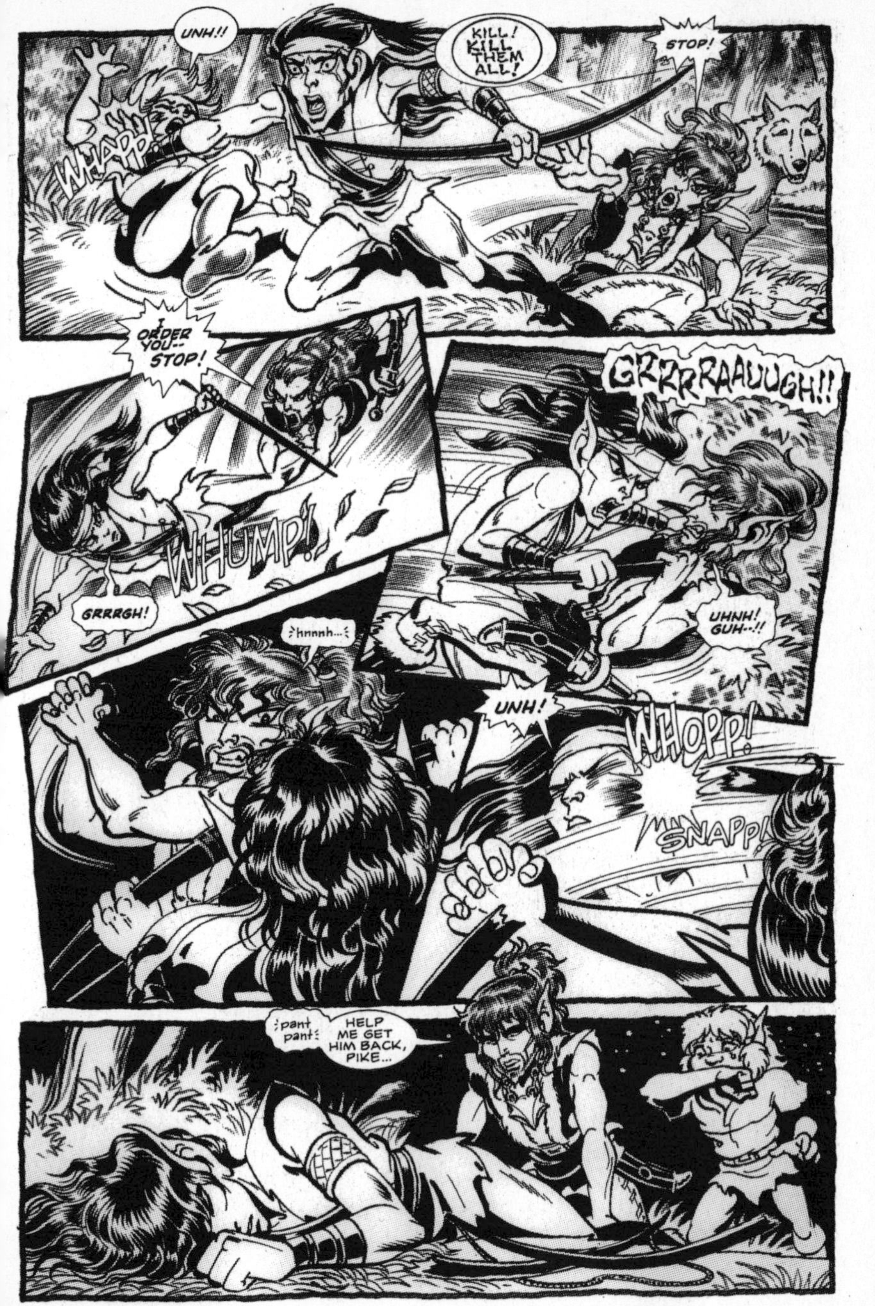
UNH!!
WHAPP!
KILL! KILL THEM ALL!
STOP!
I ORDER YOU-- STOP!
WHUMP!
GRRRGH!
GRRRRAAUUGH!!
UHNH! GUH--!!
hnnnh...
UNH!
WHOPP!
SNAPP!
pant pant
HELP ME GET HIM BACK, PIKE...

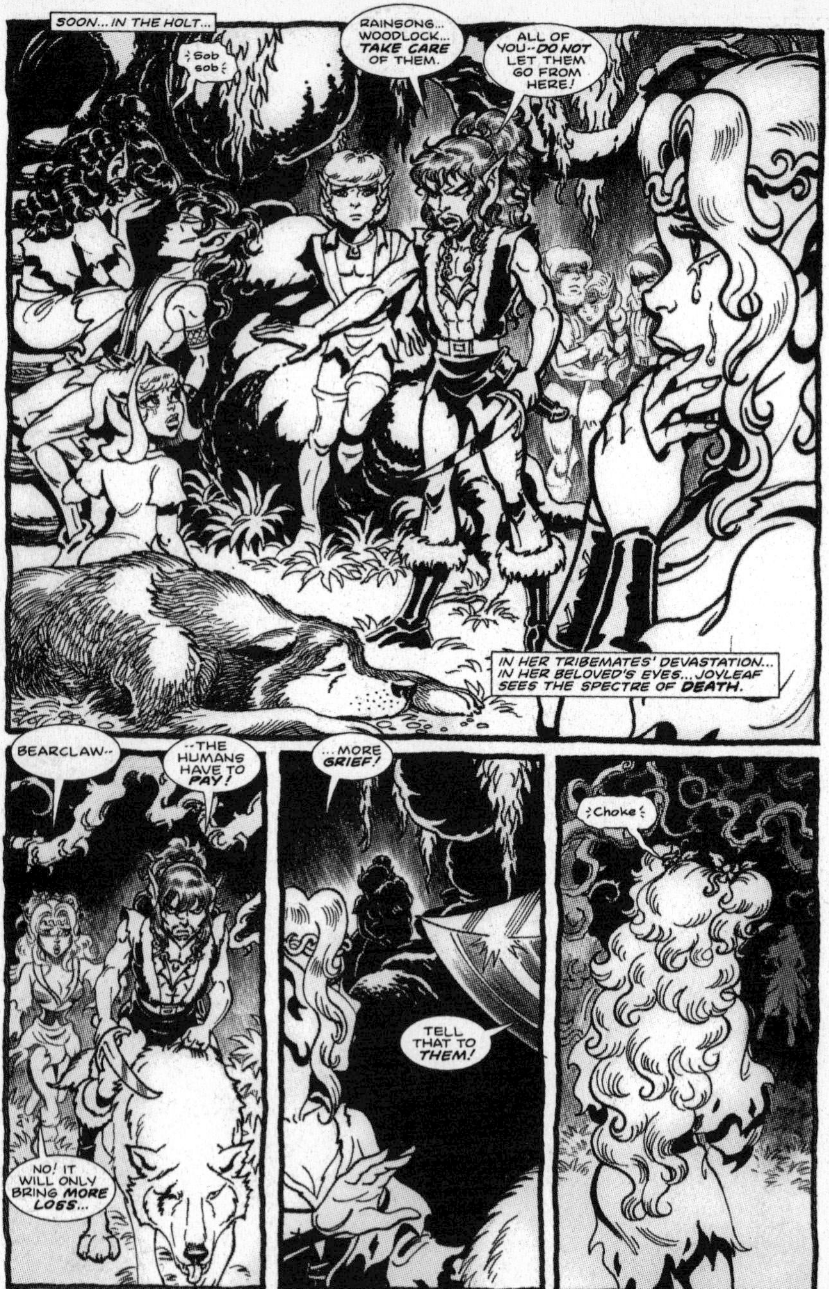
SOON... IN THE HOLT...
Sob sob
RAINSONG... WOODLOCK... TAKE CARE OF THEM.
ALL OF YOU--DO NOT LET THEM GO FROM HERE!
IN HER TRIBEMATES' DEVASTATION... IN HER BELOVED'S EYES... JOYLEAF SEES THE SPECTRE OF DEATH.
BEARCLAW--
--THE HUMANS HAVE TO PAY!
NO! IT WILL ONLY BRING MORE LOSS...
...MORE GRIEF!
TELL THAT TO THEM!
Choke

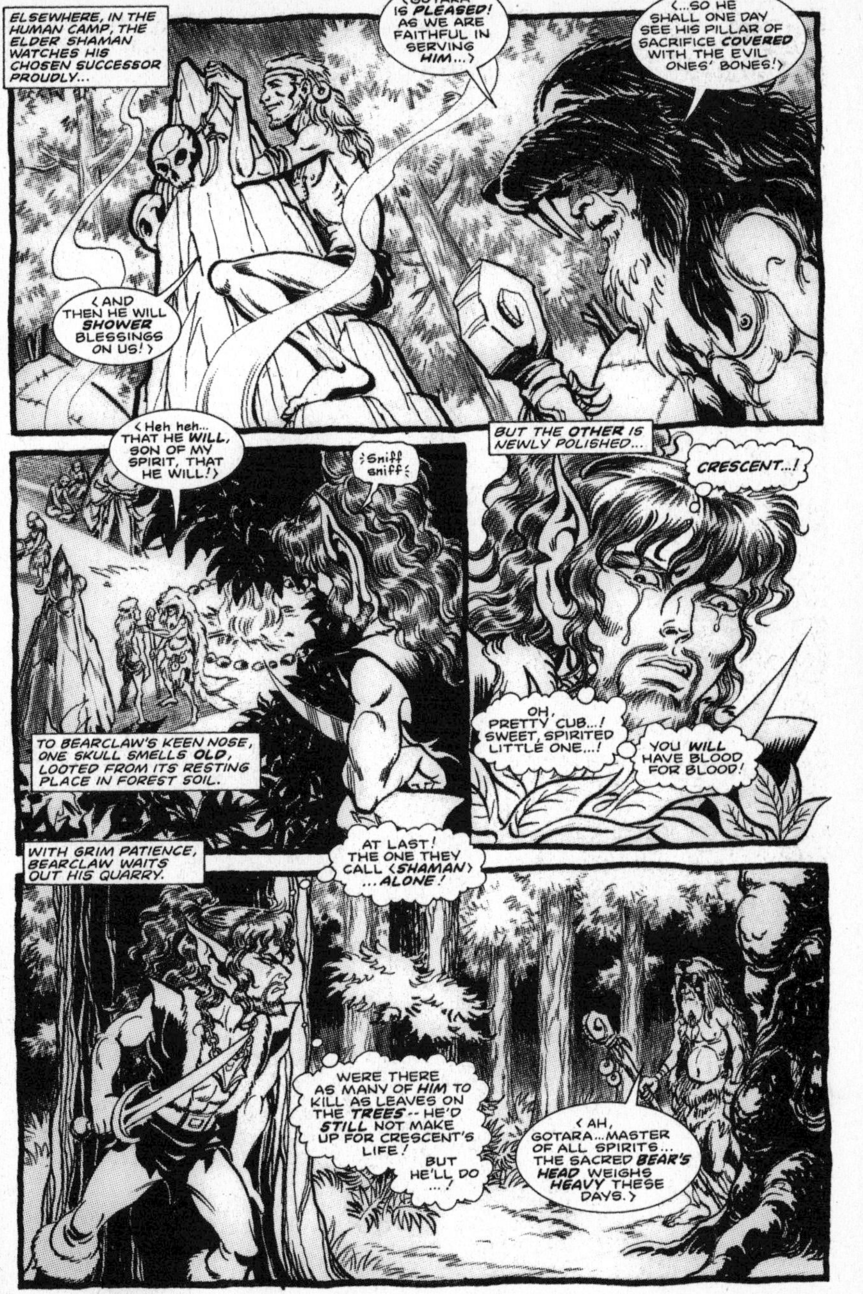
ELSEWHERE, IN THE HUMAN CAMP, THE ELDER SHAMAN WATCHES HIS CHOSEN SUCCESSOR PROUDLY...
‹GOTARA IS PLEASED! AS WE ARE FAITHFUL IN SERVING HIM...›
‹...SO HE SHALL ONE DAY SEE HIS PILLAR OF SACRIFICE COVERED WITH THE EVIL ONES' BONES!›
‹AND THEN HE WILL SHOWER BLESSINGS ON US!›
‹Heh heh... THAT HE WILL, SON OF MY SPIRIT, THAT HE WILL!›
‹Sniff sniff›
TO BEARCLAW'S KEEN NOSE, ONE SKULL SMELLS OLD, LOOTED FROM ITS RESTING PLACE IN FOREST SOIL.
BUT THE OTHER IS NEWLY POLISHED...
CRESCENT...!
OH, PRETTY CUB...! SWEET, SPIRITED LITTLE ONE...!
YOU WILL HAVE BLOOD FOR BLOOD!
WITH GRIM PATIENCE, BEARCLAW WAITS OUT HIS QUARRY.
AT LAST! THE ONE THEY CALL ‹SHAMAN› ...ALONE!
WERE THERE AS MANY OF HIM TO KILL AS LEAVES ON THE TREES -- HE'D STILL NOT MAKE UP FOR CRESCENT'S LIFE!
BUT HE'LL DO ...!
‹AH, GOTARA... MASTER OF ALL SPIRITS... THE SACRED BEAR'S HEAD WEIGHS HEAVY THESE DAYS.›

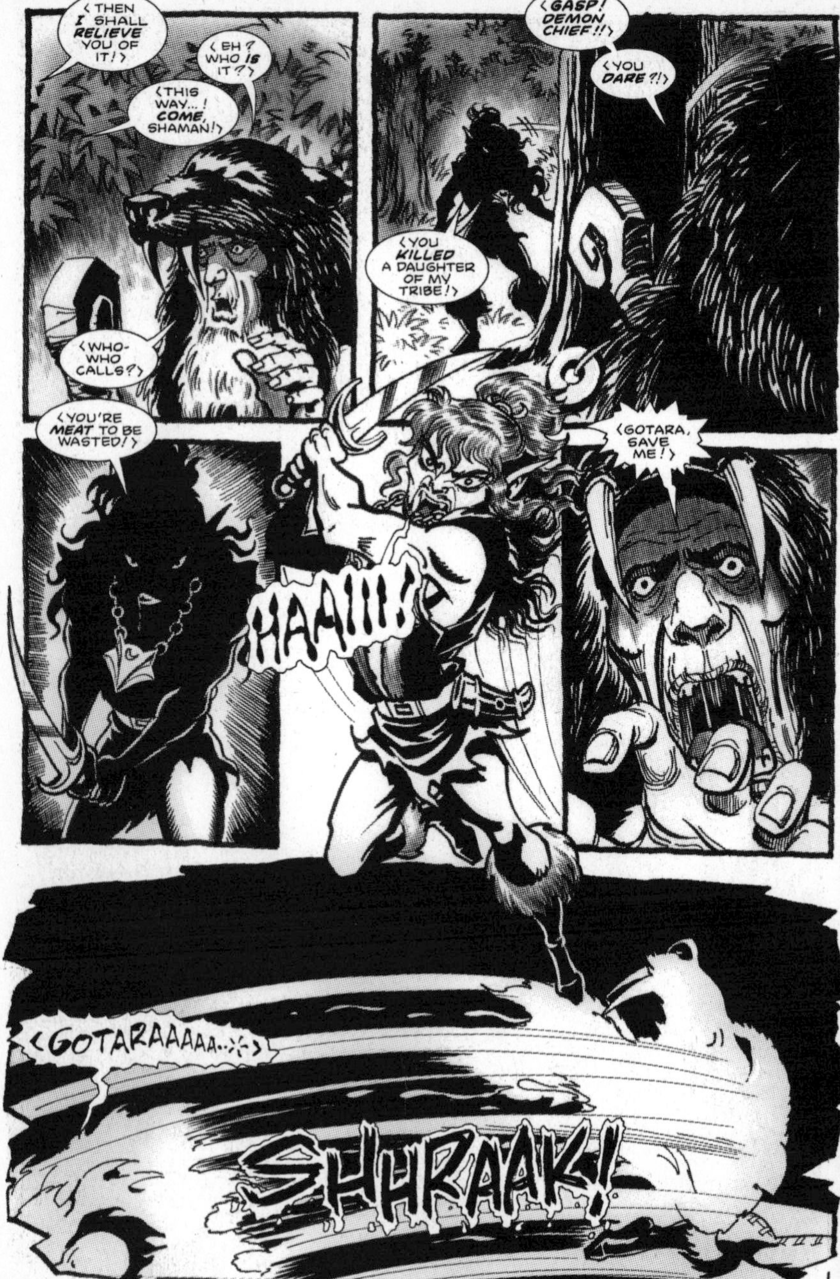

‹THEN I SHALL RELIEVE YOU OF IT!›
‹EH? WHO IS IT?›
‹THIS WAY...! COME, SHAMAN!›
‹WHO-WHO CALLS?›
‹GASP! DEMON CHIEF!!›
‹YOU DARE?!›
‹YOU KILLED A DAUGHTER OF MY TRIBE!›
‹YOU'RE MEAT TO BE WASTED!›
‹GOTARA, SAVE ME!›
HAAIII!
‹GOTARAAAAA..!›
SHHRAAK!

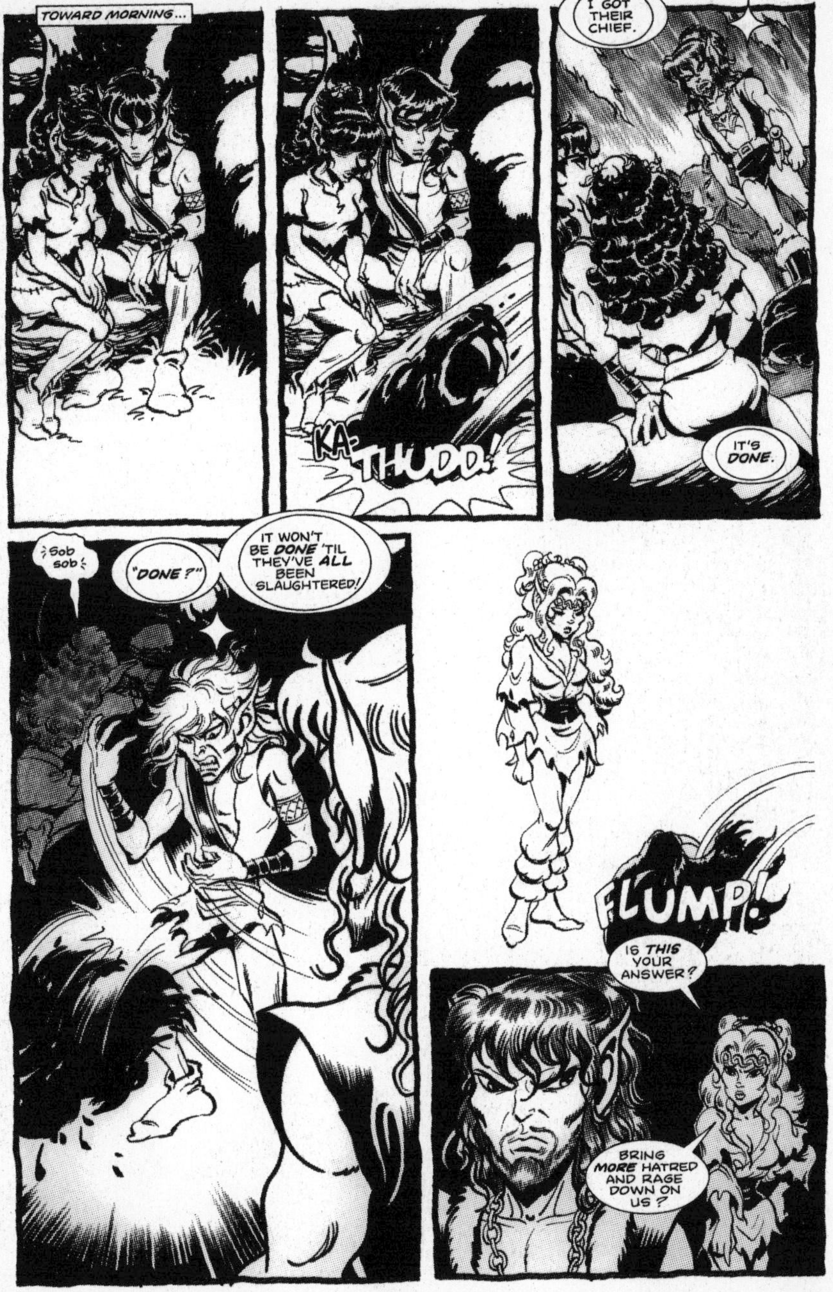
TOWARD MORNING...
KA-THUDD!
I GOT THEIR CHIEF.
IT'S DONE.
Sob sob
"DONE?"
IT WON'T BE DONE 'TIL THEY'VE ALL BEEN SLAUGHTERED!
FLUMP!
IS THIS YOUR ANSWER?
BRING MORE HATRED AND RAGE DOWN ON US?

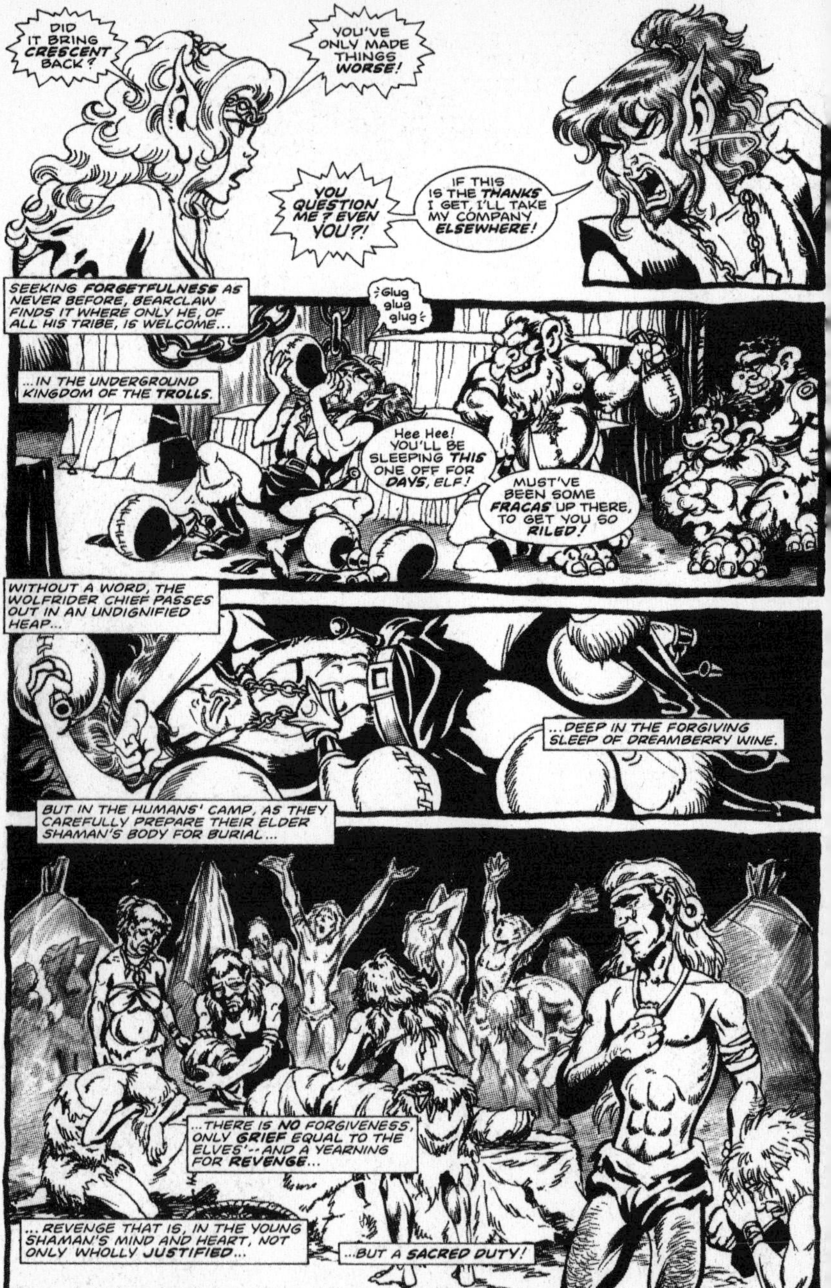

DID IT BRING CRESCENT BACK?
YOU'VE ONLY MADE THINGS WORSE!
YOU QUESTION ME? EVEN YOU?!
IF THIS IS THE THANKS I GET, I'LL TAKE MY COMPANY ELSEWHERE!
SEEKING FORGETFULNESS AS NEVER BEFORE, BEARCLAW FINDS IT WHERE ONLY HE, OF ALL HIS TRIBE, IS WELCOME...
Glug glug glug
...IN THE UNDERGROUND KINGDOM OF THE TROLLS.
Hee Hee! YOU'LL BE SLEEPING THIS ONE OFF FOR DAYS, ELF!
MUST'VE BEEN SOME FRACAS UP THERE, TO GET YOU SO RILED!
WITHOUT A WORD, THE WOLFRIDER CHIEF PASSES OUT IN AN UNDIGNIFIED HEAP...
...DEEP IN THE FORGIVING SLEEP OF DREAMBERRY WINE.
BUT IN THE HUMANS' CAMP, AS THEY CAREFULLY PREPARE THEIR ELDER SHAMAN'S BODY FOR BURIAL...
...THERE IS NO FORGIVENESS, ONLY GRIEF EQUAL TO THE ELVES'--AND A YEARNING FOR REVENGE...
...REVENGE THAT IS, IN THE YOUNG SHAMAN'S MIND AND HEART, NOT ONLY WHOLLY JUSTIFIED...
...BUT A SACRED DUTY!

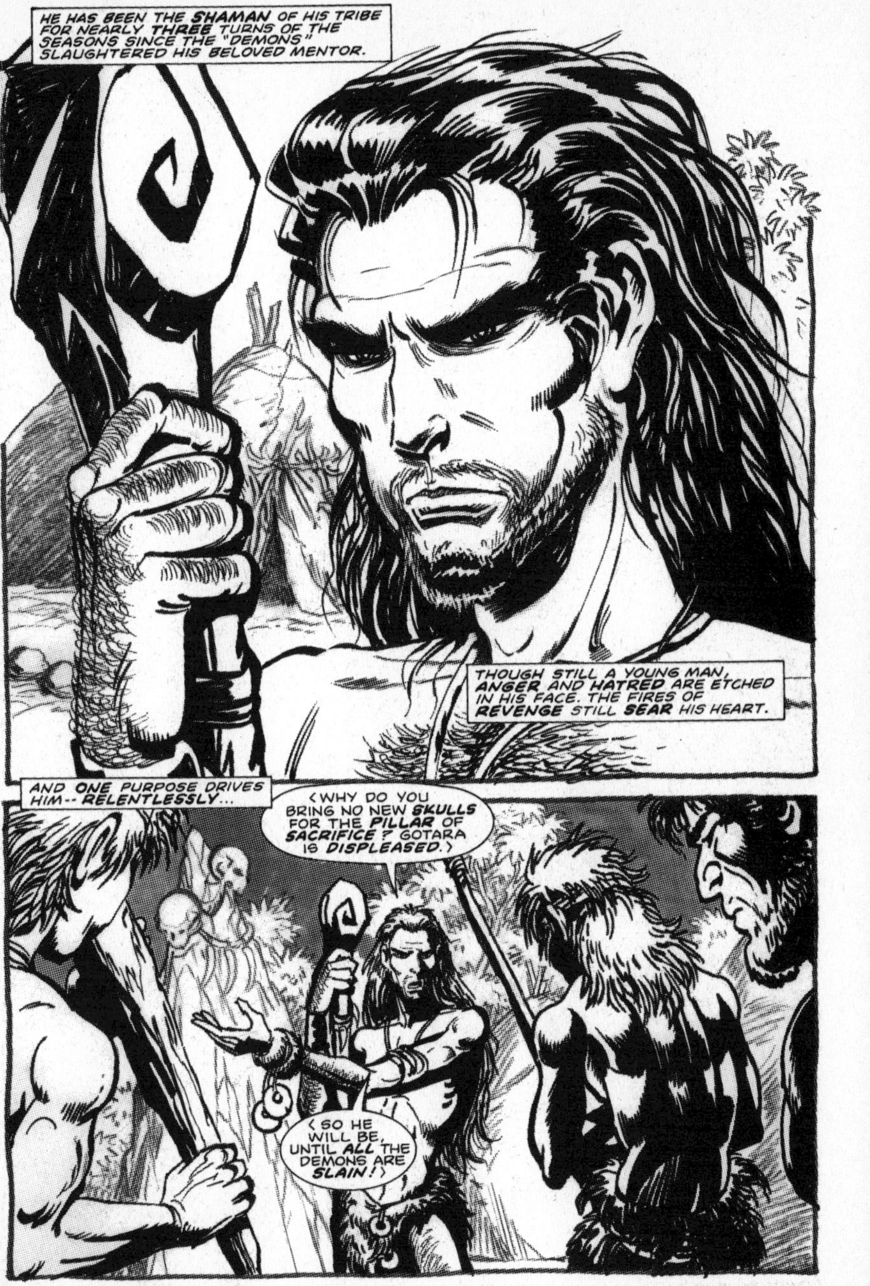
HE HAS BEEN THE SHAMAN OF HIS TRIBE FOR NEARLY THREE TURNS OF THE SEASONS SINCE THE "DEMONS" SLAUGHTERED HIS BELOVED MENTOR.
THOUGH STILL A YOUNG MAN, ANGER AND HATRED ARE ETCHED IN HIS FACE. THE FIRES OF REVENGE STILL SEAR HIS HEART.
AND ONE PURPOSE DRIVES HIM-- RELENTLESSLY...
<WHY DO YOU BRING NO NEW SKULLS FOR THE PILLAR OF SACRIFICE? GOTARA IS DISPLEASED.>
<SO HE WILL BE, UNTIL ALL THE DEMONS ARE SLAIN!>

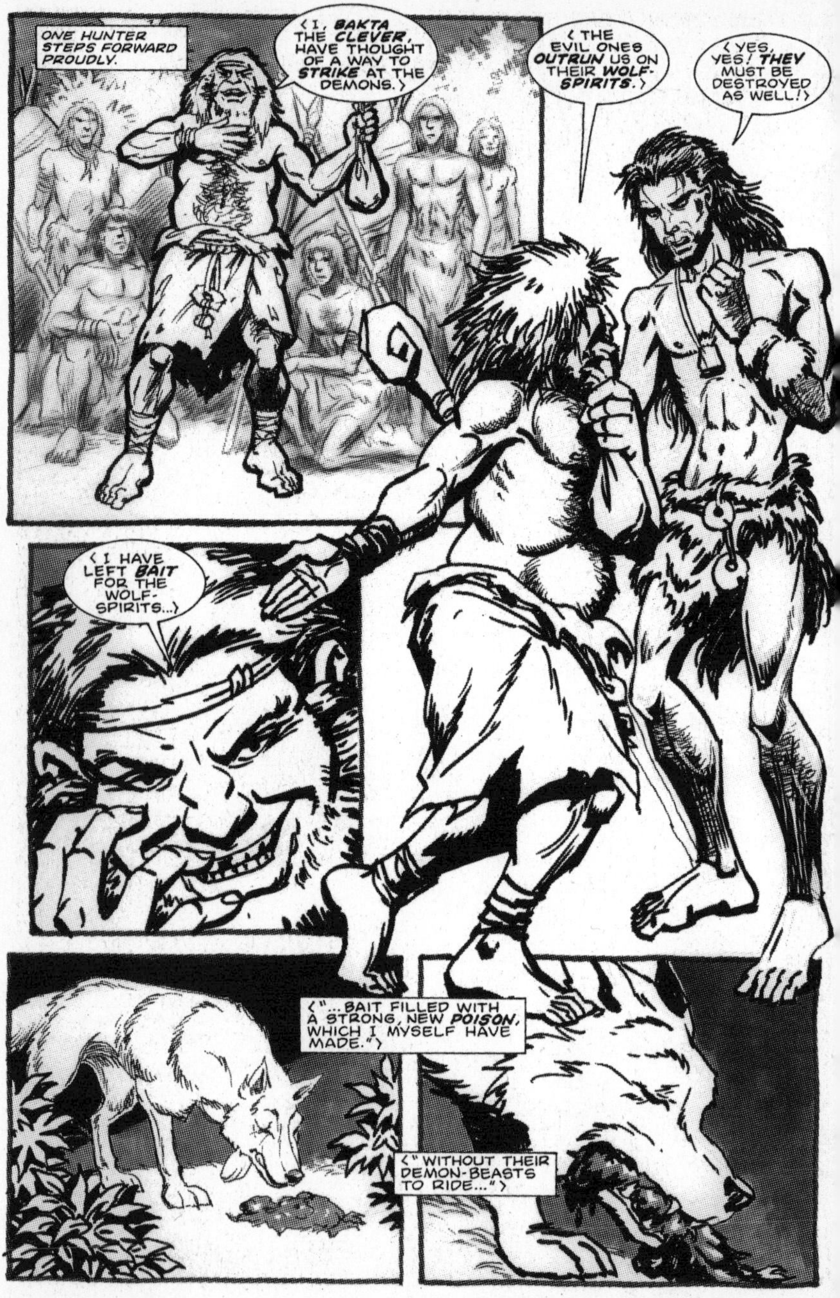
ONE HUNTER STEPS FORWARD PROUDLY.
‹I, BAKTA THE CLEVER, HAVE THOUGHT OF A WAY TO STRIKE AT THE DEMONS.›
‹THE EVIL ONES OUTRUN US ON THEIR WOLF-SPIRITS.›
‹YES, YES! THEY MUST BE DESTROYED AS WELL!›
‹I HAVE LEFT BAIT FOR THE WOLF-SPIRITS...›
‹"...BAIT FILLED WITH A STRONG, NEW POISON, WHICH I MYSELF HAVE MADE."›
‹"WITHOUT THEIR DEMON-BEASTS TO RIDE..."›

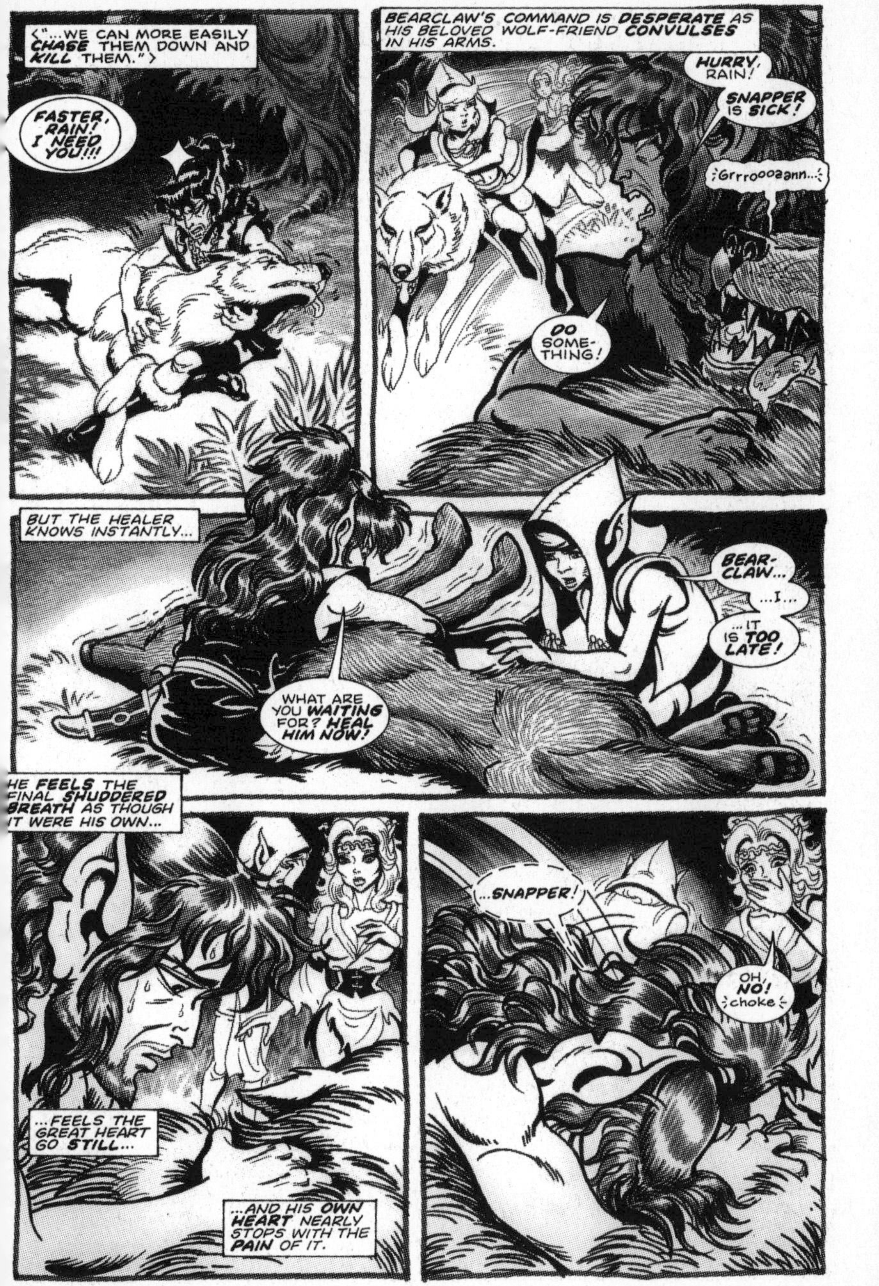

<"...WE CAN MORE EASILY CHASE THEM DOWN AND KILL THEM.">
FASTER, RAIN! I NEED YOU!!!
BEARCLAW'S COMMAND IS DESPERATE AS HIS BELOVED WOLF-FRIEND CONVULSES IN HIS ARMS.
HURRY, RAIN!
SNAPPER IS SICK!
Grrroooaann...
DO SOMETHING!
BUT THE HEALER KNOWS INSTANTLY...
BEAR-CLAW...
...I...
...IT IS TOO LATE!
WHAT ARE YOU WAITING FOR? HEAL HIM NOW!
HE FEELS THE FINAL SHUDDERED BREATH AS THOUGH IT WERE HIS OWN...
...FEELS THE GREAT HEART GO STILL...
...AND HIS OWN HEART NEARLY STOPS WITH THE PAIN OF IT.
...SNAPPER!
OH, NO! choke

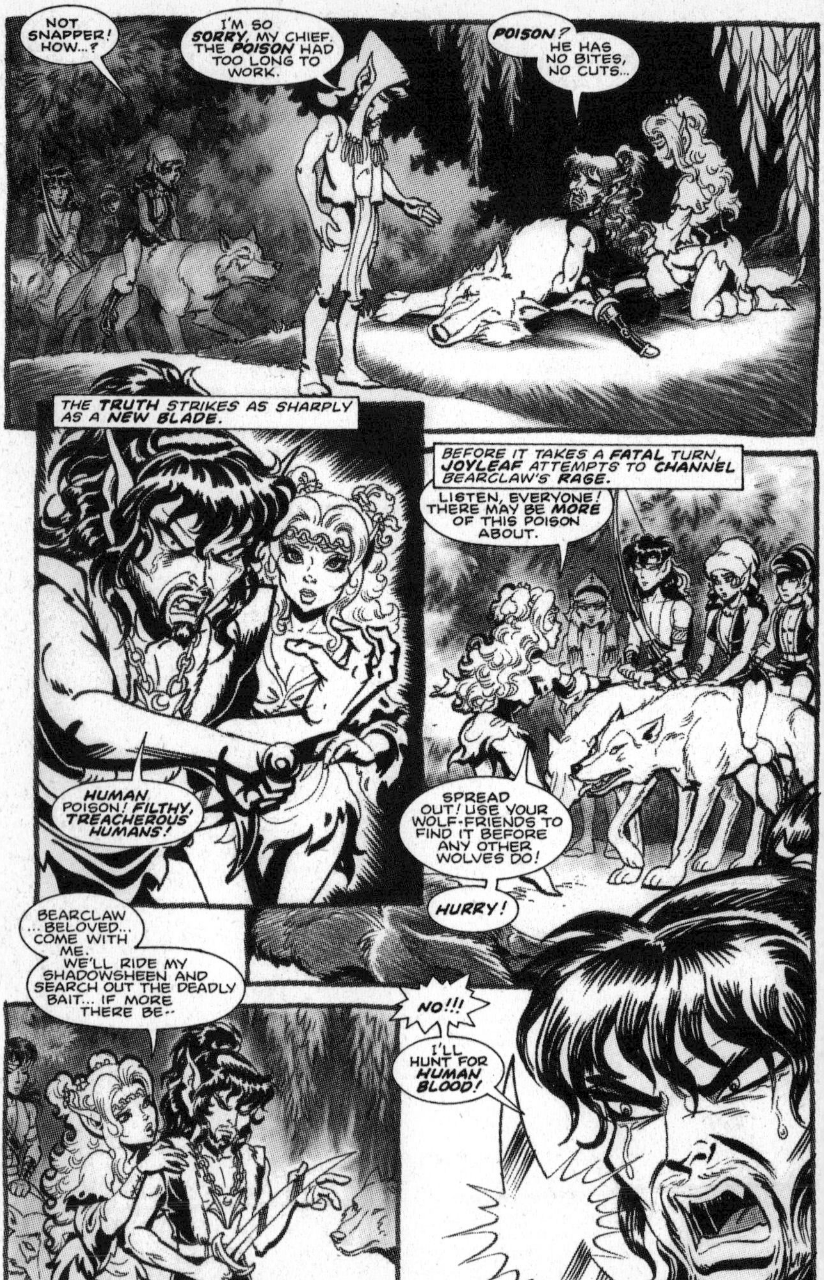

NOT SNAPPER! HOW...?
I'M SO SORRY, MY CHIEF. THE POISON HAD TOO LONG TO WORK.
POISON? HE HAS NO BITES, NO CUTS...
THE TRUTH STRIKES AS SHARPLY AS A NEW BLADE.
HUMAN POISON! FILTHY, TREACHEROUS HUMANS!
BEFORE IT TAKES A FATAL TURN, JOYLEAF ATTEMPTS TO CHANNEL BEARCLAW'S RAGE.
LISTEN, EVERYONE! THERE MAY BE MORE OF THIS POISON ABOUT.
SPREAD OUT! USE YOUR WOLF-FRIENDS TO FIND IT BEFORE ANY OTHER WOLVES DO!
HURRY!
BEARCLAW ...BELOVED... COME WITH ME. WE'LL RIDE MY SHADOWSHEEN AND SEARCH OUT THE DEADLY BAIT... IF MORE THERE BE--
NO!!!
I'LL HUNT FOR HUMAN BLOOD!

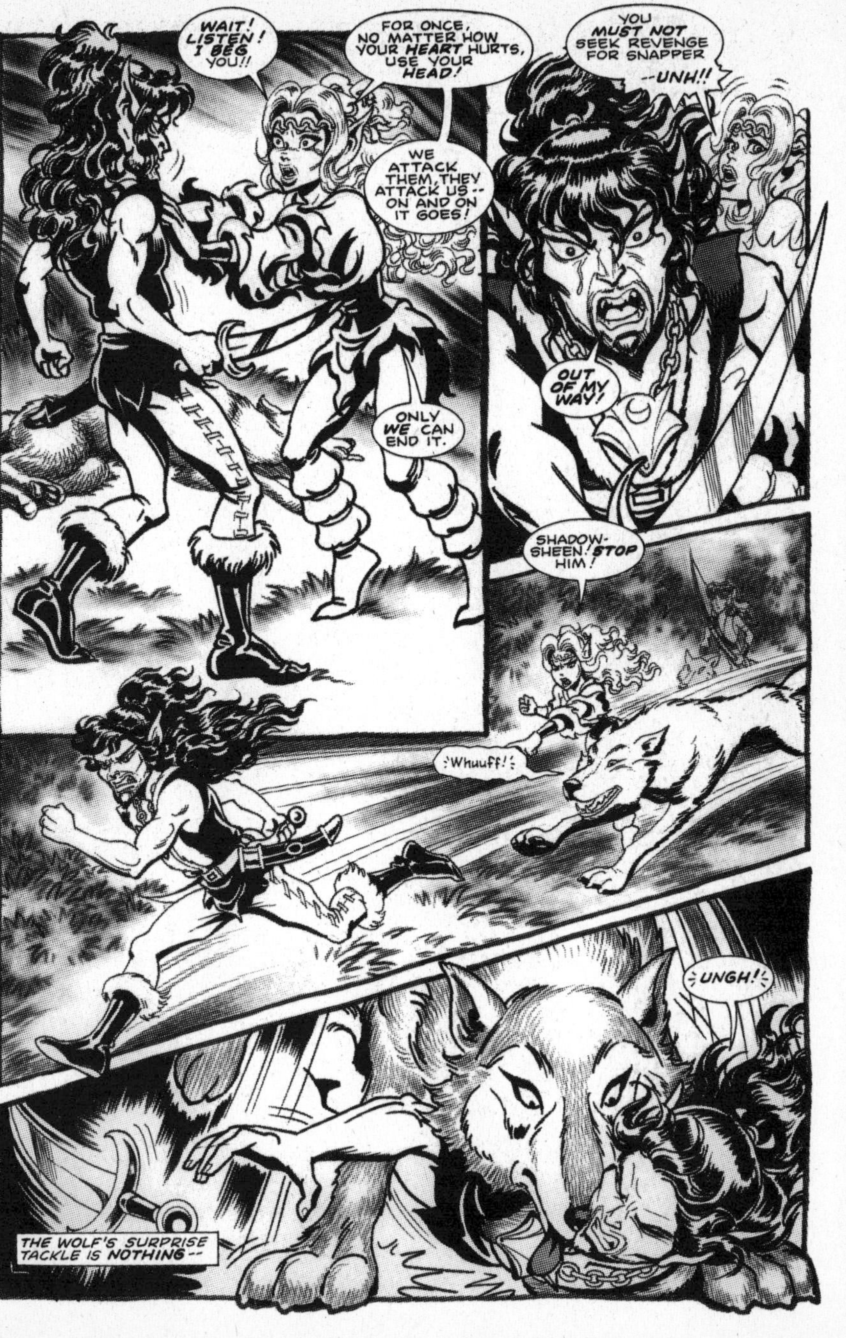
WAIT! LISTEN! I BEG YOU!!
FOR ONCE, NO MATTER HOW YOUR HEART HURTS, USE YOUR HEAD!
WE ATTACK THEM, THEY ATTACK US -- ON AND ON IT GOES!
ONLY WE CAN END IT.
YOU MUST NOT SEEK REVENGE FOR SNAPPER
--UNH!!
OUT OF MY WAY!
SHADOW-SHEEN! STOP HIM!
Whuuff!
UNGH!
THE WOLF'S SURPRISE TACKLE IS NOTHING --

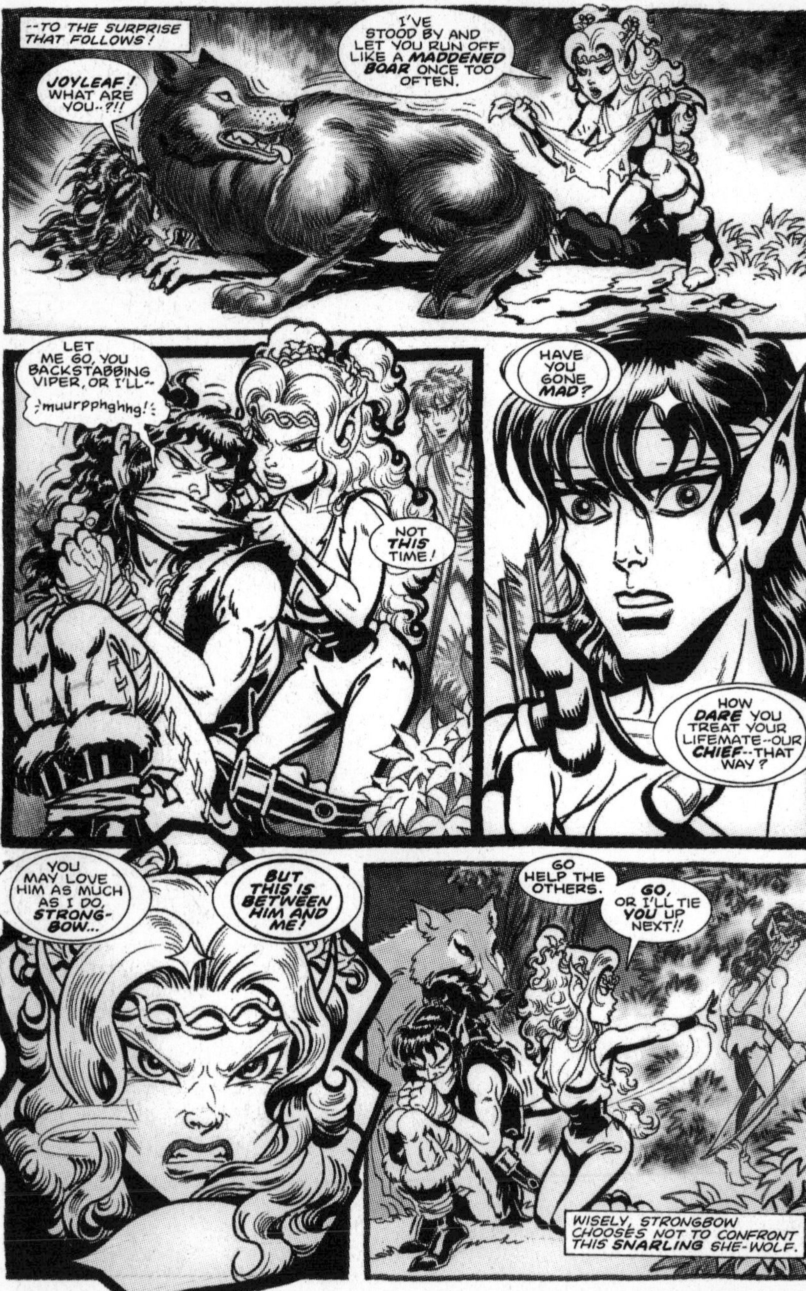
--TO THE SURPRISE THAT FOLLOWS!
JOYLEAF! WHAT ARE YOU--?!!
I'VE STOOD BY AND LET YOU RUN OFF LIKE A MADDENED BOAR ONCE TOO OFTEN.
LET ME GO, YOU BACKSTABBING VIPER, OR I'LL--
mmurpphghhg!
NOT THIS TIME!
HAVE YOU GONE MAD?
HOW DARE YOU TREAT YOUR LIFEMATE--OUR CHIEF--THAT WAY?
YOU MAY LOVE HIM AS MUCH AS I DO, STRONG-BOW...
BUT THIS IS BETWEEN HIM AND ME!
GO HELP THE OTHERS.
GO, OR I'LL TIE YOU UP NEXT!!
WISELY, STRONGBOW CHOOSES NOT TO CONFRONT THIS SNARLING SHE-WOLF.

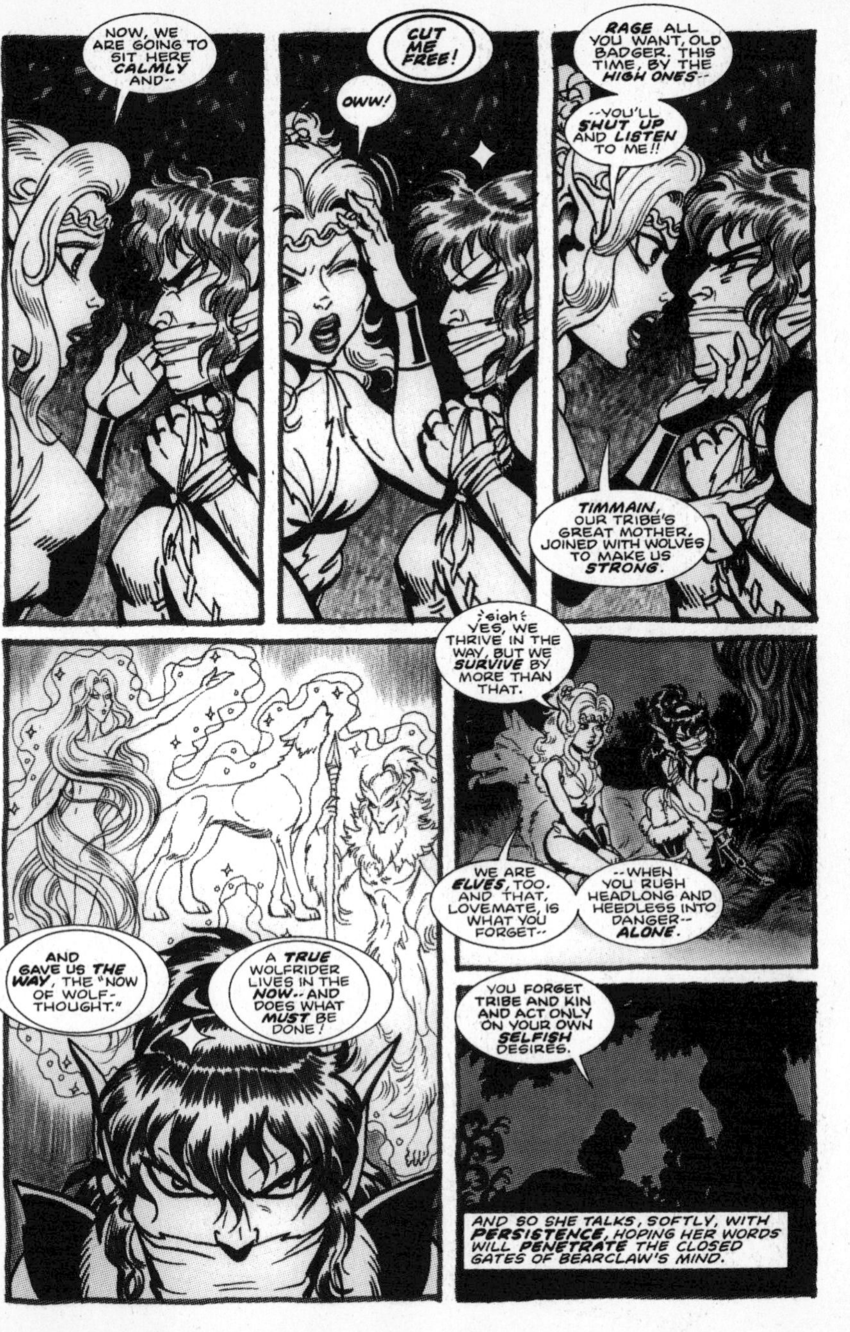
NOW, WE ARE GOING TO SIT HERE CALMLY AND--
CUT ME FREE!
OWW!
RAGE ALL YOU WANT, OLD BADGER. THIS TIME, BY THE HIGH ONES--
--YOU'LL SHUT UP AND LISTEN TO ME!!
TIMMAIN, OUR TRIBE'S GREAT MOTHER, JOINED WITH WOLVES TO MAKE US STRONG.
AND GAVE US THE WAY, THE "NOW OF WOLF-THOUGHT."
A TRUE WOLFRIDER LIVES IN THE NOW-- AND DOES WHAT MUST BE DONE!
sigh YES, WE THRIVE IN THE WAY, BUT WE SURVIVE BY MORE THAN THAT.
WE ARE ELVES, TOO. AND THAT, LOVEMATE, IS WHAT YOU FORGET--
--WHEN YOU RUSH HEADLONG AND HEEDLESS INTO DANGER-- ALONE.
YOU FORGET TRIBE AND KIN AND ACT ONLY ON YOUR OWN SELFISH DESIRES.
AND SO SHE TALKS, SOFTLY, WITH PERSISTENCE, HOPING HER WORDS WILL PENETRATE THE CLOSED GATES OF BEARCLAW'S MIND.

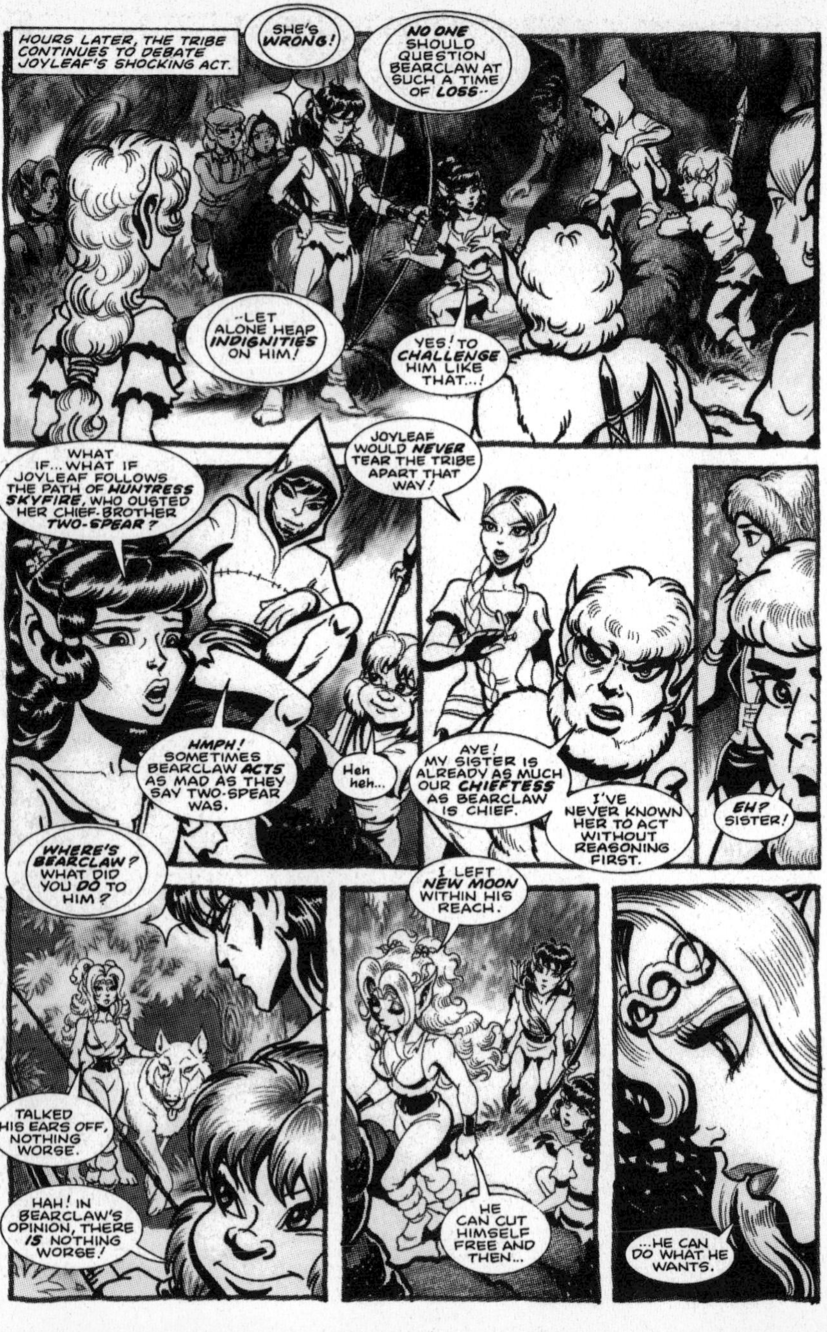
HOURS LATER, THE TRIBE CONTINUES TO DEBATE JOYLEAF'S SHOCKING ACT.
SHE'S WRONG!
NO ONE SHOULD QUESTION BEARCLAW AT SUCH A TIME OF LOSS--
--LET ALONE HEAP INDIGNITIES ON HIM!
YES! TO CHALLENGE HIM LIKE THAT...!
WHAT IF... WHAT IF JOYLEAF FOLLOWS THE PATH OF HUNTRESS SKYFIRE, WHO OUSTED HER CHIEF-BROTHER TWO-SPEAR?
HMPH! SOMETIMES BEARCLAW ACTS AS MAD AS THEY SAY TWO-SPEAR WAS.
Heh heh...
JOYLEAF WOULD NEVER TEAR THE TRIBE APART THAT WAY!
AYE! MY SISTER IS ALREADY AS MUCH OUR CHIEFTESS AS BEARCLAW IS CHIEF.
I'VE NEVER KNOWN HER TO ACT WITHOUT REASONING FIRST.
EH? SISTER!
WHERE'S BEARCLAW? WHAT DID YOU DO TO HIM?
TALKED HIS EARS OFF, NOTHING WORSE.
HAH! IN BEARCLAW'S OPINION, THERE IS NOTHING WORSE!
I LEFT NEW MOON WITHIN HIS REACH.
HE CAN CUT HIMSELF FREE AND THEN...
...HE CAN DO WHAT HE WANTS.

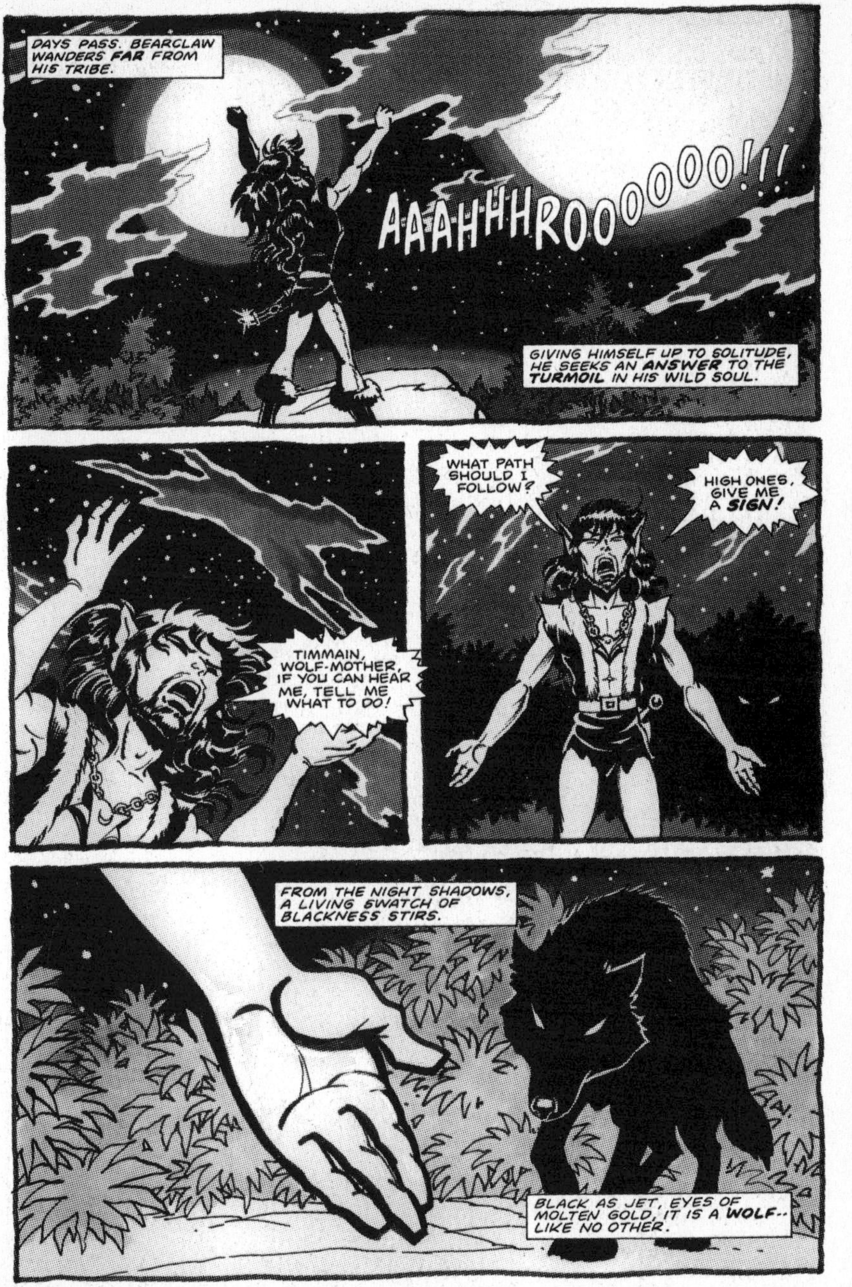
DAYS PASS. BEARCLAW WANDERS FAR FROM HIS TRIBE.
AAAHHHROOOOOOO!!!
GIVING HIMSELF UP TO SOLITUDE, HE SEEKS AN ANSWER TO THE TURMOIL IN HIS WILD SOUL.
TIMMAIN, WOLF-MOTHER, IF YOU CAN HEAR ME, TELL ME WHAT TO DO!
WHAT PATH SHOULD I FOLLOW?
HIGH ONES, GIVE ME A SIGN!
FROM THE NIGHT SHADOWS, A LIVING SWATCH OF BLACKNESS STIRS.
BLACK AS JET, EYES OF MOLTEN GOLD, IT IS A WOLF-- LIKE NO OTHER.

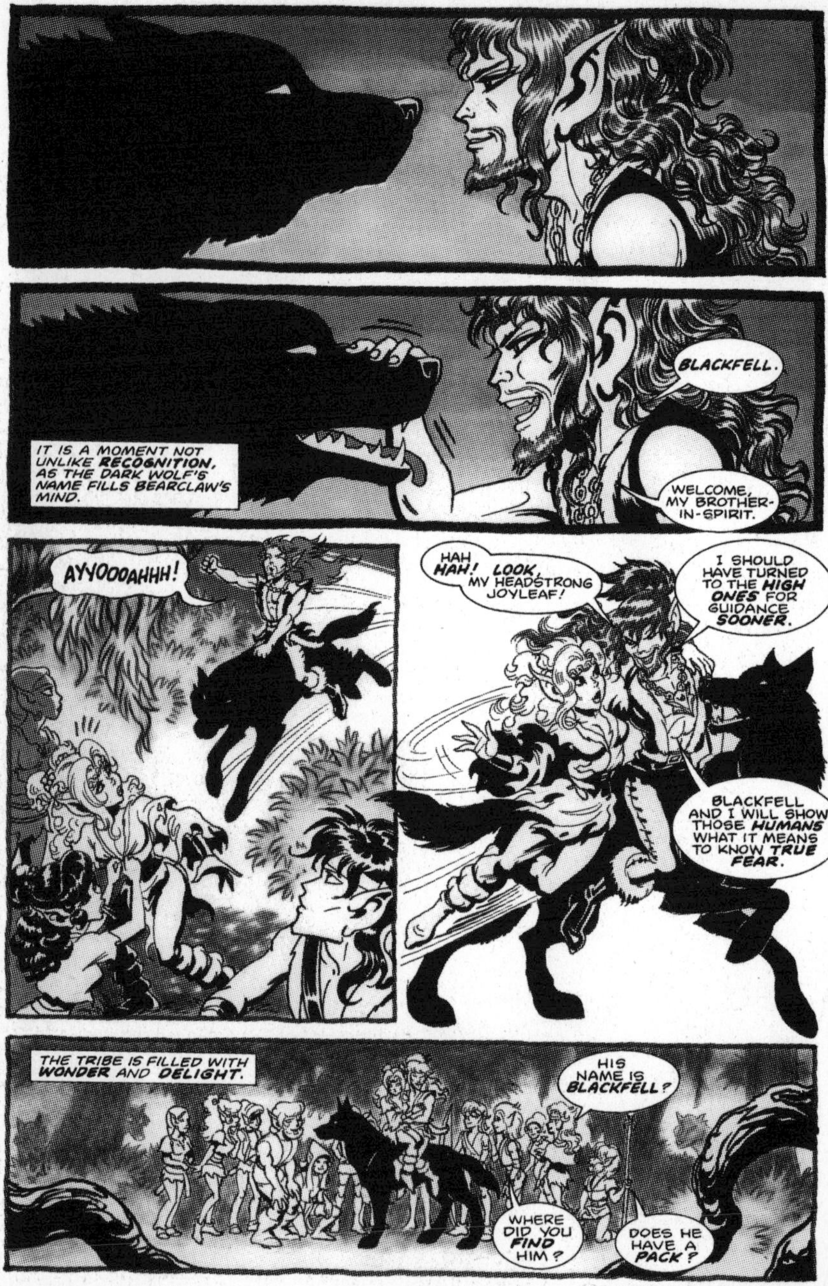
BLACKFELL.
IT IS A MOMENT NOT UNLIKE RECOGNITION, AS THE DARK WOLF'S NAME FILLS BEARCLAW'S MIND.
WELCOME, MY BROTHER-IN-SPIRIT.
AYYOOOAHHH!
HAH HAH! LOOK, MY HEADSTRONG JOYLEAF!
I SHOULD HAVE TURNED TO THE HIGH ONES FOR GUIDANCE SOONER.
BLACKFELL AND I WILL SHOW THOSE HUMANS WHAT IT MEANS TO KNOW TRUE FEAR.
THE TRIBE IS FILLED WITH WONDER AND DELIGHT.
HIS NAME IS BLACKFELL?
WHERE DID YOU FIND HIM?
DOES HE HAVE A PACK?

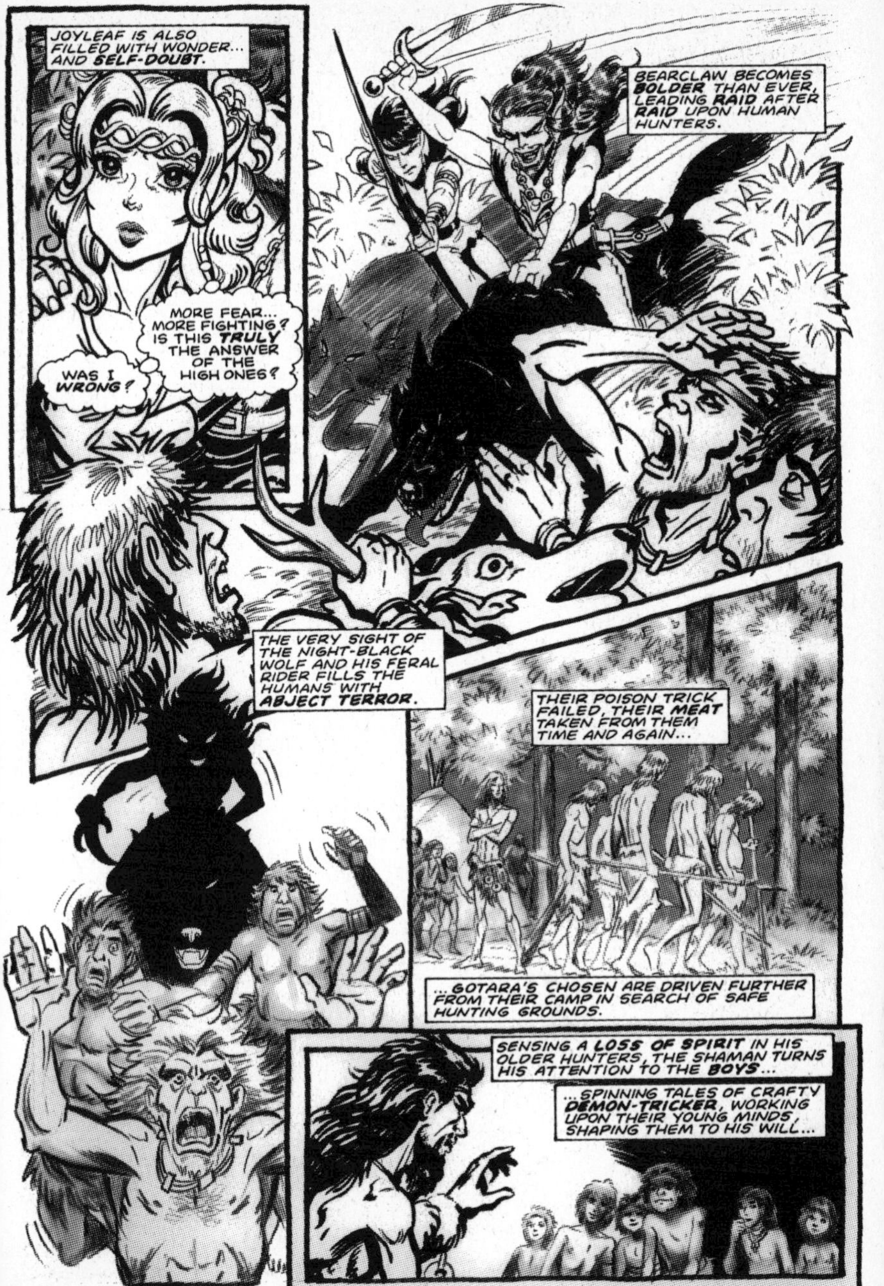
JOYLEAF IS ALSO FILLED WITH WONDER... AND SELF-DOUBT.
MORE FEAR... MORE FIGHTING? IS THIS TRULY THE ANSWER OF THE HIGH ONES?
WAS I WRONG?
BEARCLAW BECOMES BOLDER THAN EVER, LEADING RAID AFTER RAID UPON HUMAN HUNTERS.
THE VERY SIGHT OF THE NIGHT-BLACK WOLF AND HIS FERAL RIDER FILLS THE HUMANS WITH ABJECT TERROR.
THEIR POISON TRICK FAILED, THEIR MEAT TAKEN FROM THEM TIME AND AGAIN...
...GOTARA'S CHOSEN ARE DRIVEN FURTHER FROM THEIR CAMP IN SEARCH OF SAFE HUNTING GROUNDS.
SENSING A LOSS OF SPIRIT IN HIS OLDER HUNTERS, THE SHAMAN TURNS HIS ATTENTION TO THE BOYS...
...SPINNING TALES OF CRAFTY DEMON-TRICKER, WORKING UPON THEIR YOUNG MINDS, SHAPING THEM TO HIS WILL...

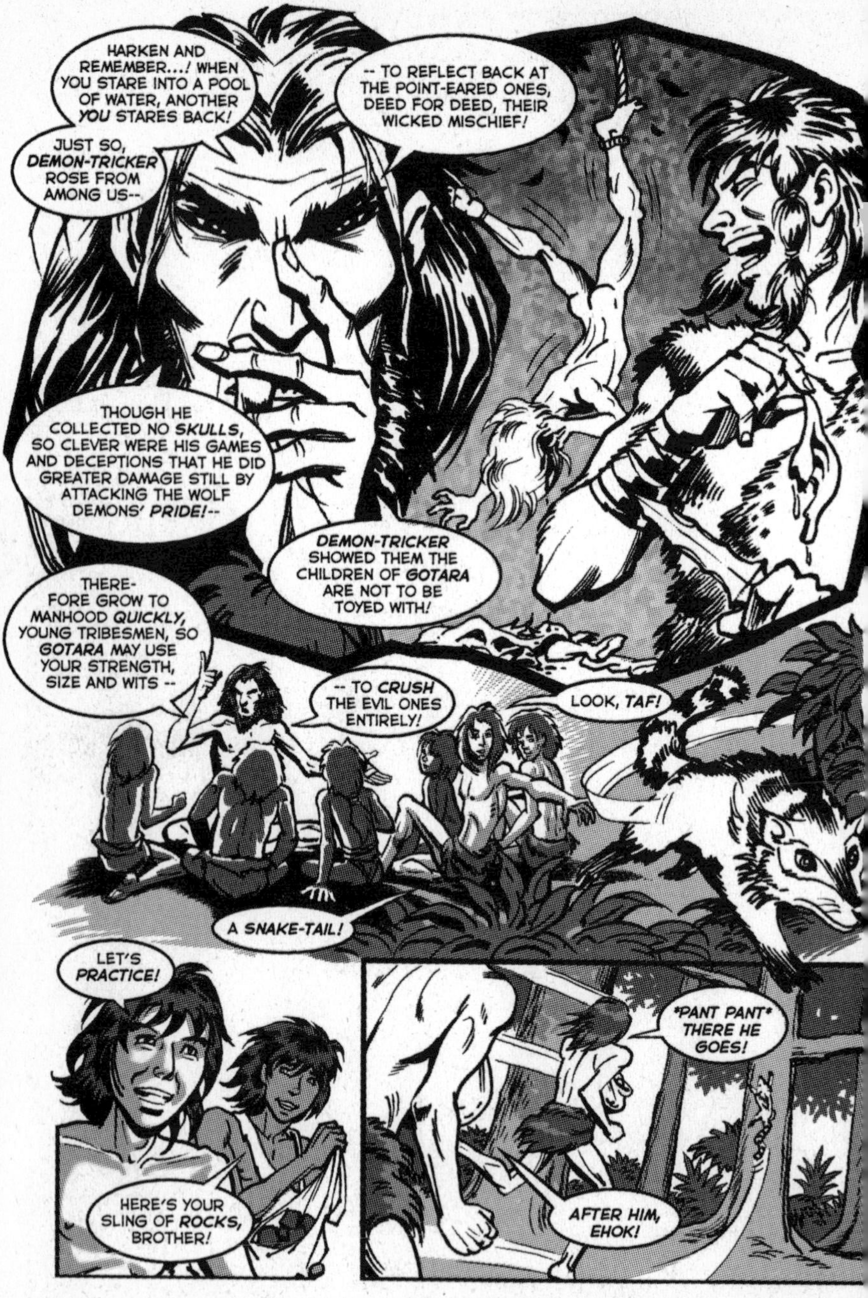
HARKEN AND REMEMBER...! WHEN YOU STARE INTO A POOL OF WATER, ANOTHER YOU STARES BACK!
JUST SO, DEMON-TRICKER ROSE FROM AMONG US--
-- TO REFLECT BACK AT THE POINT-EARED ONES, DEED FOR DEED, THEIR WICKED MISCHIEF!
THOUGH HE COLLECTED NO SKULLS, SO CLEVER WERE HIS GAMES AND DECEPTIONS THAT HE DID GREATER DAMAGE STILL BY ATTACKING THE WOLF DEMONS' PRIDE!--
DEMON-TRICKER SHOWED THEM THE CHILDREN OF GOTARA ARE NOT TO BE TOYED WITH!
THERE-FORE GROW TO MANHOOD QUICKLY, YOUNG TRIBESMEN, SO GOTARA MAY USE YOUR STRENGTH, SIZE AND WITS --
-- TO CRUSH THE EVIL ONES ENTIRELY!
LOOK, TAF!
A SNAKE-TAIL!
LET'S PRACTICE!
HERE'S YOUR SLING OF ROCKS, BROTHER!
PANT PANT THERE HE GOES!
AFTER HIM, EHOK!

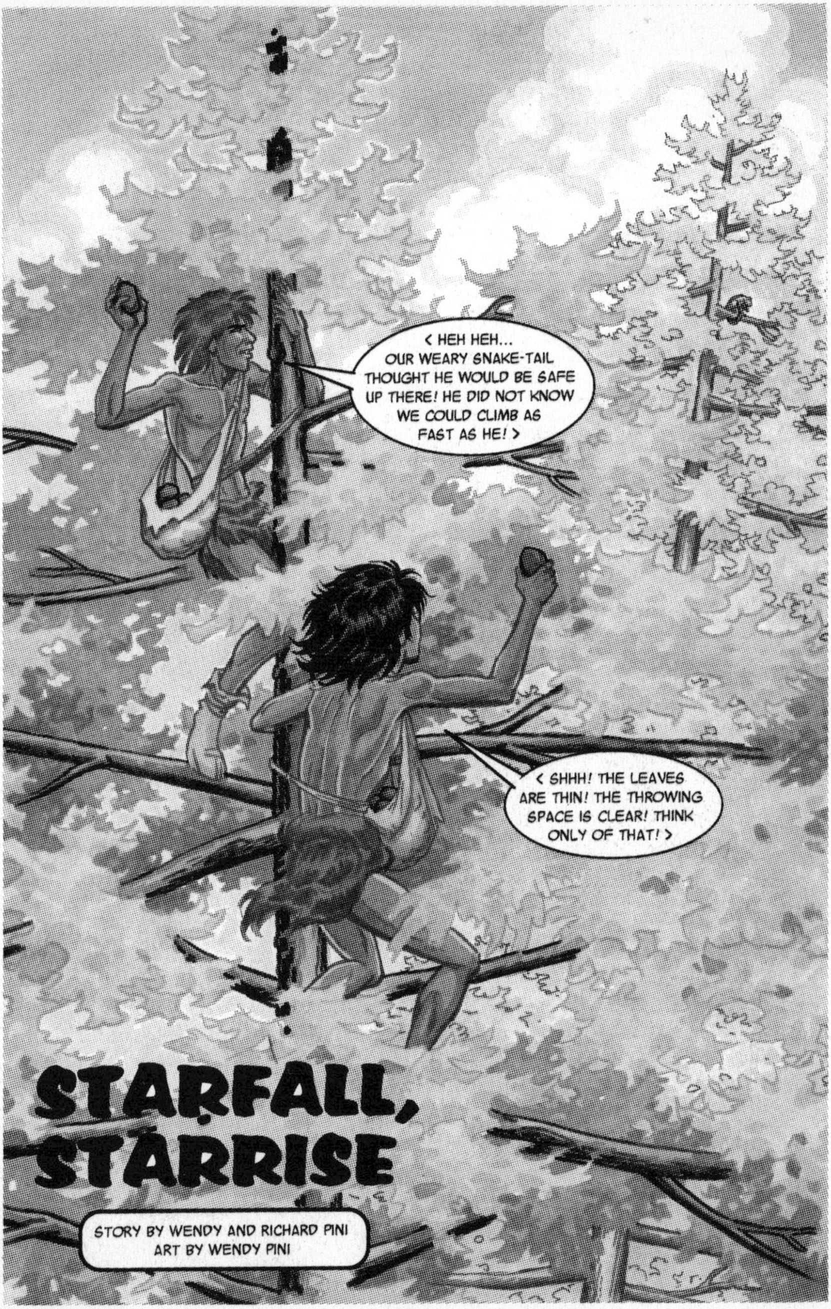
< HEH HEH... OUR WEARY SNAKE-TAIL THOUGHT HE WOULD BE SAFE UP THERE! HE DID NOT KNOW WE COULD CLIMB AS FAST AS HE! >
< SHHH! THE LEAVES ARE THIN! THE THROWING SPACE IS CLEAR! THINK ONLY OF THAT! >
STARFALL, STARRISE
STORY BY WENDY AND RICHARD PINI
ART BY WENDY PINI

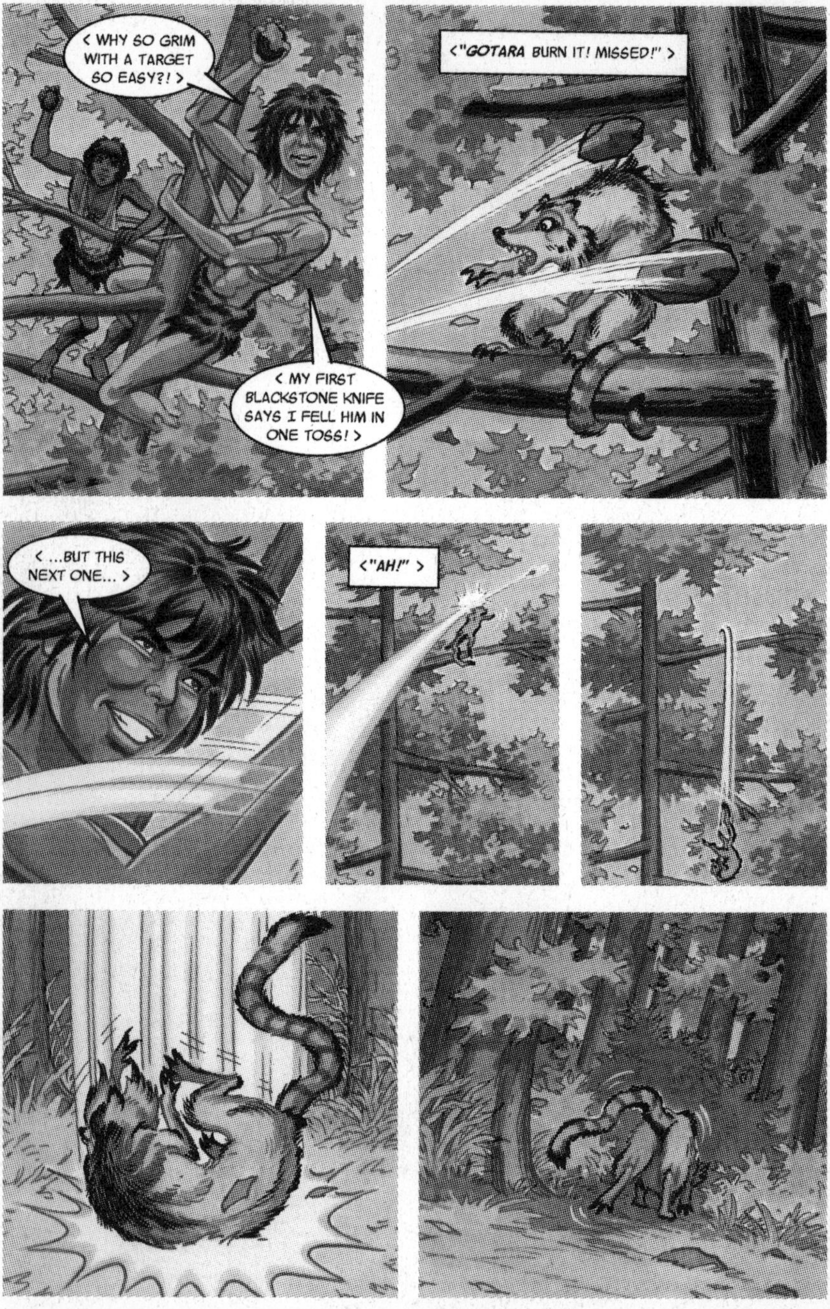
< WHY SO GRIM WITH A TARGET SO EASY?! >
< MY FIRST BLACKSTONE KNIFE SAYS I FELL HIM IN ONE TOSS! >
<"GOTARA BURN IT! MISSED!" >
< ...BUT THIS NEXT ONE... >
<"AH!" >

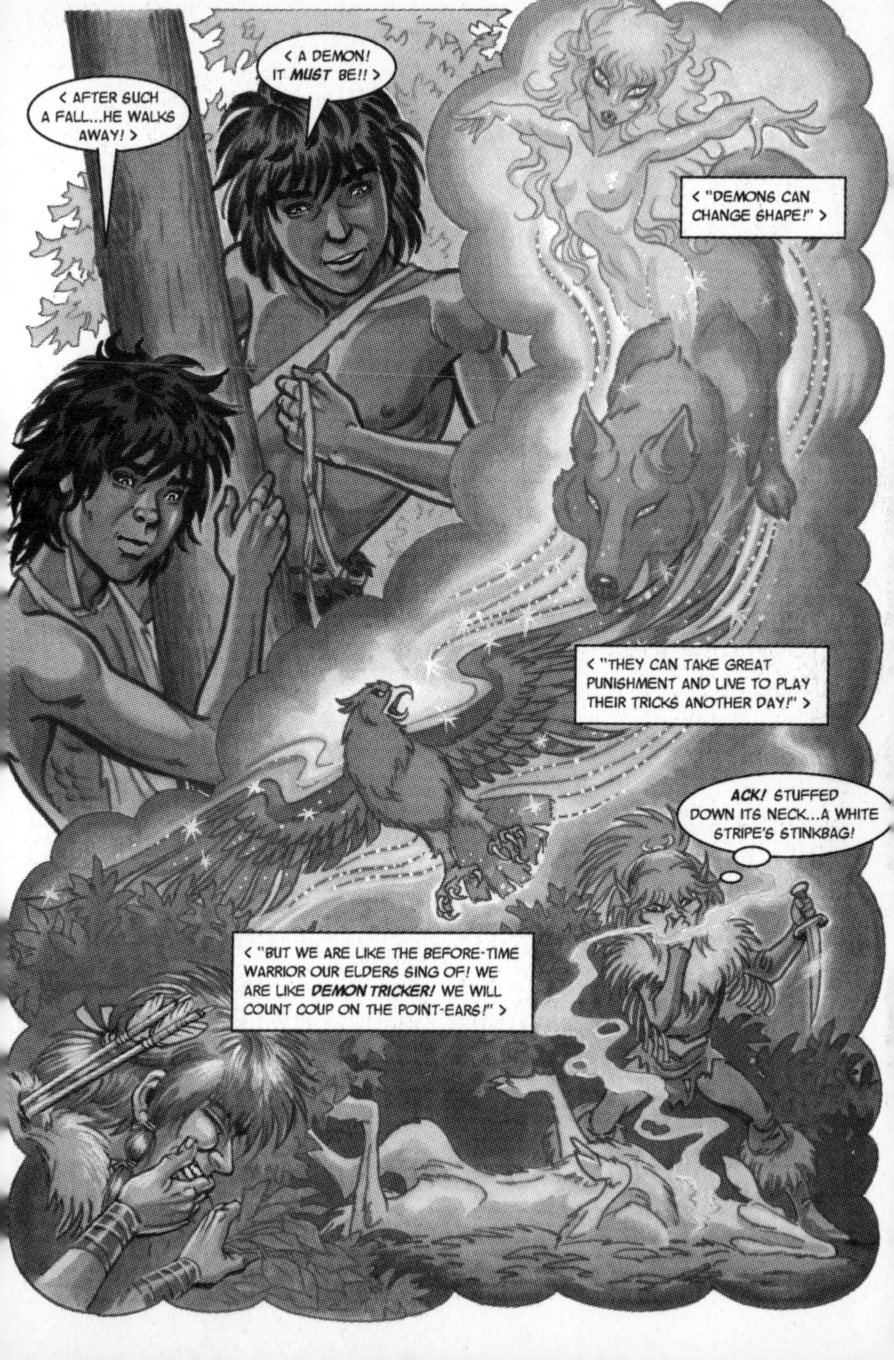
< AFTER SUCH A FALL...HE WALKS AWAY! >
< A DEMON! IT MUST BE!! >
< "DEMONS CAN CHANGE SHAPE!" >
< "THEY CAN TAKE GREAT PUNISHMENT AND LIVE TO PLAY THEIR TRICKS ANOTHER DAY!" >
ACK! STUFFED DOWN ITS NECK...A WHITE STRIPE'S STINKBAG!
< "BUT WE ARE LIKE THE BEFORE-TIME WARRIOR OUR ELDERS SING OF! WE ARE LIKE DEMON TRICKER! WE WILL COUNT COUP ON THE POINT-EARS!" >

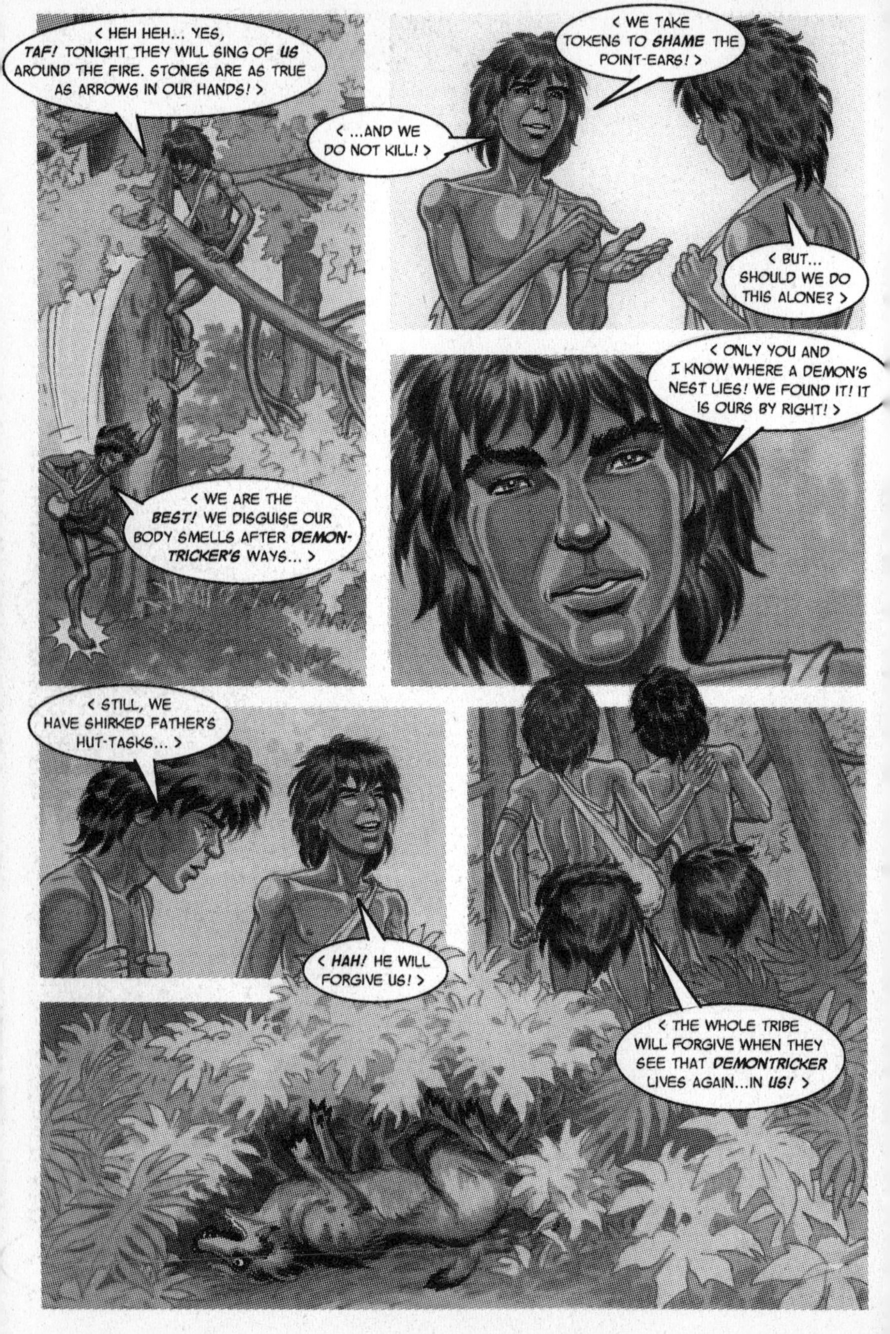

< HEH HEH... YES, TAF! TONIGHT THEY WILL SING OF US AROUND THE FIRE. STONES ARE AS TRUE AS ARROWS IN OUR HANDS! >
< WE TAKE TOKENS TO SHAME THE POINT-EARS! >
< ...AND WE DO NOT KILL! >
< BUT... SHOULD WE DO THIS ALONE? >
< WE ARE THE BEST! WE DISGUISE OUR BODY SMELLS AFTER DEMON-TRICKER'S WAYS... >
< ONLY YOU AND I KNOW WHERE A DEMON'S NEST LIES! WE FOUND IT! IT IS OURS BY RIGHT! >
< STILL, WE HAVE SHIRKED FATHER'S HUT-TASKS... >
< HAH! HE WILL FORGIVE US! >
< THE WHOLE TRIBE WILL FORGIVE WHEN THEY SEE THAT DEMONTRICKER LIVES AGAIN...IN US! >

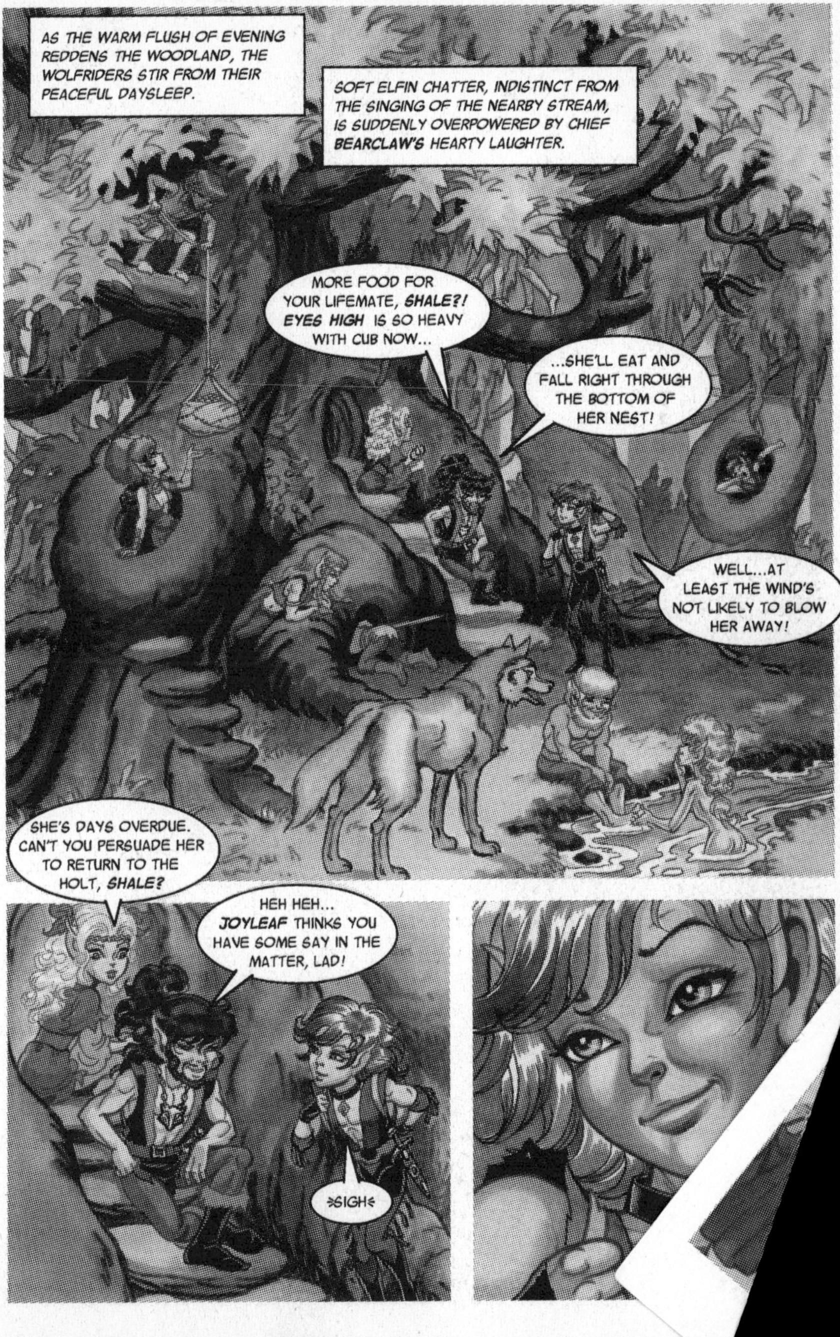
AS THE WARM FLUSH OF EVENING REDDENS THE WOODLAND, THE WOLFRIDERS STIR FROM THEIR PEACEFUL DAYSLEEP.
SOFT ELFIN CHATTER, INDISTINCT FROM THE SINGING OF THE NEARBY STREAM, IS SUDDENLY OVERPOWERED BY CHIEF BEARCLAW'S HEARTY LAUGHTER.
MORE FOOD FOR YOUR LIFEMATE, SHALE?! EYES HIGH IS SO HEAVY WITH CUB NOW...
...SHE'LL EAT AND FALL RIGHT THROUGH THE BOTTOM OF HER NEST!
WELL...AT LEAST THE WIND'S NOT LIKELY TO BLOW HER AWAY!
SHE'S DAYS OVERDUE. CAN'T YOU PERSUADE HER TO RETURN TO THE HOLT, SHALE?
HEH HEH... JOYLEAF THINKS YOU HAVE SOME SAY IN THE MATTER, LAD!
>SIGH<

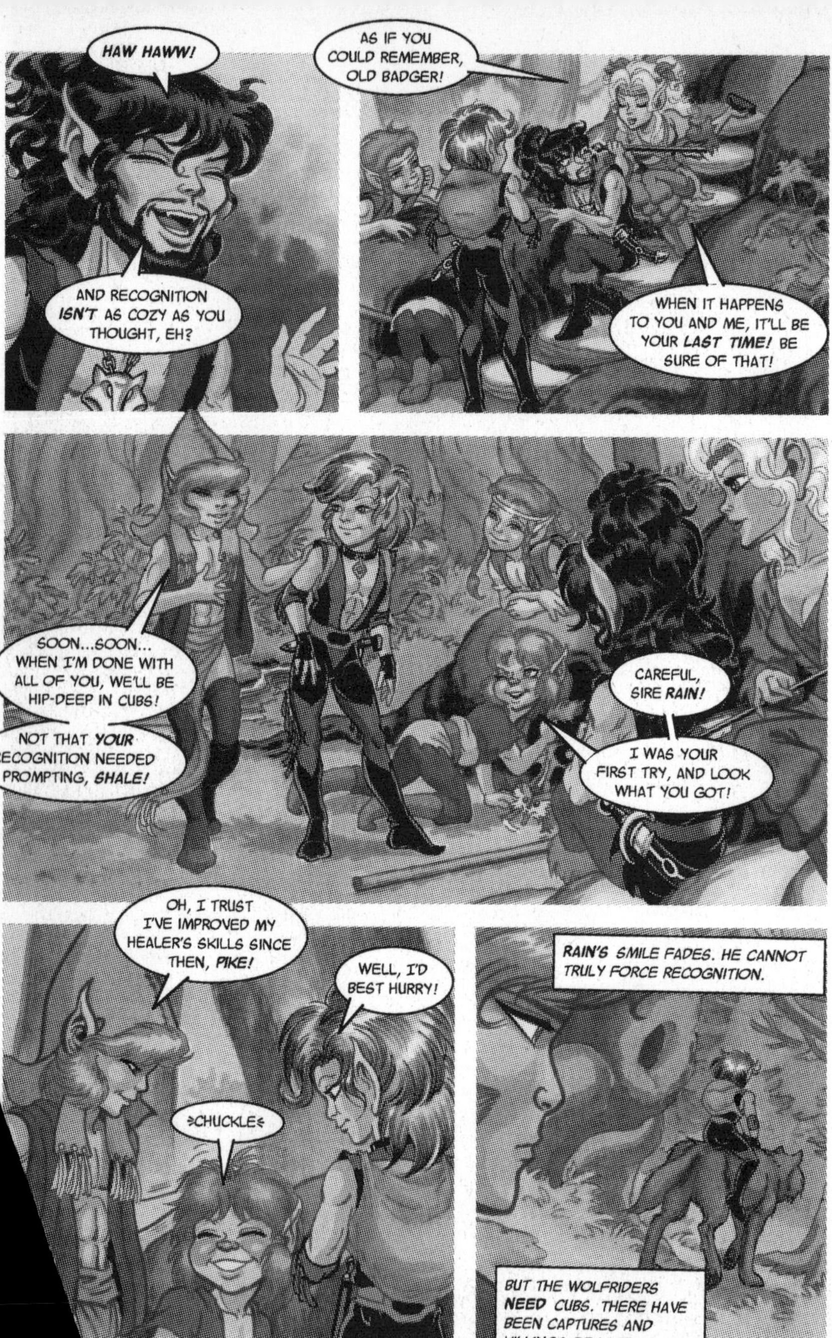
HAW HAWW!
AND RECOGNITION ISN'T AS COZY AS YOU THOUGHT, EH?
AS IF YOU COULD REMEMBER, OLD BADGER!
WHEN IT HAPPENS TO YOU AND ME, IT'LL BE YOUR LAST TIME! BE SURE OF THAT!
SOON...SOON... WHEN I'M DONE WITH ALL OF YOU, WE'LL BE HIP-DEEP IN CUBS!
NOT THAT YOUR RECOGNITION NEEDED PROMPTING, SHALE!
CAREFUL, SIRE RAIN!
I WAS YOUR FIRST TRY, AND LOOK WHAT YOU GOT!
OH, I TRUST I'VE IMPROVED MY HEALER'S SKILLS SINCE THEN, PIKE!
WELL, I'D BEST HURRY!
≈CHUCKLE≈
RAIN'S SMILE FADES. HE CANNOT TRULY FORCE RECOGNITION.
BUT THE WOLFRIDERS NEED CUBS. THERE HAVE BEEN CAPTURES AND KILLINGS OF LATE -

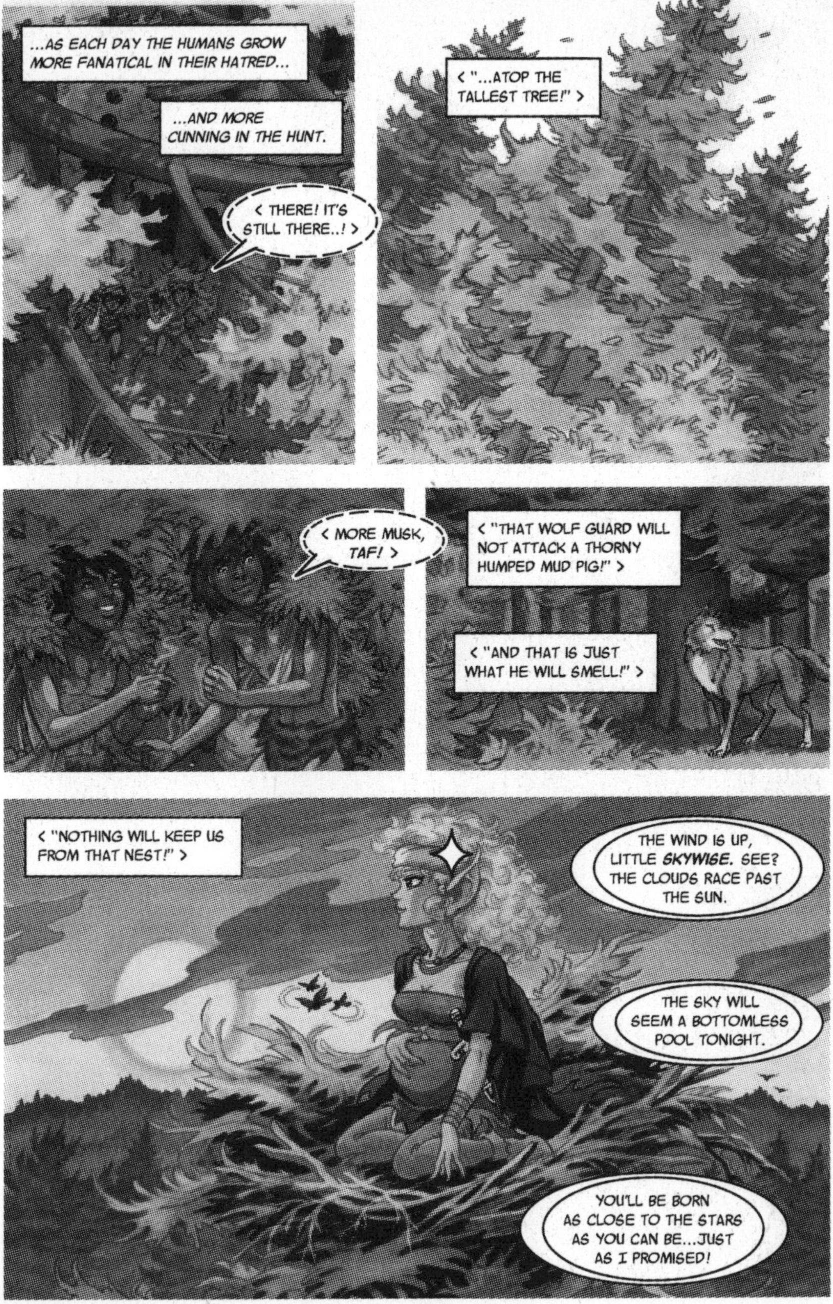

...AS EACH DAY THE HUMANS GROW MORE FANATICAL IN THEIR HATRED...
...AND MORE CUNNING IN THE HUNT.
< THERE! IT'S STILL THERE..! >
< "...ATOP THE TALLEST TREE!" >
< MORE MUSK, TAF! >
< "THAT WOLF GUARD WILL NOT ATTACK A THORNY HUMPED MUD PIG!" >
< "AND THAT IS JUST WHAT HE WILL SMELL!" >
< "NOTHING WILL KEEP US FROM THAT NEST!" >
THE WIND IS UP, LITTLE SKYWISE. SEE? THE CLOUDS RACE PAST THE SUN.
THE SKY WILL SEEM A BOTTOMLESS POOL TONIGHT.
YOU'LL BE BORN AS CLOSE TO THE STARS AS YOU CAN BE...JUST AS I PROMISED!

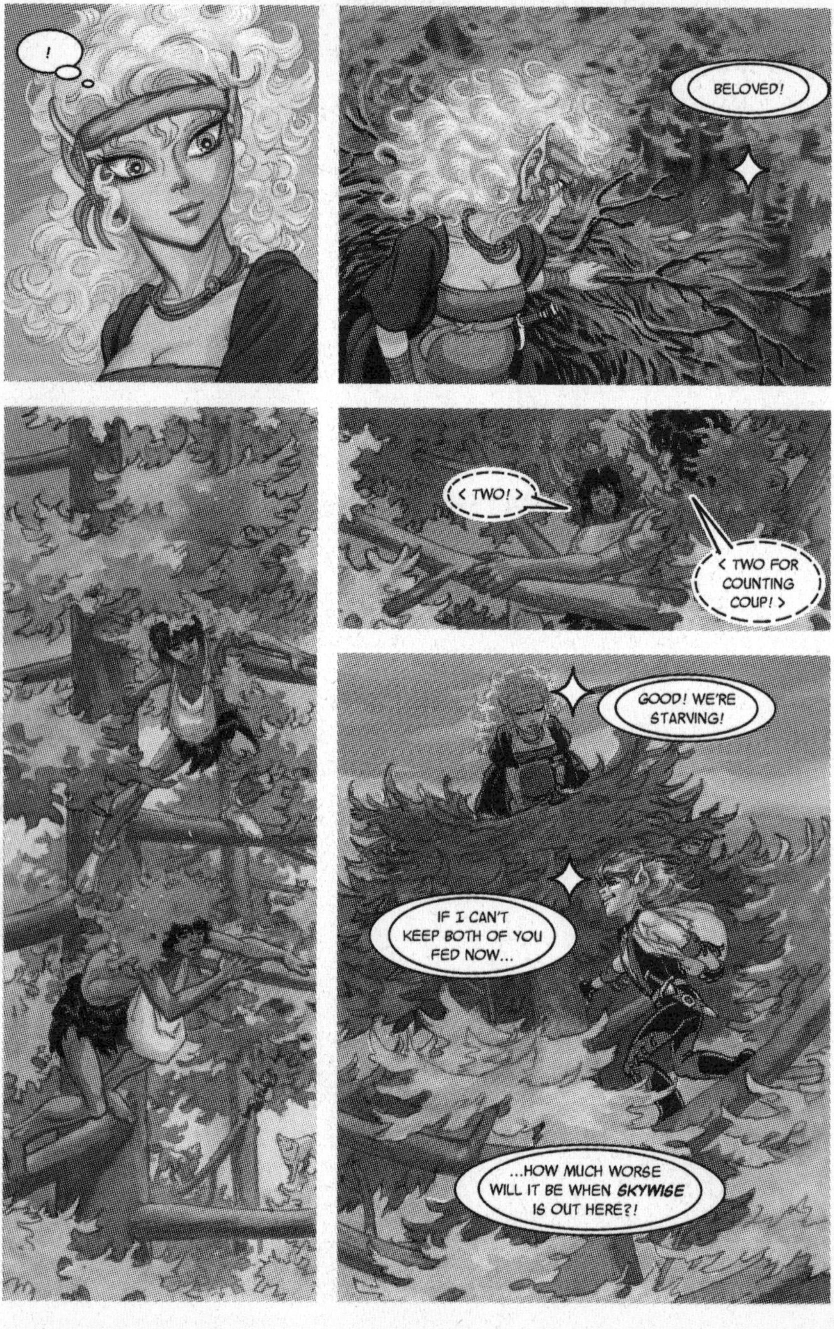

!
BELOVED!
< TWO! >
< TWO FOR COUNTING COUP! >
GOOD! WE'RE STARVING!
IF I CAN'T KEEP BOTH OF YOU FED NOW...
...HOW MUCH WORSE WILL IT BE WHEN SKYWISE IS OUT HERE?!

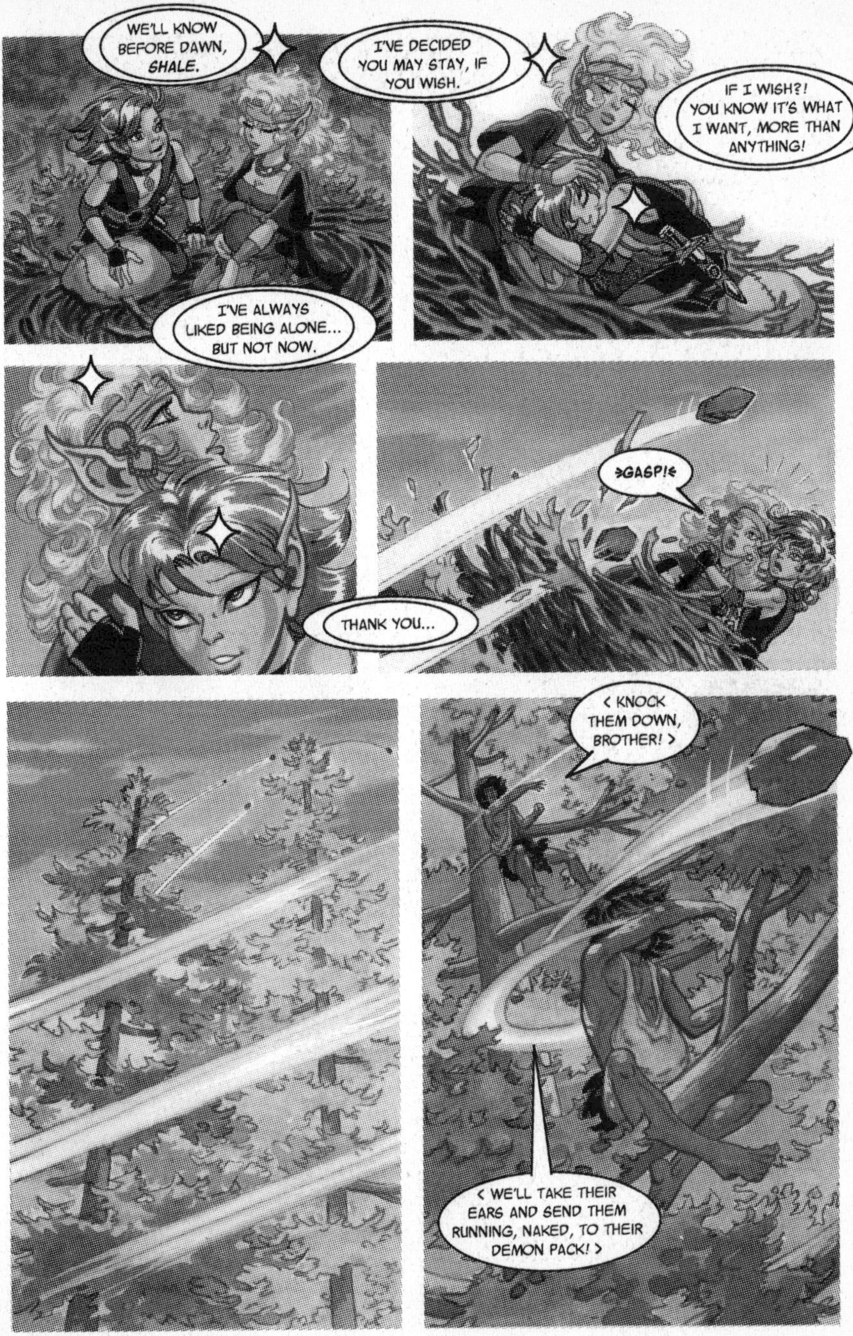
WE'LL KNOW BEFORE DAWN, SHALE.
I'VE ALWAYS LIKED BEING ALONE... BUT NOT NOW.
I'VE DECIDED YOU MAY STAY, IF YOU WISH.
IF I WISH?! YOU KNOW IT'S WHAT I WANT, MORE THAN ANYTHING!
THANK YOU...
GASP!
< KNOCK THEM DOWN, BROTHER! >
< WE'LL TAKE THEIR EARS AND SEND THEM RUNNING, NAKED, TO THEIR DEMON PACK! >

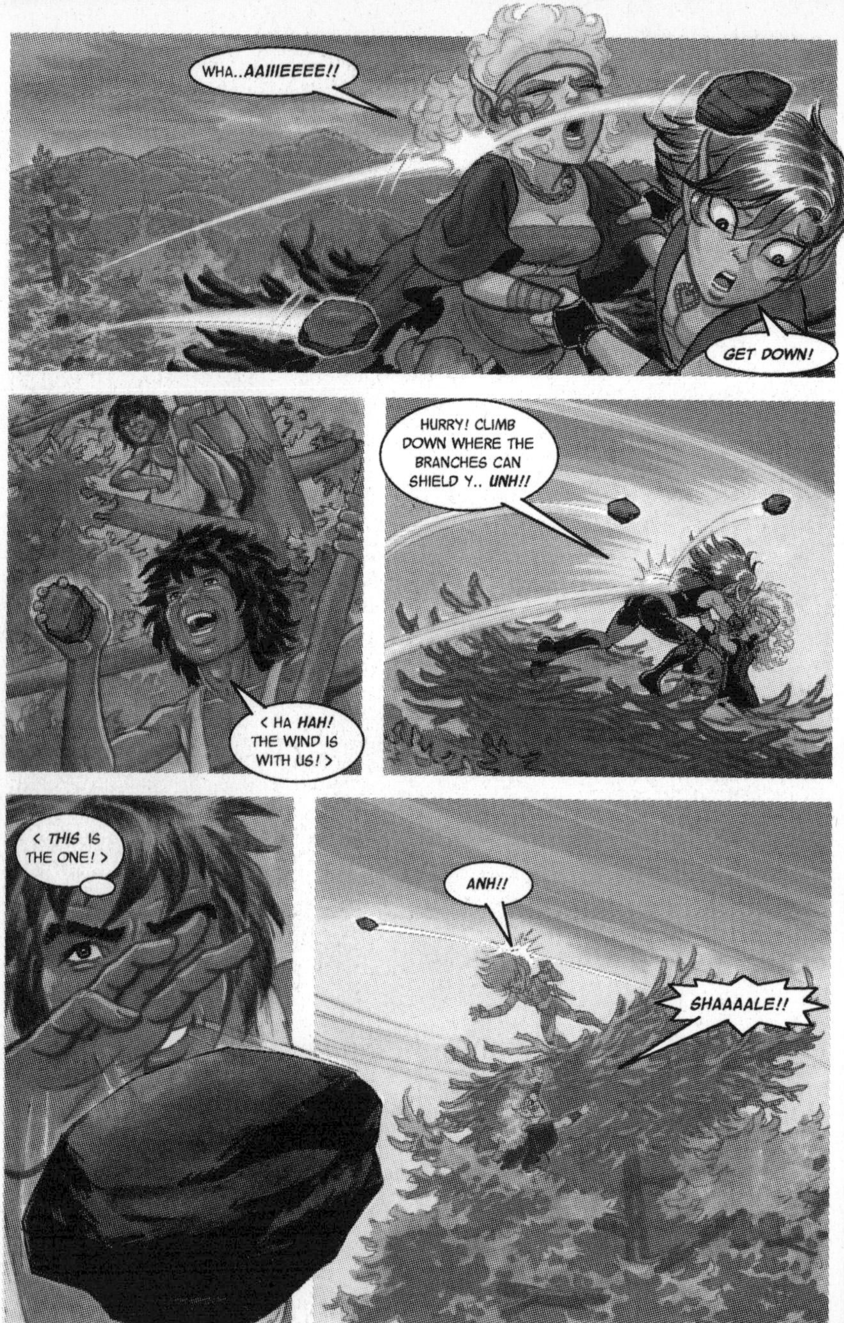
WHA.. AAIIIEEEE!!
GET DOWN!
< HA HAH! THE WIND IS WITH US! >
HURRY! CLIMB DOWN WHERE THE BRANCHES CAN SHIELD Y.. UNH!!
< THIS IS THE ONE! >
ANH!!
SHAAAALE!!

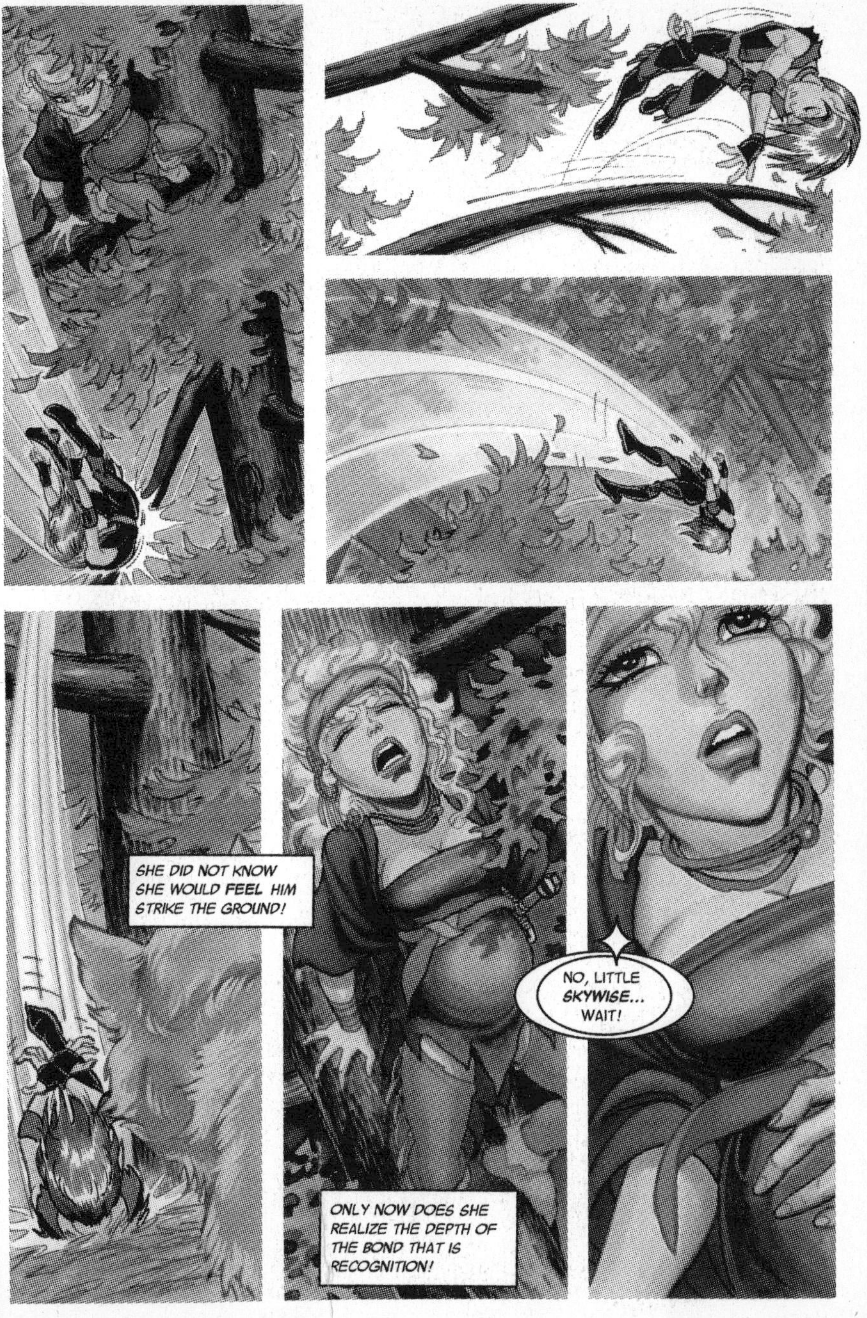
SHE DID NOT KNOW SHE WOULD FEEL HIM STRIKE THE GROUND!
ONLY NOW DOES SHE REALIZE THE DEPTH OF THE BOND THAT IS RECOGNITION!
NO, LITTLE SKYWISE... WAIT!

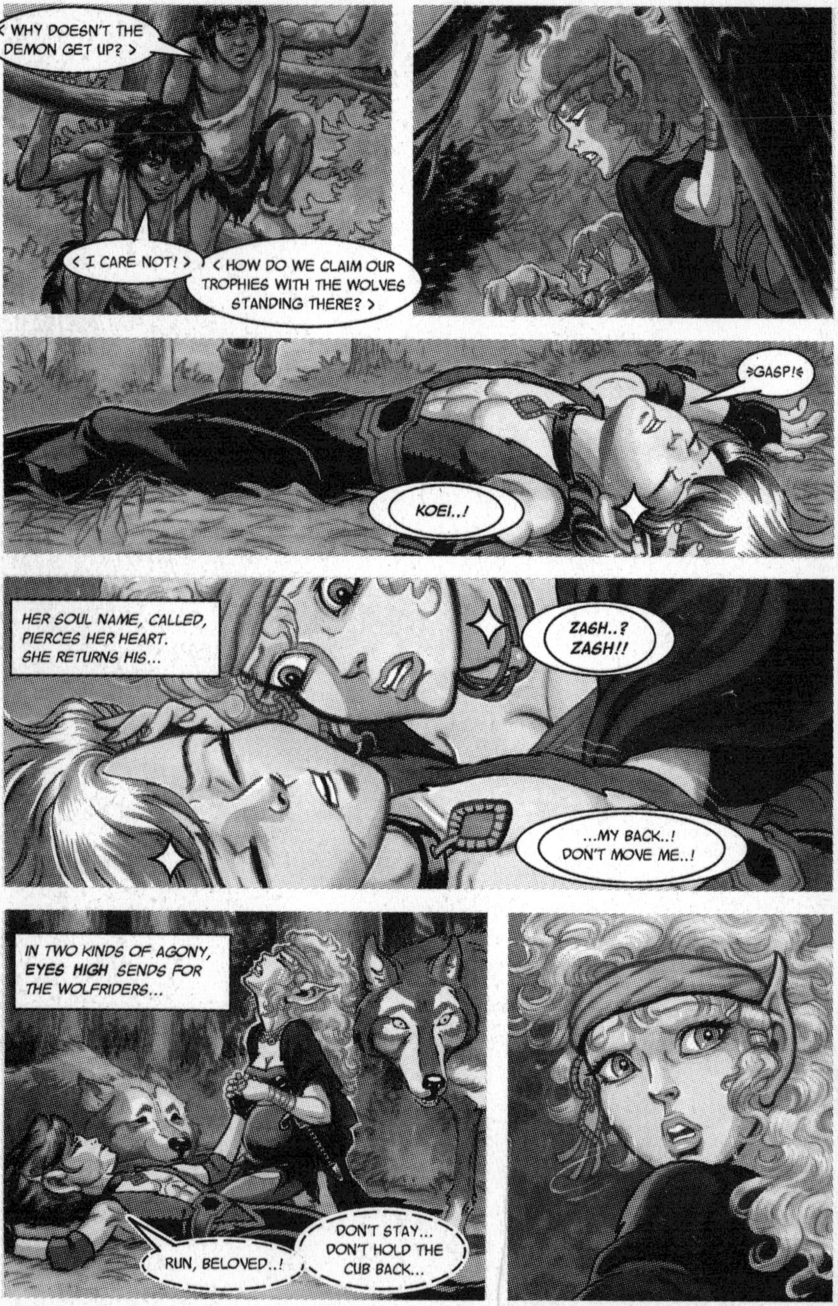
< WHY DOESN'T THE DEMON GET UP? >
< I CARE NOT! >
< HOW DO WE CLAIM OUR TROPHIES WITH THE WOLVES STANDING THERE? >
≯GASP!≮
KOEI..!
HER SOUL NAME, CALLED, PIERCES HER HEART. SHE RETURNS HIS...
ZASH..? ZASH!!
...MY BACK..! DON'T MOVE ME..!
IN TWO KINDS OF AGONY, EYES HIGH SENDS FOR THE WOLFRIDERS...
RUN, BELOVED..!
DON'T STAY... DON'T HOLD THE CUB BACK...

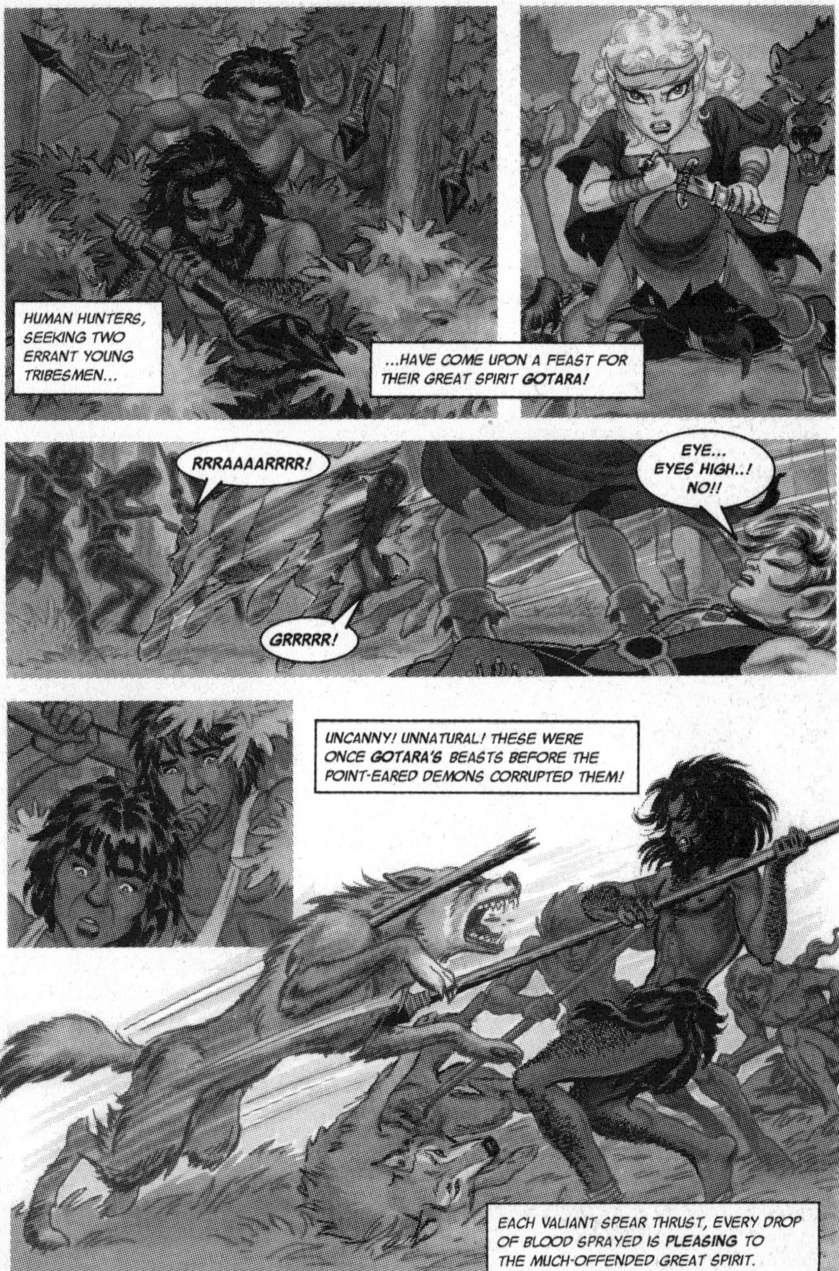
HUMAN HUNTERS, SEEKING TWO ERRANT YOUNG TRIBESMEN...
...HAVE COME UPON A FEAST FOR THEIR GREAT SPIRIT GOTARA!
RRRAAAARRRR!
GRRRRR!
EYE... EYES HIGH..! NO!!
UNCANNY! UNNATURAL! THESE WERE ONCE GOTARA'S BEASTS BEFORE THE POINT-EARED DEMONS CORRUPTED THEM!
EACH VALIANT SPEAR THRUST, EVERY DROP OF BLOOD SPRAYED IS PLEASING TO THE MUCH-OFFENDED GREAT SPIRIT.

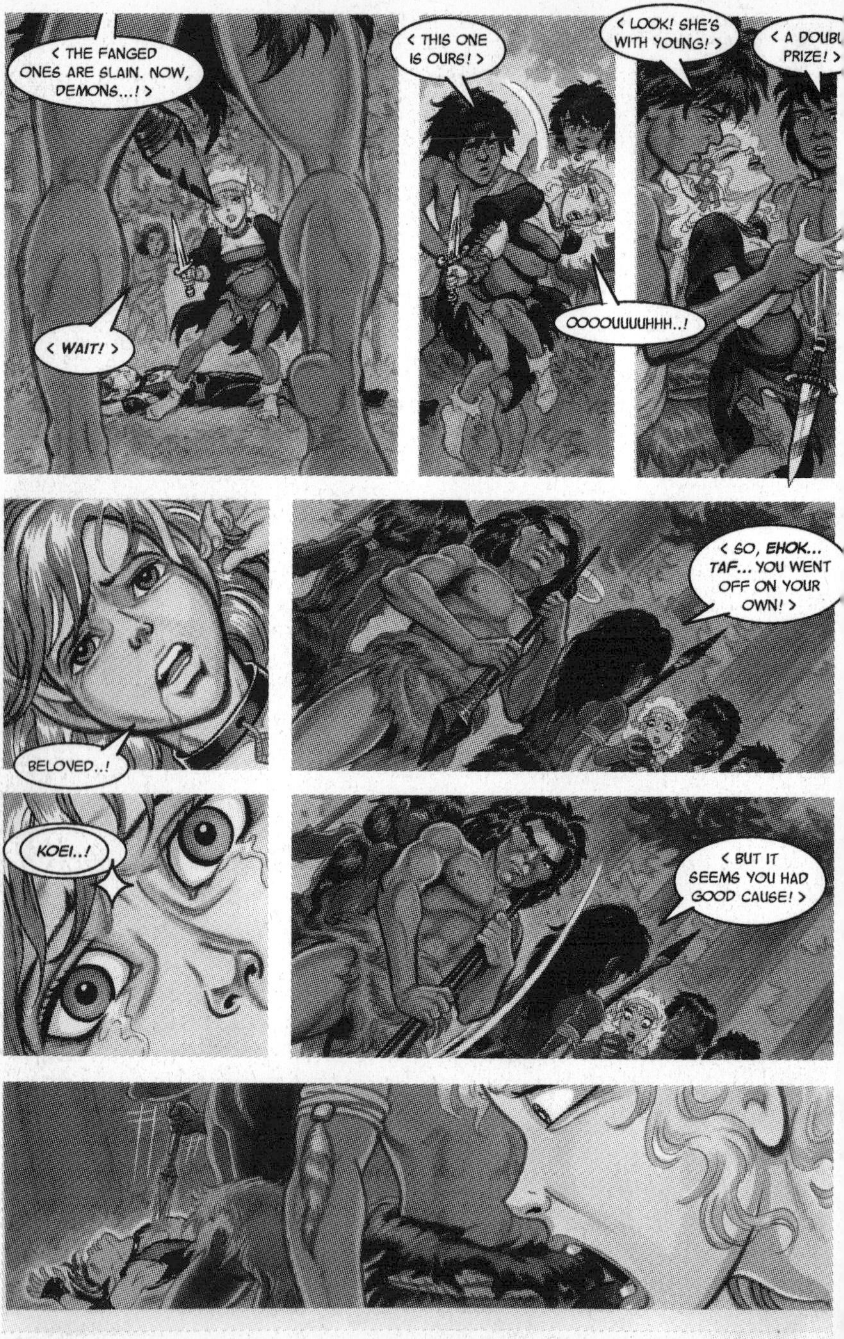

< THE FANGED ONES ARE SLAIN. NOW, DEMONS...! >
< WAIT! >
< THIS ONE IS OURS! >
OOOOUUUUHHH..!
< LOOK! SHE'S WITH YOUNG! >
< A DOUBL PRIZE! >
BELOVED..!
< SO, EHOK... TAF... YOU WENT OFF ON YOUR OWN! >
KOEI..!
< BUT IT SEEMS YOU HAD GOOD CAUSE! >

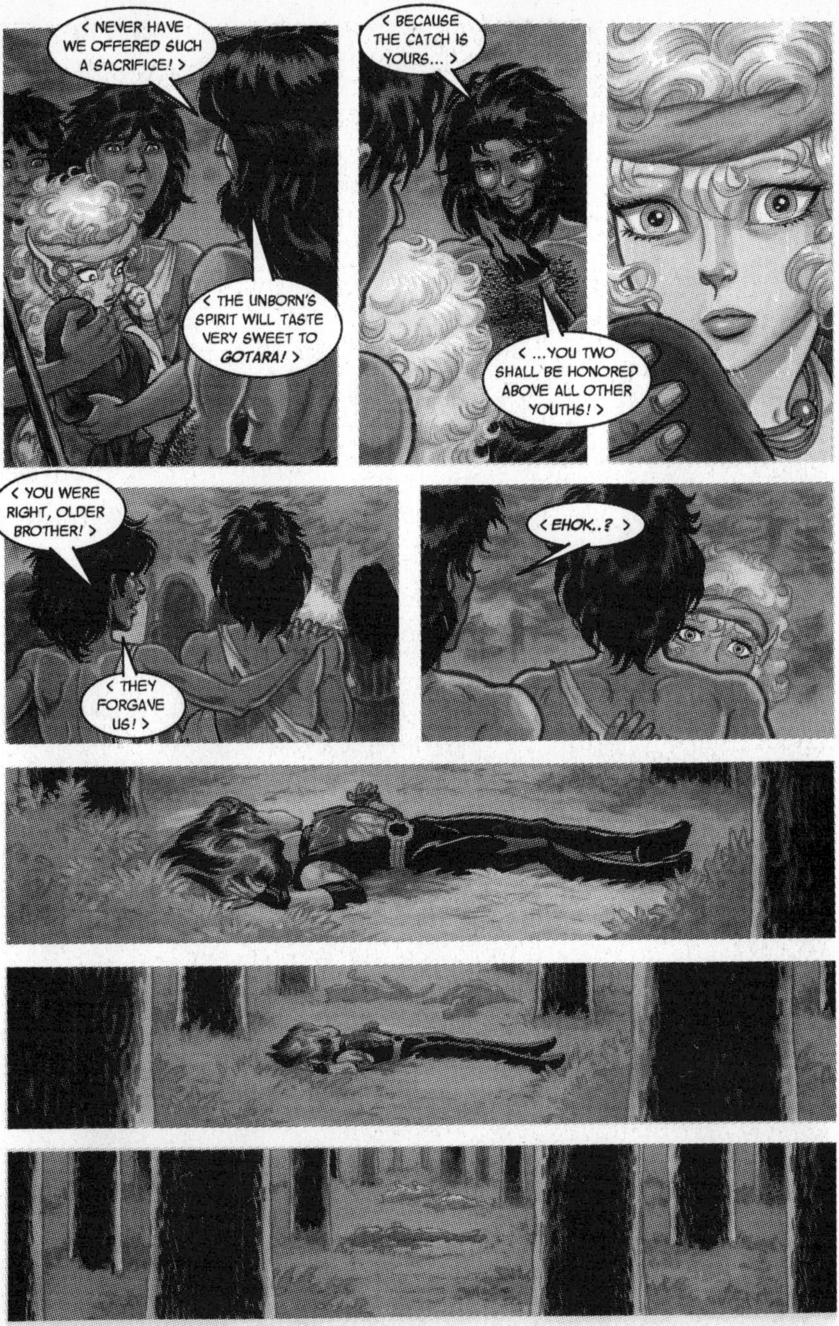
< NEVER HAVE WE OFFERED SUCH A SACRIFICE! >
< THE UNBORN'S SPIRIT WILL TASTE VERY SWEET TO GOTARA! >
< BECAUSE THE CATCH IS YOURS... >
< ...YOU TWO SHALL BE HONORED ABOVE ALL OTHER YOUTHS! >
< YOU WERE RIGHT, OLDER BROTHER! >
< THEY FORGAVE US! >
< EHOK..? >

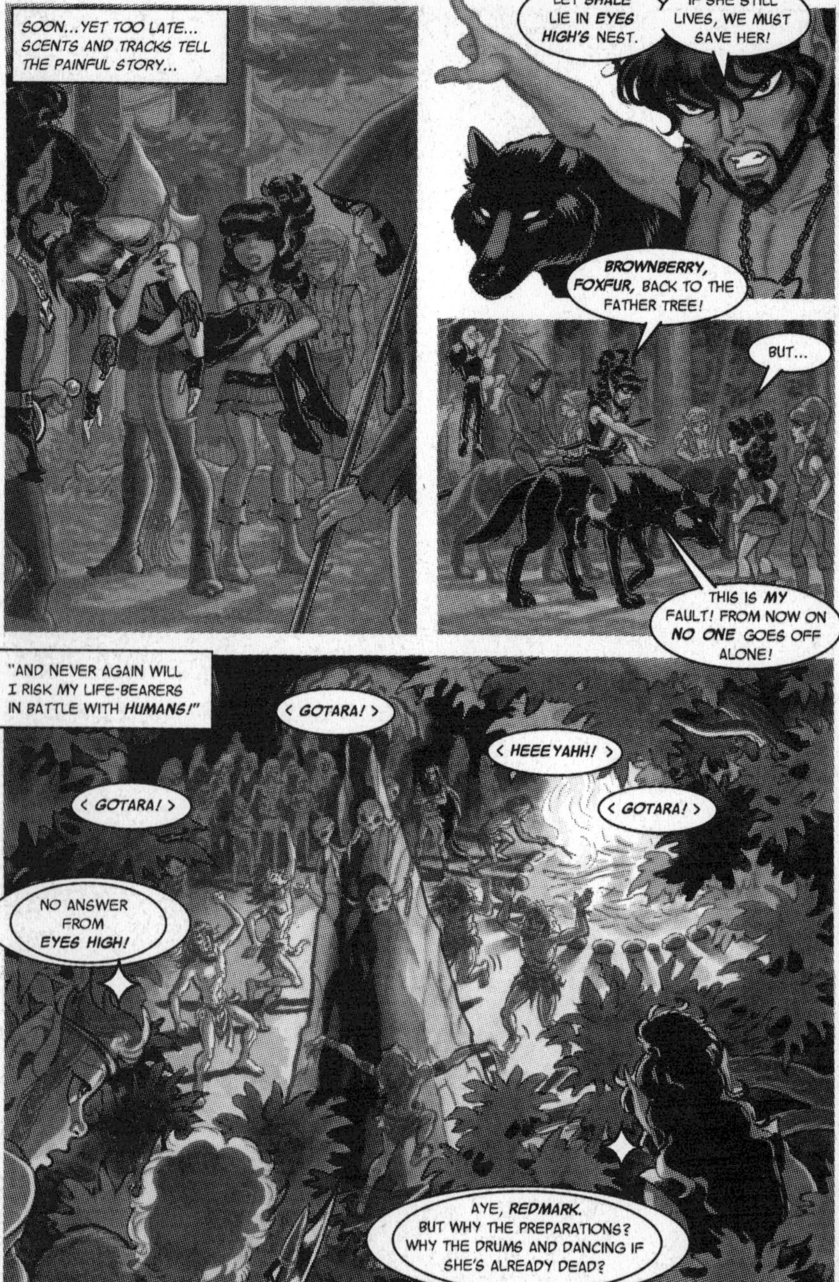
SOON...YET TOO LATE... SCENTS AND TRACKS TELL THE PAINFUL STORY...
LET SHALE LIE IN EYES HIGH'S NEST.
IF SHE STILL LIVES, WE MUST SAVE HER!
BROWNBERRY, FOXFUR, BACK TO THE FATHER TREE!
BUT...
THIS IS MY FAULT! FROM NOW ON NO ONE GOES OFF ALONE!
"AND NEVER AGAIN WILL I RISK MY LIFE-BEARERS IN BATTLE WITH HUMANS!"
< GOTARA! >
< HEEEYAHH! >
< GOTARA! >
< GOTARA! >
NO ANSWER FROM EYES HIGH!
AYE, REDMARK. BUT WHY THE PREPARATIONS? WHY THE DRUMS AND DANCING IF SHE'S ALREADY DEAD?

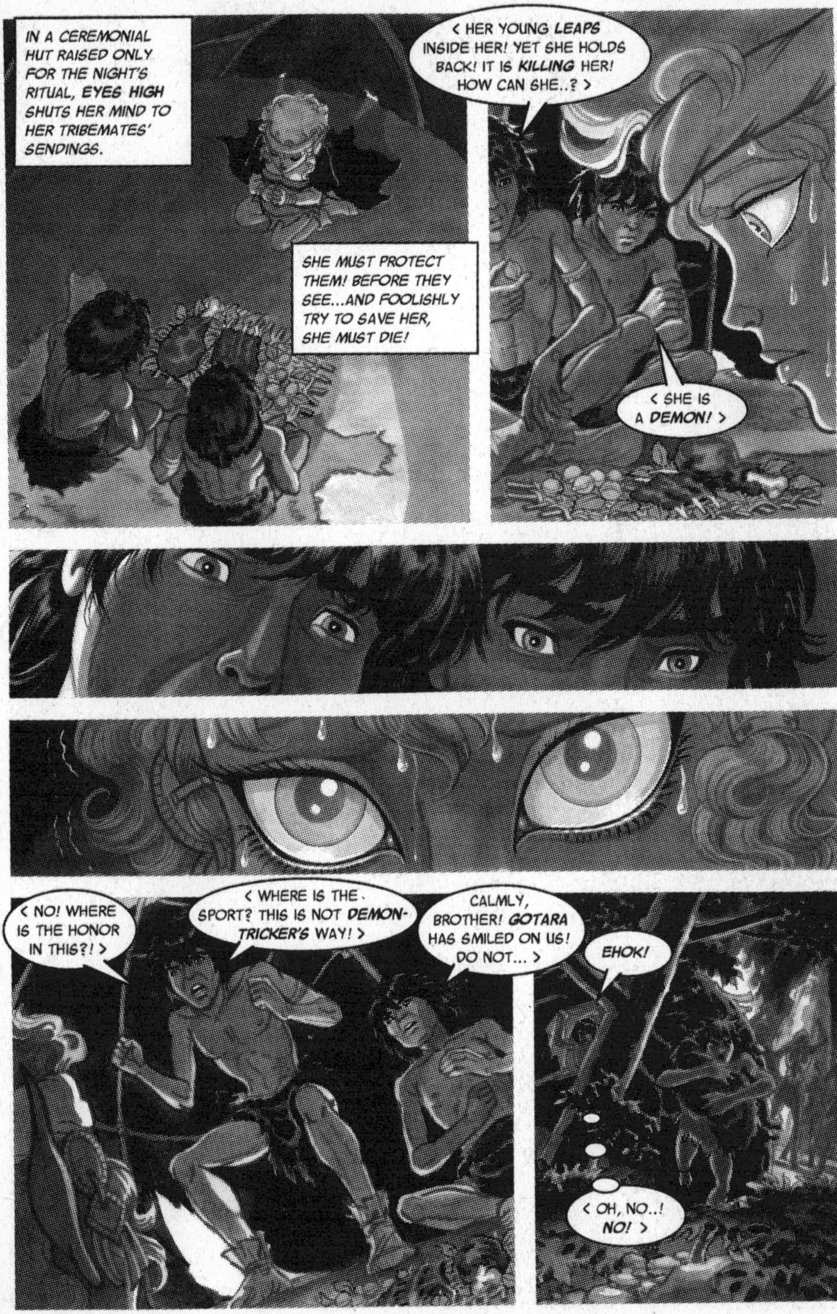
IN A CEREMONIAL HUT RAISED ONLY FOR THE NIGHT'S RITUAL, EYES HIGH SHUTS HER MIND TO HER TRIBEMATES' SENDINGS.
SHE MUST PROTECT THEM! BEFORE THEY SEE...AND FOOLISHLY TRY TO SAVE HER, SHE MUST DIE!
< HER YOUNG LEAPS INSIDE HER! YET SHE HOLDS BACK! IT IS KILLING HER! HOW CAN SHE..? >
< SHE IS A DEMON! >
< NO! WHERE IS THE HONOR IN THIS?! >
< WHERE IS THE SPORT? THIS IS NOT DEMON-TRICKER'S WAY! >
CALMLY, BROTHER! GOTARA HAS SMILED ON US! DO NOT... >
EHOK!
< OH, NO..! NO! >

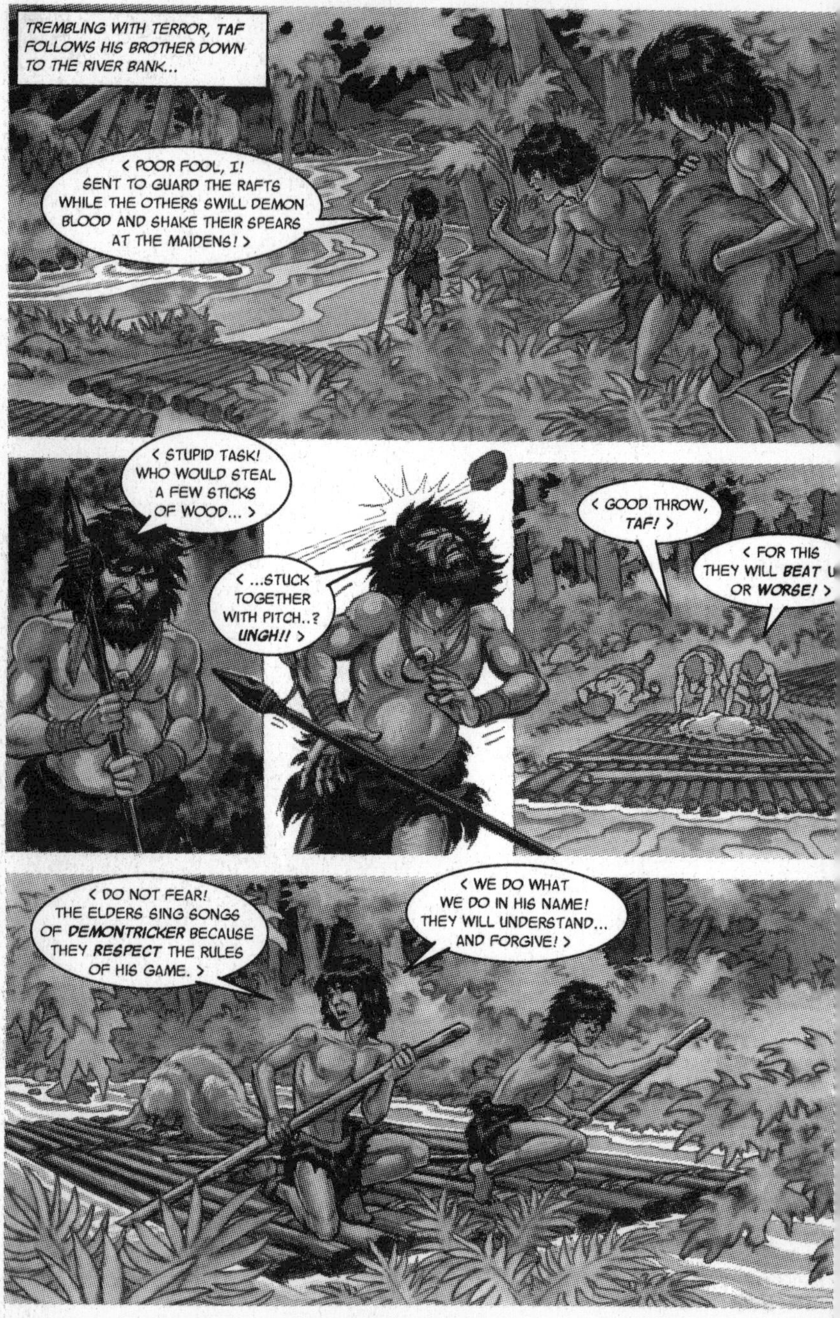
TREMBLING WITH TERROR, TAF FOLLOWS HIS BROTHER DOWN TO THE RIVER BANK...
< POOR FOOL, I! SENT TO GUARD THE RAFTS WHILE THE OTHERS SWILL DEMON BLOOD AND SHAKE THEIR SPEARS AT THE MAIDENS! >
< STUPID TASK! WHO WOULD STEAL A FEW STICKS OF WOOD... >
< ...STUCK TOGETHER WITH PITCH..? UNGH!! >
< GOOD THROW, TAF! >
< FOR THIS THEY WILL BEAT U OR WORSE! >
< DO NOT FEAR! THE ELDERS SING SONGS OF DEMONTRICKER BECAUSE THEY RESPECT THE RULES OF HIS GAME. >
< WE DO WHAT WE DO IN HIS NAME! THEY WILL UNDERSTAND... AND FORGIVE! >

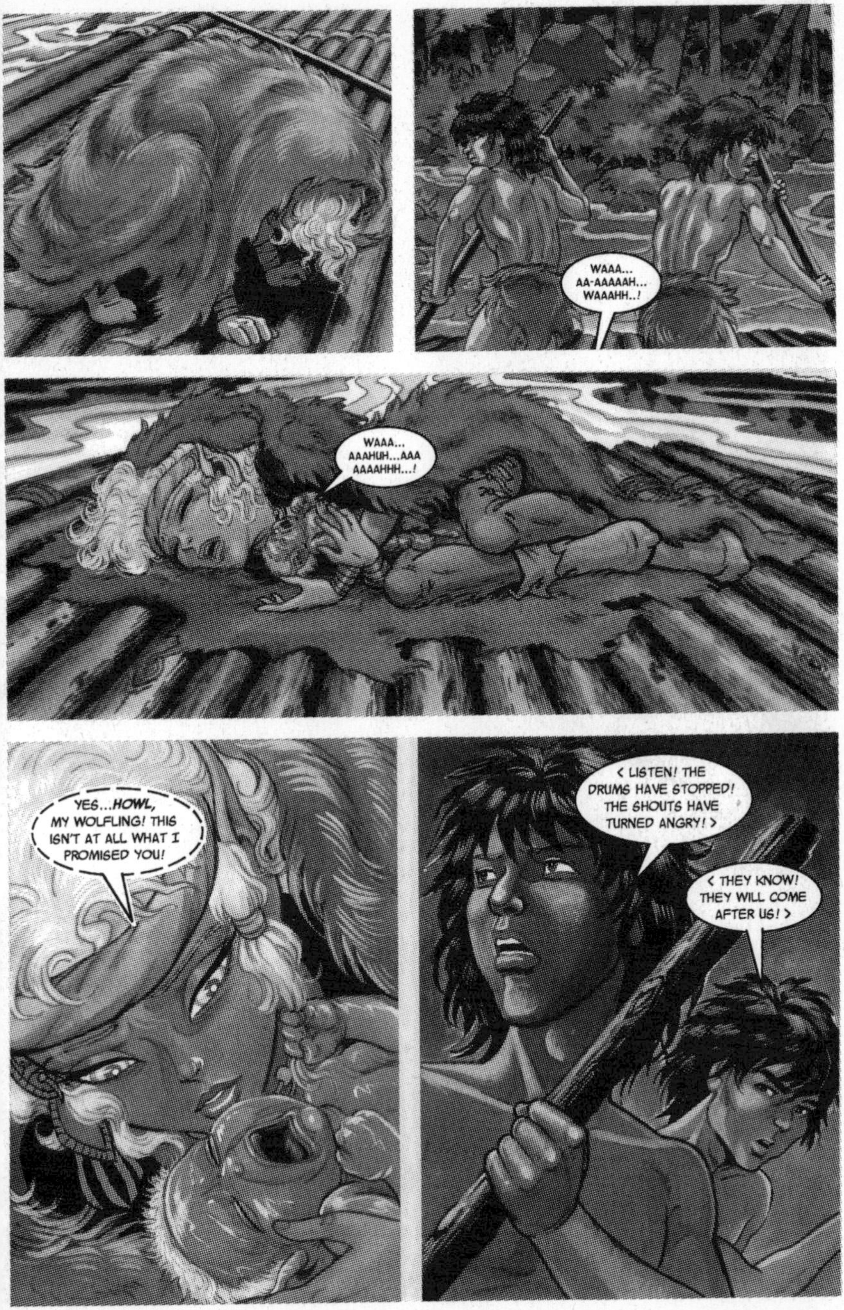
WAAA... AA-AAAAAH... WAAAHH..!
WAAA... AAAHUH...AAA AAAAHHH...!
YES...HOWL, MY WOLFLING! THIS ISN'T AT ALL WHAT I PROMISED YOU!
< LISTEN! THE DRUMS HAVE STOPPED! THE SHOUTS HAVE TURNED ANGRY! >
< THEY KNOW! THEY WILL COME AFTER US! >

AND...

SOMETHING'S MADE THEM FURIOUS!

FOLLOW THEM! IT *HAS* TO DO WITH EYES HIGH!

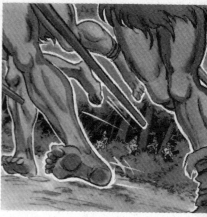

THE RIVER FORKS AND THE BROTHERS CAREFULLY POLE TO THE LEFT.

THE WAY IS WILDER, NARROWER, ROCKIER THAN BEFORE...AN UPSTREAM STRUGGLE.

BUT IT WILL TAKE THEM INTO THE FORBIDDEN TERRITORY OF THE WOLFRIDERS WHERE THEY CAN LEAVE THE MOTHER AND HER NEWBORN IN PEACE.

EYES HIGH KNOWS THIS PLACE...KNOWS THE YOUTHS SEEK TO AID HER...KNOWS PURSUERS COME...

HER STRENGTH EBBING, SHE BUNDLES SKYWISE IN HER OILED LEATHER CLOAK...

...AND CALLS ONE LAST TIME!

BEARCLAW! COME ALONE...AHEAD OF THE HUMANS! WATCH THE WATER! HURRY!

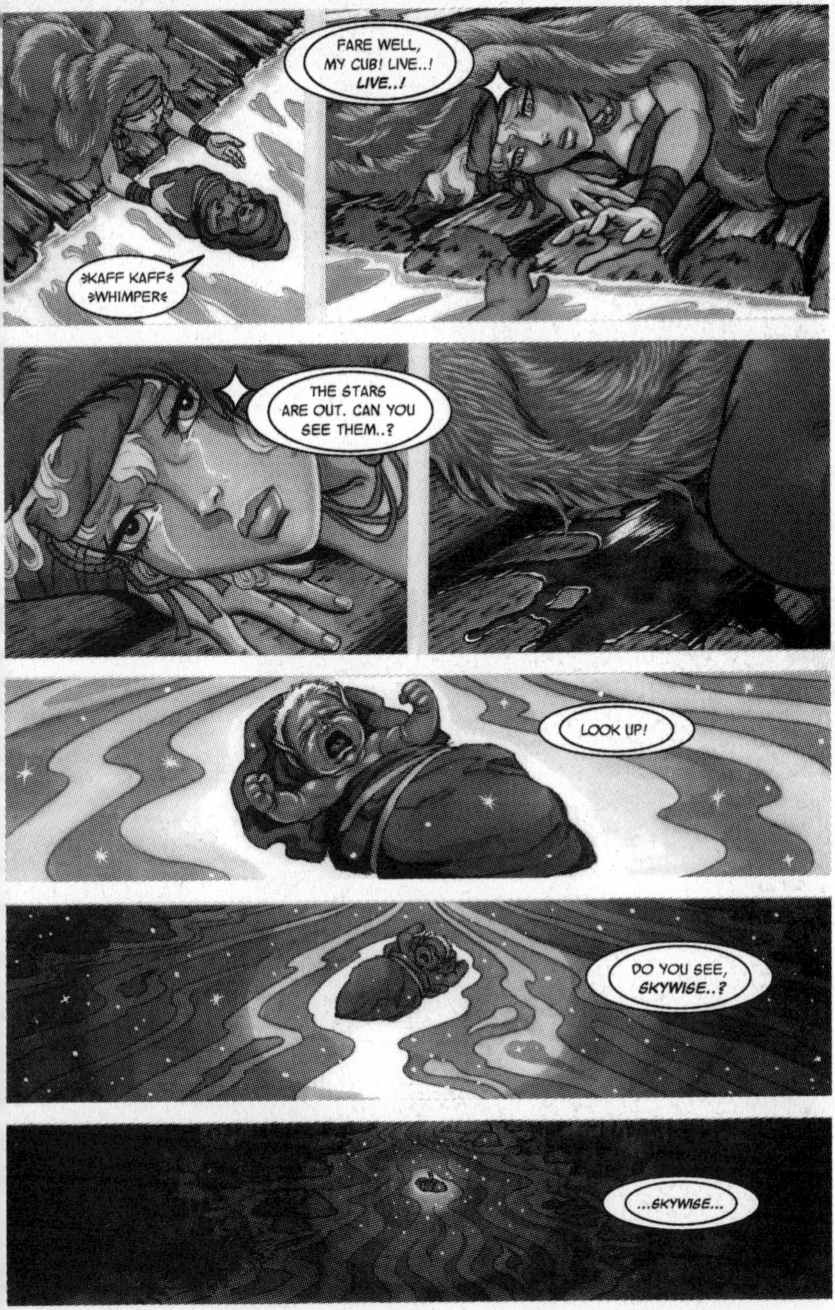
FARE WELL, MY CUB! LIVE..! LIVE..!
≈KAFF KAFF≈ ≈WHIMPER≈
THE STARS ARE OUT. CAN YOU SEE THEM..?
LOOK UP!
DO YOU SEE, SKYWISE..?
...SKYWISE...

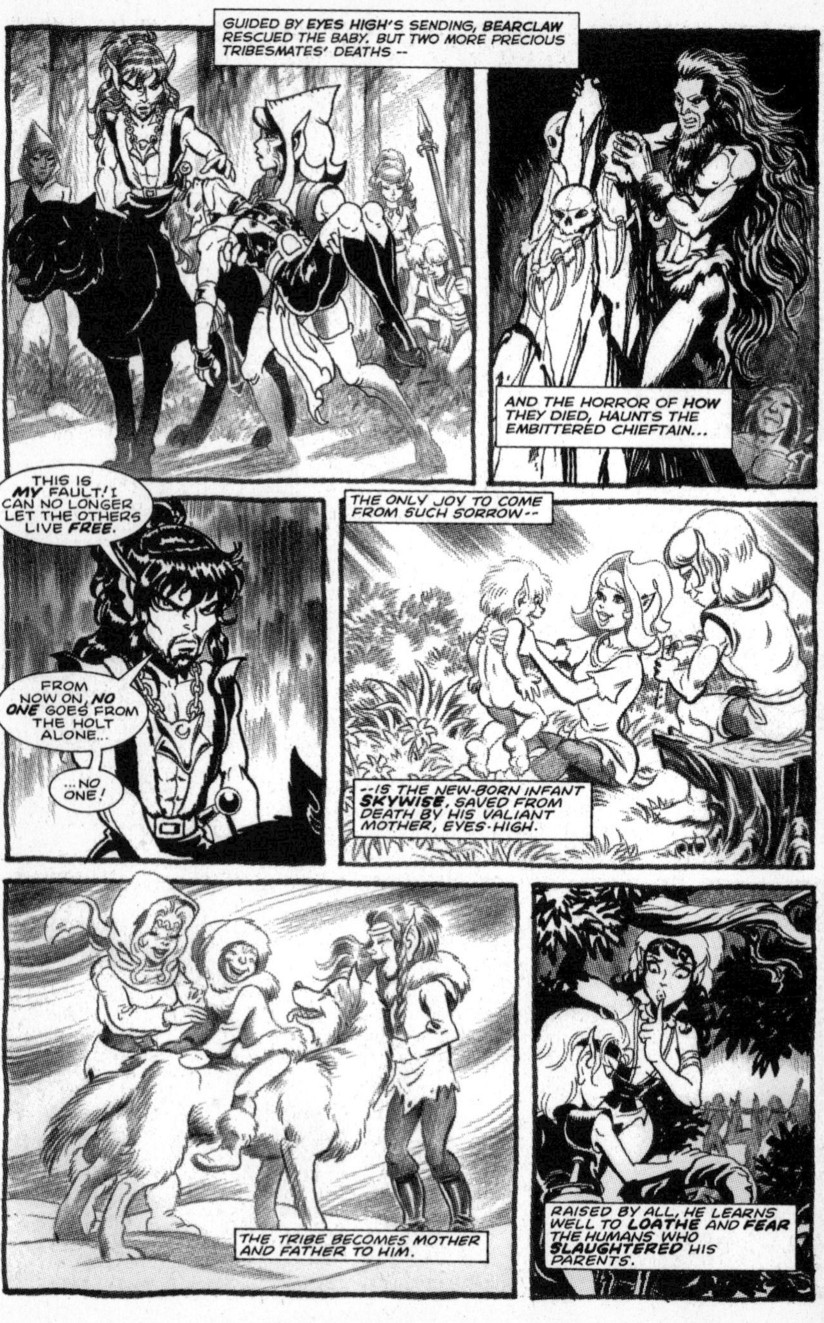
GUIDED BY EYES HIGH'S SENDING, BEARCLAW RESCUED THE BABY. BUT TWO MORE PRECIOUS TRIBESMATES' DEATHS --
AND THE HORROR OF HOW THEY DIED, HAUNTS THE EMBITTERED CHIEFTAIN...
THIS IS MY FAULT! I CAN NO LONGER LET THE OTHERS LIVE FREE.
FROM NOW ON, NO ONE GOES FROM THE HOLT ALONE...
...NO ONE!
THE ONLY JOY TO COME FROM SUCH SORROW--
--IS THE NEW-BORN INFANT SKYWISE, SAVED FROM DEATH BY HIS VALIANT MOTHER, EYES-HIGH.
THE TRIBE BECOMES MOTHER AND FATHER TO HIM.
RAISED BY ALL, HE LEARNS WELL TO LOATHE AND FEAR THE HUMANS WHO SLAUGHTERED HIS PARENTS.

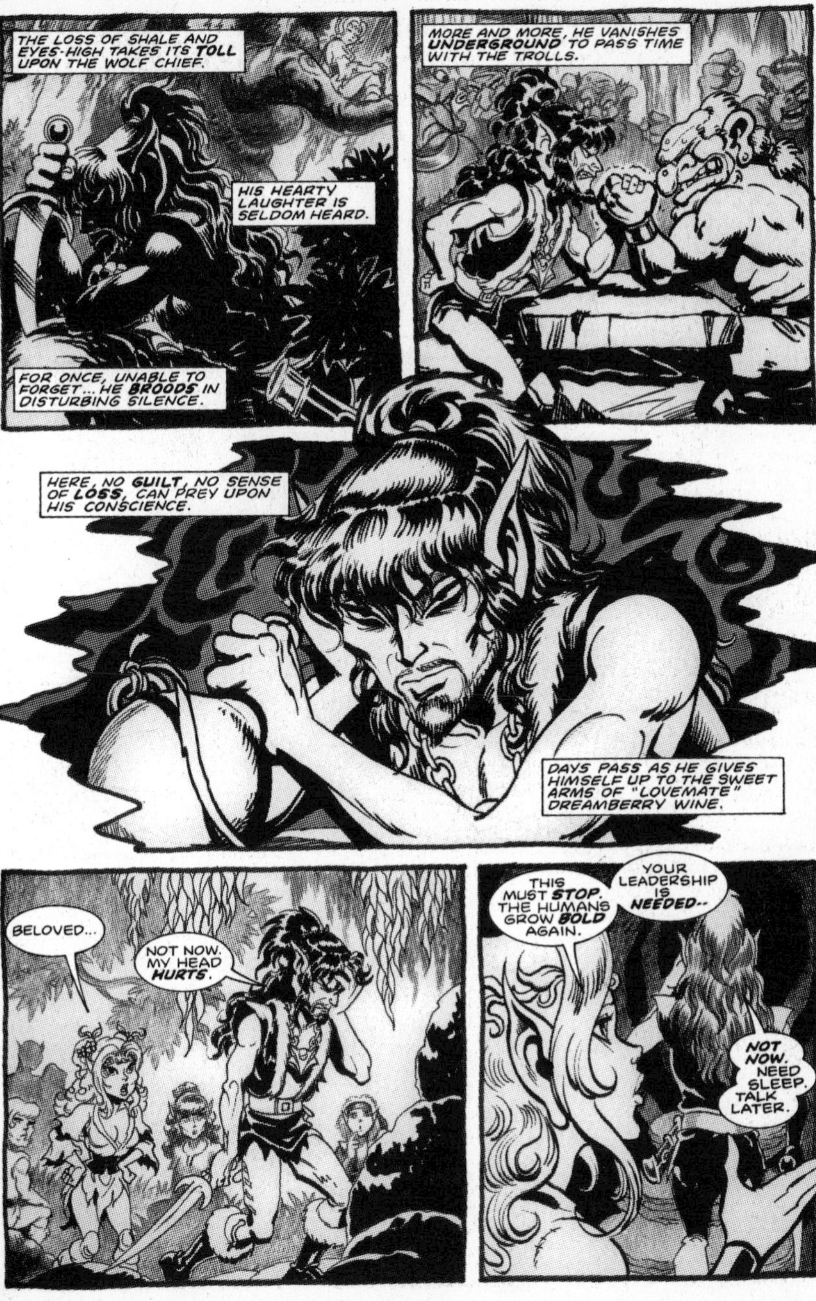

THE LOSS OF SHALE AND EYES-HIGH TAKES ITS TOLL UPON THE WOLF CHIEF.
HIS HEARTY LAUGHTER IS SELDOM HEARD.
FOR ONCE, UNABLE TO FORGET... HE BROODS IN DISTURBING SILENCE.
MORE AND MORE, HE VANISHES UNDERGROUND TO PASS TIME WITH THE TROLLS.
HERE, NO GUILT, NO SENSE OF LOSS, CAN PREY UPON HIS CONSCIENCE.
DAYS PASS AS HE GIVES HIMSELF UP TO THE SWEET ARMS OF "LOVEMATE" DREAMBERRY WINE.
BELOVED...
NOT NOW. MY HEAD HURTS.
THIS MUST STOP. THE HUMANS GROW BOLD AGAIN.
YOUR LEADERSHIP IS NEEDED--
NOT NOW. NEED SLEEP. TALK LATER.

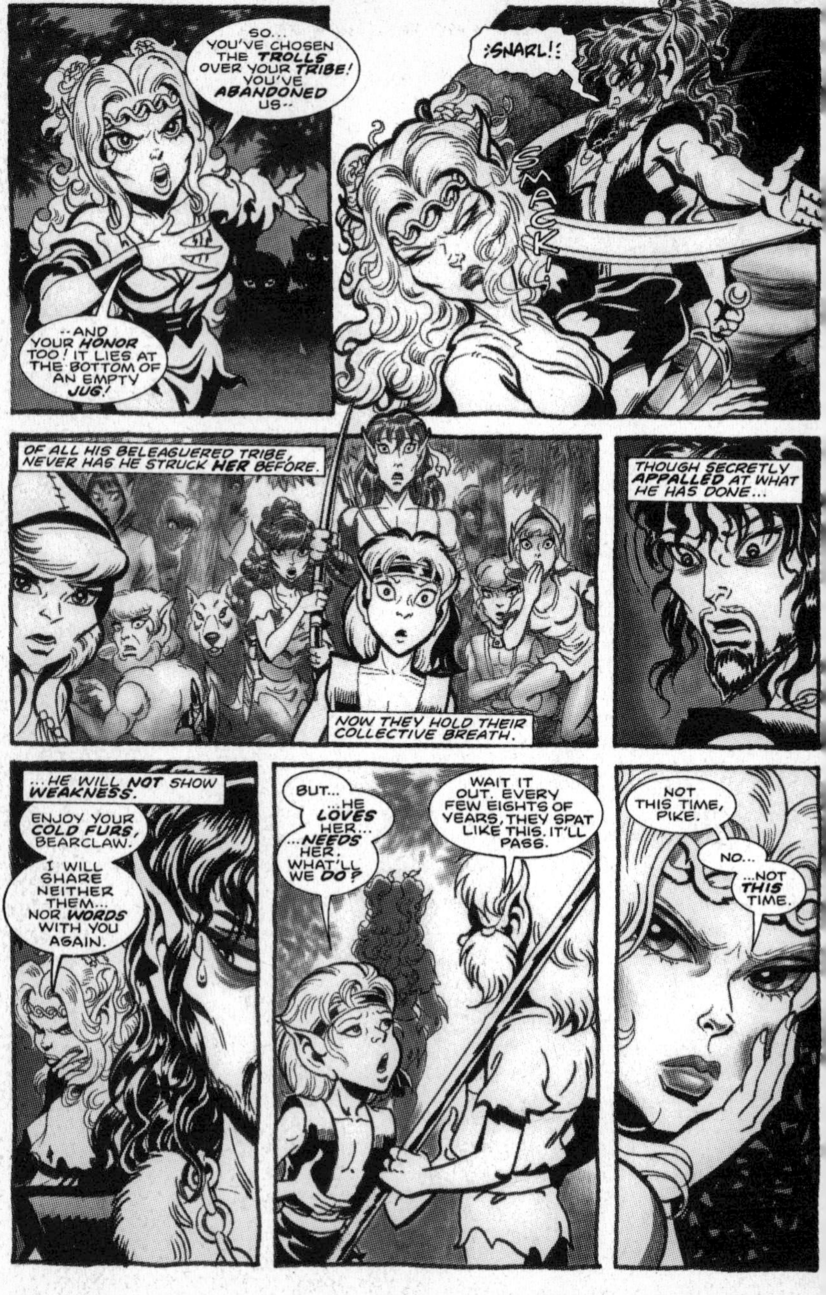
SO... YOU'VE CHOSEN THE TROLLS OVER YOUR TRIBE! YOU'VE ABANDONED US--
--AND YOUR HONOR TOO! IT LIES AT THE BOTTOM OF AN EMPTY JUG!
:SNARL!:
SMACK!
OF ALL HIS BELEAGUERED TRIBE, NEVER HAS HE STRUCK HER BEFORE.
NOW THEY HOLD THEIR COLLECTIVE BREATH.
THOUGH SECRETLY APPALLED AT WHAT HE HAS DONE...
...HE WILL NOT SHOW WEAKNESS.
ENJOY YOUR COLD FURS, BEARCLAW.
I WILL SHARE NEITHER THEM... NOR WORDS WITH YOU AGAIN.
BUT... ...HE LOVES HER... ...NEEDS HER. WHAT'LL WE DO?
WAIT IT OUT. EVERY FEW EIGHTS OF YEARS, THEY SPAT LIKE THIS. IT'LL PASS.
NOT THIS TIME, PIKE.
NO... ...NOT THIS TIME.

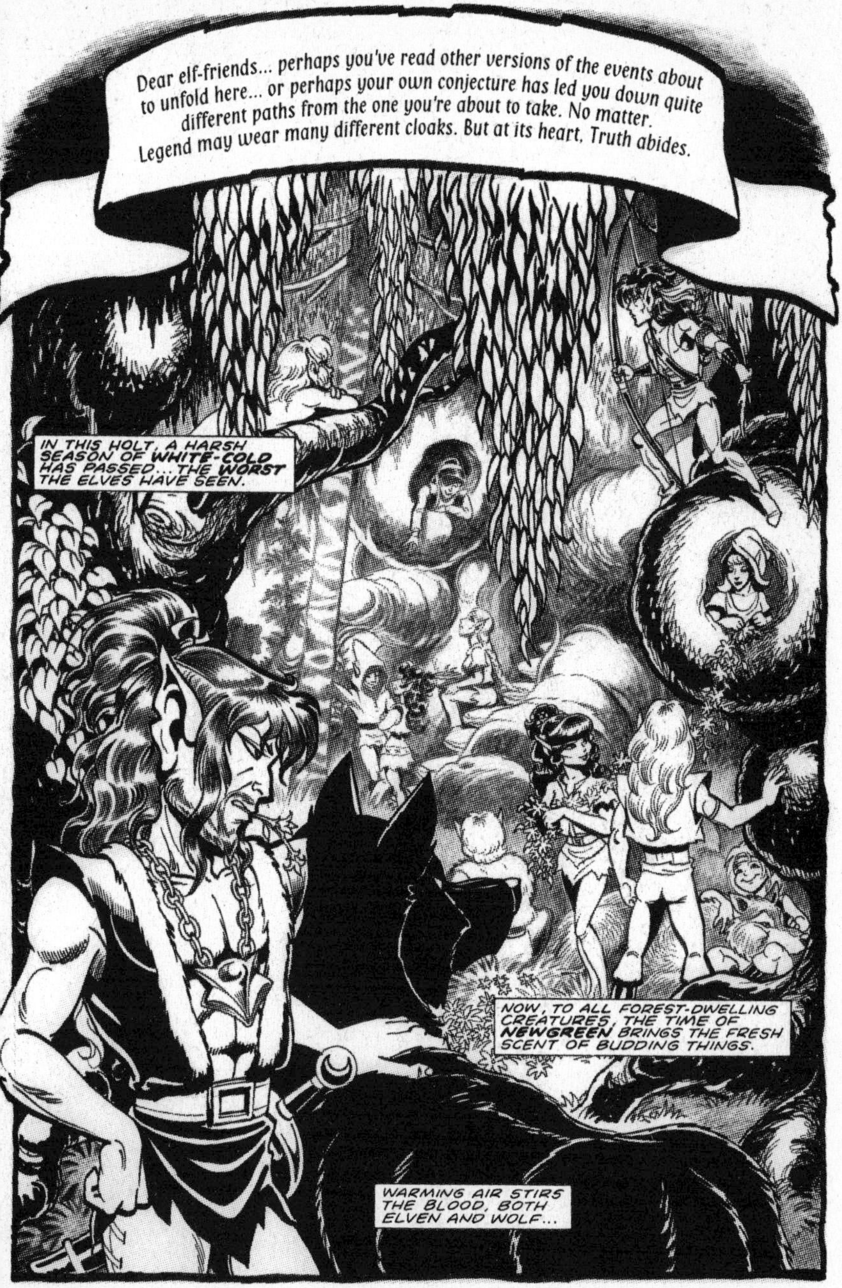
Dear elf-friends... perhaps you've read other versions of the events about to unfold here... or perhaps your own conjecture has led you down quite different paths from the one you're about to take. No matter. Legend may wear many different cloaks. But at its heart, Truth abides.
IN THIS HOLT, A HARSH SEASON OF WHITE-COLD HAS PASSED... THE WORST THE ELVES HAVE SEEN.
NOW, TO ALL FOREST-DWELLING CREATURES, THE TIME OF NEWGREEN BRINGS THE FRESH SCENT OF BUDDING THINGS.
WARMING AIR STIRS THE BLOOD, BOTH ELVEN AND WOLF...

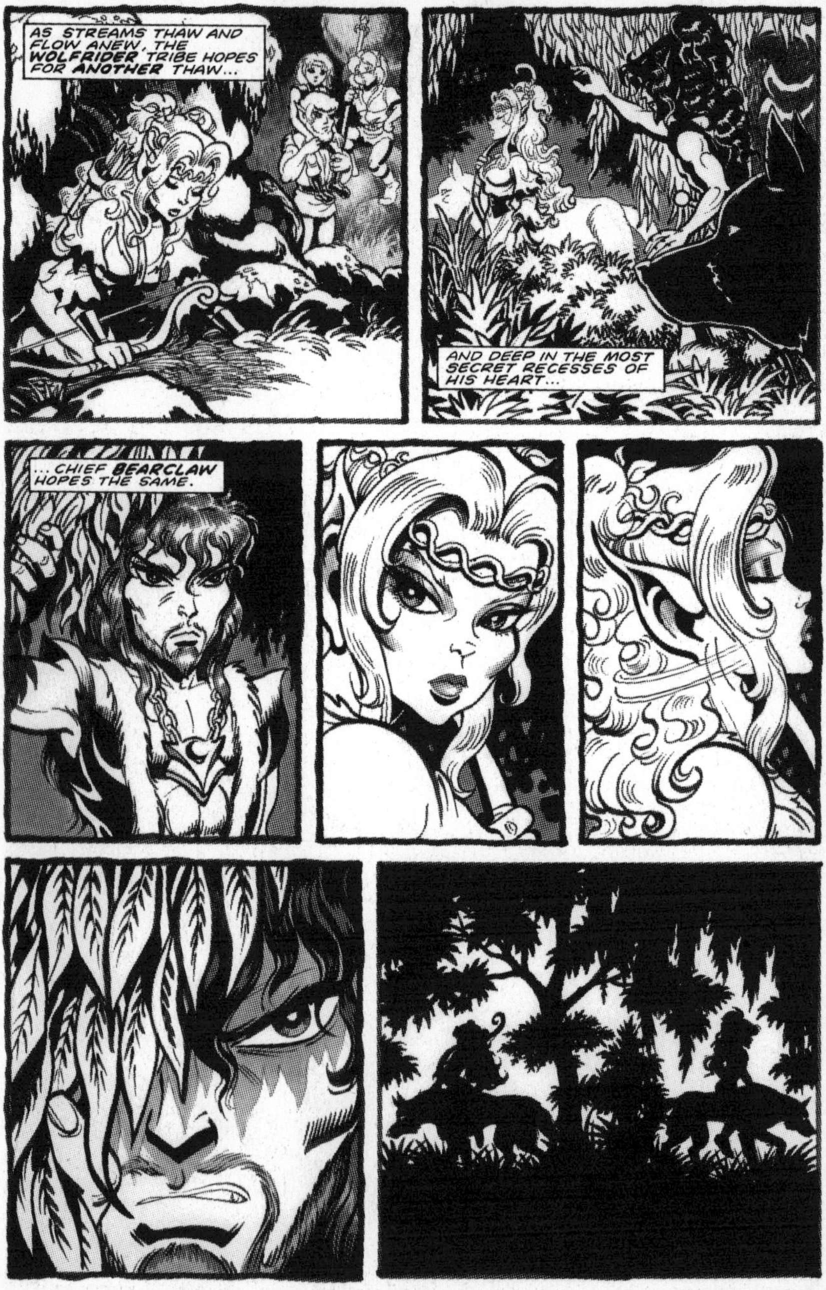
AS STREAMS THAW AND FLOW ANEW, THE WOLFRIDER TRIBE HOPES FOR ANOTHER THAW...
AND DEEP IN THE MOST SECRET RECESSES OF HIS HEART...
...CHIEF BEARCLAW HOPES THE SAME.

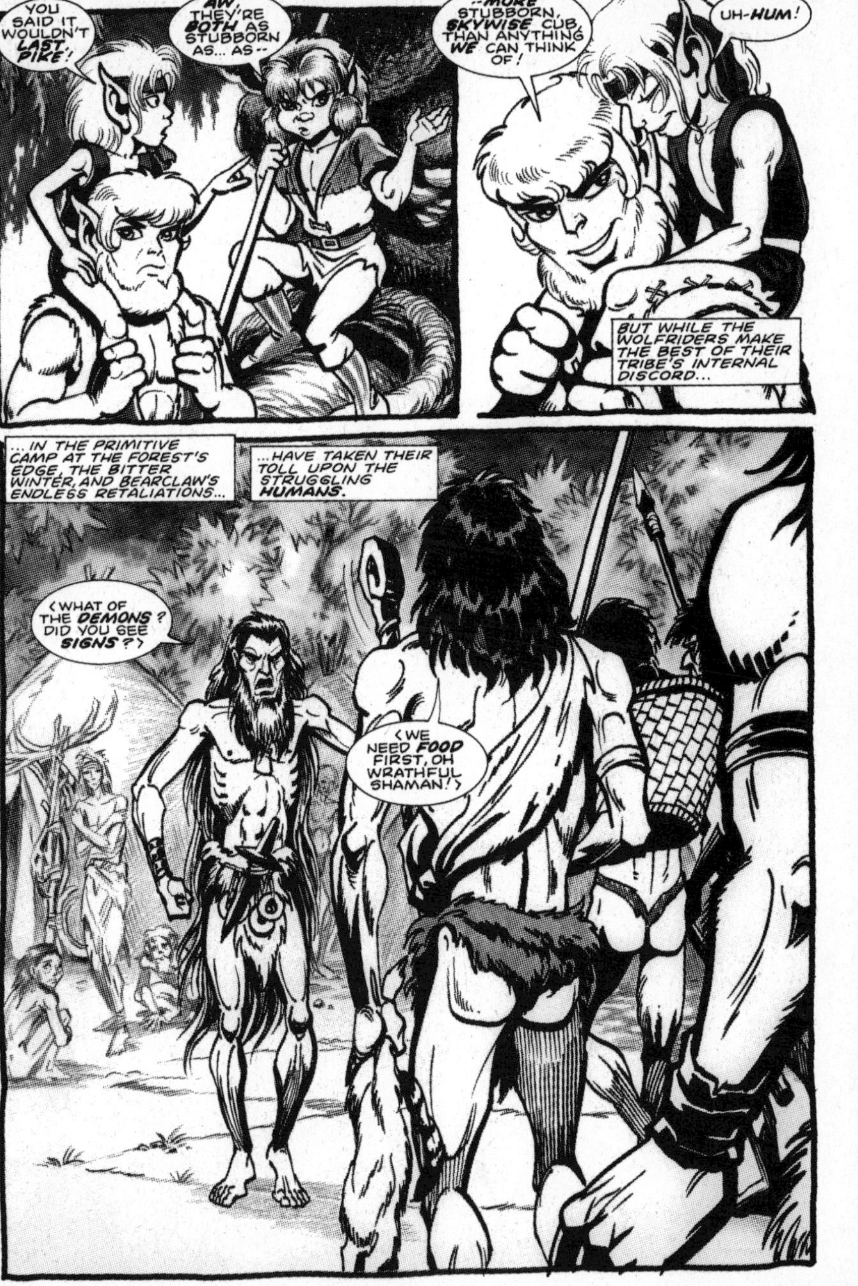

YOU SAID IT WOULDN'T LAST, PIKE!
AW, THEY'RE BOTH AS STUBBORN AS... AS--
--MORE STUBBORN, SKYWISE CUB, THAN ANYTHING WE CAN THINK OF!
UH-HUM!
BUT WHILE THE WOLFRIDERS MAKE THE BEST OF THEIR TRIBE'S INTERNAL DISCORD...
...IN THE PRIMITIVE CAMP AT THE FOREST'S EDGE, THE BITTER WINTER, AND BEARCLAW'S ENDLESS RETALIATIONS...
...HAVE TAKEN THEIR TOLL UPON THE STRUGGLING HUMANS.
<WHAT OF THE DEMONS? DID YOU SEE SIGNS?>
<WE NEED FOOD FIRST, OH WRATHFUL SHAMAN!>

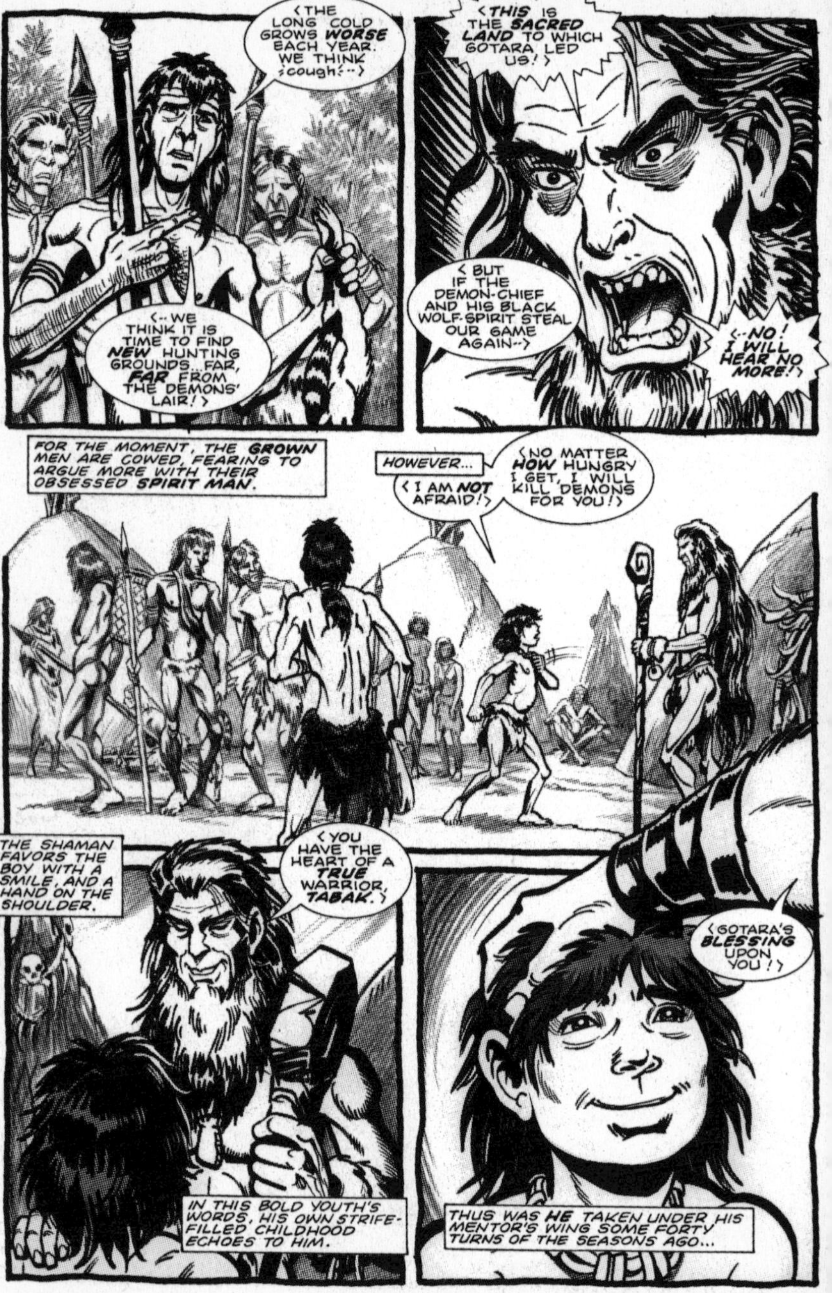

‹THE LONG COLD GROWS WORSE EACH YEAR. WE THINK ‹cough›--›
‹--WE THINK IT IS TIME TO FIND NEW HUNTING GROUNDS...FAR, FAR FROM THE DEMONS' LAIR!›
‹THIS IS THE SACRED LAND TO WHICH GOTARA LED US!›
‹BUT IF THE DEMON-CHIEF AND HIS BLACK WOLF-SPIRIT STEAL OUR GAME AGAIN--›
‹--NO! I WILL HEAR NO MORE!›
FOR THE MOMENT, THE GROWN MEN ARE COWED, FEARING TO ARGUE MORE WITH THEIR OBSESSED SPIRIT MAN.
HOWEVER...
‹I AM NOT AFRAID!›
‹NO MATTER HOW HUNGRY I GET, I WILL KILL DEMONS FOR YOU!›
THE SHAMAN FAVORS THE BOY WITH A SMILE, AND A HAND ON THE SHOULDER.
‹YOU HAVE THE HEART OF A TRUE WARRIOR, TABAK.›
IN THIS BOLD YOUTH'S WORDS, HIS OWN STRIFE-FILLED CHILDHOOD ECHOES TO HIM.
‹GOTARA'S BLESSING UPON YOU!›
THUS WAS HE TAKEN UNDER HIS MENTOR'S WING SOME FORTY TURNS OF THE SEASONS AGO...

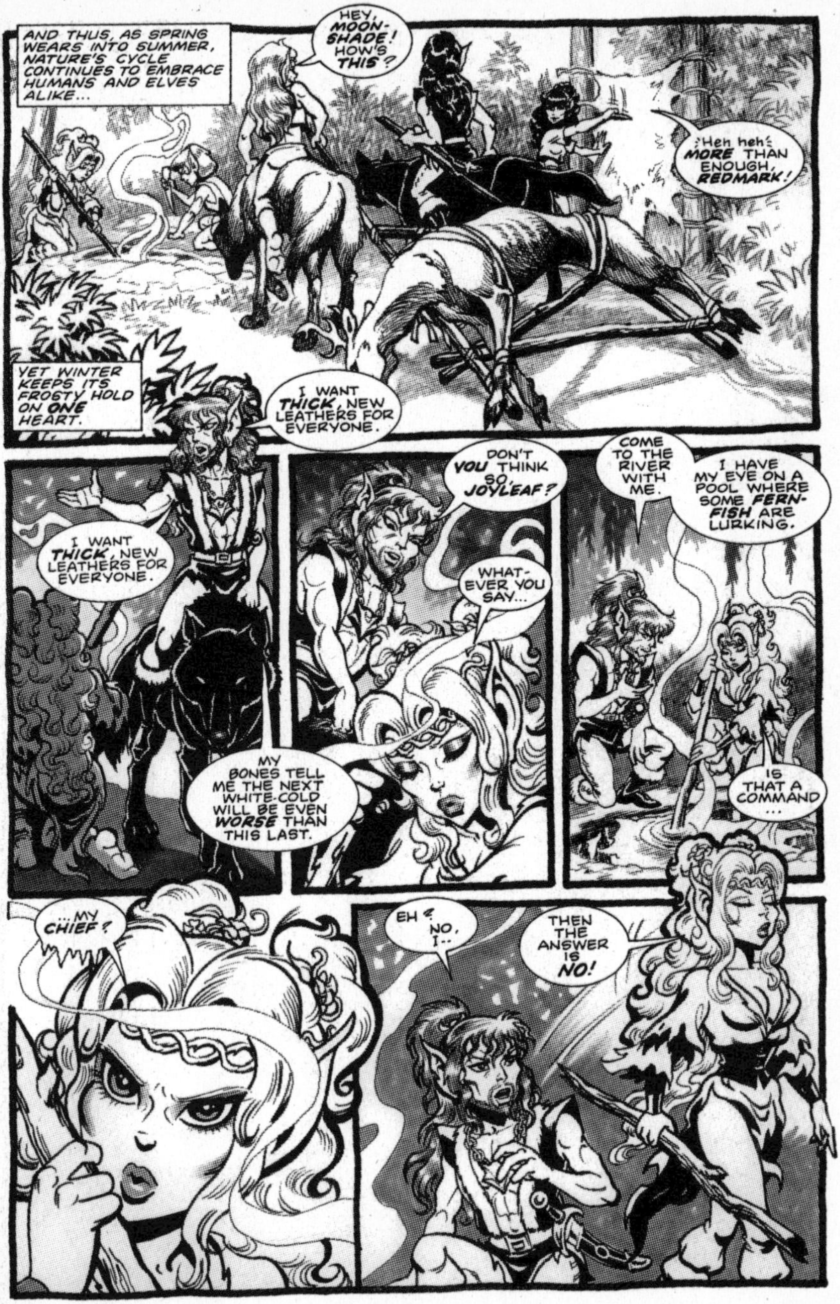
AND THUS, AS SPRING WEARS INTO SUMMER, NATURE'S CYCLE CONTINUES TO EMBRACE HUMANS AND ELVES ALIKE...
HEY, MOON-SHADE! HOW'S THIS?
Heh heh MORE THAN ENOUGH, REDMARK!
YET WINTER KEEPS ITS FROSTY HOLD ON ONE HEART.
I WANT THICK, NEW LEATHERS FOR EVERYONE.
I WANT THICK, NEW LEATHERS FOR EVERYONE.
MY BONES TELL ME THE NEXT WHITE-COLD WILL BE EVEN WORSE THAN THIS LAST.
DON'T YOU THINK SO, JOYLEAF?
WHAT-EVER YOU SAY...
COME TO THE RIVER WITH ME.
I HAVE MY EYE ON A POOL WHERE SOME FERN-FISH ARE LURKING.
IS THAT A COMMAND ...
... MY CHIEF?
EH? NO, I--
THEN THE ANSWER IS NO!

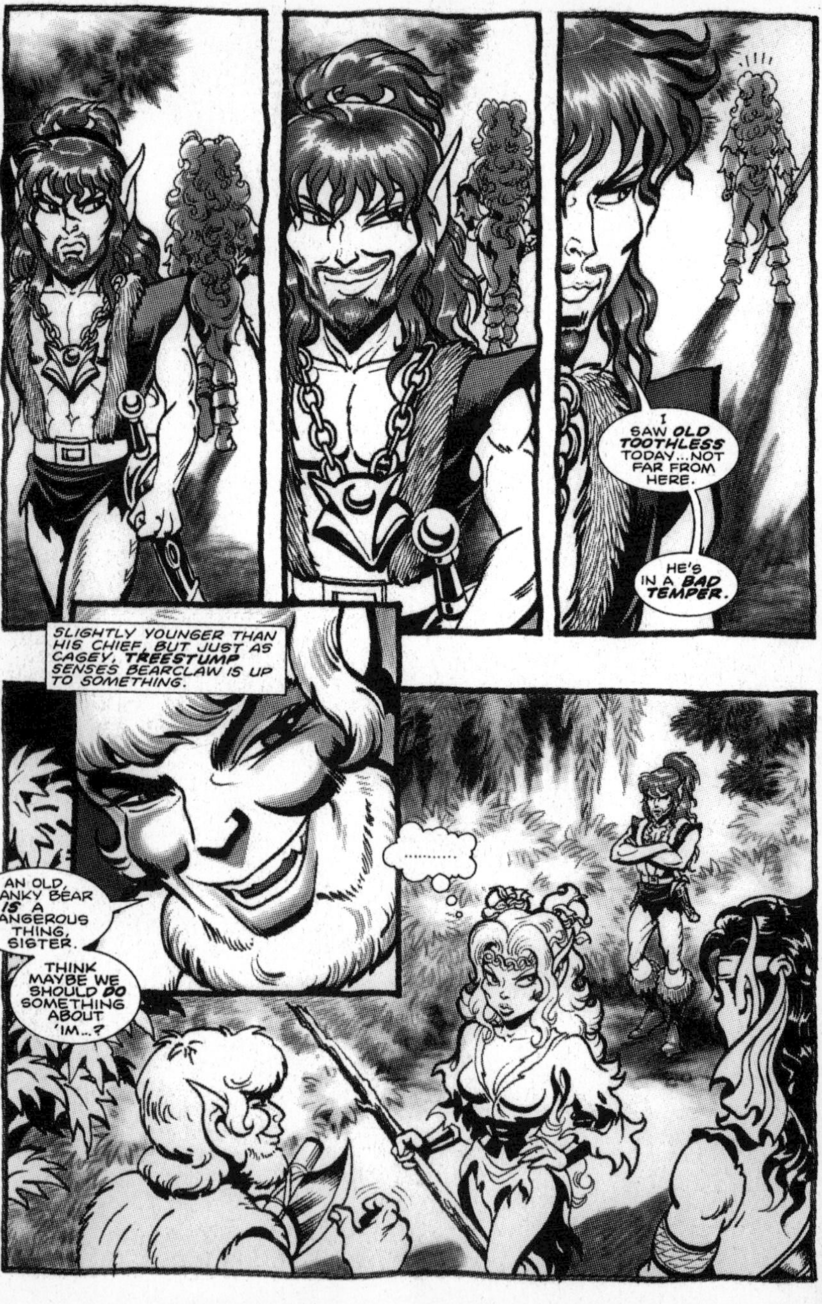

I SAW OLD TOOTHLESS TODAY...NOT FAR FROM HERE.
HE'S IN A BAD TEMPER.
SLIGHTLY YOUNGER THAN HIS CHIEF, BUT JUST AS CAGEY, TREESTUMP SENSES BEARCLAW IS UP TO SOMETHING.
....
AN OLD, CRANKY BEAR IS A DANGEROUS THING, SISTER.
THINK MAYBE WE SHOULD DO SOMETHING ABOUT 'IM...?

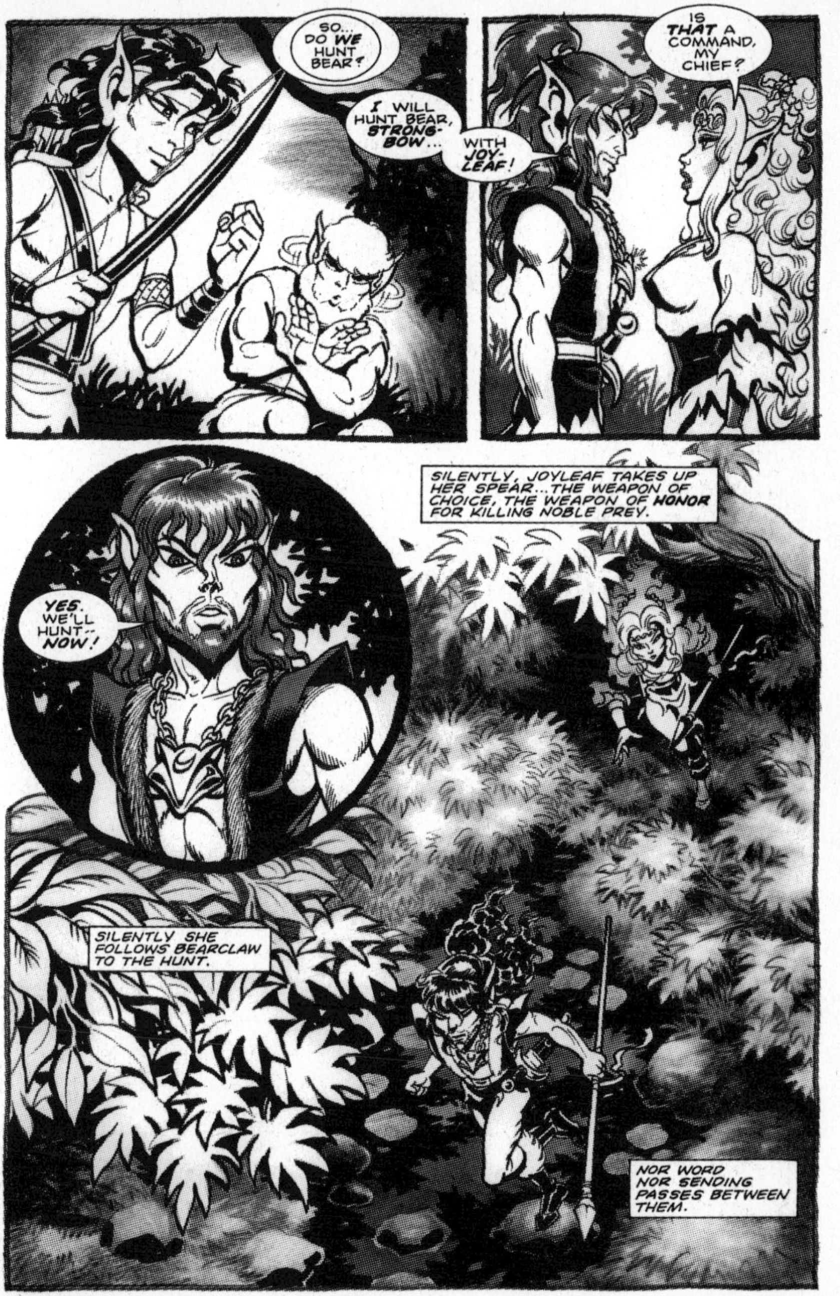
SO... DO WE HUNT BEAR?
I WILL HUNT BEAR, STRONGBOW...
WITH JOYLEAF!
IS THAT A COMMAND, MY CHIEF?
YES. WE'LL HUNT-- NOW!
SILENTLY, JOYLEAF TAKES UP HER SPEAR...THE WEAPON OF CHOICE, THE WEAPON OF HONOR FOR KILLING NOBLE PREY.
SILENTLY SHE FOLLOWS BEARCLAW TO THE HUNT.
NOR WORD NOR SENDING PASSES BETWEEN THEM.

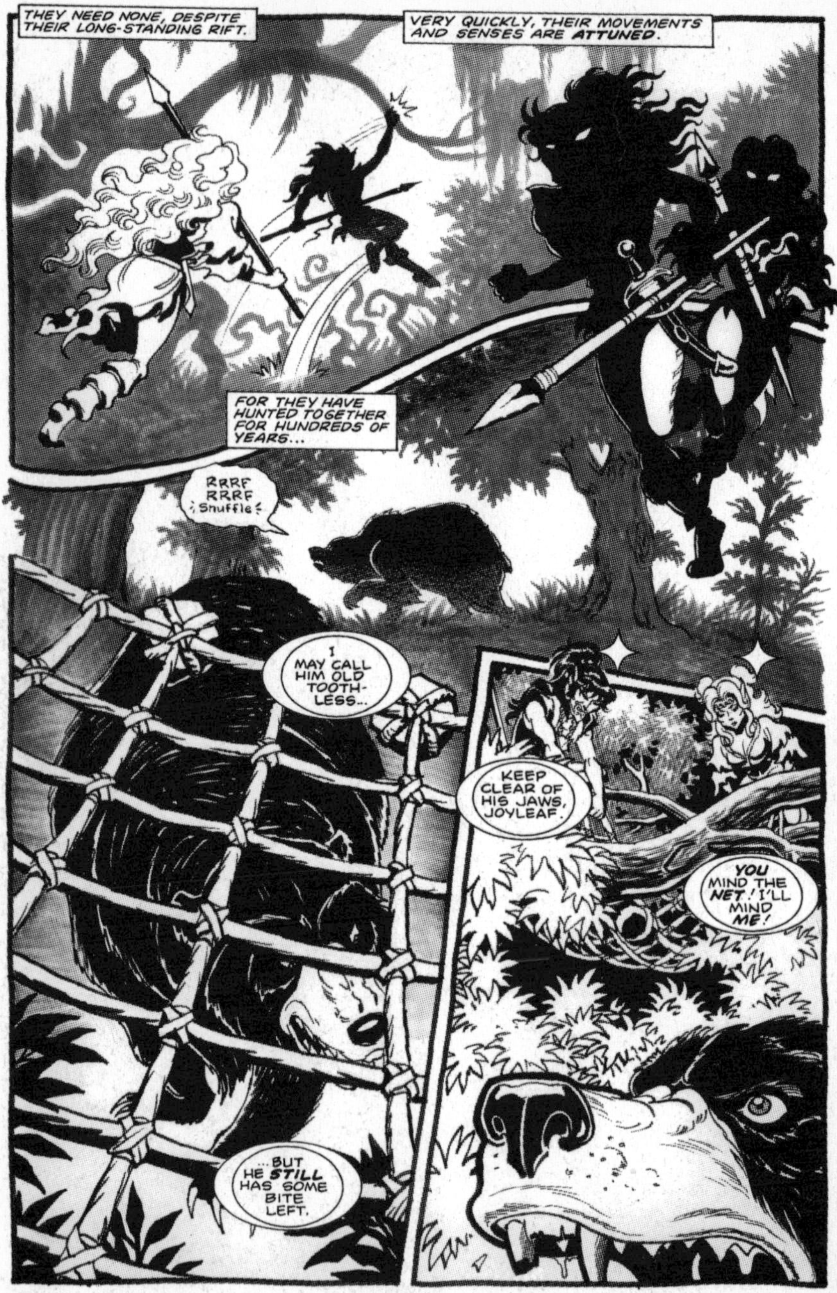
THEY NEED NONE, DESPITE THEIR LONG-STANDING RIFT.
VERY QUICKLY, THEIR MOVEMENTS AND SENSES ARE ATTUNED.
FOR THEY HAVE HUNTED TOGETHER FOR HUNDREDS OF YEARS...
RRRF RRRF Snuffle
I MAY CALL HIM OLD TOOTH-LESS...
...BUT HE STILL HAS SOME BITE LEFT.
KEEP CLEAR OF HIS JAWS, JOYLEAF.
YOU MIND THE NET! I'LL MIND ME!

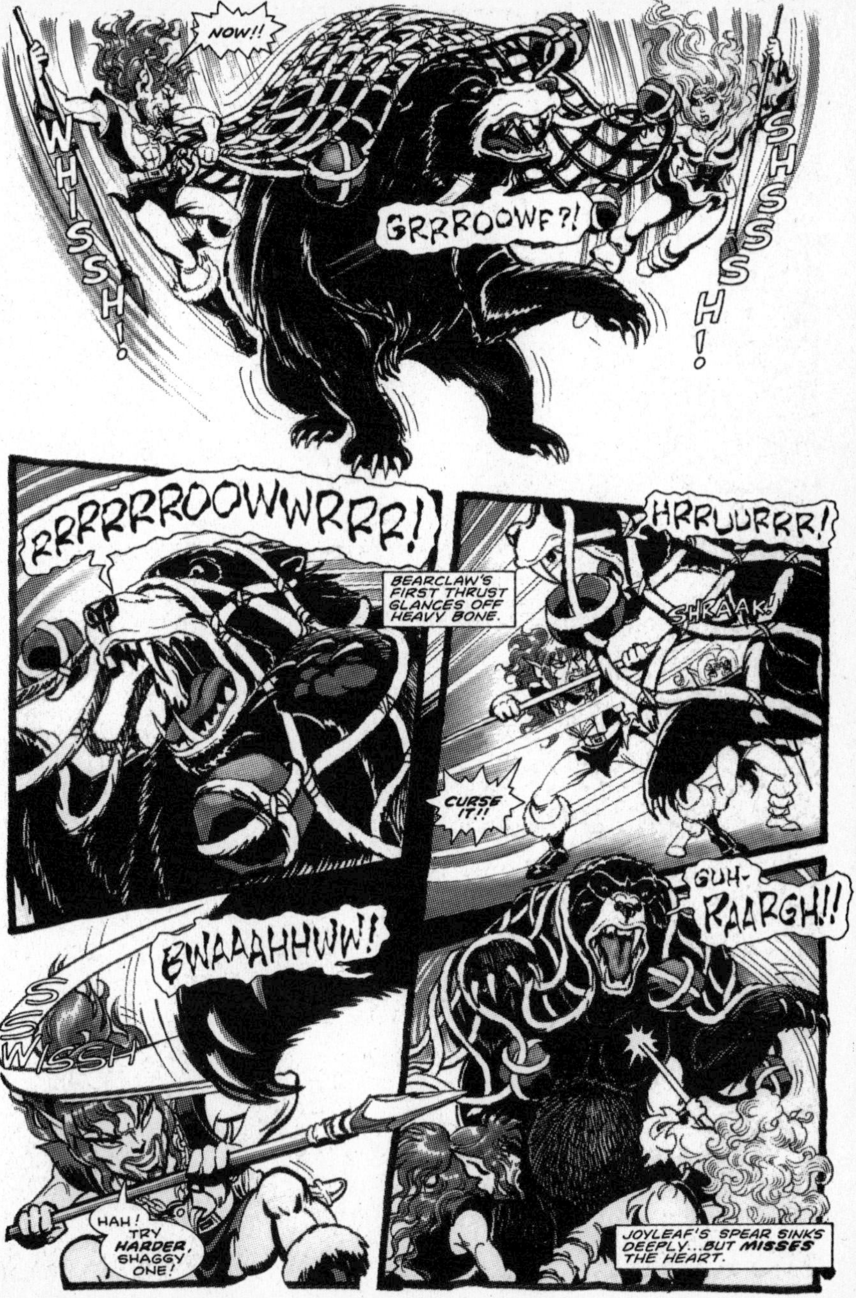
NOW!!
WHISSSH!
GRRROOWF?!
SHSSSSH!
RRRRRROOWWRRRR!
BEARCLAW'S FIRST THRUST GLANCES OFF HEAVY BONE.
HRRUURRR!
SHRAAK!
CURSE IT!!
BWAAAHHWW!
SSWISSH
HAH! TRY HARDER, SHAGGY ONE!
GUH-RAARGH!!
JOYLEAF'S SPEAR SINKS DEEPLY... BUT MISSES THE HEART.

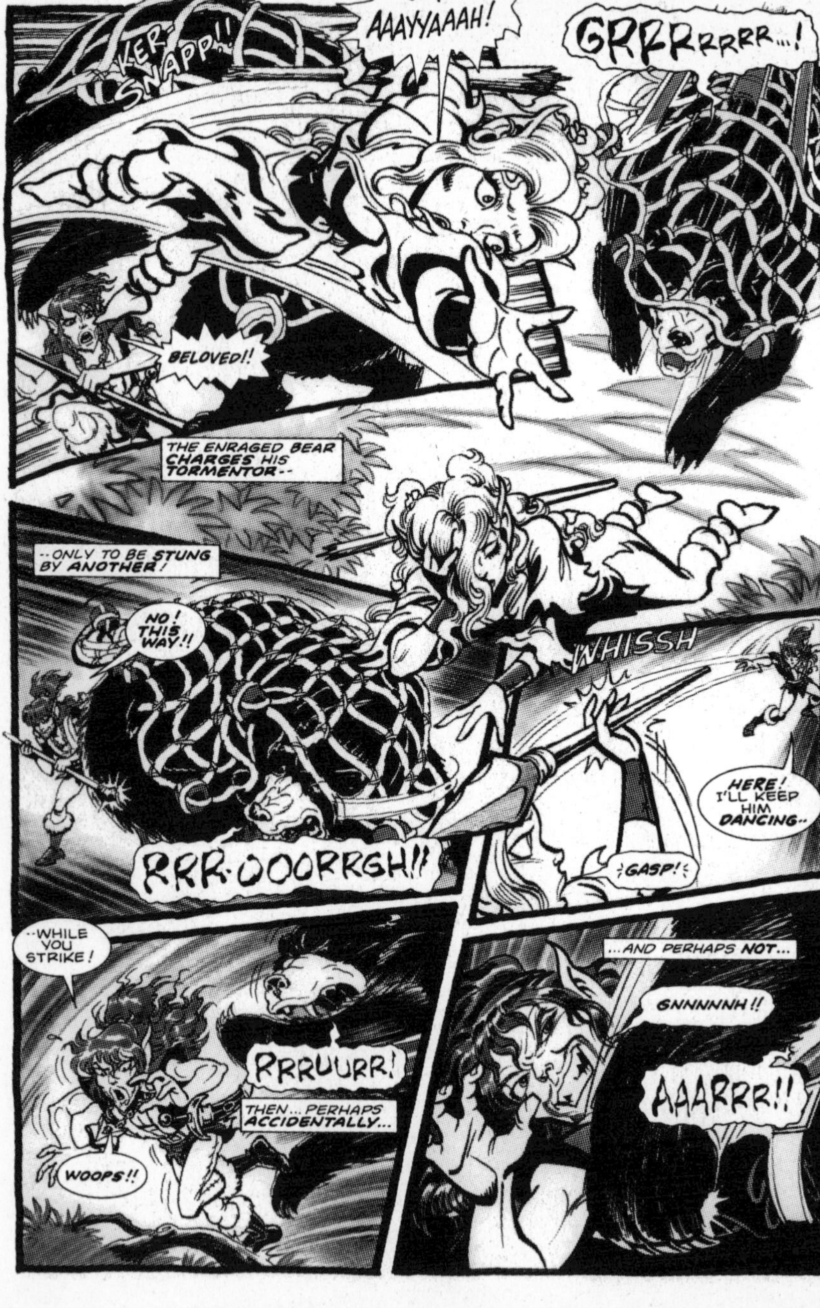

KER-SNAPP!!
AAAYYAAAH!
GRRRrrrrr...!
BELOVED!!
THE ENRAGED BEAR CHARGES HIS TORMENTOR--
..ONLY TO BE STUNG BY ANOTHER!
NO! THIS WAY!!
WHISSH
HERE! I'LL KEEP HIM DANCING..
RRR-OOORRGH!!
GASP!
..WHILE YOU STRIKE!
RRRUURR!
THEN... PERHAPS ACCIDENTALLY...
WOOPS!!
...AND PERHAPS NOT...
GNNNNNH!!
AAARRR!!

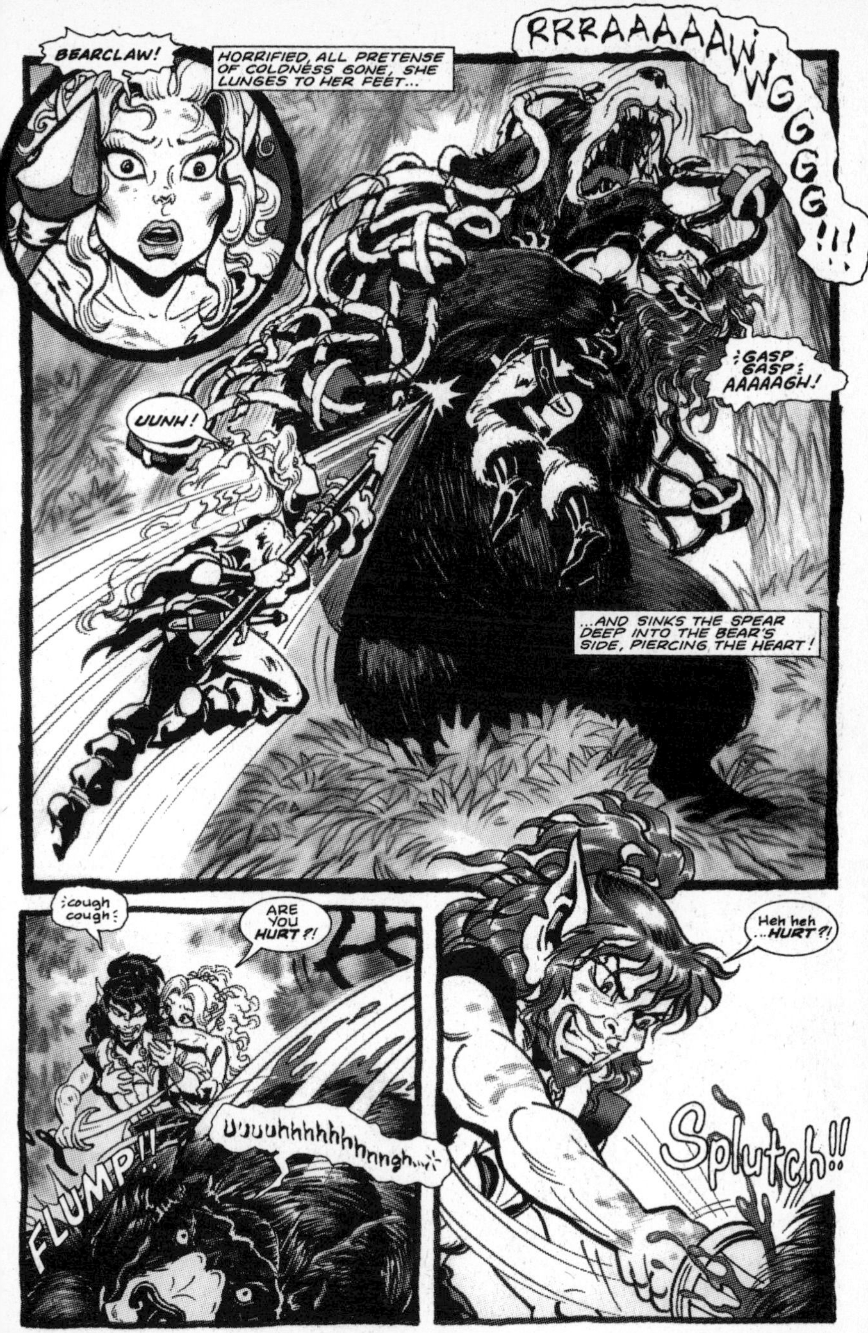

BEARCLAW!
HORRIFIED, ALL PRETENSE OF COLDNESS GONE, SHE LUNGES TO HER FEET...
RRRAAAAAAWWGGGG!!!
UUNH!
GASP GASP AAAAAGH!
...AND SINKS THE SPEAR DEEP INTO THE BEAR'S SIDE, PIERCING THE HEART!
cough cough
ARE YOU HURT?!
U'uuuhhhhhhhnngh...
FLUMP!!
Heh heh ...HURT?!
Splutch!!

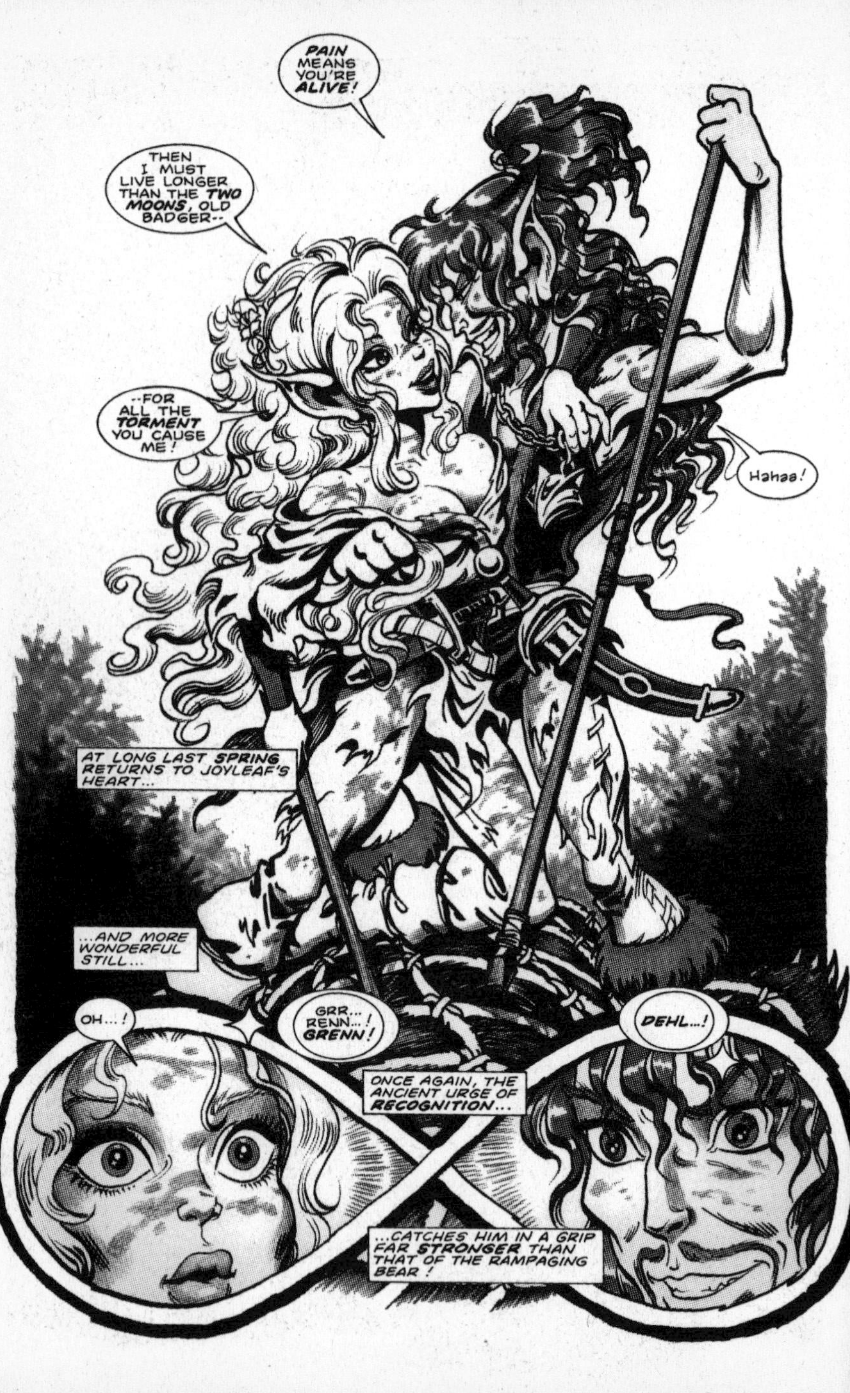
PAIN MEANS YOU'RE ALIVE!
THEN I MUST LIVE LONGER THAN THE TWO MOONS, OLD BADGER--
--FOR ALL THE TORMENT YOU CAUSE ME!
Hahaa!
AT LONG LAST SPRING RETURNS TO JOYLEAF'S HEART...
...AND MORE WONDERFUL STILL...
OH...!
GRR... RENN...! GRENN!
DEHL...!
ONCE AGAIN, THE ANCIENT URGE OF RECOGNITION...
...CATCHES HIM IN A GRIP FAR STRONGER THAN THAT OF THE RAMPAGING BEAR!

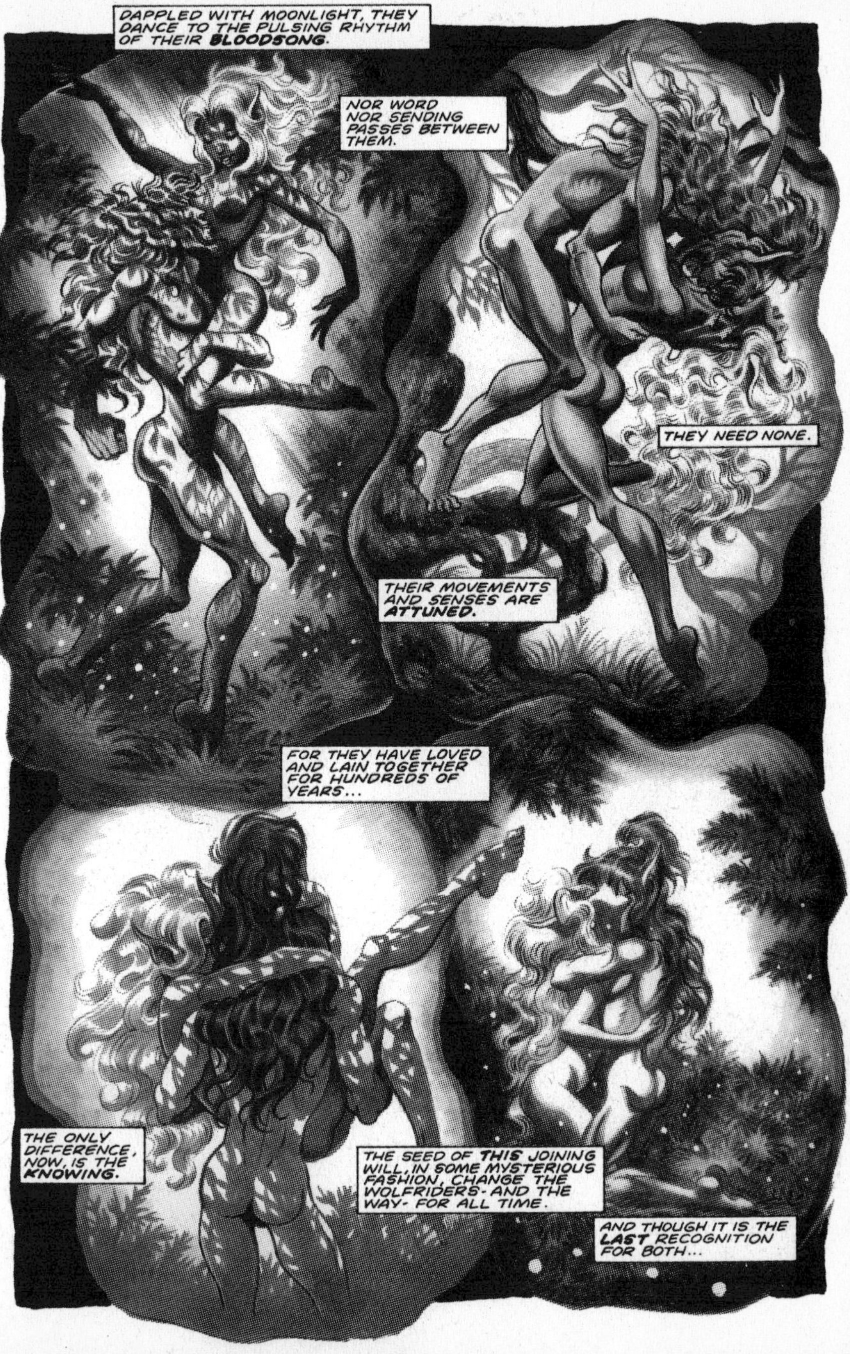
DAPPLED WITH MOONLIGHT, THEY DANCE TO THE PULSING RHYTHM OF THEIR BLOODSONG.
NOR WORD NOR SENDING PASSES BETWEEN THEM.
THEY NEED NONE.
THEIR MOVEMENTS AND SENSES ARE ATTUNED.
FOR THEY HAVE LOVED AND LAIN TOGETHER FOR HUNDREDS OF YEARS...
THE ONLY DIFFERENCE, NOW, IS THE KNOWING.
THE SEED OF THIS JOINING WILL, IN SOME MYSTERIOUS FASHION, CHANGE THE WOLFRIDERS- AND THE WAY- FOR ALL TIME.
AND THOUGH IT IS THE LAST RECOGNITION FOR BOTH...

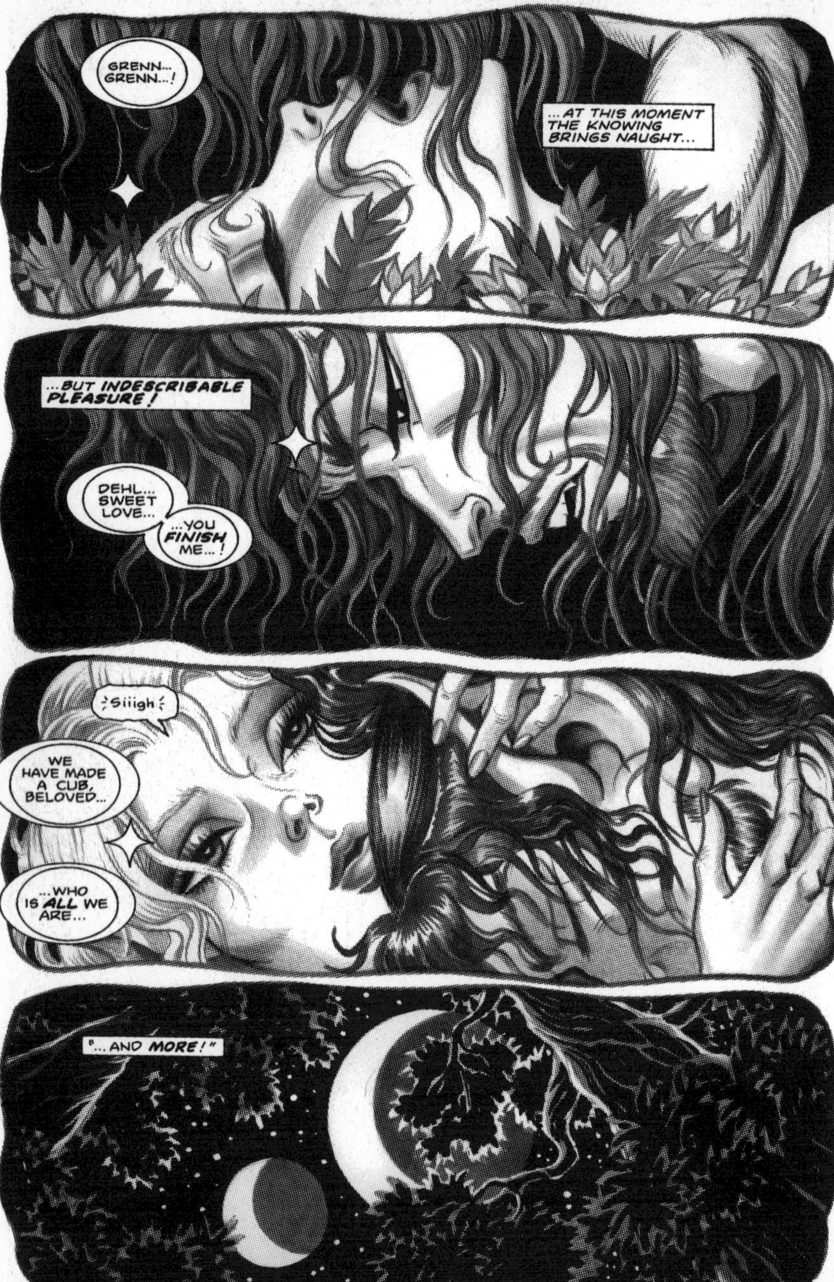
GRENN... GRENN...!
...AT THIS MOMENT THE KNOWING BRINGS NAUGHT...
...BUT INDESCRIBABLE PLEASURE!
DEHL... SWEET LOVE...
...YOU FINISH ME...!
Siiigh
WE HAVE MADE A CUB, BELOVED...
...WHO IS ALL WE ARE...
"...AND MORE!"

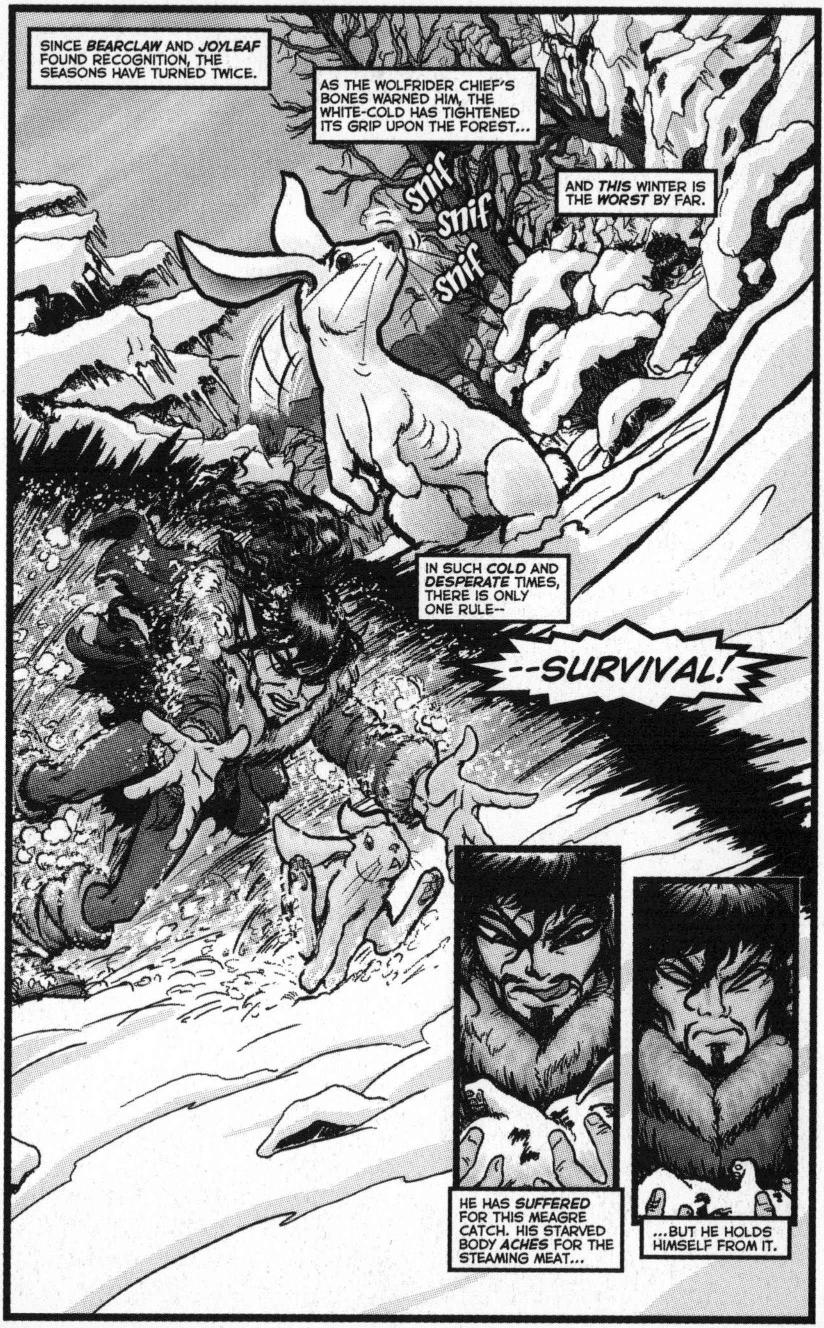
SINCE BEARCLAW AND JOYLEAF FOUND RECOGNITION, THE SEASONS HAVE TURNED TWICE.
AS THE WOLFRIDER CHIEF'S BONES WARNED HIM, THE WHITE-COLD HAS TIGHTENED ITS GRIP UPON THE FOREST...
snif
snif
snif
AND THIS WINTER IS THE WORST BY FAR.
IN SUCH COLD AND DESPERATE TIMES, THERE IS ONLY ONE RULE--
--SURVIVAL!
HE HAS SUFFERED FOR THIS MEAGRE CATCH. HIS STARVED BODY ACHES FOR THE STEAMING MEAT...
...BUT HE HOLDS HIMSELF FROM IT.

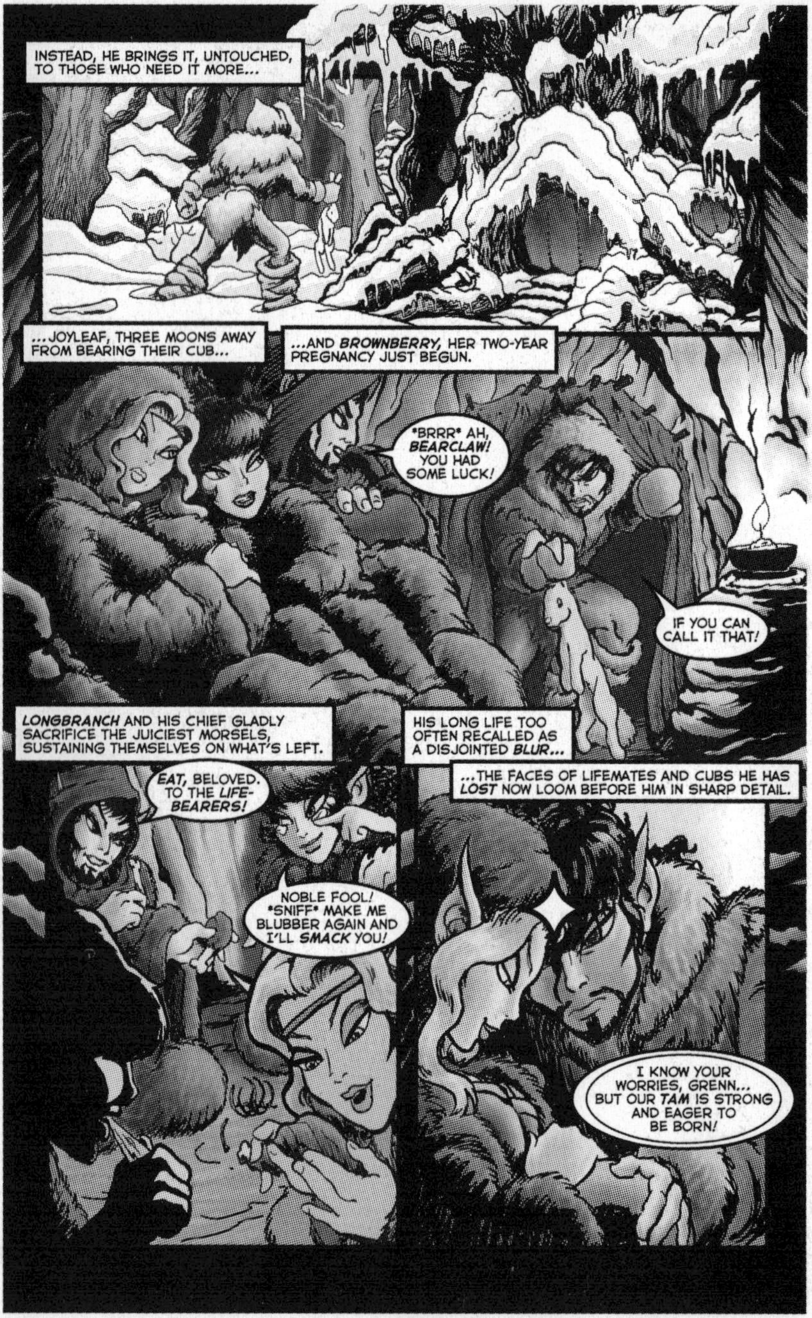
INSTEAD, HE BRINGS IT, UNTOUCHED, TO THOSE WHO NEED IT MORE...
...JOYLEAF, THREE MOONS AWAY FROM BEARING THEIR CUB...
...AND BROWNBERRY, HER TWO-YEAR PREGNANCY JUST BEGUN.
BRRR AH, BEARCLAW! YOU HAD SOME LUCK!
IF YOU CAN CALL IT THAT!
LONGBRANCH AND HIS CHIEF GLADLY SACRIFICE THE JUICIEST MORSELS, SUSTAINING THEMSELVES ON WHAT'S LEFT.
EAT, BELOVED. TO THE LIFE-BEARERS!
NOBLE FOOL! *SNIFF* MAKE ME BLUBBER AGAIN AND I'LL SMACK YOU!
HIS LONG LIFE TOO OFTEN RECALLED AS A DISJOINTED BLUR...
...THE FACES OF LIFEMATES AND CUBS HE HAS LOST NOW LOOM BEFORE HIM IN SHARP DETAIL.
I KNOW YOUR WORRIES, GRENN... BUT OUR TAM IS STRONG AND EAGER TO BE BORN!

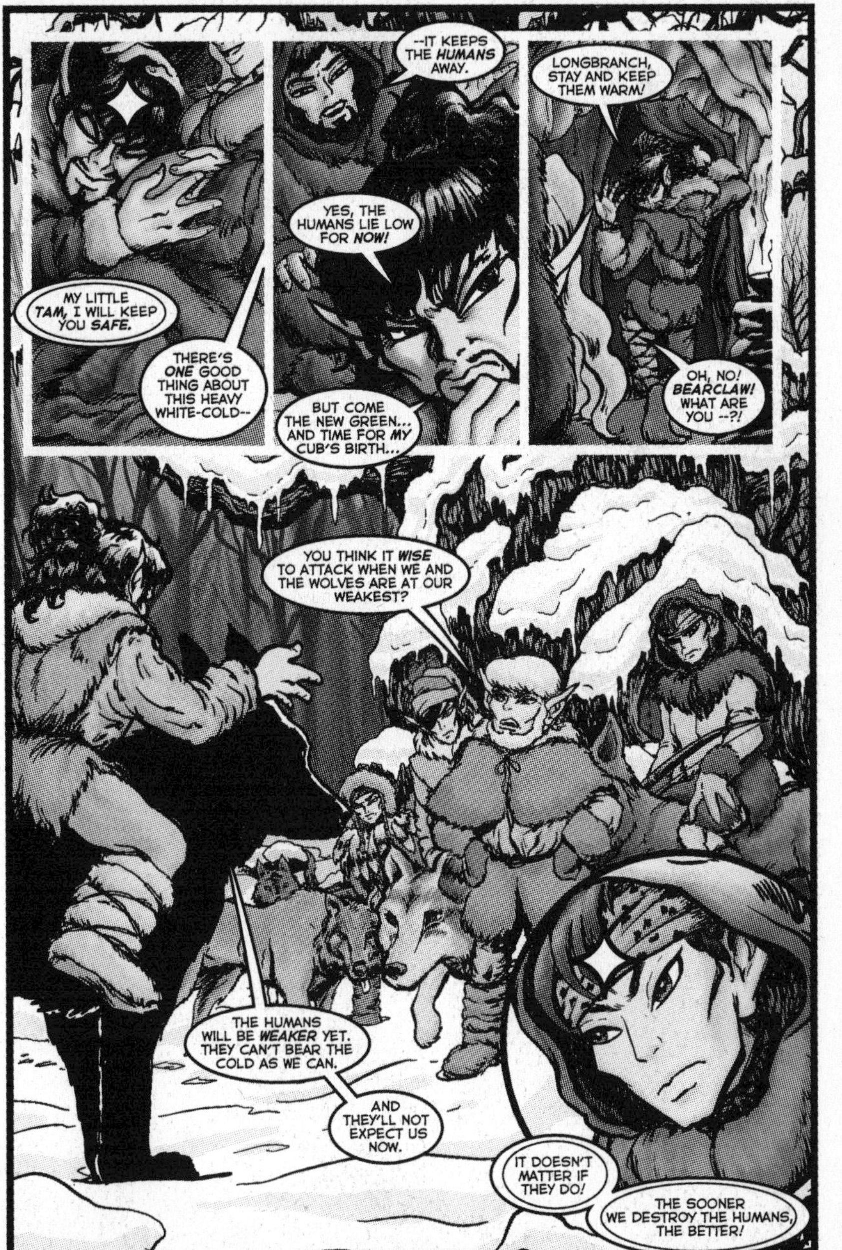
MY LITTLE TAM, I WILL KEEP YOU SAFE.
THERE'S ONE GOOD THING ABOUT THIS HEAVY WHITE-COLD--
--IT KEEPS THE HUMANS AWAY.
YES, THE HUMANS LIE LOW FOR NOW!
BUT COME THE NEW GREEN... AND TIME FOR MY CUB'S BIRTH...
LONGBRANCH, STAY AND KEEP THEM WARM!
OH, NO! BEARCLAW! WHAT ARE YOU --?!
YOU THINK IT WISE TO ATTACK WHEN WE AND THE WOLVES ARE AT OUR WEAKEST?
THE HUMANS WILL BE WEAKER YET. THEY CAN'T BEAR THE COLD AS WE CAN.
AND THEY'LL NOT EXPECT US NOW.
IT DOESN'T MATTER IF THEY DO!
THE SOONER WE DESTROY THE HUMANS, THE BETTER!

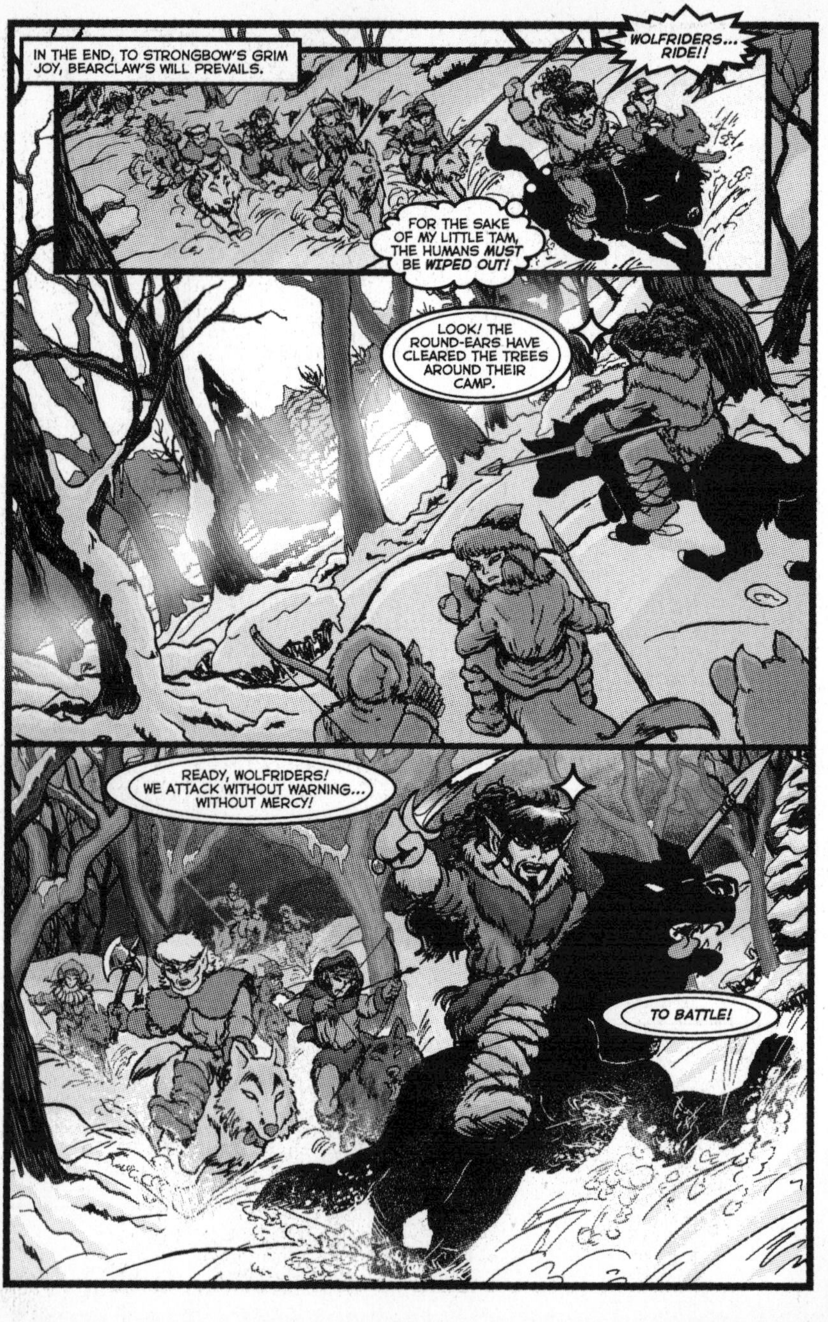
IN THE END, TO STRONGBOW'S GRIM JOY, BEARCLAW'S WILL PREVAILS.
WOLFRIDERS... RIDE!!
FOR THE SAKE OF MY LITTLE TAM, THE HUMANS *MUST* BE *WIPED OUT!*
LOOK! THE ROUND-EARS HAVE CLEARED THE TREES AROUND THEIR CAMP.
READY, WOLFRIDERS! WE ATTACK WITHOUT WARNING... WITHOUT MERCY!
TO BATTLE!

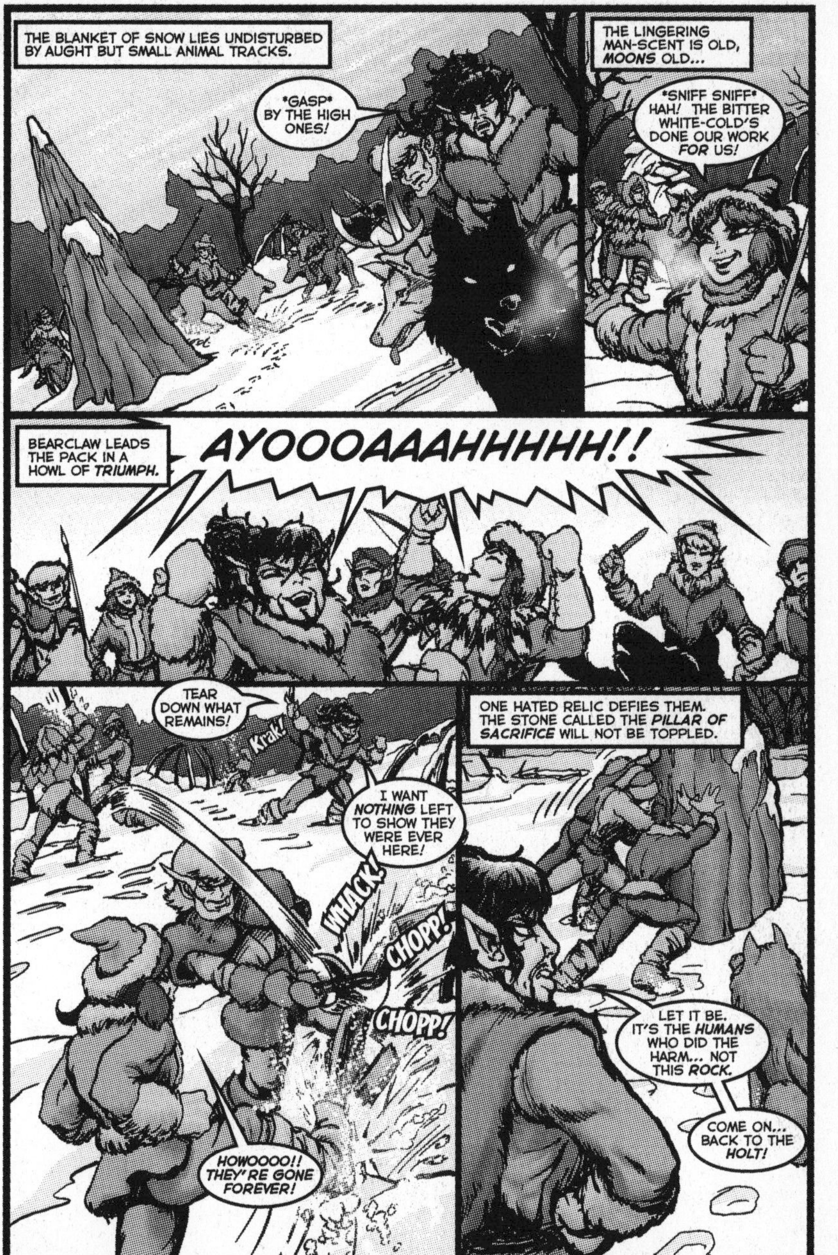
THE BLANKET OF SNOW LIES UNDISTURBED BY AUGHT BUT SMALL ANIMAL TRACKS.
GASP BY THE HIGH ONES!
THE LINGERING MAN-SCENT IS OLD, MOONS OLD...
SNIFF SNIFF HAH! THE BITTER WHITE-COLD'S DONE OUR WORK FOR US!
BEARCLAW LEADS THE PACK IN A HOWL OF TRIUMPH.
AYOOOAAAHHHHH!!
TEAR DOWN WHAT REMAINS!
KRAK!
I WANT NOTHING LEFT TO SHOW THEY WERE EVER HERE!
WHACK!
CHOPP!
CHOPP!
HOWOOOO!! THEY'RE GONE FOREVER!
ONE HATED RELIC DEFIES THEM. THE STONE CALLED THE PILLAR OF SACRIFICE WILL NOT BE TOPPLED.
LET IT BE. IT'S THE HUMANS WHO DID THE HARM... NOT THIS ROCK.
COME ON... BACK TO THE HOLT!

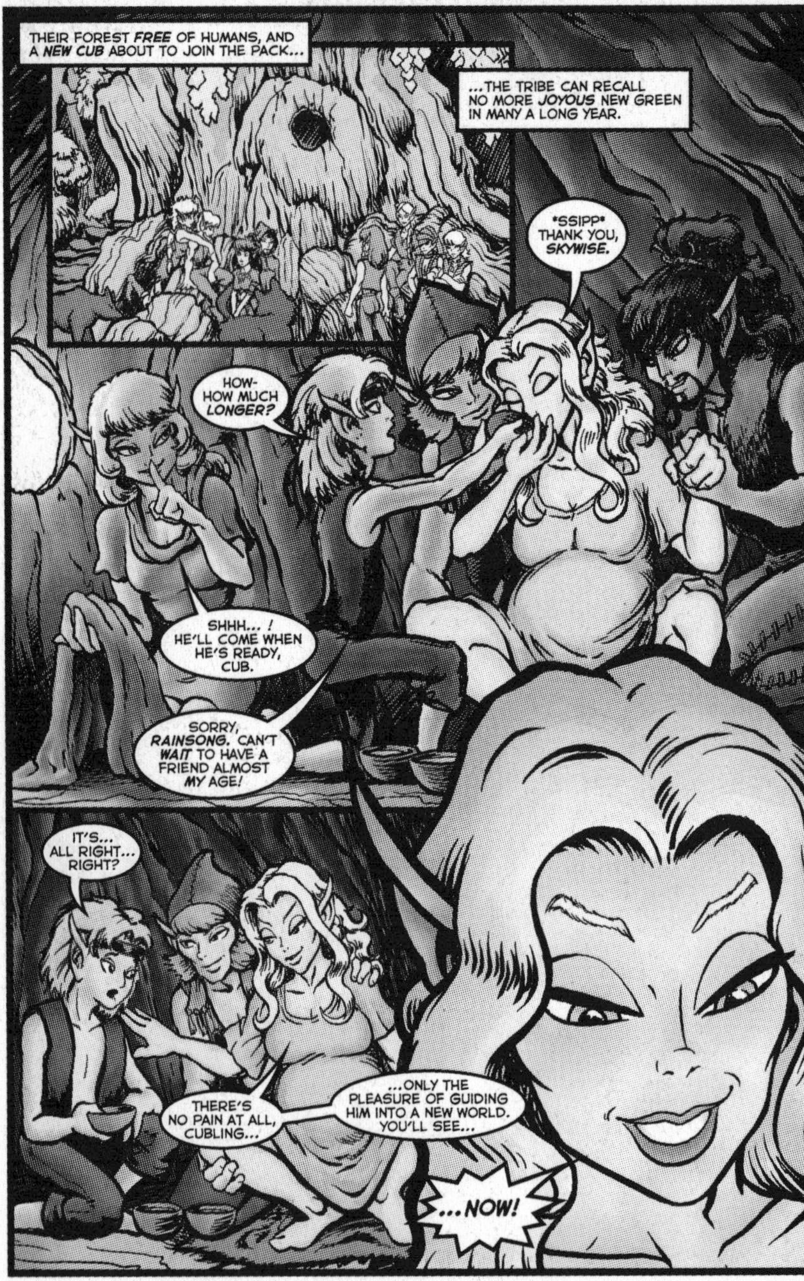
THEIR FOREST *FREE* OF HUMANS, AND A *NEW CUB* ABOUT TO JOIN THE PACK...
...THE TRIBE CAN RECALL NO MORE *JOYOUS* NEW GREEN IN MANY A LONG YEAR.
SSIPP THANK YOU, *SKYWISE.*
HOW- HOW MUCH *LONGER?*
SHHH... ! HE'LL COME WHEN HE'S READY, CUB.
SORRY, *RAINSONG.* CAN'T *WAIT* TO HAVE A FRIEND ALMOST *MY* AGE!
IT'S... ALL RIGHT... RIGHT?
THERE'S NO PAIN AT ALL, CUBLING...
...ONLY THE PLEASURE OF GUIDING HIM INTO A NEW WORLD. YOU'LL SEE...
...NOW!

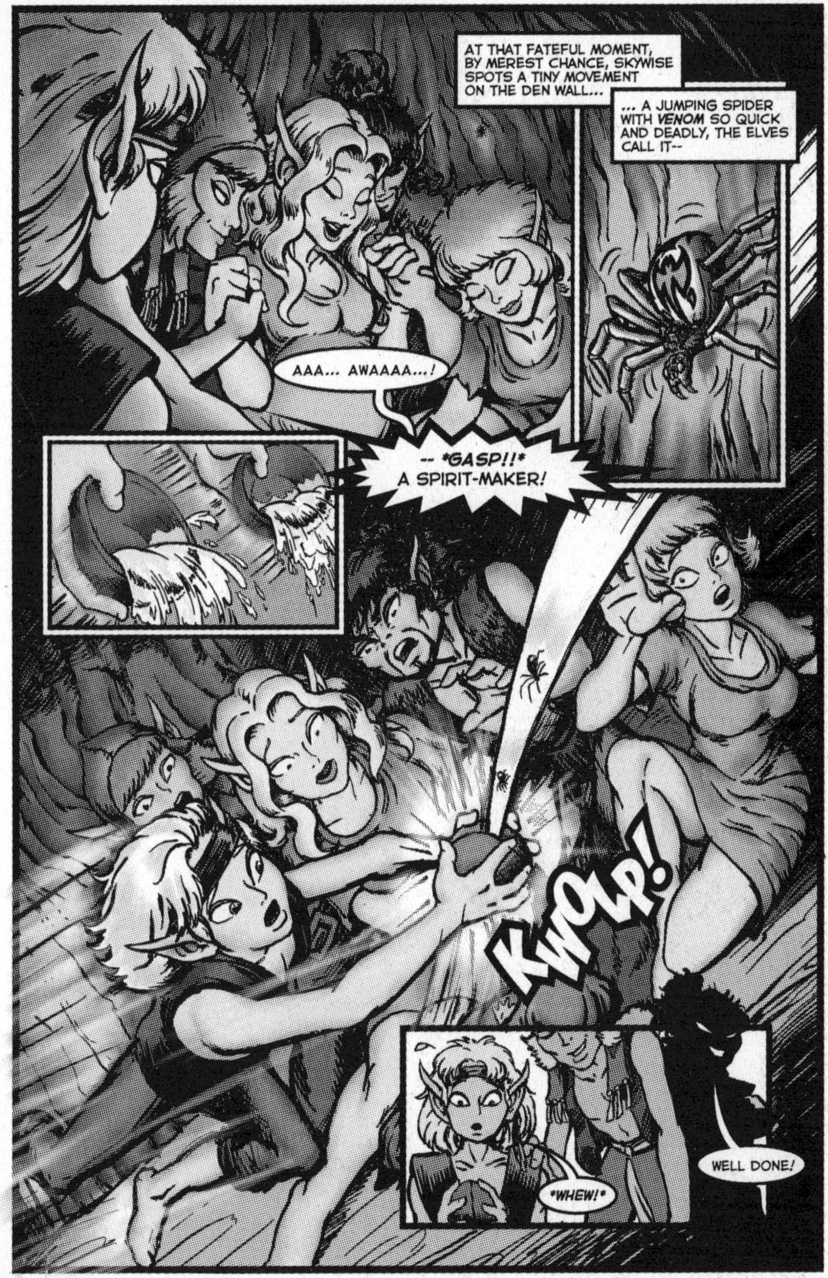
AT THAT FATEFUL MOMENT, BY MEREST CHANCE, SKYWISE SPOTS A TINY MOVEMENT ON THE DEN WALL...
... A JUMPING SPIDER WITH VENOM SO QUICK AND DEADLY, THE ELVES CALL IT--
AAA... AWAAAA...!
-- *GASP!!* A SPIRIT-MAKER!
KWOLP!
WHEW!
WELL DONE!

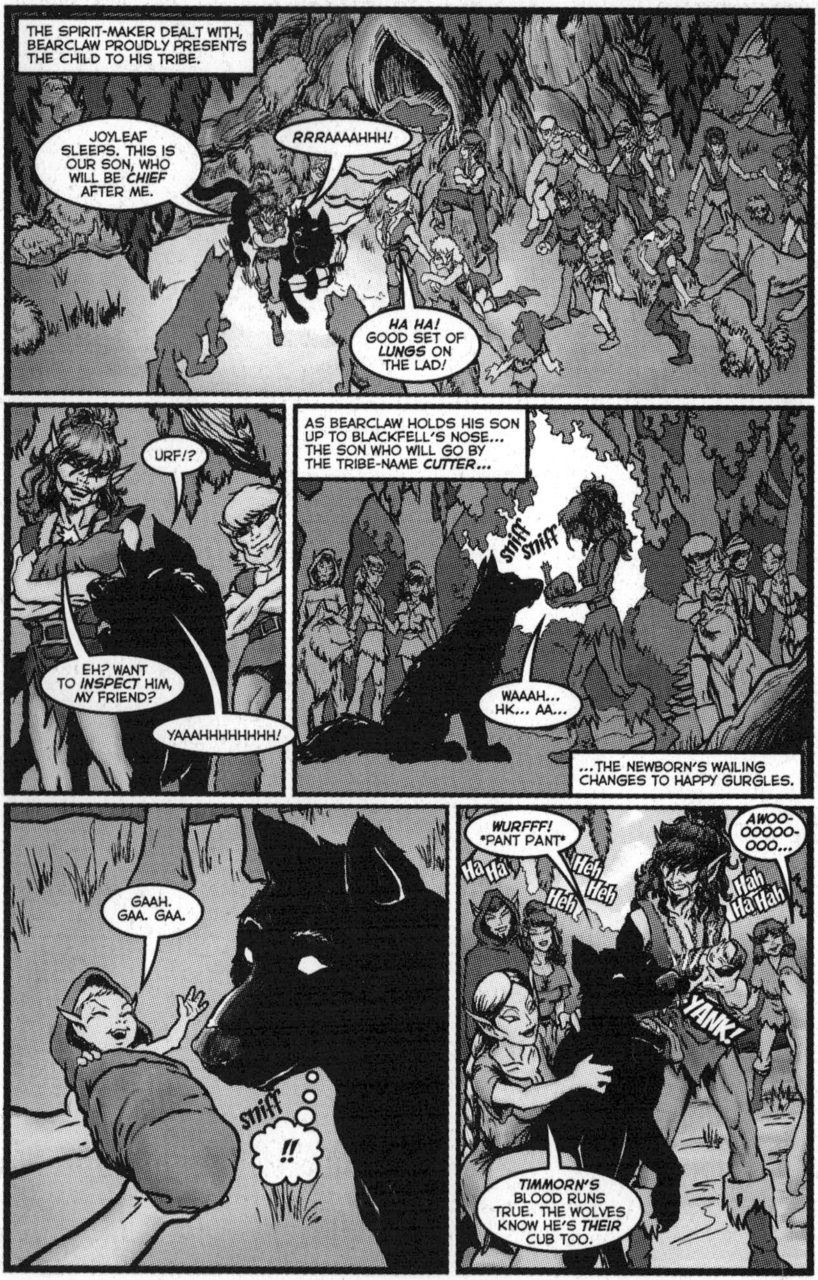
THE SPIRIT-MAKER DEALT WITH, BEARCLAW PROUDLY PRESENTS THE CHILD TO HIS TRIBE.
JOYLEAF SLEEPS. THIS IS OUR SON, WHO WILL BE CHIEF AFTER ME.
RRRAAAAHHH!
HA HA! GOOD SET OF LUNGS ON THE LAD!
URF!?
EH? WANT TO INSPECT HIM, MY FRIEND?
YAAAHHHHHHHH!
AS BEARCLAW HOLDS HIS SON UP TO BLACKFELL'S NOSE... THE SON WHO WILL GO BY THE TRIBE-NAME CUTTER...
sniff sniff
WAAAH... HK... AA...
...THE NEWBORN'S WAILING CHANGES TO HAPPY GURGLES.
GAAH. GAA. GAA.
sniff
!!
WURFFF! *PANT PANT*
AWOO-OOOOO-OOO...
Ha Ha
Heh Heh Heh
Hah Ha Hah
YANK!
TIMMORN'S BLOOD RUNS TRUE. THE WOLVES KNOW HE'S THEIR CUB TOO.

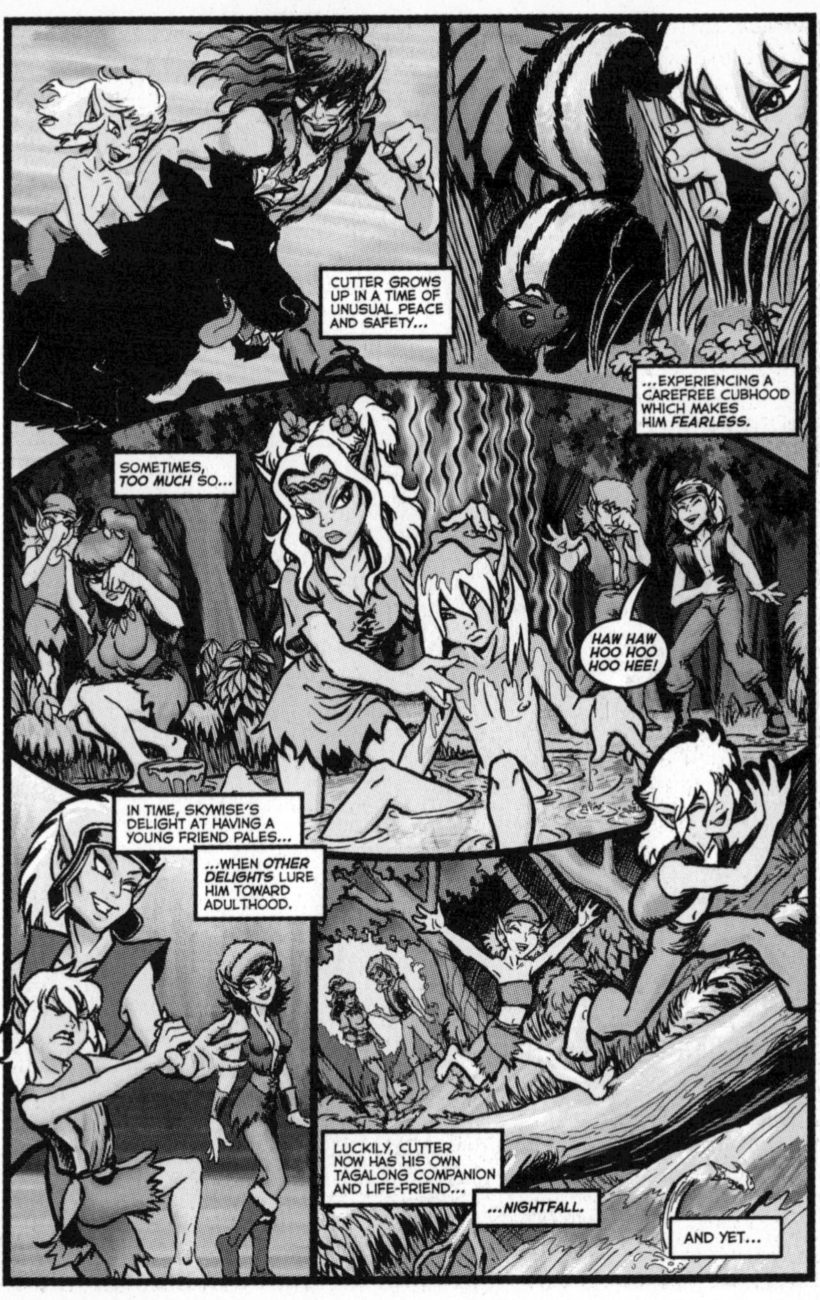
CUTTER GROWS UP IN A TIME OF UNUSUAL PEACE AND SAFETY...
...EXPERIENCING A CAREFREE CUBHOOD WHICH MAKES HIM FEARLESS.
SOMETIMES, TOO MUCH SO...
HAW HAW HOO HOO HOO HEE!
IN TIME, SKYWISE'S DELIGHT AT HAVING A YOUNG FRIEND PALES...
...WHEN OTHER DELIGHTS LURE HIM TOWARD ADULTHOOD.
LUCKILY, CUTTER NOW HAS HIS OWN TAGALONG COMPANION AND LIFE-FRIEND...
...NIGHTFALL.
AND YET...

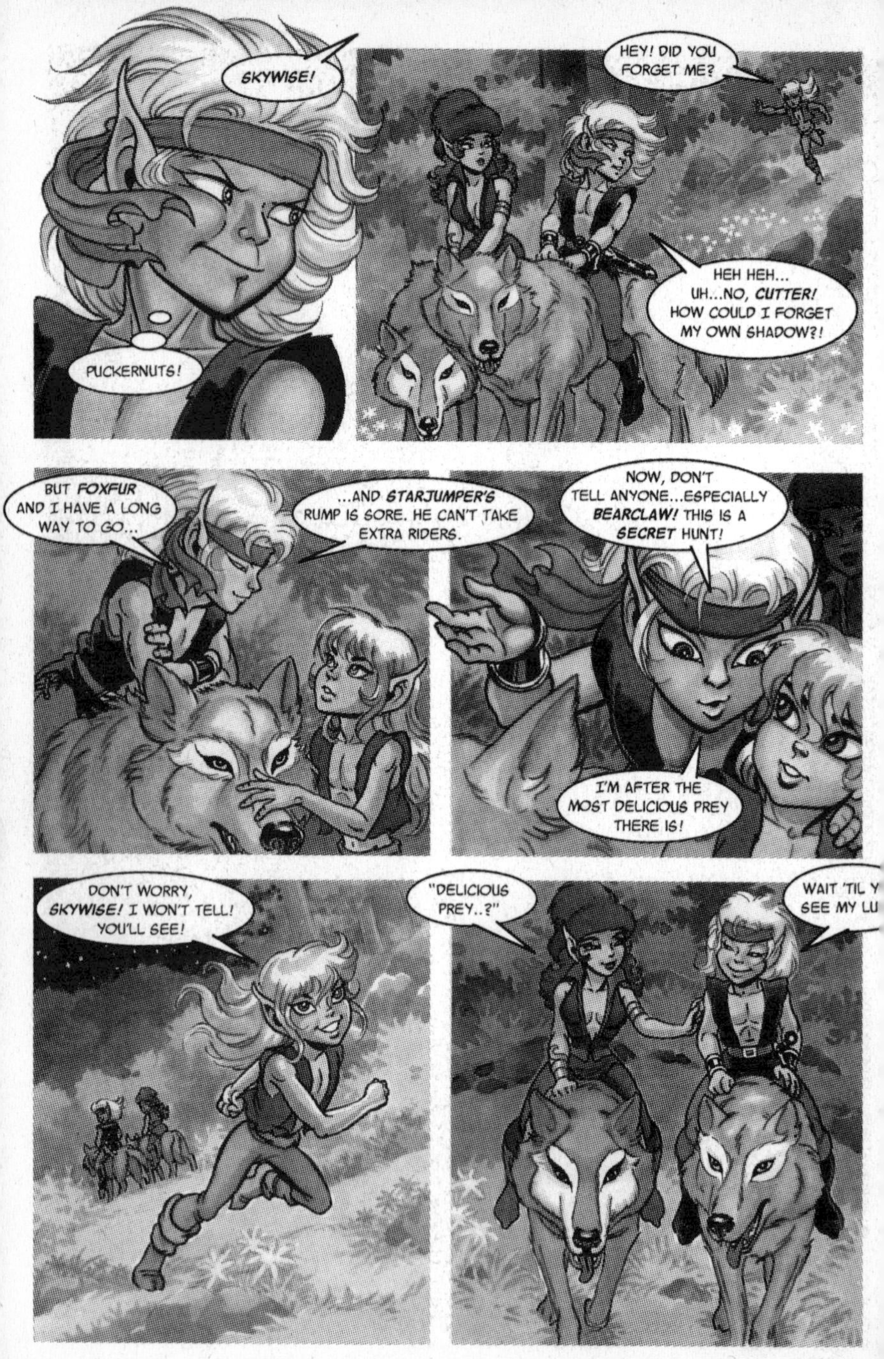
SKYWISE!
PUCKERNUTS!
HEY! DID YOU FORGET ME?
HEH HEH... UH...NO, CUTTER! HOW COULD I FORGET MY OWN SHADOW?!
BUT FOXFUR AND I HAVE A LONG WAY TO GO...
...AND STARJUMPER'S RUMP IS SORE. HE CAN'T TAKE EXTRA RIDERS.
NOW, DON'T TELL ANYONE...ESPECIALLY BEARCLAW! THIS IS A SECRET HUNT!
I'M AFTER THE MOST DELICIOUS PREY THERE IS!
DON'T WORRY, SKYWISE! I WON'T TELL! YOU'LL SEE!
"DELICIOUS PREY..?"

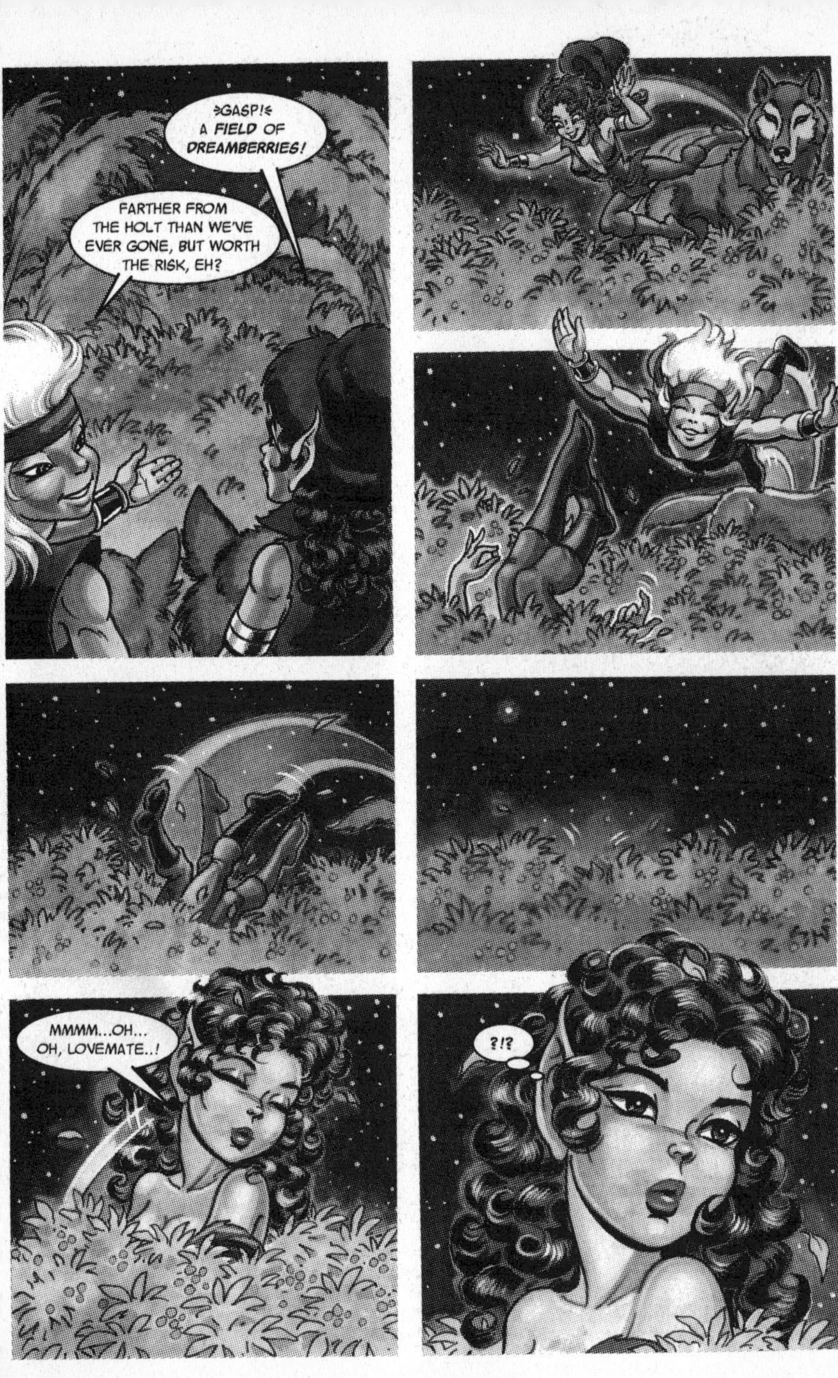
FARTHER FROM THE HOLT THAN WE'VE EVER GONE, BUT WORTH THE RISK, EH?
≥GASP!≤ A FIELD OF DREAMBERRIES!
MMMM...OH... OH, LOVEMATE..!
?!?

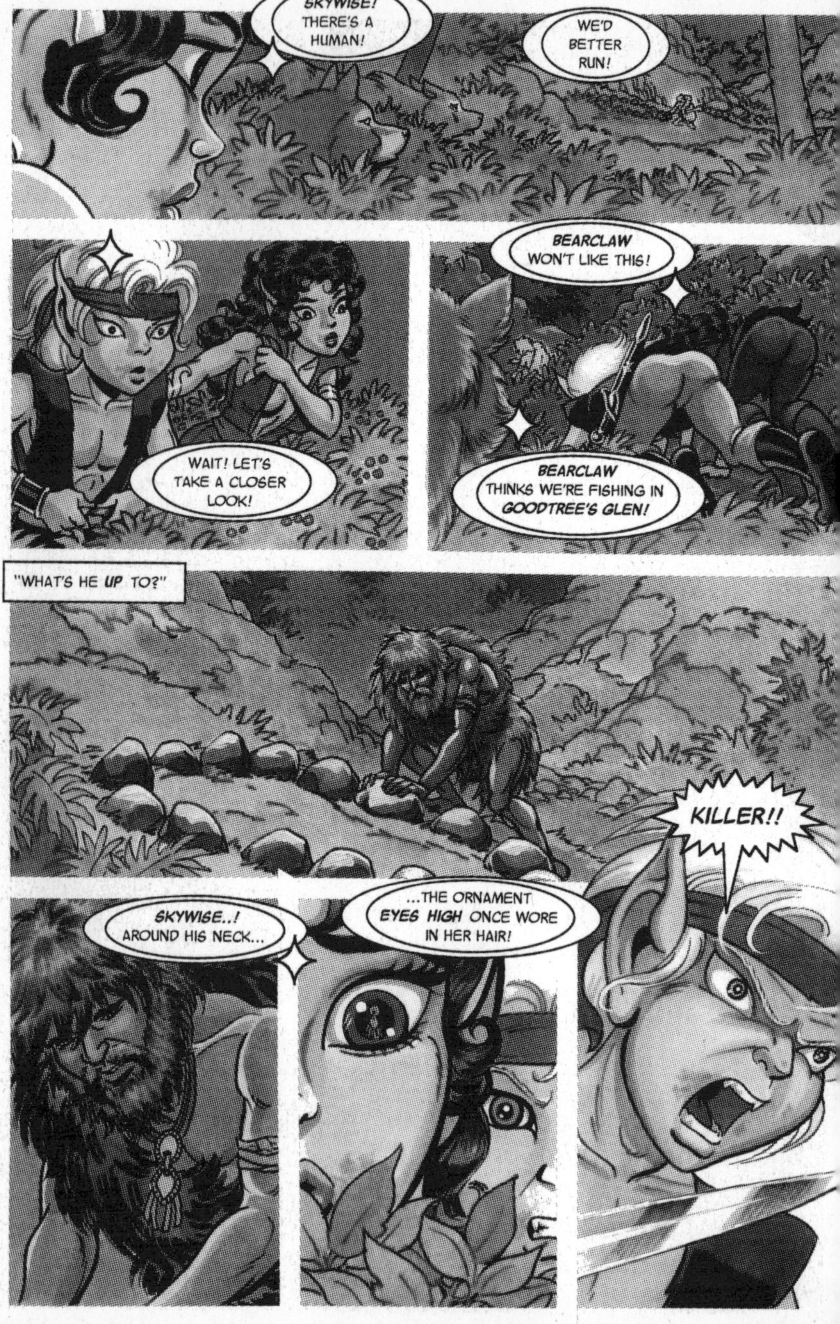
SKYWISE! THERE'S A HUMAN!
WE'D BETTER RUN!
WAIT! LET'S TAKE A CLOSER LOOK!
BEARCLAW WON'T LIKE THIS!
BEARCLAW THINKS WE'RE FISHING IN GOODTREE'S GLEN!
"WHAT'S HE UP TO?"
SKYWISE..! AROUND HIS NECK...
...THE ORNAMENT EYES HIGH ONCE WORE IN HER HAIR!
KILLER!!

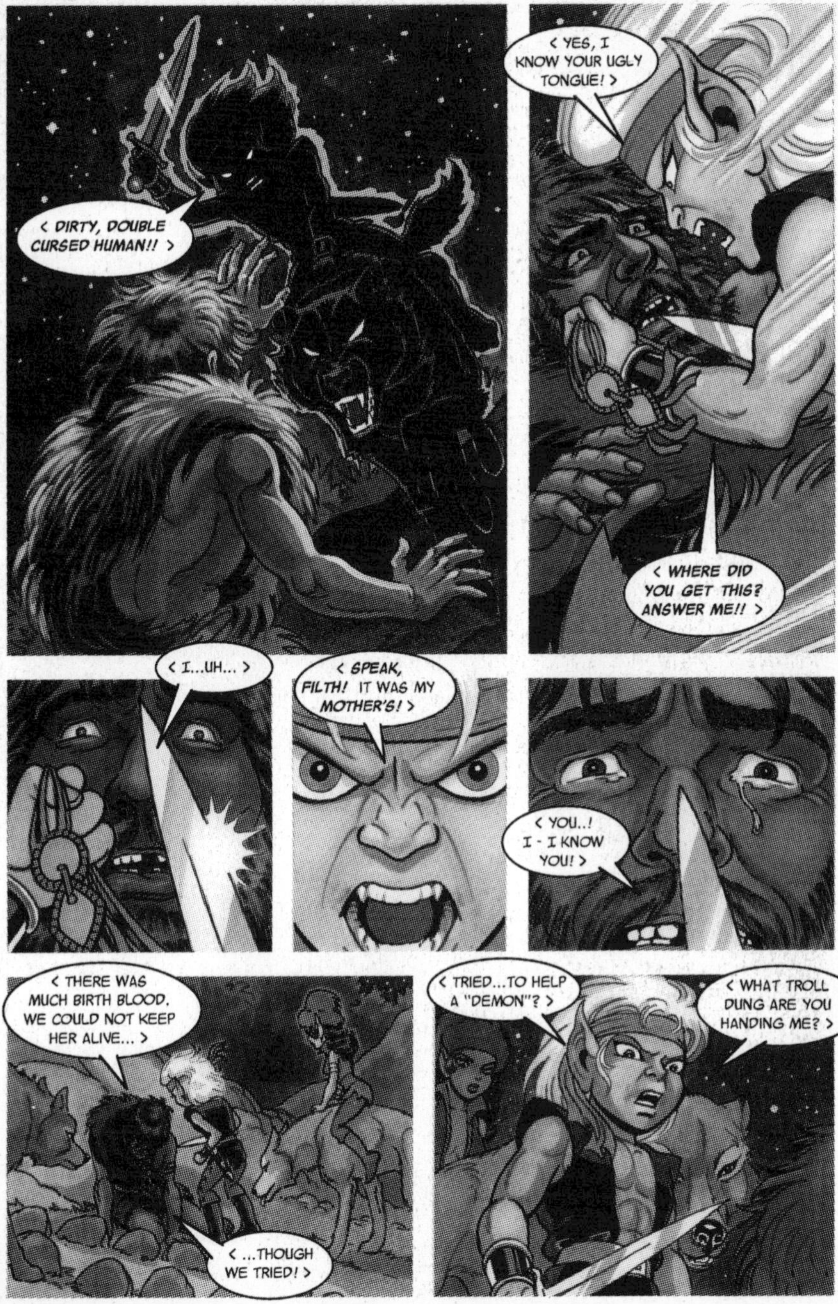
< DIRTY, DOUBLE CURSED HUMAN!! >
< YES, I KNOW YOUR UGLY TONGUE! >
< WHERE DID YOU GET THIS? ANSWER ME!! >
< I...UH... >
< SPEAK, FILTH! IT WAS MY MOTHER'S! >
< YOU..! I - I KNOW YOU! >
< THERE WAS MUCH BIRTH BLOOD. WE COULD NOT KEEP HER ALIVE... >
< ...THOUGH WE TRIED! >
< TRIED...TO HELP A "DEMON"? >
< WHAT TROLL DUNG ARE YOU HANDING ME? >

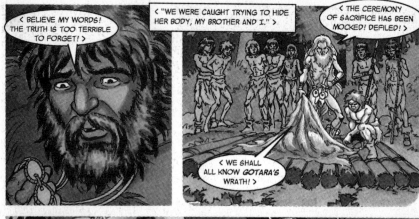

< BELIEVE MY WORDS! THE TRUTH IS TOO TERRIBLE TO FORGET! >

< "WE WERE CAUGHT TRYING TO HIDE HER BODY, MY BROTHER AND I." >

< THE CEREMONY OF SACRIFICE HAS BEEN MOCKED! DEFILED! >

< WE SHALL ALL KNOW GOTARA'S WRATH! >

< LIAR! YOU KILLED MY MOTHER! NOW IT'S YOUR TURN! >

< NO! NO! YOU ARE ALREADY AVENGED! LISTEN! >

< "WE WERE MADE TO DRAW LOTS!" >

< "MY BROTHER LOST!" >

< TAF!! >

< BUT...YOU SAID...THEY WOULD FORGIVE!! >

< "I WAS FORCED TO WATCH...AS TAF TOOK YOUR MOTHER'S PLACE ON THE PILLAR OF SACRIFICE!" >

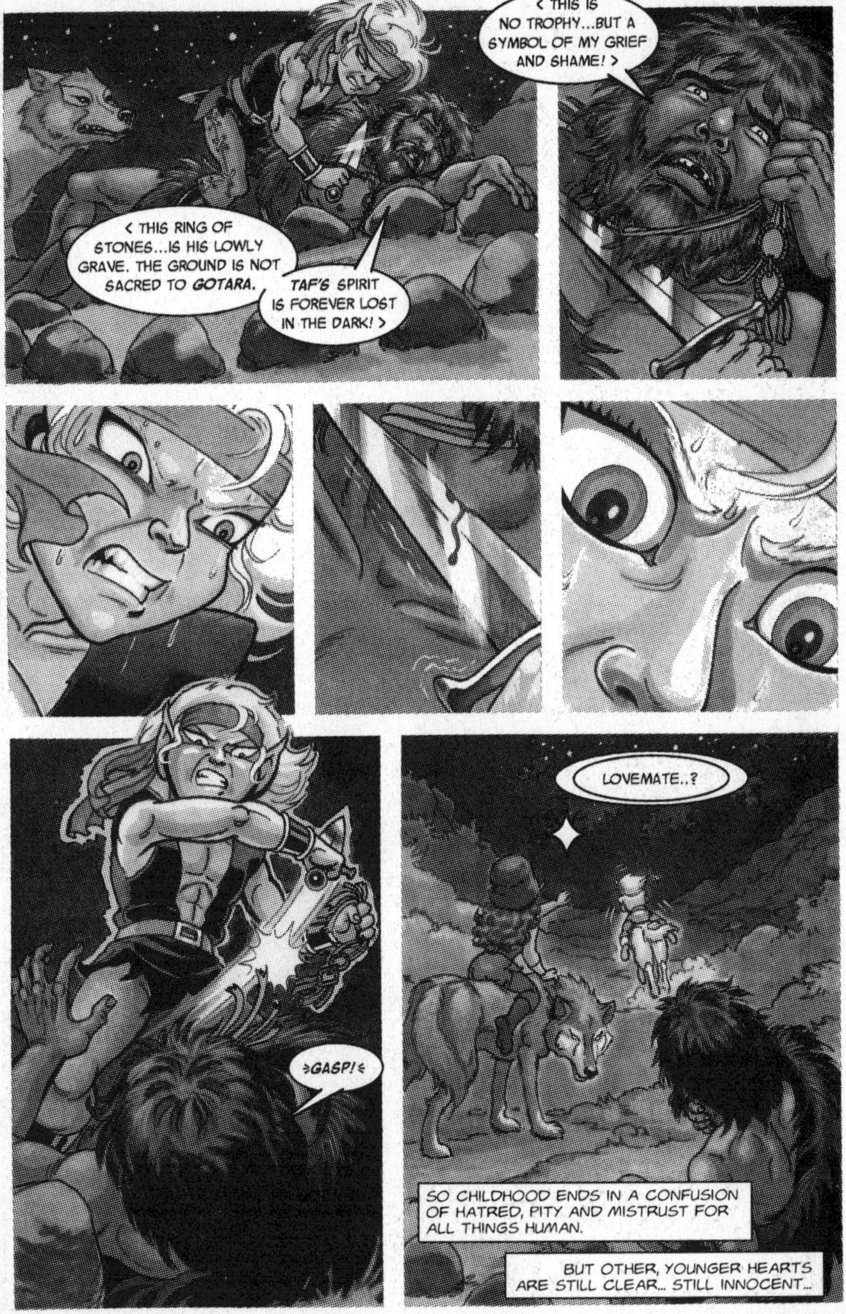

< THIS RING OF STONES...IS HIS LOWLY GRAVE. THE GROUND IS NOT SACRED TO GOTARA.
TAF'S SPIRIT IS FOREVER LOST IN THE DARK! >
< THIS IS NO TROPHY...BUT A SYMBOL OF MY GRIEF AND SHAME! >
GASP!
LOVEMATE..?
SO CHILDHOOD ENDS IN A CONFUSION OF HATRED, PITY AND MISTRUST FOR ALL THINGS HUMAN.
BUT OTHER, YOUNGER HEARTS ARE STILL CLEAR... STILL INNOCENT...

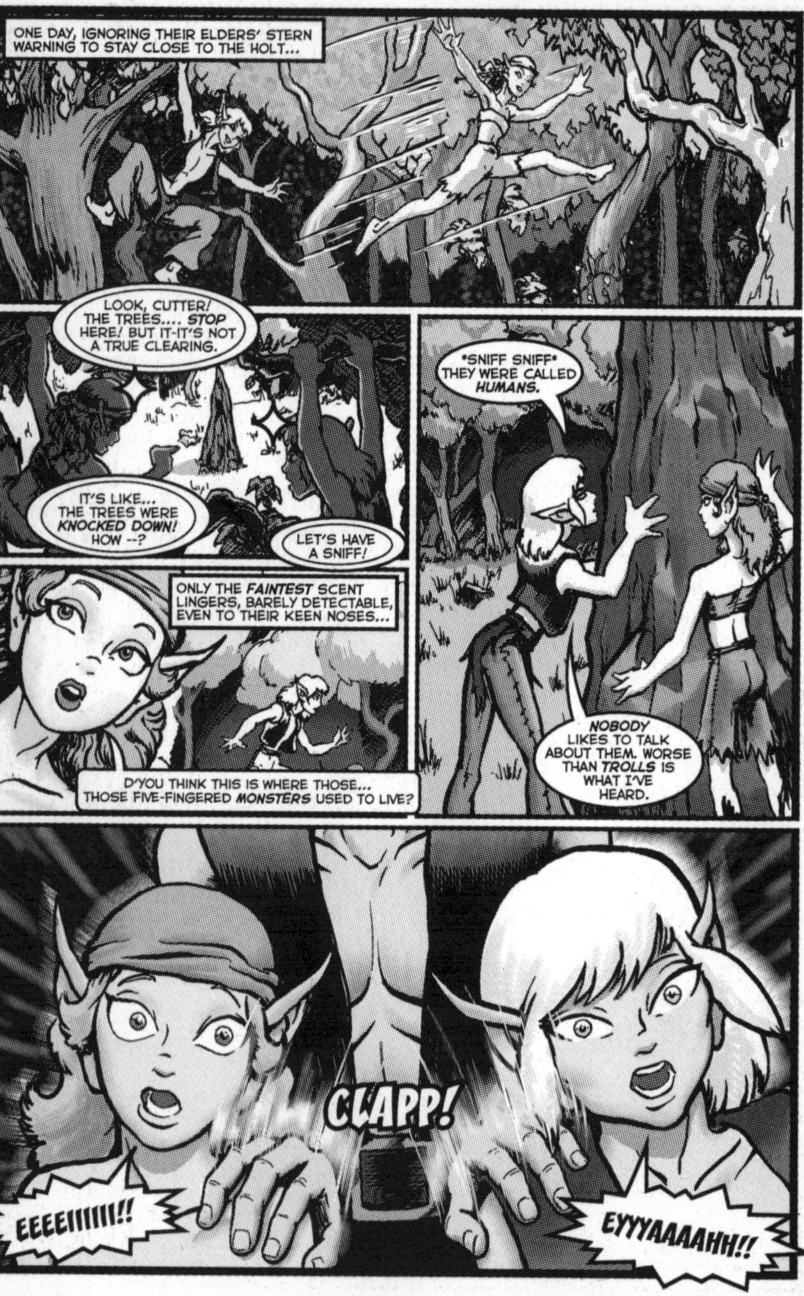
ONE DAY, IGNORING THEIR ELDERS' STERN WARNING TO STAY CLOSE TO THE HOLT...
LOOK, CUTTER! THE TREES.... STOP HERE! BUT IT-IT'S NOT A TRUE CLEARING.
IT'S LIKE... THE TREES WERE KNOCKED DOWN! HOW --?
LET'S HAVE A SNIFF!
SNIFF SNIFF THEY WERE CALLED HUMANS.
ONLY THE FAINTEST SCENT LINGERS, BARELY DETECTABLE, EVEN TO THEIR KEEN NOSES...
D'YOU THINK THIS IS WHERE THOSE... THOSE FIVE-FINGERED MONSTERS USED TO LIVE?
NOBODY LIKES TO TALK ABOUT THEM. WORSE THAN TROLLS IS WHAT I'VE HEARD.
CLAPP!
EEEEIIIIIII!!
EYYYAAAAAHH!!

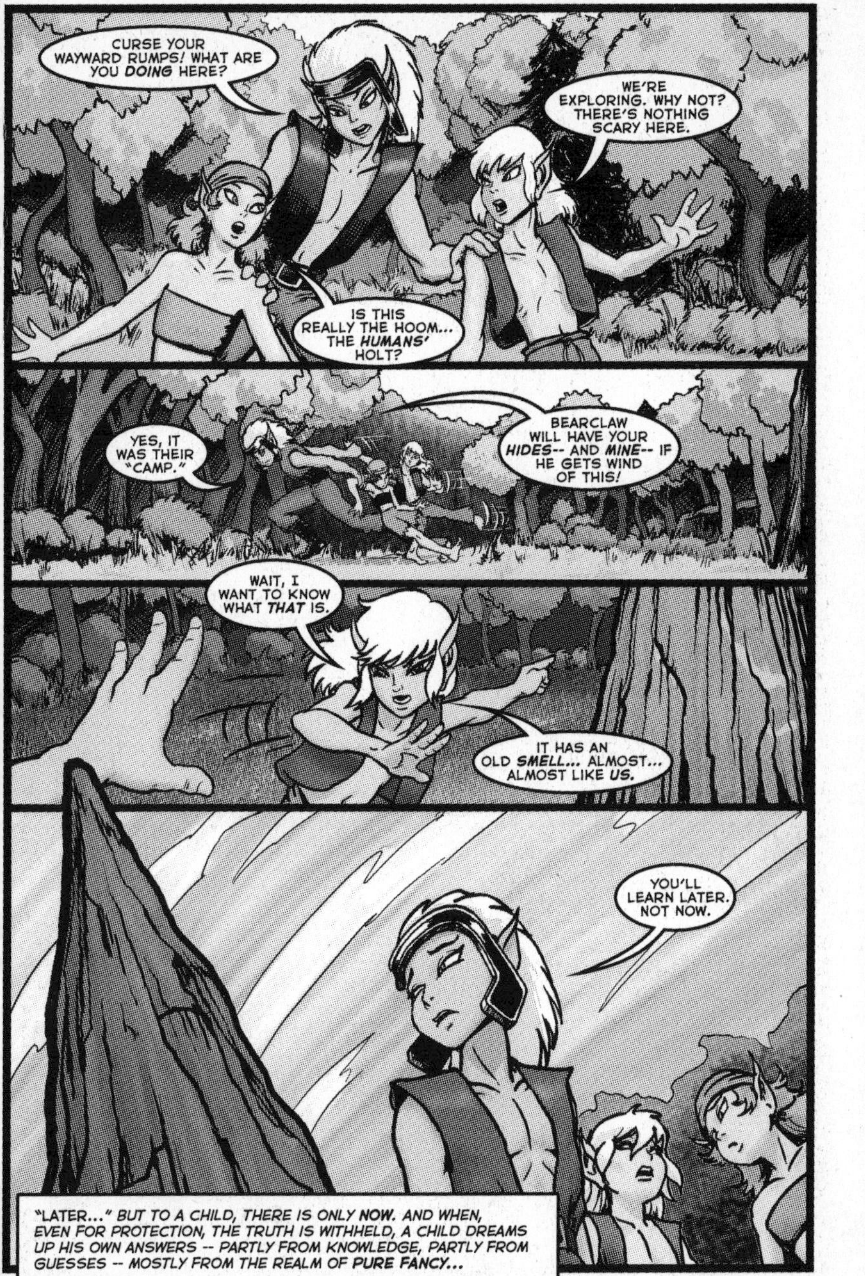
CURSE YOUR WAYWARD RUMPS! WHAT ARE YOU *DOING* HERE?
WE'RE EXPLORING. WHY NOT? THERE'S NOTHING SCARY HERE.
IS THIS REALLY THE HOOM... THE *HUMANS'* HOLT?
YES, IT WAS THEIR "CAMP."
BEARCLAW WILL HAVE YOUR *HIDES*-- AND *MINE*-- IF HE GETS WIND OF THIS!
WAIT, I WANT TO KNOW WHAT *THAT* IS.
IT HAS AN OLD *SMELL*... ALMOST... ALMOST LIKE *US.*
YOU'LL LEARN LATER. NOT NOW.
*"LATER..." BUT TO A CHILD, THERE IS ONLY **NOW.** AND WHEN, EVEN FOR PROTECTION, THE TRUTH IS WITHHELD, A CHILD DREAMS UP HIS OWN ANSWERS -- PARTLY FROM KNOWLEDGE, PARTLY FROM GUESSES -- MOSTLY FROM THE REALM OF **PURE FANCY...***

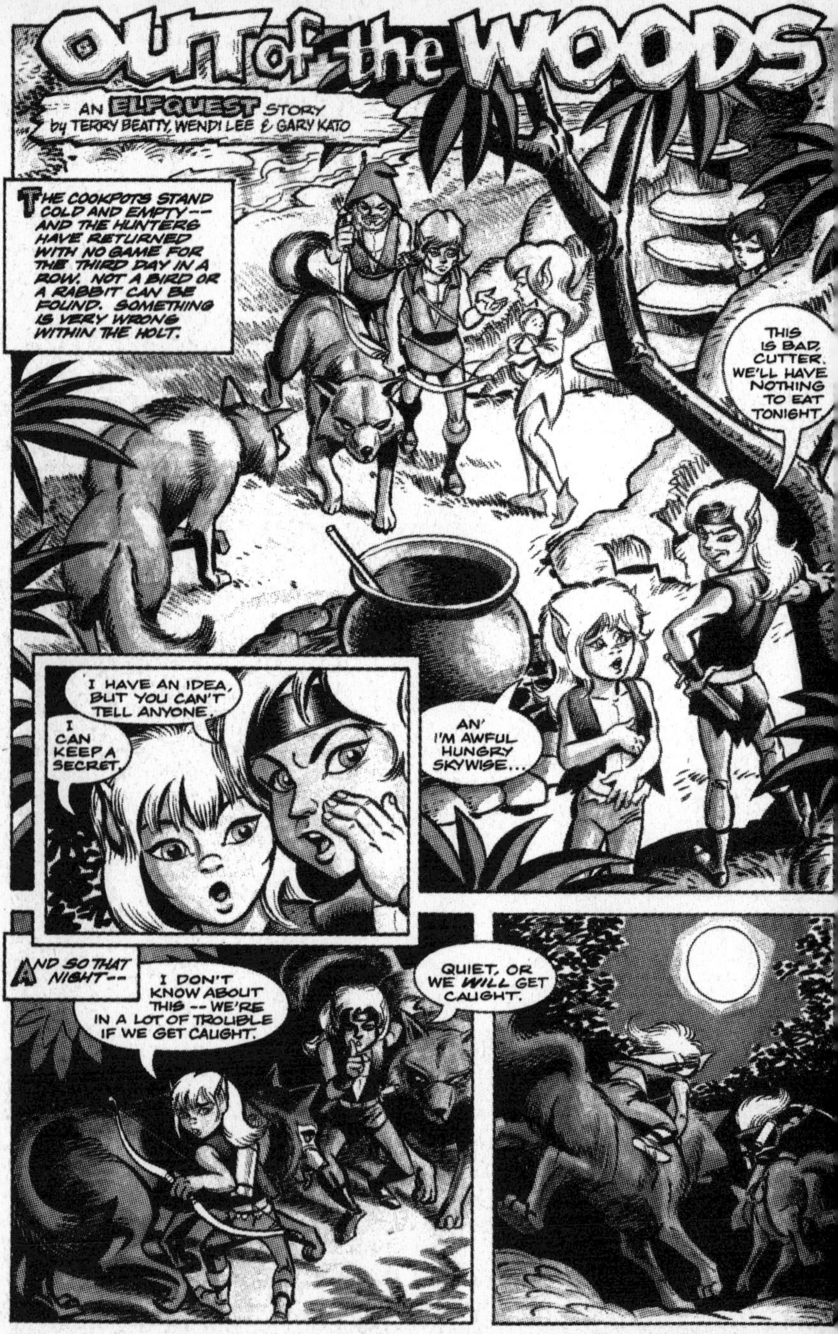
OUT of the WOODS
AN ELFQUEST STORY
by TERRY BEATTY, WENDI LEE & GARY KATO
THE COOKPOTS STAND COLD AND EMPTY -- AND THE HUNTERS HAVE RETURNED WITH NO GAME FOR THE THIRD DAY IN A ROW. NOT A BIRD OR A RABBIT CAN BE FOUND. SOMETHING IS VERY WRONG WITHIN THE HOLT.
THIS IS BAD, CUTTER. WE'LL HAVE NOTHING TO EAT TONIGHT.
AN' I'M AWFUL HUNGRY SKYWISE...
I HAVE AN IDEA, BUT YOU CAN'T TELL ANYONE.
I CAN KEEP A SECRET.
AND SO THAT NIGHT--
I DON'T KNOW ABOUT THIS -- WE'RE IN A LOT OF TROUBLE IF WE GET CAUGHT.
QUIET, OR WE WILL GET CAUGHT.

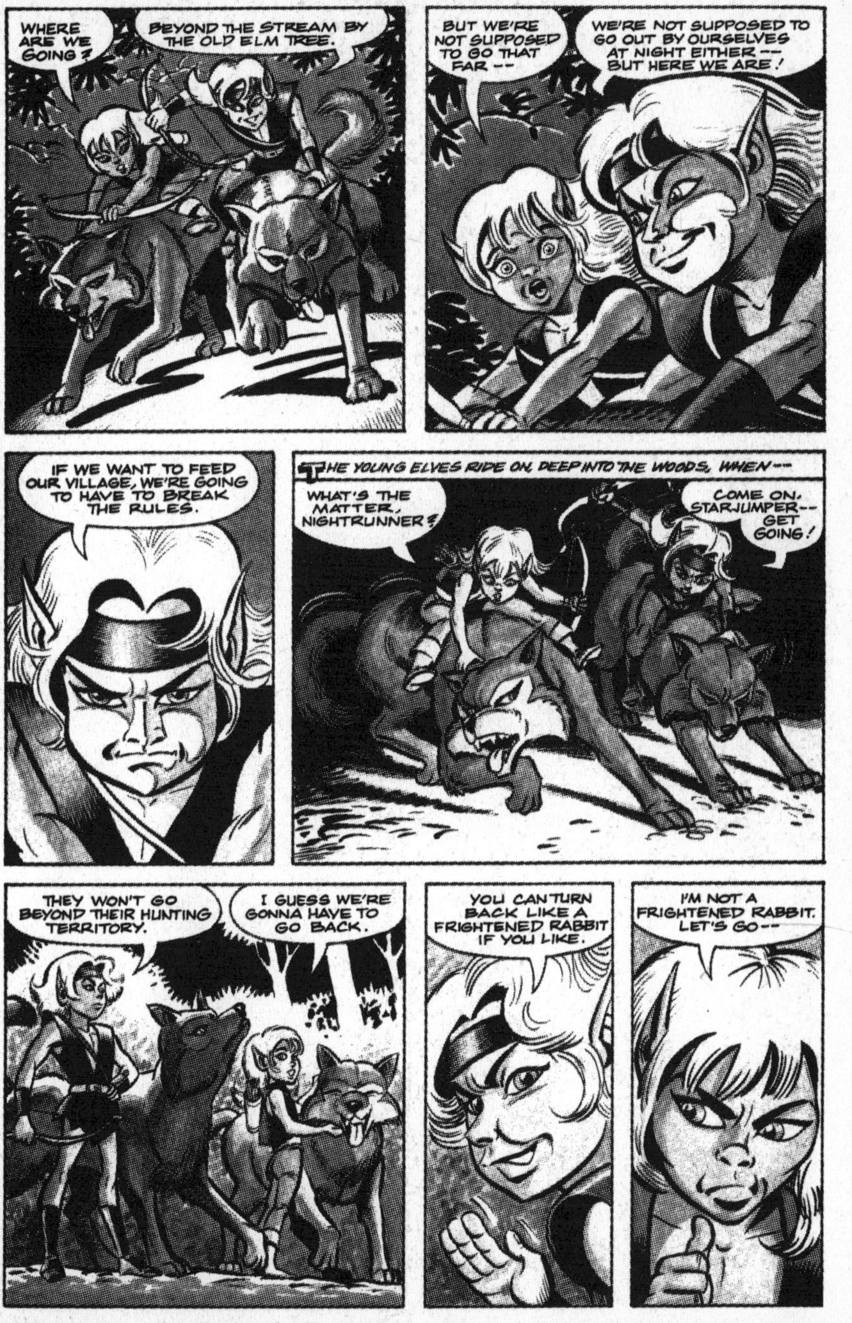
WHERE ARE WE GOING?
BEYOND THE STREAM BY THE OLD ELM TREE.
BUT WE'RE NOT SUPPOSED TO GO THAT FAR --
WE'RE NOT SUPPOSED TO GO OUT BY OURSELVES AT NIGHT EITHER -- BUT HERE WE ARE!
IF WE WANT TO FEED OUR VILLAGE, WE'RE GOING TO HAVE TO BREAK THE RULES.
THE YOUNG ELVES RIDE ON, DEEP INTO THE WOODS, WHEN --
WHAT'S THE MATTER, NIGHTRUNNER?
COME ON, STARJUMPER -- GET GOING!
THEY WON'T GO BEYOND THEIR HUNTING TERRITORY.
I GUESS WE'RE GONNA HAVE TO GO BACK.
YOU CAN TURN BACK LIKE A FRIGHTENED RABBIT IF YOU LIKE.
I'M NOT A FRIGHTENED RABBIT. LET'S GO --

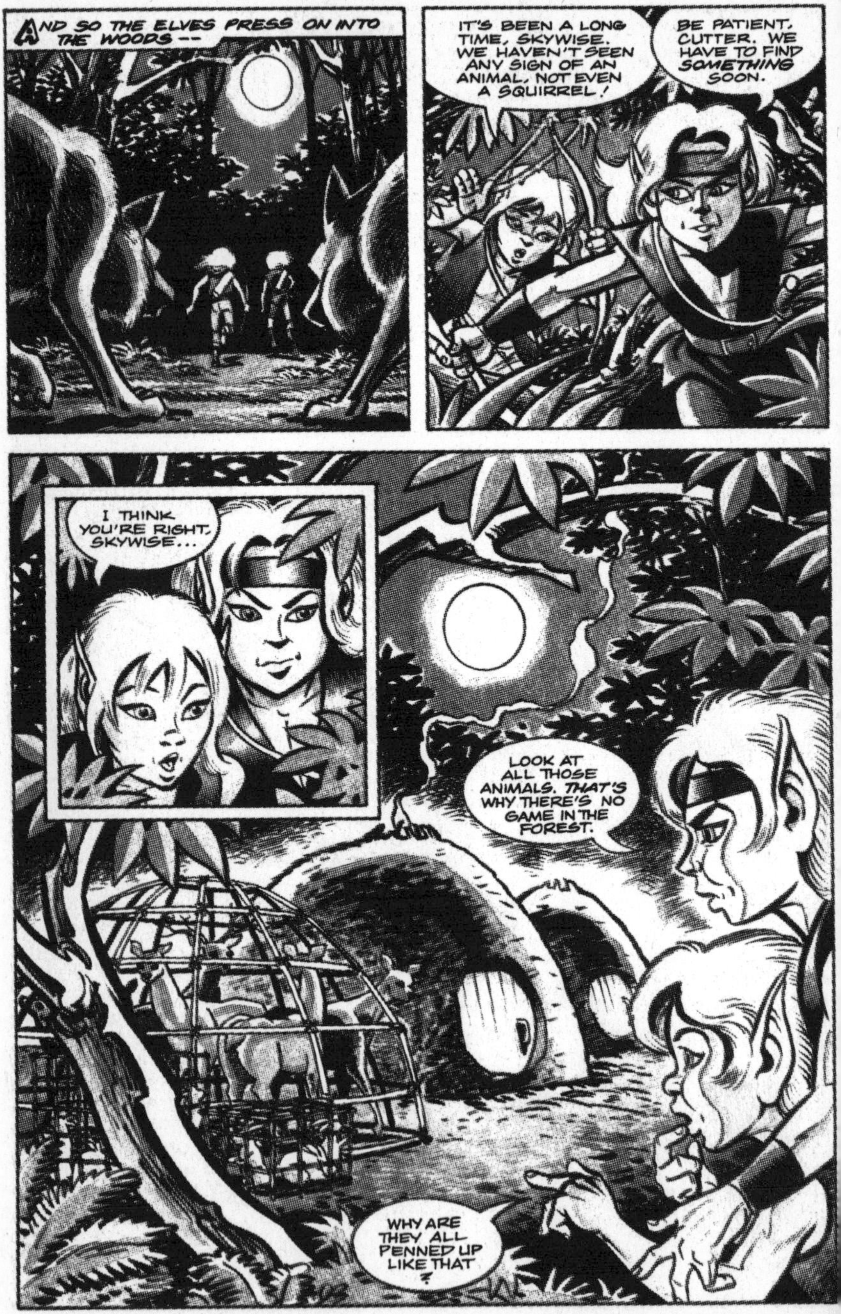
AND SO THE ELVES PRESS ON INTO THE WOODS --
IT'S BEEN A LONG TIME, SKYWISE. WE HAVEN'T SEEN ANY SIGN OF AN ANIMAL, NOT EVEN A SQUIRREL!
BE PATIENT, CUTTER. WE HAVE TO FIND SOMETHING SOON.
I THINK YOU'RE RIGHT, SKYWISE...
LOOK AT ALL THOSE ANIMALS. THAT'S WHY THERE'S NO GAME IN THE FOREST.
WHY ARE THEY ALL PENNED UP LIKE THAT?

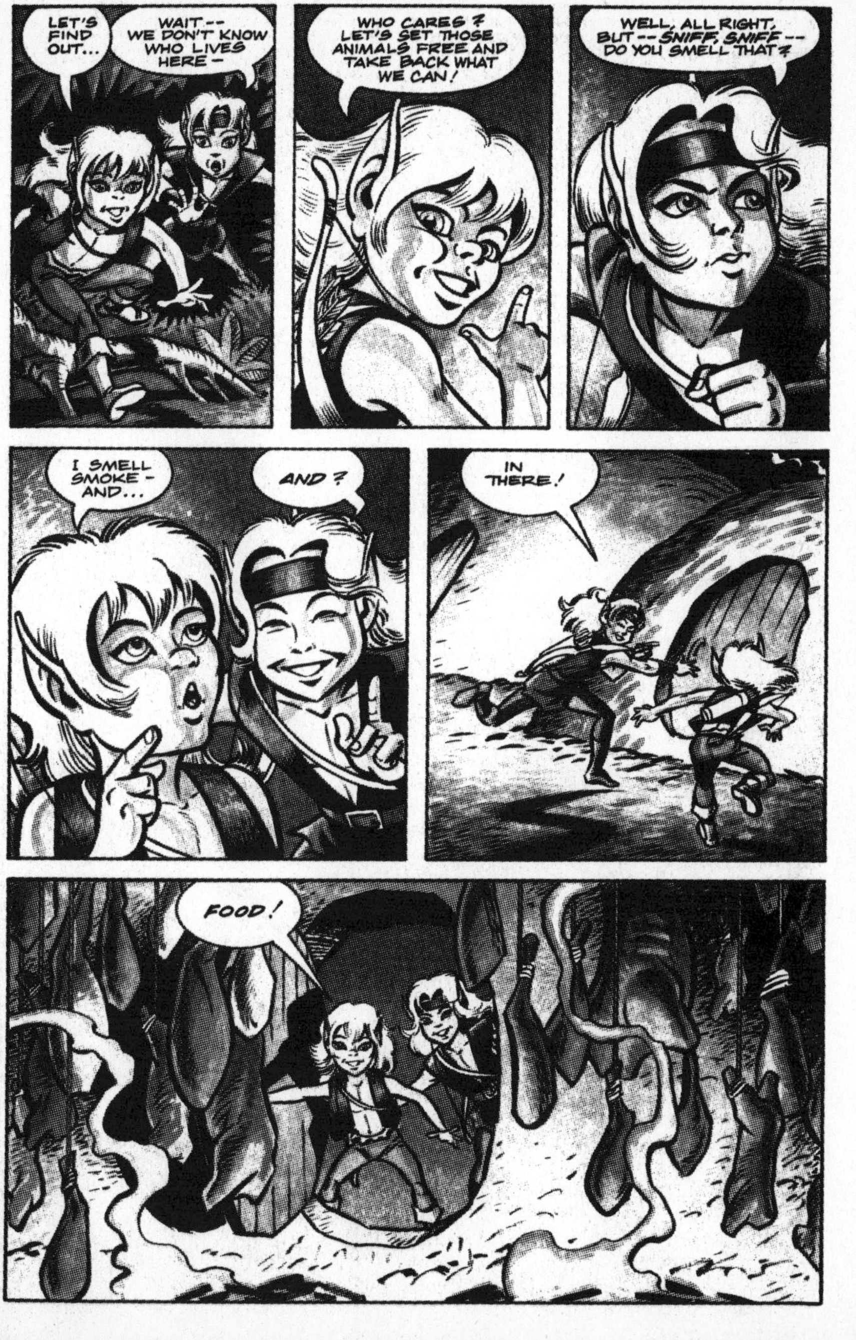
LET'S FIND OUT...
WAIT-- WE DON'T KNOW WHO LIVES HERE–
WHO CARES? LET'S SET THOSE ANIMALS FREE AND TAKE BACK WHAT WE CAN!
WELL, ALL RIGHT, BUT --SNIFF, SNIFF-- DO YOU SMELL THAT?
I SMELL SMOKE– AND...
AND?
IN THERE!
FOOD!

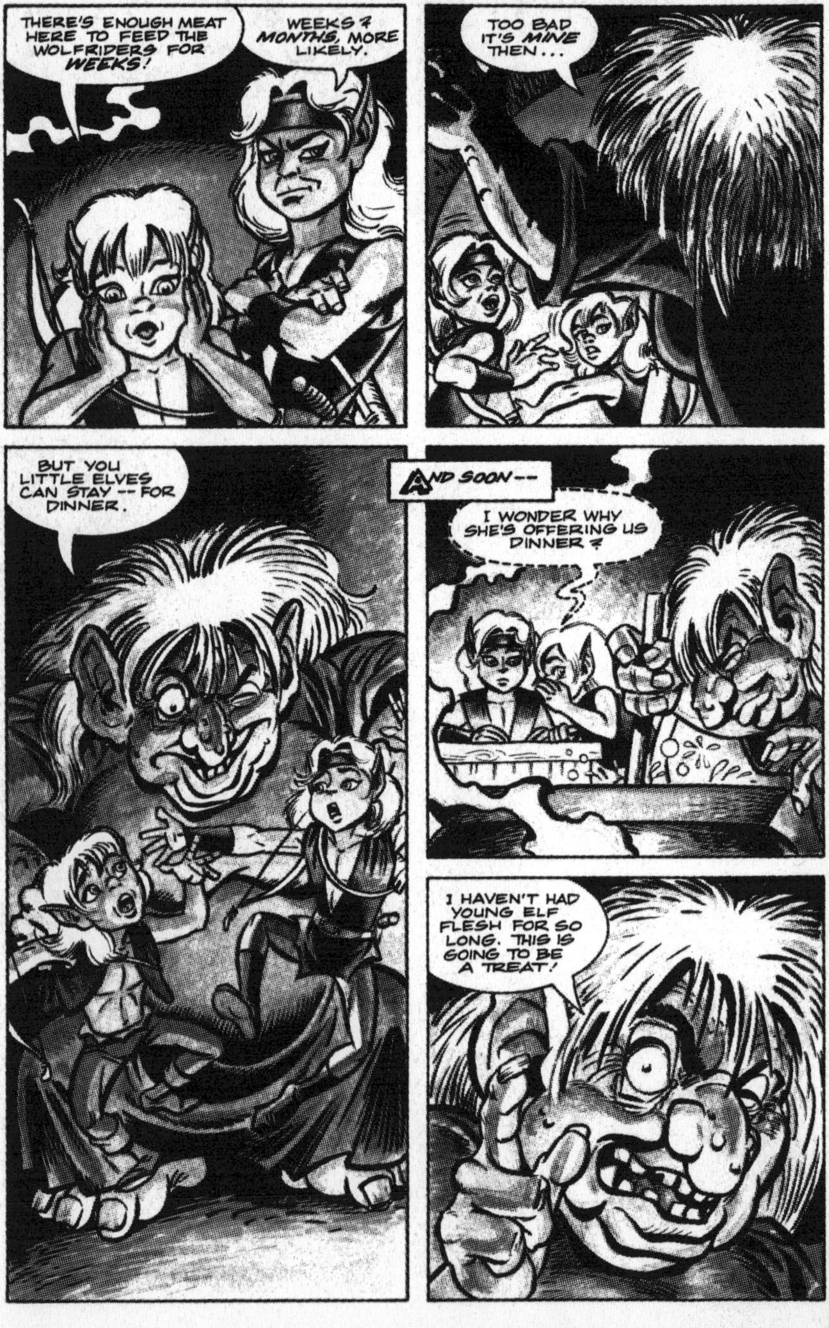

THERE'S ENOUGH MEAT HERE TO FEED THE WOLFRIDERS FOR WEEKS!
WEEKS? MONTHS, MORE LIKELY.
TOO BAD IT'S MINE THEN...
BUT YOU LITTLE ELVES CAN STAY -- FOR DINNER.
AND SOON --
I WONDER WHY SHE'S OFFERING US DINNER?
I HAVEN'T HAD YOUNG ELF FLESH FOR SO LONG. THIS IS GOING TO BE A TREAT!

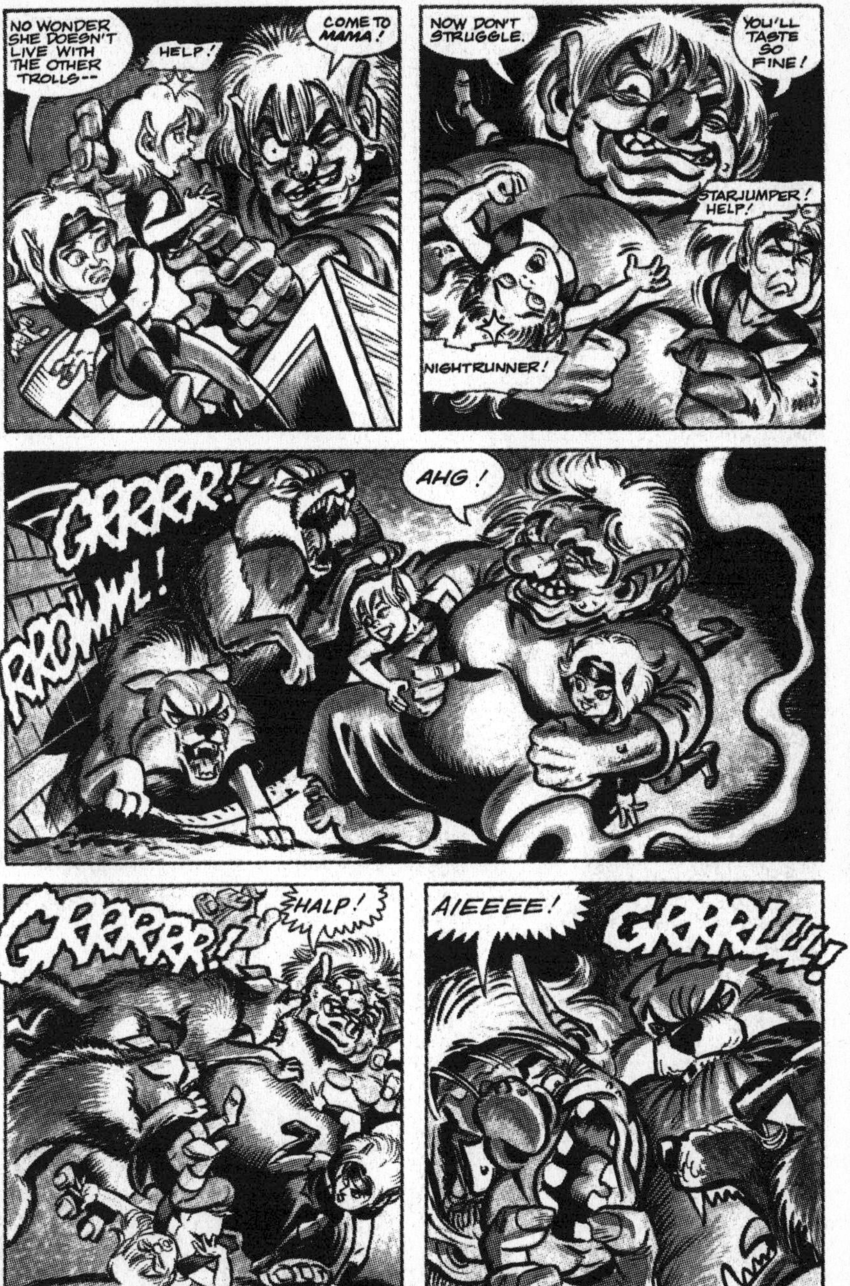
NO WONDER SHE DOESN'T LIVE WITH THE OTHER TROLLS--
HELP!
COME TO MAMA!
NOW DON'T STRUGGLE.
YOU'LL TASTE SO FINE!
STARJUMPER! HELP!
NIGHTRUNNER!
GRRRRR!
RROWWWL!
AHG!
GRRRRRR!
HALP!
AIEEEEE!
GRRRLL!!

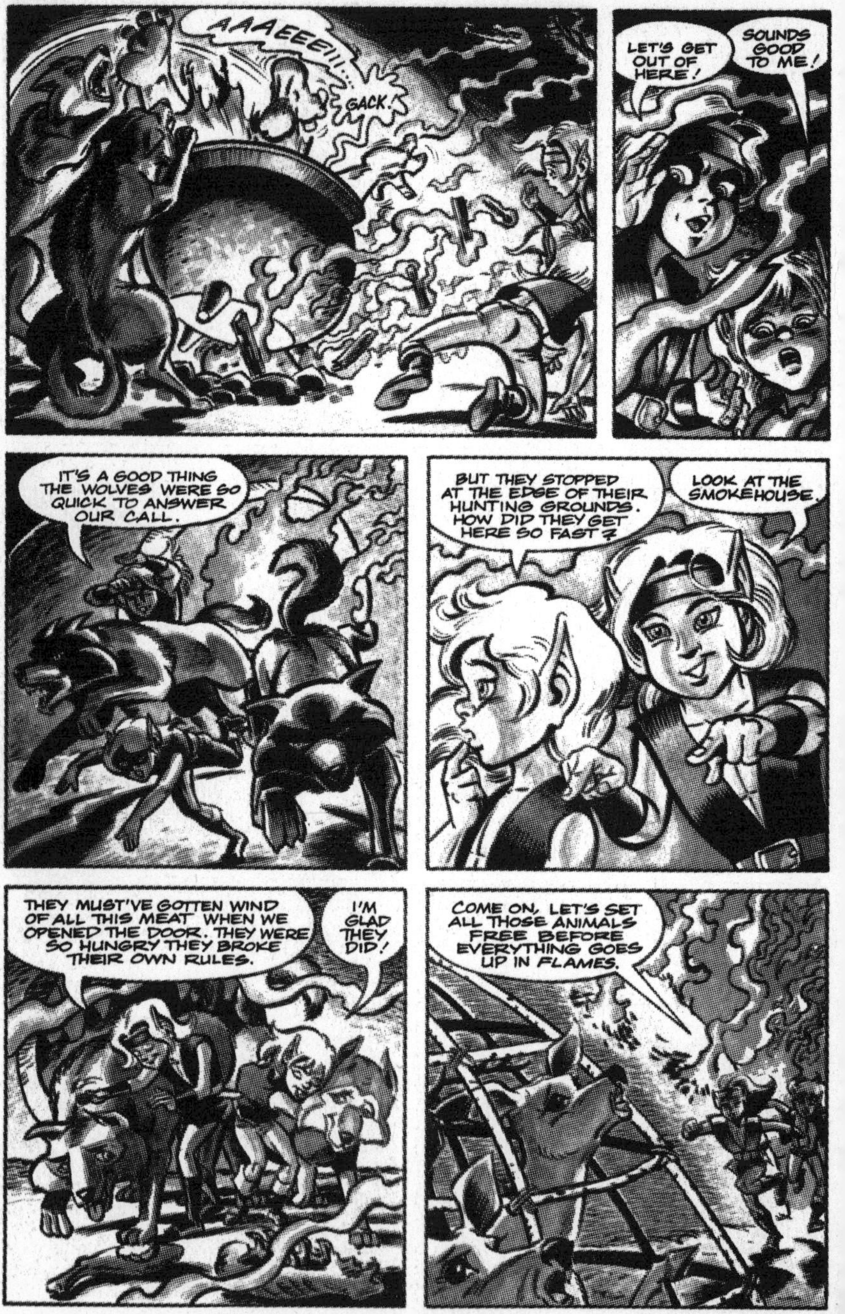
AAAAEEE!!!
GACK!
LET'S GET OUT OF HERE!
SOUNDS GOOD TO ME!
IT'S A GOOD THING THE WOLVES WERE SO QUICK TO ANSWER OUR CALL.
BUT THEY STOPPED AT THE EDGE OF THEIR HUNTING GROUNDS. HOW DID THEY GET HERE SO FAST?
LOOK AT THE SMOKEHOUSE.
THEY MUST'VE GOTTEN WIND OF ALL THIS MEAT WHEN WE OPENED THE DOOR. THEY WERE SO HUNGRY THEY BROKE THEIR OWN RULES.
I'M GLAD THEY DID!
COME ON, LET'S SET ALL THOSE ANIMALS FREE BEFORE EVERYTHING GOES UP IN FLAMES.

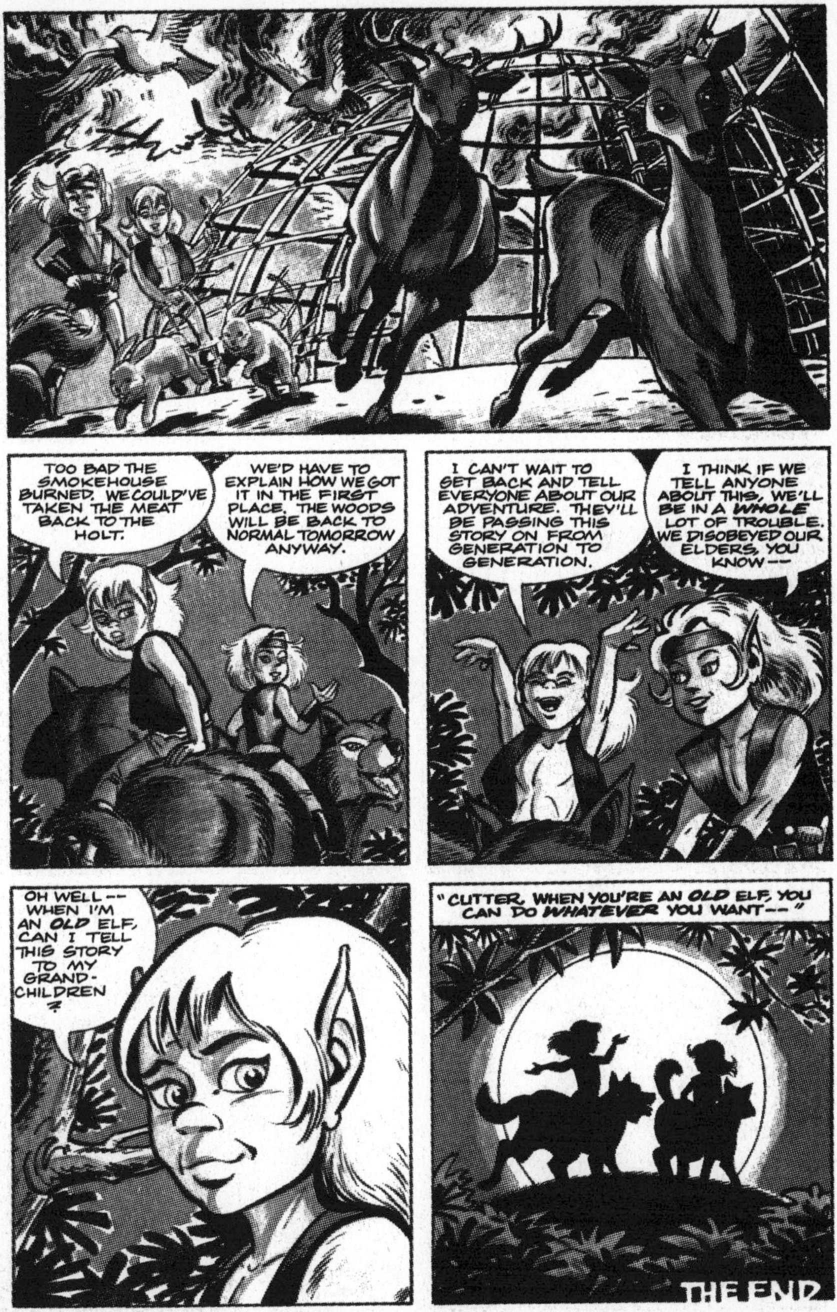
TOO BAD THE SMOKEHOUSE BURNED. WE COULD'VE TAKEN THE MEAT BACK TO THE HOLT.
WE'D HAVE TO EXPLAIN HOW WE GOT IT IN THE FIRST PLACE. THE WOODS WILL BE BACK TO NORMAL TOMORROW ANYWAY.
I CAN'T WAIT TO GET BACK AND TELL EVERYONE ABOUT OUR ADVENTURE. THEY'LL BE PASSING THIS STORY ON FROM GENERATION TO GENERATION.
I THINK IF WE TELL ANYONE ABOUT THIS, WE'LL BE IN A *WHOLE* LOT OF TROUBLE. WE DISOBEYED OUR ELDERS, YOU KNOW--
OH WELL-- WHEN I'M AN *OLD* ELF, CAN I TELL THIS STORY TO MY GRAND-CHILDREN?
"CUTTER, WHEN YOU'RE AN *OLD* ELF, YOU CAN DO *WHATEVER* YOU WANT--"
THE END

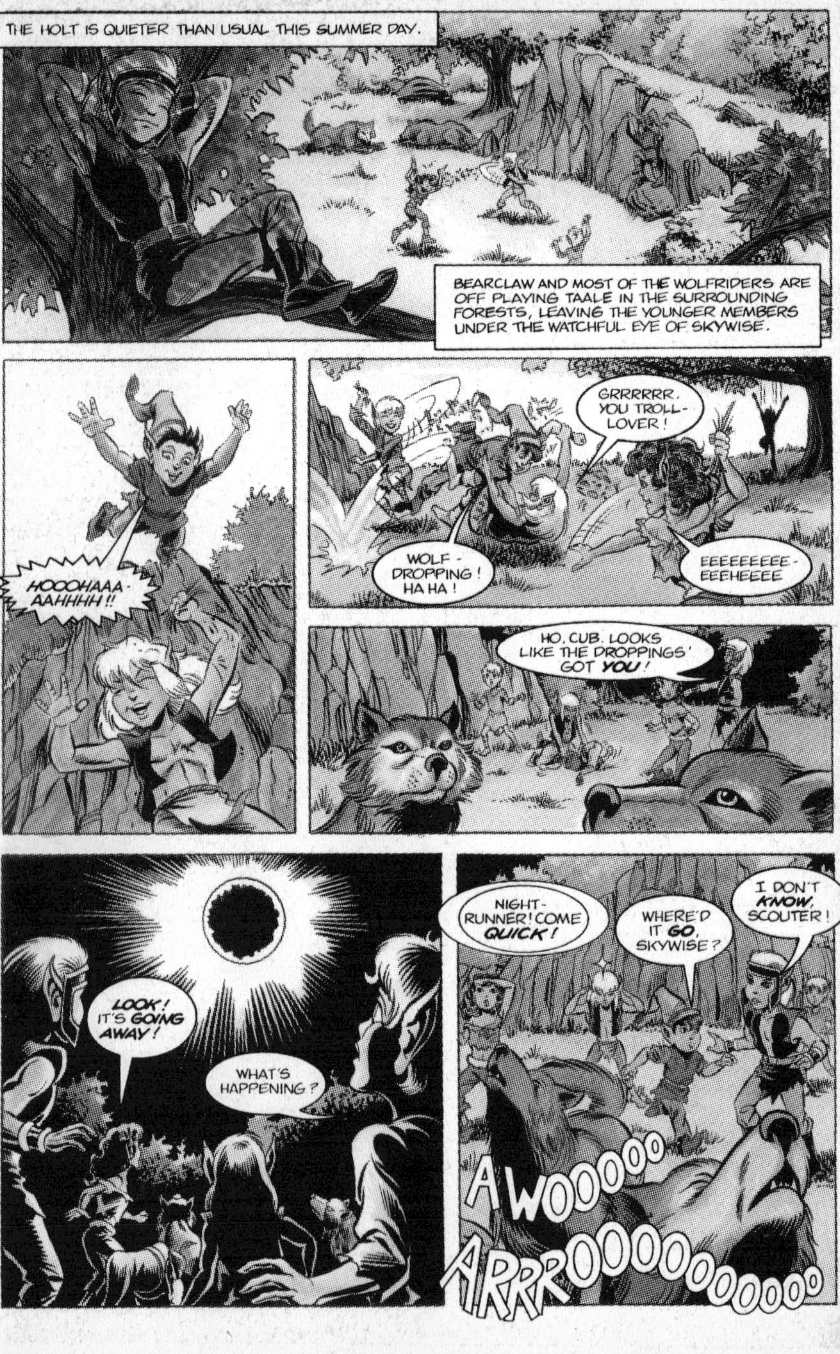
THE HOLT IS QUIETER THAN USUAL THIS SUMMER DAY.
BEARCLAW AND MOST OF THE WOLFRIDERS ARE OFF PLAYING TAALE IN THE SURROUNDING FORESTS, LEAVING THE YOUNGER MEMBERS UNDER THE WATCHFUL EYE OF SKYWISE.
HOOOHAAA-AAHHHH!!
GRRRRRR. YOU TROLL-LOVER!
WOLF-DROPPING! HA HA!
EEEEEEEEE-EEEHEEEE
HO, CUB. LOOKS LIKE THE DROPPINGS' GOT YOU!
LOOK! IT'S GOING AWAY!
WHAT'S HAPPENING?
NIGHT-RUNNER! COME QUICK!
WHERE'D IT GO, SKYWISE?
I DON'T KNOW, SCOUTER!
AWOOOOO
ARRROOOOOOOOOOO

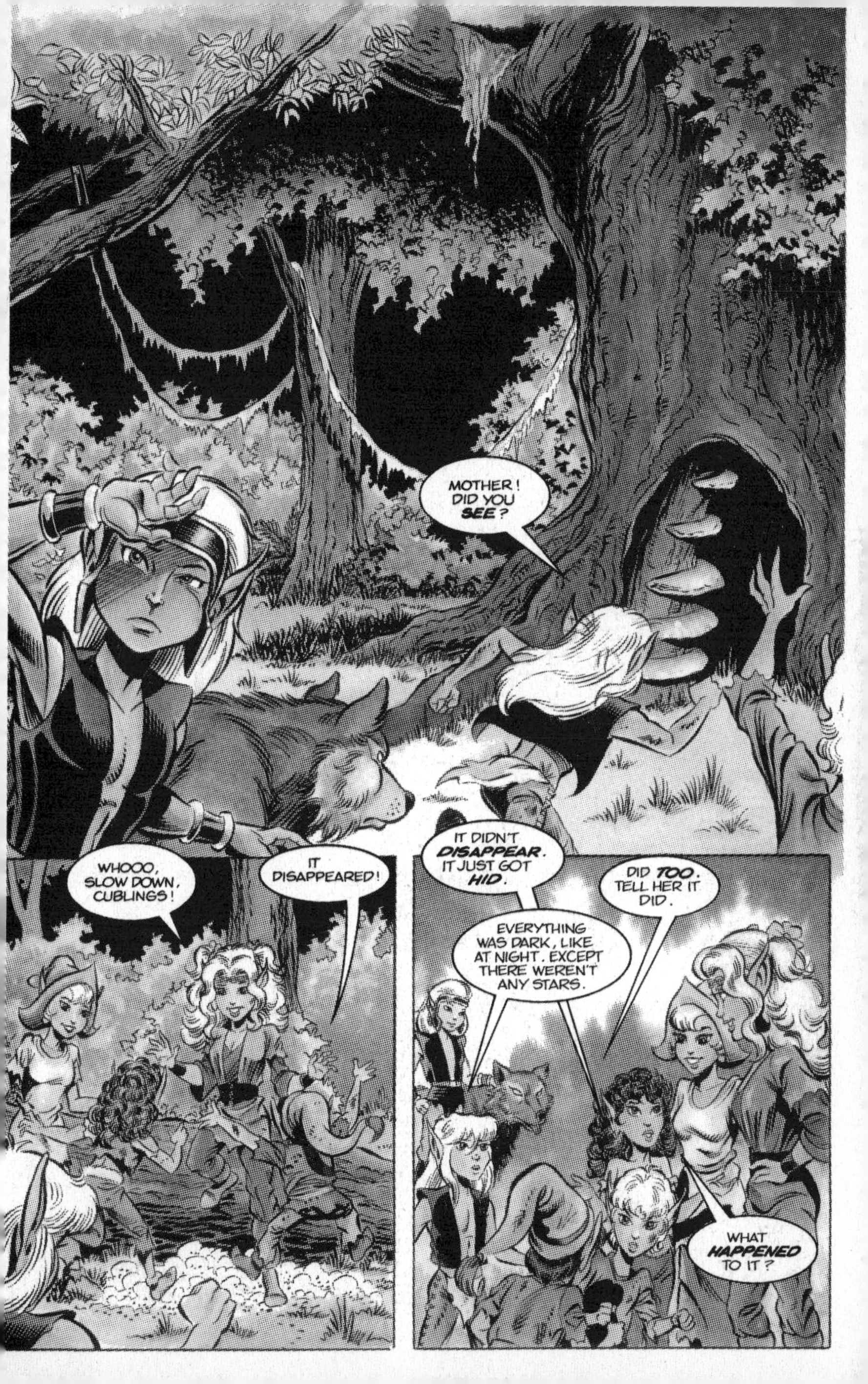
MOTHER! DID YOU SEE?
WHOOO, SLOW DOWN, CUBLINGS!
IT DISAPPEARED!
IT DIDN'T DISAPPEAR. IT JUST GOT HID.
DID TOO. TELL HER IT DID.
EVERYTHING WAS DARK, LIKE AT NIGHT. EXCEPT THERE WEREN'T ANY STARS.
WHAT HAPPENED TO IT?

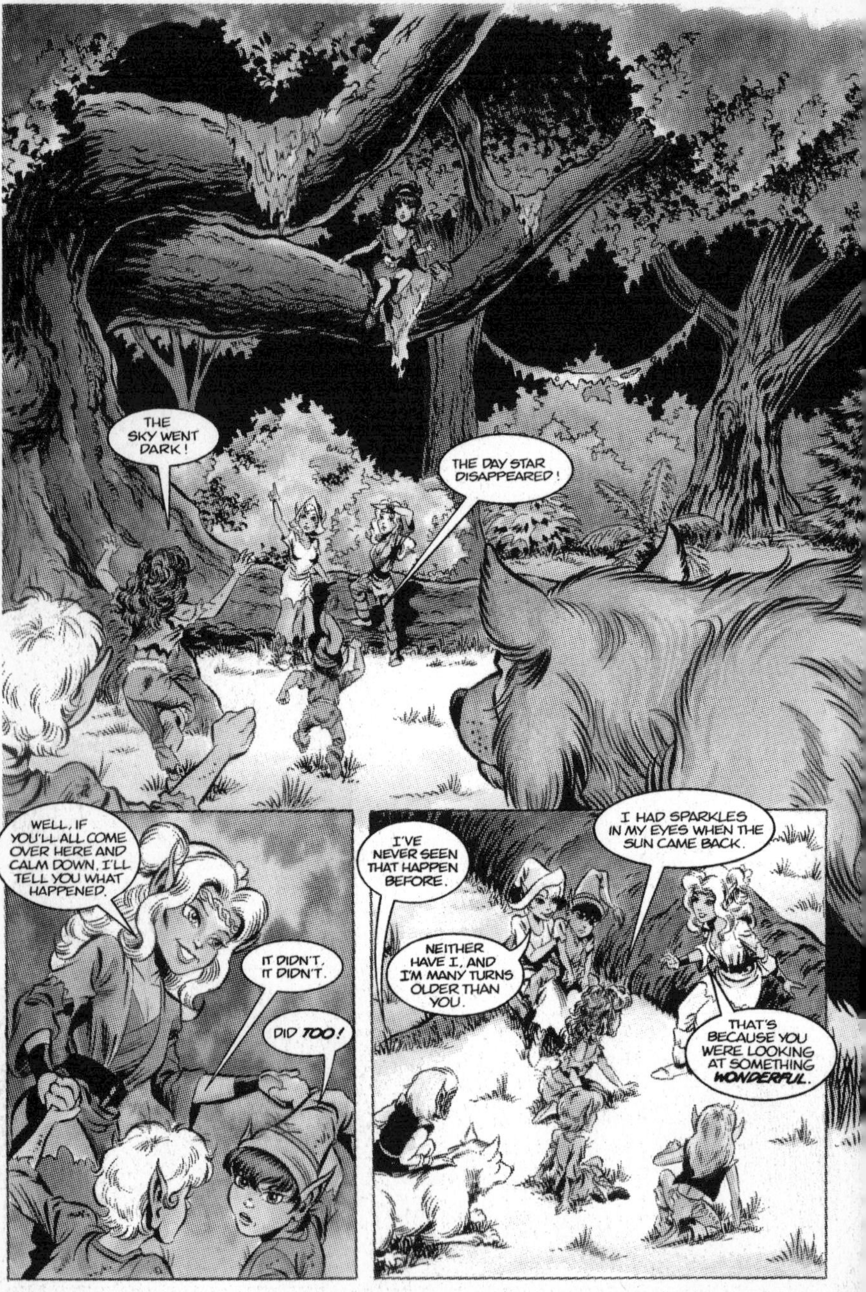
THE SKY WENT DARK!
THE DAY STAR DISAPPEARED!
WELL, IF YOU'LL ALL COME OVER HERE AND CALM DOWN, I'LL TELL YOU WHAT HAPPENED.
IT DIDN'T, IT DIDN'T.
DID **TOO**!
I'VE NEVER SEEN THAT HAPPEN BEFORE.
NEITHER HAVE I, AND I'M MANY TURNS OLDER THAN YOU.
I HAD SPARKLES IN MY EYES WHEN THE SUN CAME BACK.
THAT'S BECAUSE YOU WERE LOOKING AT SOMETHING **WONDERFUL**.

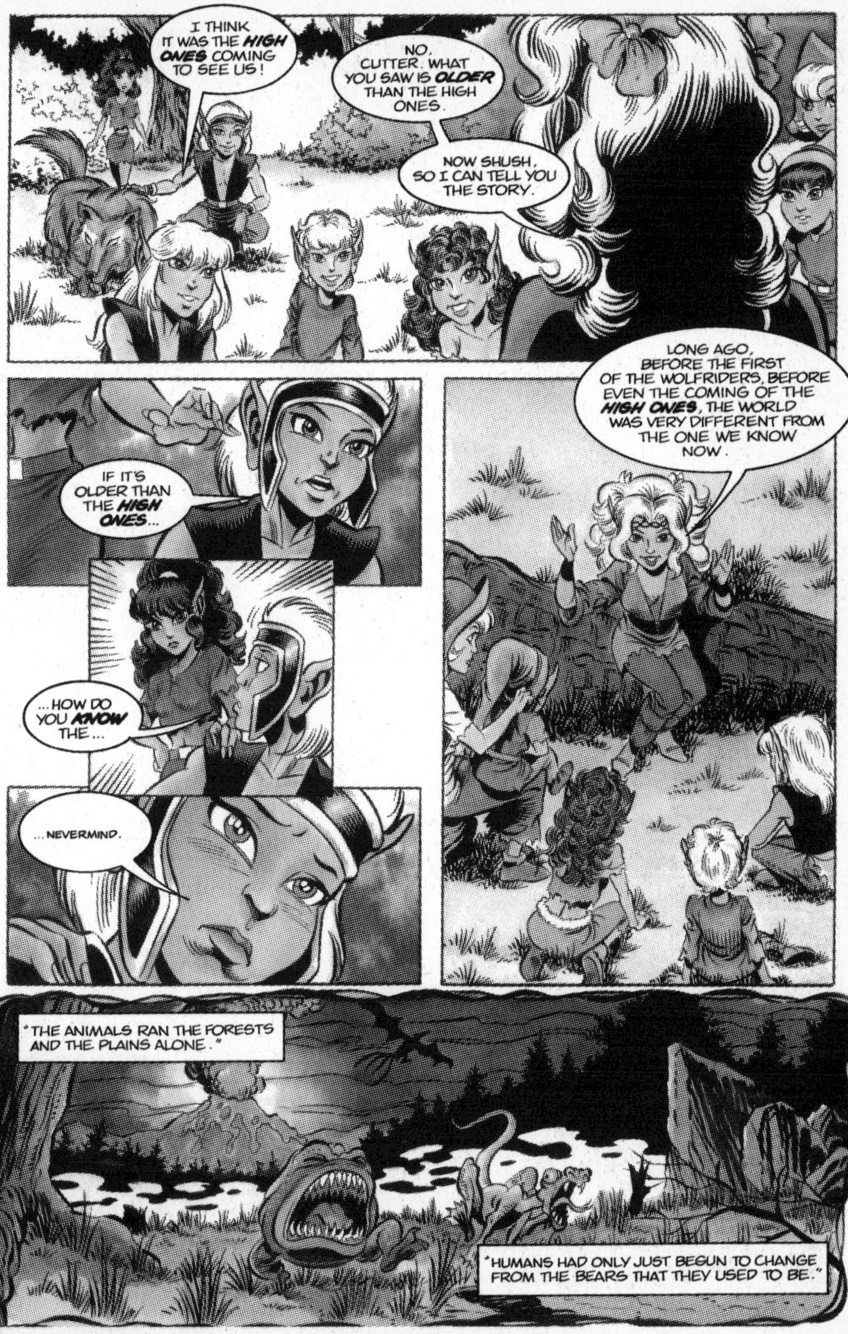
I THINK IT WAS THE HIGH ONES COMING TO SEE US!
NO, CUTTER. WHAT YOU SAW IS OLDER THAN THE HIGH ONES.
NOW SHUSH, SO I CAN TELL YOU THE STORY.
IF IT'S OLDER THAN THE HIGH ONES...
...HOW DO YOU KNOW THE...
...NEVERMIND.
LONG AGO, BEFORE THE FIRST OF THE WOLFRIDERS, BEFORE EVEN THE COMING OF THE HIGH ONES, THE WORLD WAS VERY DIFFERENT FROM THE ONE WE KNOW NOW.
"THE ANIMALS RAN THE FORESTS AND THE PLAINS ALONE."
"HUMANS HAD ONLY JUST BEGUN TO CHANGE FROM THE BEARS THAT THEY USED TO BE."

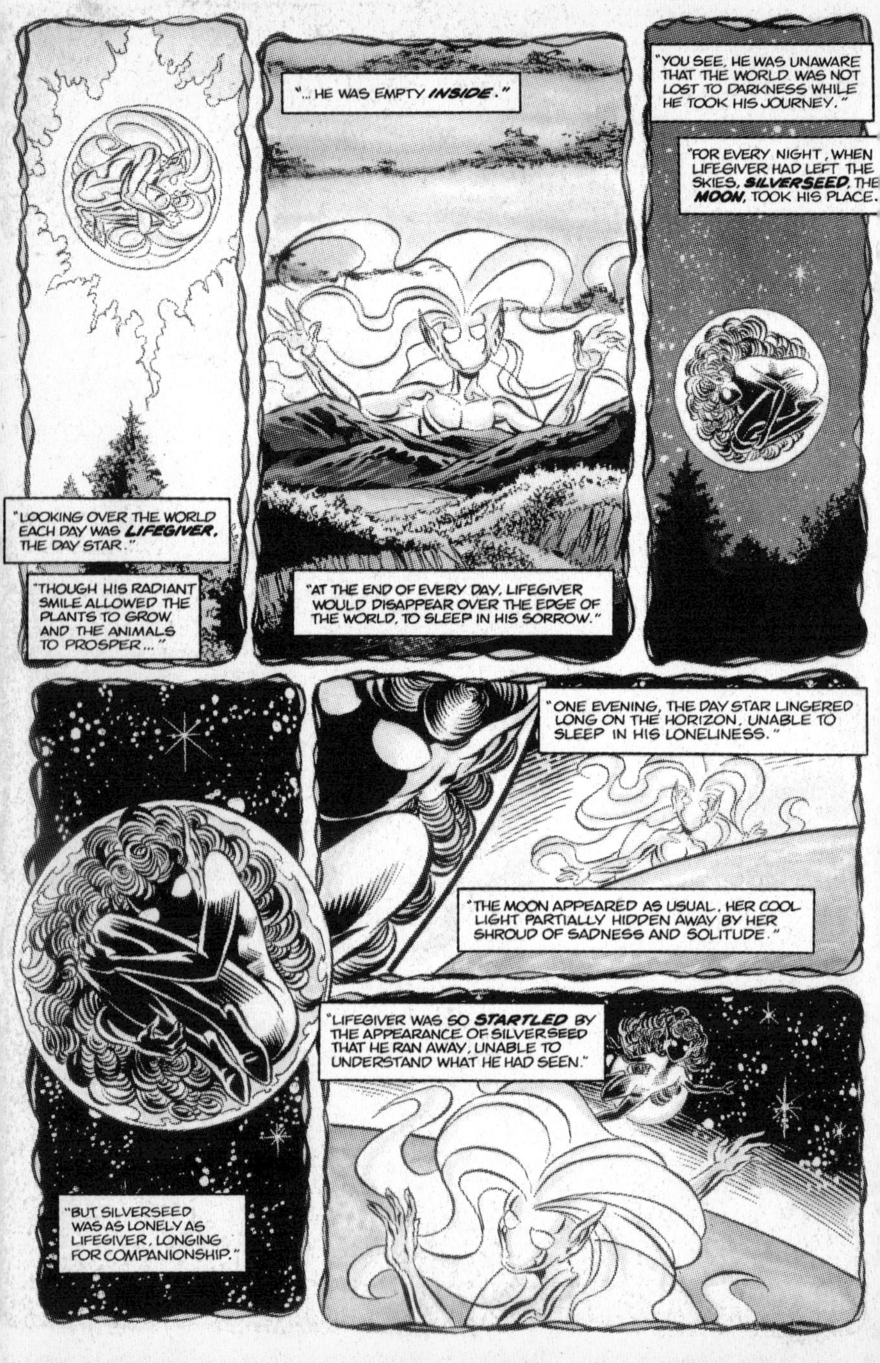
"LOOKING OVER THE WORLD EACH DAY WAS **LIFEGIVER**, THE DAY STAR."
"THOUGH HIS RADIANT SMILE ALLOWED THE PLANTS TO GROW AND THE ANIMALS TO PROSPER..."
"...HE WAS EMPTY **INSIDE**."
"AT THE END OF EVERY DAY, LIFEGIVER WOULD DISAPPEAR OVER THE EDGE OF THE WORLD, TO SLEEP IN HIS SORROW."
"YOU SEE, HE WAS UNAWARE THAT THE WORLD WAS NOT LOST TO DARKNESS WHILE HE TOOK HIS JOURNEY."
"FOR EVERY NIGHT, WHEN LIFEGIVER HAD LEFT THE SKIES, **SILVERSEED**, THE **MOON**, TOOK HIS PLACE.
"ONE EVENING, THE DAY STAR LINGERED LONG ON THE HORIZON, UNABLE TO SLEEP IN HIS LONELINESS."
"THE MOON APPEARED AS USUAL, HER COOL LIGHT PARTIALLY HIDDEN AWAY BY HER SHROUD OF SADNESS AND SOLITUDE."
"BUT SILVERSEED WAS AS LONELY AS LIFEGIVER, LONGING FOR COMPANIONSHIP."
"LIFEGIVER WAS SO **STARTLED** BY THE APPEARANCE OF SILVERSEED THAT HE RAN AWAY, UNABLE TO UNDERSTAND WHAT HE HAD SEEN."

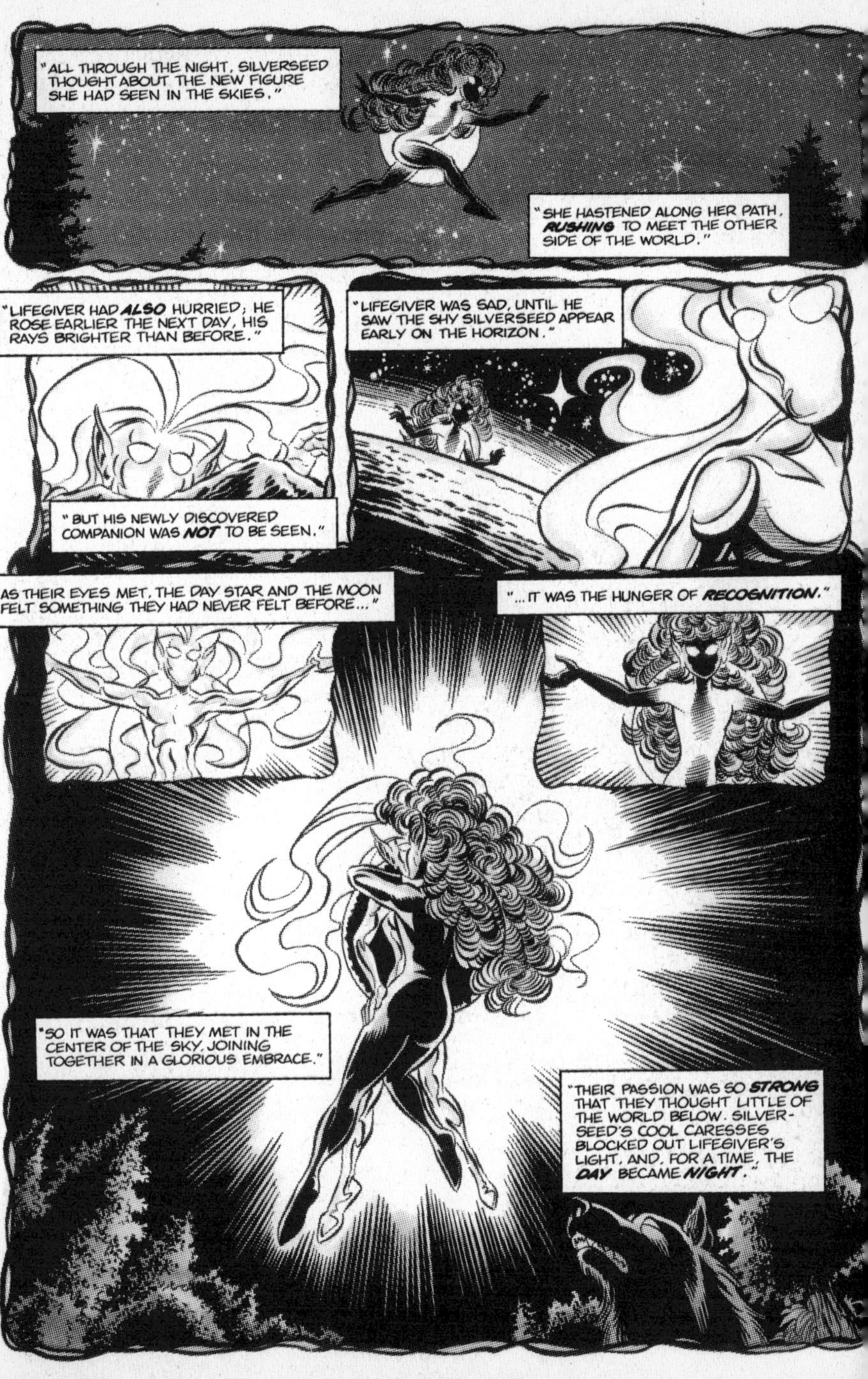
"ALL THROUGH THE NIGHT, SILVERSEED THOUGHT ABOUT THE NEW FIGURE SHE HAD SEEN IN THE SKIES."
"SHE HASTENED ALONG HER PATH, RUSHING TO MEET THE OTHER SIDE OF THE WORLD."
"LIFEGIVER HAD ALSO HURRIED; HE ROSE EARLIER THE NEXT DAY, HIS RAYS BRIGHTER THAN BEFORE."
"BUT HIS NEWLY DISCOVERED COMPANION WAS NOT TO BE SEEN."
"LIFEGIVER WAS SAD, UNTIL HE SAW THE SHY SILVERSEED APPEAR EARLY ON THE HORIZON."
"AS THEIR EYES MET, THE DAY STAR AND THE MOON FELT SOMETHING THEY HAD NEVER FELT BEFORE..."
"...IT WAS THE HUNGER OF RECOGNITION."
"SO IT WAS THAT THEY MET IN THE CENTER OF THE SKY, JOINING TOGETHER IN A GLORIOUS EMBRACE."
"THEIR PASSION WAS SO STRONG THAT THEY THOUGHT LITTLE OF THE WORLD BELOW. SILVER-SEED'S COOL CARESSES BLOCKED OUT LIFEGIVER'S LIGHT, AND, FOR A TIME, THE DAY BECAME NIGHT."

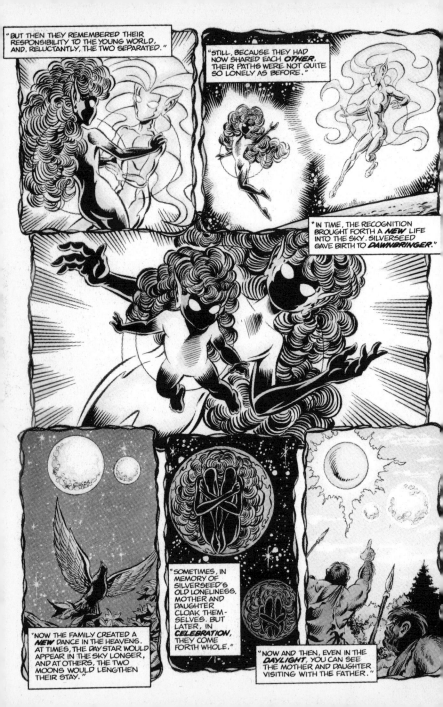

"BUT THEN THEY REMEMBERED THEIR RESPONSIBILITY TO THE YOUNG WORLD, AND, RELUCTANTLY, THE TWO SEPARATED."

"STILL, BECAUSE THEY HAD NOW SHARED EACH *OTHER*, THEIR PATHS WERE NOT QUITE SO LONELY AS BEFORE."

"IN TIME, THE RECOGNITION BROUGHT FORTH A *NEW* LIFE INTO THE SKY. SILVERSEED GAVE BIRTH TO *DAWNBRINGER*."

"NOW THE FAMILY CREATED A *NEW* DANCE IN THE HEAVENS. AT TIMES, THE *DAY STAR* WOULD APPEAR IN THE SKY LONGER, AND AT OTHERS, THE TWO MOONS WOULD LENGTHEN THEIR STAY."

"SOMETIMES, IN MEMORY OF SILVERSEED'S OLD LONELINESS, MOTHER AND DAUGHTER CLOAK THEM- SELVES. BUT LATER, IN *CELEBRATION*, THEY COME FORTH WHOLE."

"NOW AND THEN, EVEN IN THE *DAYLIGHT*, YOU CAN SEE THE MOTHER AND DAUGHTER VISITING WITH THE FATHER."

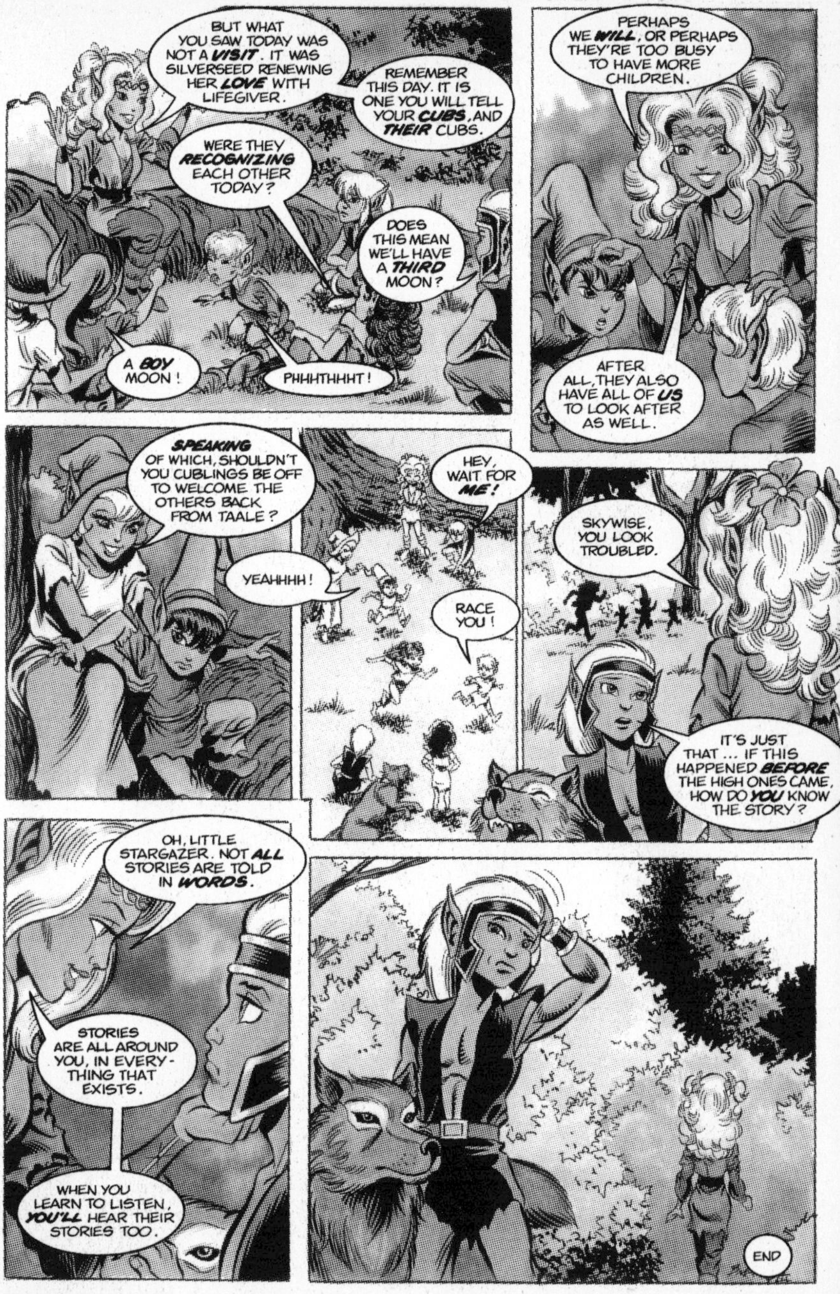
BUT WHAT YOU SAW TODAY WAS NOT A VISIT. IT WAS SILVERSEED RENEWING HER LOVE WITH LIFEGIVER.
REMEMBER THIS DAY. IT IS ONE YOU WILL TELL YOUR CUBS, AND THEIR CUBS.
WERE THEY RECOGNIZING EACH OTHER TODAY?
DOES THIS MEAN WE'LL HAVE A THIRD MOON?
A BOY MOON!
PHHHTHHHT!
PERHAPS WE WILL, OR PERHAPS THEY'RE TOO BUSY TO HAVE MORE CHILDREN.
AFTER ALL, THEY ALSO HAVE ALL OF US TO LOOK AFTER AS WELL.
SPEAKING OF WHICH, SHOULDN'T YOU CUBLINGS BE OFF TO WELCOME THE OTHERS BACK FROM TAALE?
YEAHHHH!
HEY, WAIT FOR ME!
RACE YOU!
SKYWISE, YOU LOOK TROUBLED.
IT'S JUST THAT ... IF THIS HAPPENED BEFORE THE HIGH ONES CAME, HOW DO YOU KNOW THE STORY?
OH, LITTLE STARGAZER. NOT ALL STORIES ARE TOLD IN WORDS.
STORIES ARE ALL AROUND YOU, IN EVERY-THING THAT EXISTS.
WHEN YOU LEARN TO LISTEN, YOU'LL HEAR THEIR STORIES TOO.
END

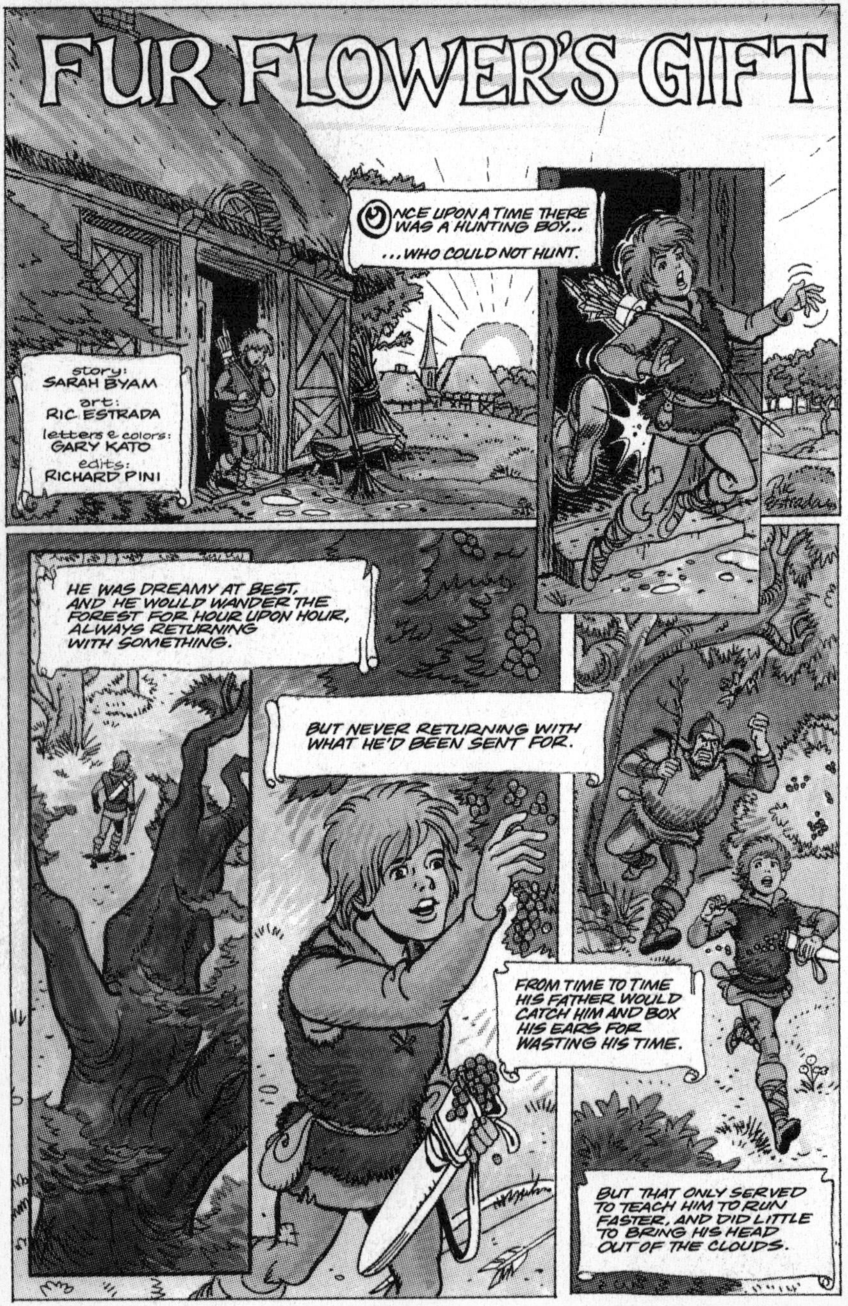
FUR FLOWER'S GIFT
ONCE UPON A TIME THERE WAS A HUNTING BOY...
...WHO COULD NOT HUNT.
story: SARAH BYAM
art: RIC ESTRADA
letters & colors: GARY KATO
edits: RICHARD PINI
HE WAS DREAMY AT BEST, AND HE WOULD WANDER THE FOREST FOR HOUR UPON HOUR, ALWAYS RETURNING WITH SOMETHING.
BUT NEVER RETURNING WITH WHAT HE'D BEEN SENT FOR.
FROM TIME TO TIME HIS FATHER WOULD CATCH HIM AND BOX HIS EARS FOR WASTING HIS TIME.
BUT THAT ONLY SERVED TO TEACH HIM TO RUN FASTER, AND DID LITTLE TO BRING HIS HEAD OUT OF THE CLOUDS.

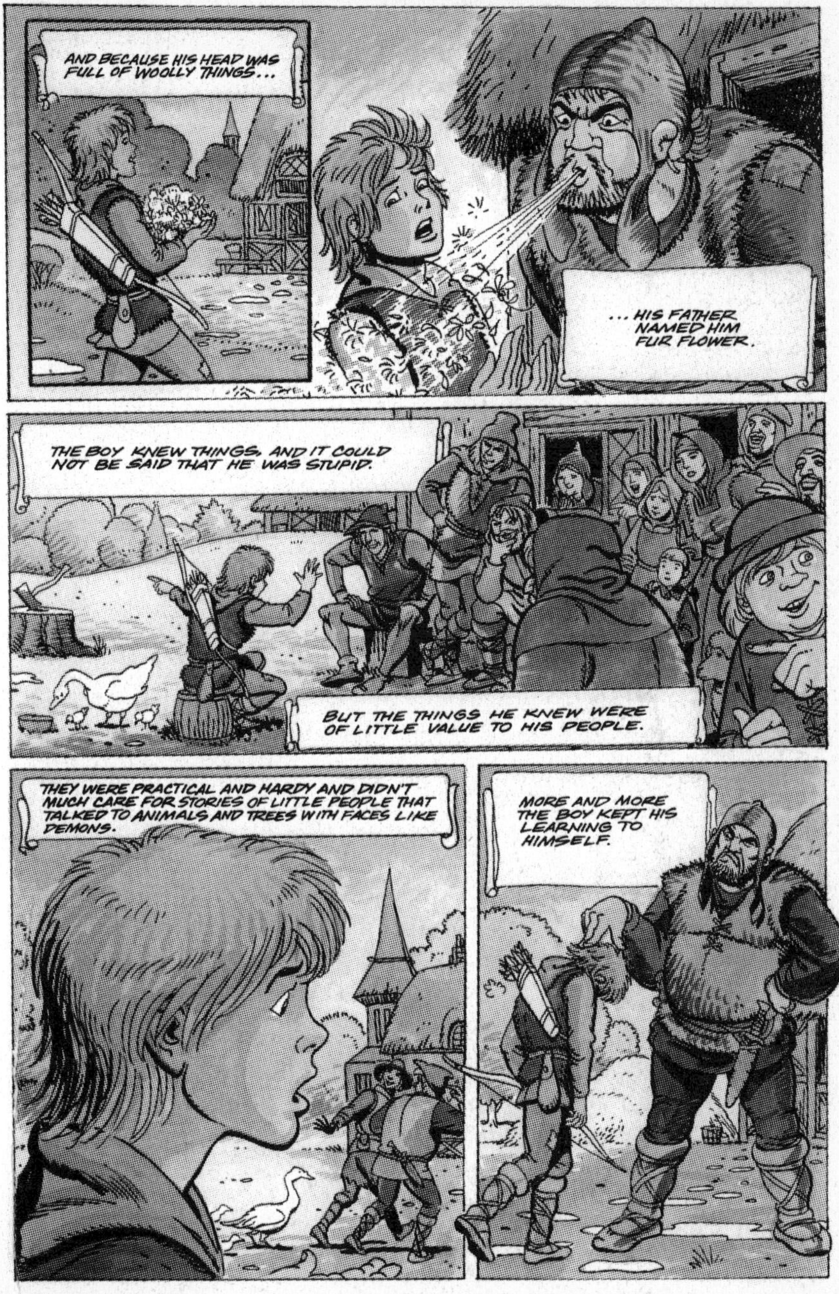
AND BECAUSE HIS HEAD WAS FULL OF WOOLLY THINGS...
...HIS FATHER NAMED HIM FUR FLOWER.
THE BOY KNEW THINGS, AND IT COULD NOT BE SAID THAT HE WAS STUPID.
BUT THE THINGS HE KNEW WERE OF LITTLE VALUE TO HIS PEOPLE.
THEY WERE PRACTICAL AND HARDY AND DIDN'T MUCH CARE FOR STORIES OF LITTLE PEOPLE THAT TALKED TO ANIMALS AND TREES WITH FACES LIKE DEMONS.
MORE AND MORE THE BOY KEPT HIS LEARNING TO HIMSELF.

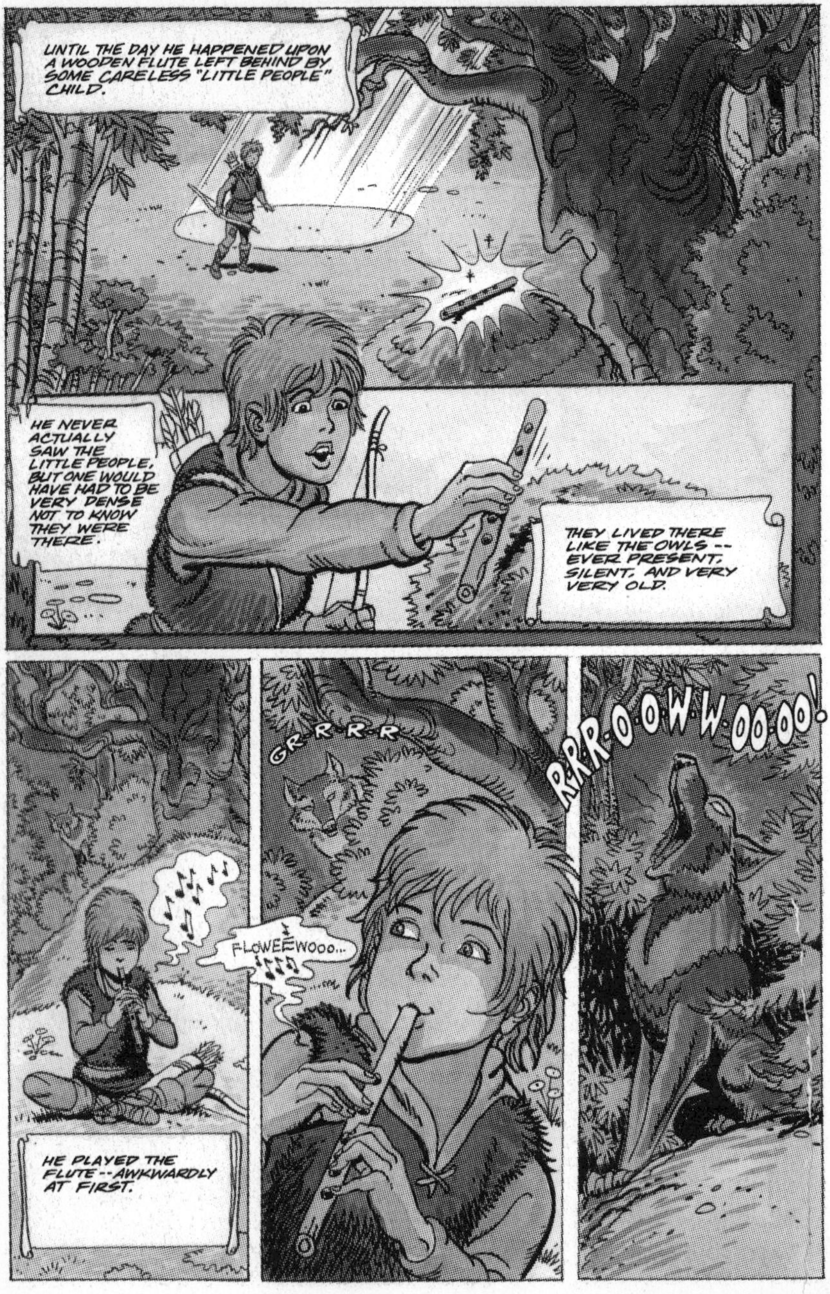
UNTIL THE DAY HE HAPPENED UPON A WOODEN FLUTE LEFT BEHIND BY SOME CARELESS "LITTLE PEOPLE" CHILD.
HE NEVER ACTUALLY SAW THE LITTLE PEOPLE, BUT ONE WOULD HAVE HAD TO BE VERY DENSE NOT TO KNOW THEY WERE THERE.
THEY LIVED THERE LIKE THE OWLS -- EVER PRESENT, SILENT, AND VERY VERY OLD.
HE PLAYED THE FLUTE -- AWKWARDLY AT FIRST.
FLOWEEWOOO...
GR-R-R-R
RRR-O-O-W-W-OO-OO!

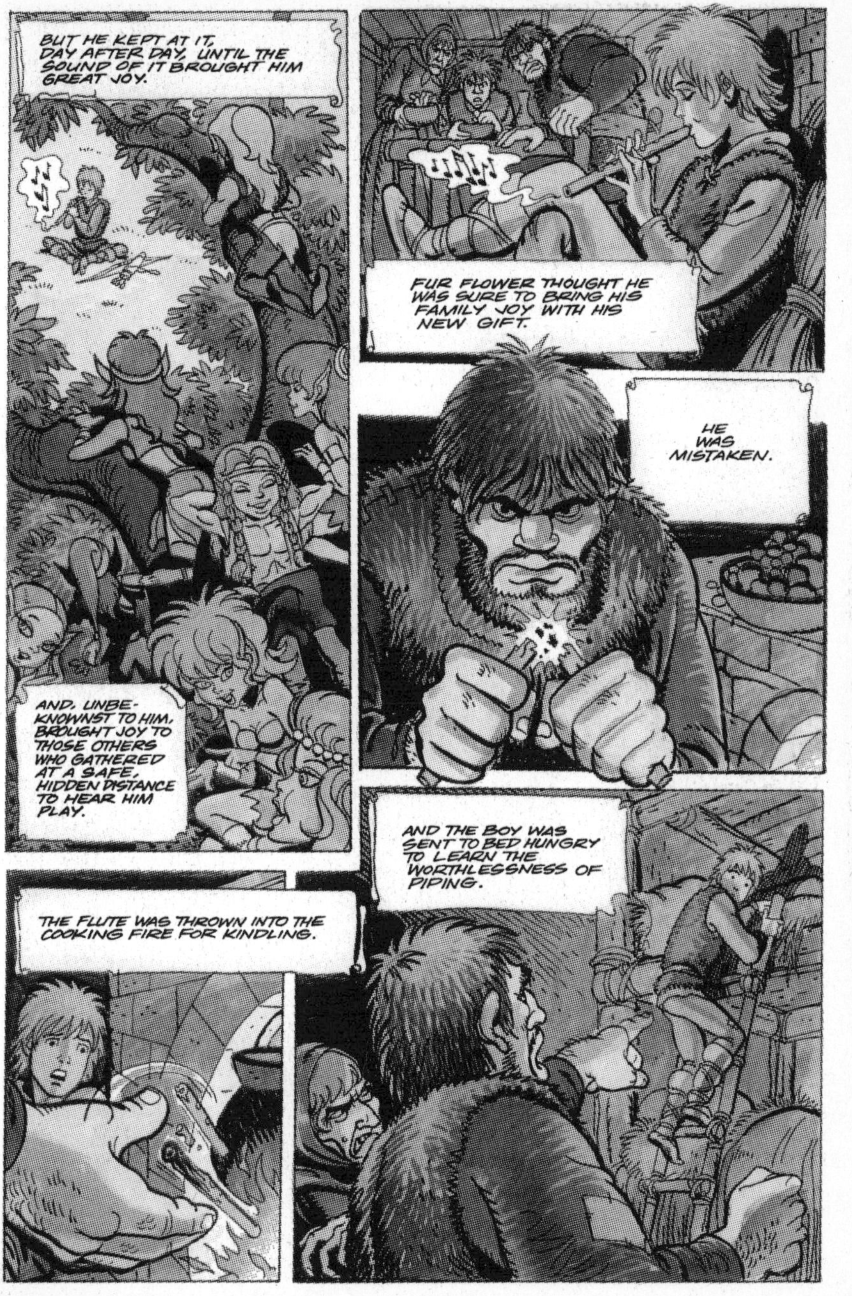
BUT HE KEPT AT IT, DAY AFTER DAY, UNTIL THE SOUND OF IT BROUGHT HIM GREAT JOY.
AND, UNBE-KNOWNST TO HIM, BROUGHT JOY TO THOSE OTHERS WHO GATHERED AT A SAFE, HIDDEN DISTANCE TO HEAR HIM PLAY.
FUR FLOWER THOUGHT HE WAS SURE TO BRING HIS FAMILY JOY WITH HIS NEW GIFT.
HE WAS MISTAKEN.
THE FLUTE WAS THROWN INTO THE COOKING FIRE FOR KINDLING.
AND THE BOY WAS SENT TO BED HUNGRY TO LEARN THE WORTHLESSNESS OF PIPING.

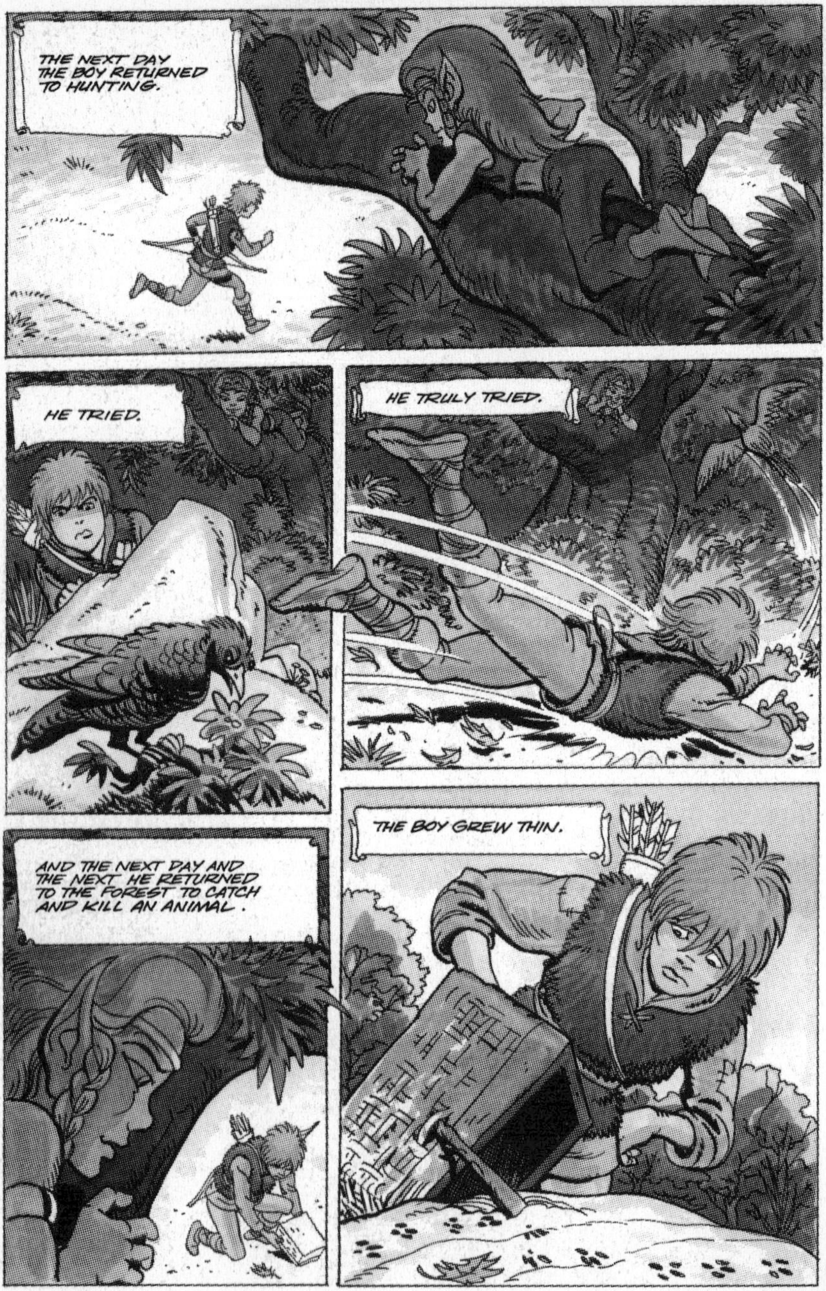
THE NEXT DAY THE BOY RETURNED TO HUNTING.
HE TRIED.
HE TRULY TRIED.
AND THE NEXT DAY AND THE NEXT HE RETURNED TO THE FOREST TO CATCH AND KILL AN ANIMAL.
THE BOY GREW THIN.

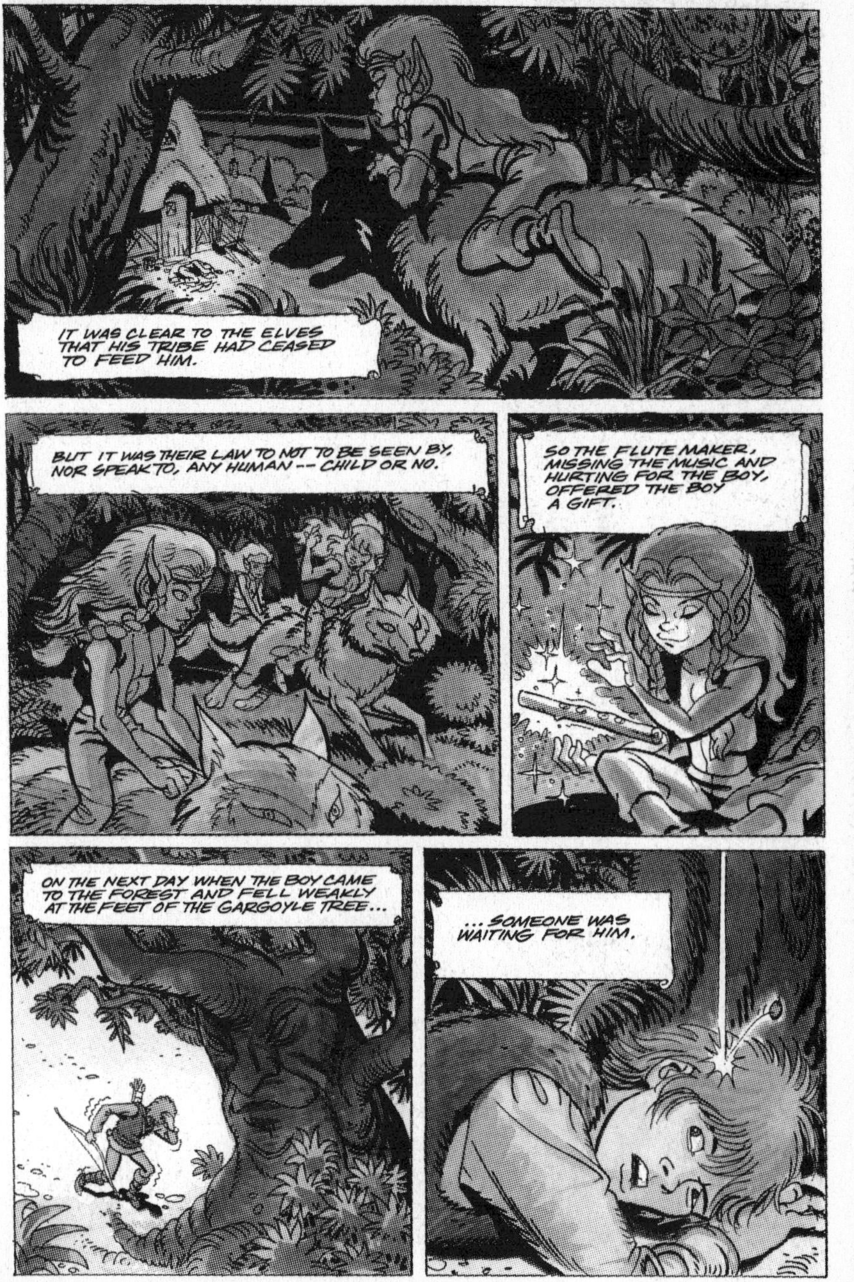
IT WAS CLEAR TO THE ELVES THAT HIS TRIBE HAD CEASED TO FEED HIM.
BUT IT WAS THEIR LAW TO NOT TO BE SEEN BY, NOR SPEAK TO, ANY HUMAN -- CHILD OR NO.
SO THE FLUTE MAKER, MISSING THE MUSIC AND HURTING FOR THE BOY, OFFERED THE BOY A GIFT.
ON THE NEXT DAY WHEN THE BOY CAME TO THE FOREST AND FELL WEAKLY AT THE FEET OF THE GARGOYLE TREE...
...SOMEONE WAS WAITING FOR HIM.

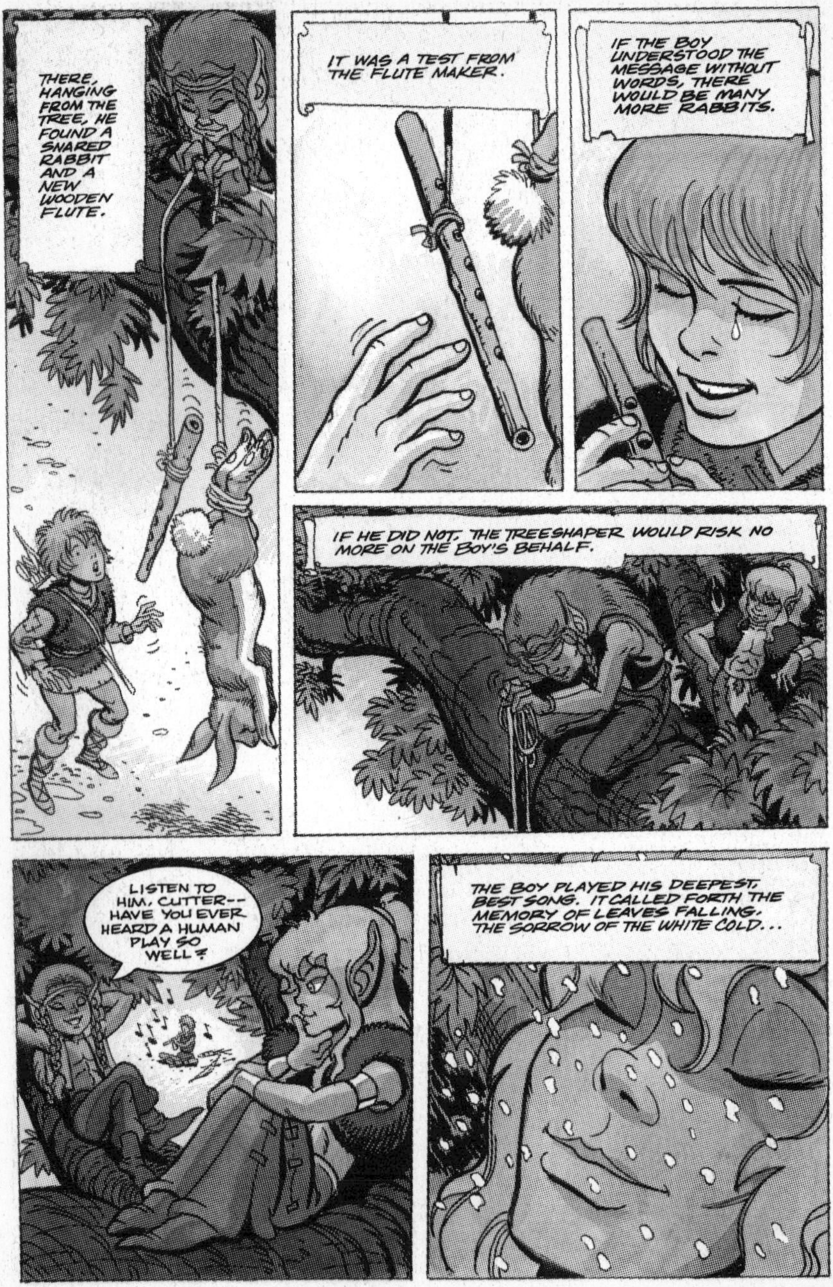
THERE, HANGING FROM THE TREE, HE FOUND A SNARED RABBIT AND A NEW WOODEN FLUTE.
IT WAS A TEST FROM THE FLUTE MAKER.
IF THE BOY UNDERSTOOD THE MESSAGE WITHOUT WORDS, THERE WOULD BE MANY MORE RABBITS.
IF HE DID NOT, THE TREESHAPER WOULD RISK NO MORE ON THE BOY'S BEHALF.
LISTEN TO HIM, CUTTER-- HAVE YOU EVER HEARD A HUMAN PLAY SO WELL?
THE BOY PLAYED HIS DEEPEST, BEST SONG. IT CALLED FORTH THE MEMORY OF LEAVES FALLING. THE SORROW OF THE WHITE COLD...

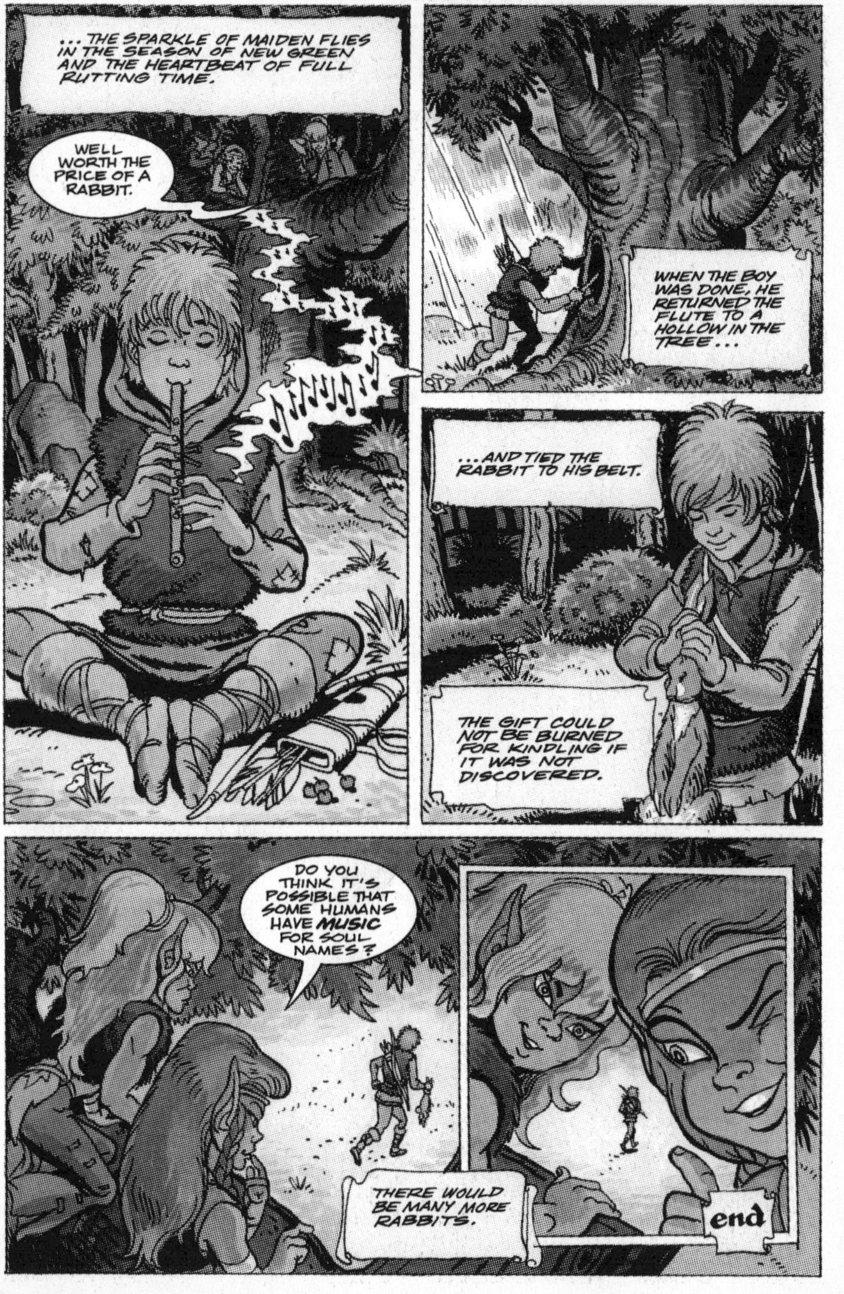

... THE SPARKLE OF MAIDEN FLIES IN THE SEASON OF NEW GREEN AND THE HEARTBEAT OF FULL RUTTING TIME.
WELL WORTH THE PRICE OF A RABBIT.
WHEN THE BOY WAS DONE, HE RETURNED THE FLUTE TO A HOLLOW IN THE TREE...
...AND TIED THE RABBIT TO HIS BELT.
THE GIFT COULD NOT BE BURNED FOR KINDLING IF IT WAS NOT DISCOVERED.
DO YOU THINK IT'S POSSIBLE THAT SOME HUMANS HAVE MUSIC FOR SOUL NAMES?
THERE WOULD BE MANY MORE RABBITS.
end

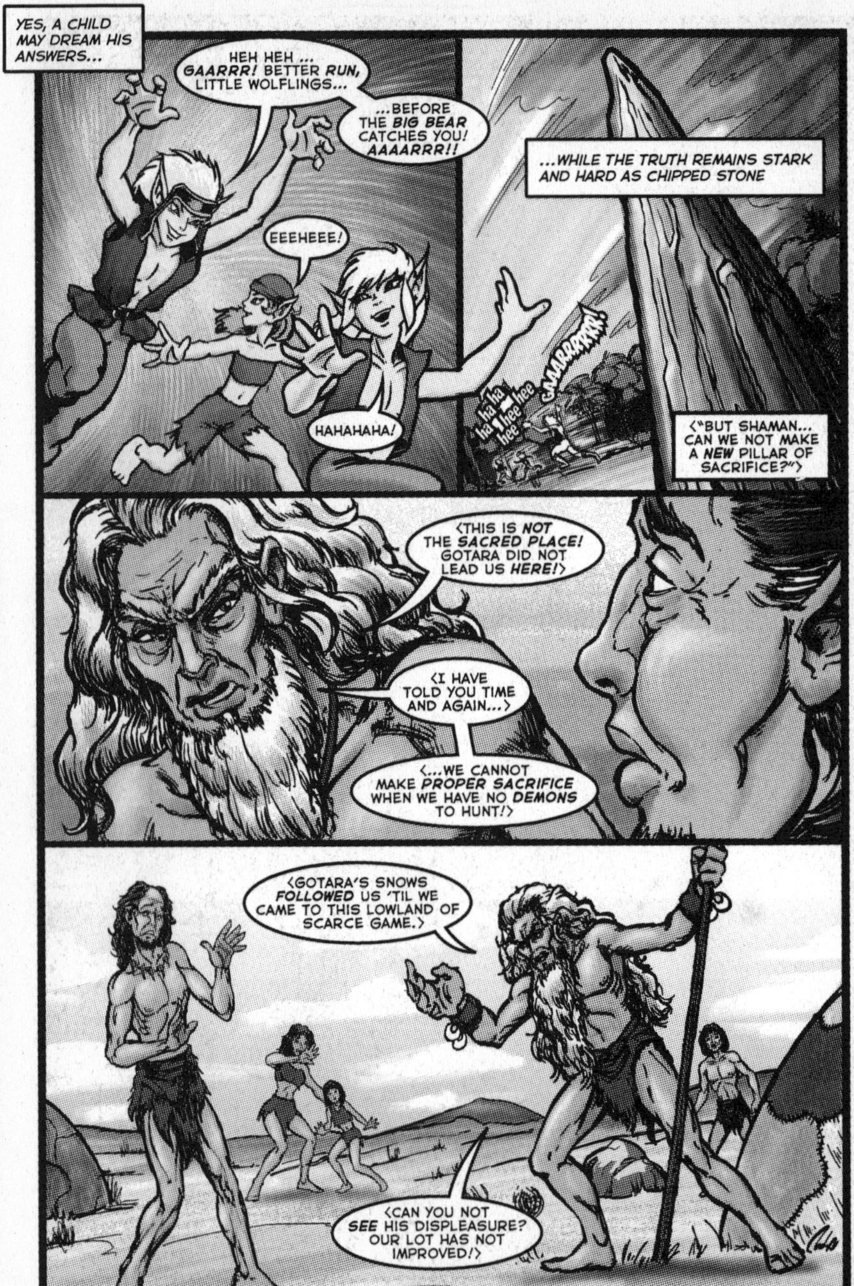
YES, A CHILD MAY DREAM HIS ANSWERS...
HEH HEH ... GAARRR! BETTER RUN, LITTLE WOLFLINGS...
...BEFORE THE BIG BEAR CATCHES YOU! AAAARRR!!
EEEHEEE!
HAHAHAHA!
...WHILE THE TRUTH REMAINS STARK AND HARD AS CHIPPED STONE
ha ha ha hee hee hee
GAAARRRRRR!
<"BUT SHAMAN... CAN WE NOT MAKE A NEW PILLAR OF SACRIFICE?">
<THIS IS NOT THE SACRED PLACE! GOTARA DID NOT LEAD US HERE!>
<I HAVE TOLD YOU TIME AND AGAIN...>
<...WE CANNOT MAKE PROPER SACRIFICE WHEN WE HAVE NO DEMONS TO HUNT!>
<GOTARA'S SNOWS FOLLOWED US 'TIL WE CAME TO THIS LOWLAND OF SCARCE GAME.>
<CAN YOU NOT SEE HIS DISPLEASURE? OUR LOT HAS NOT IMPROVED!>

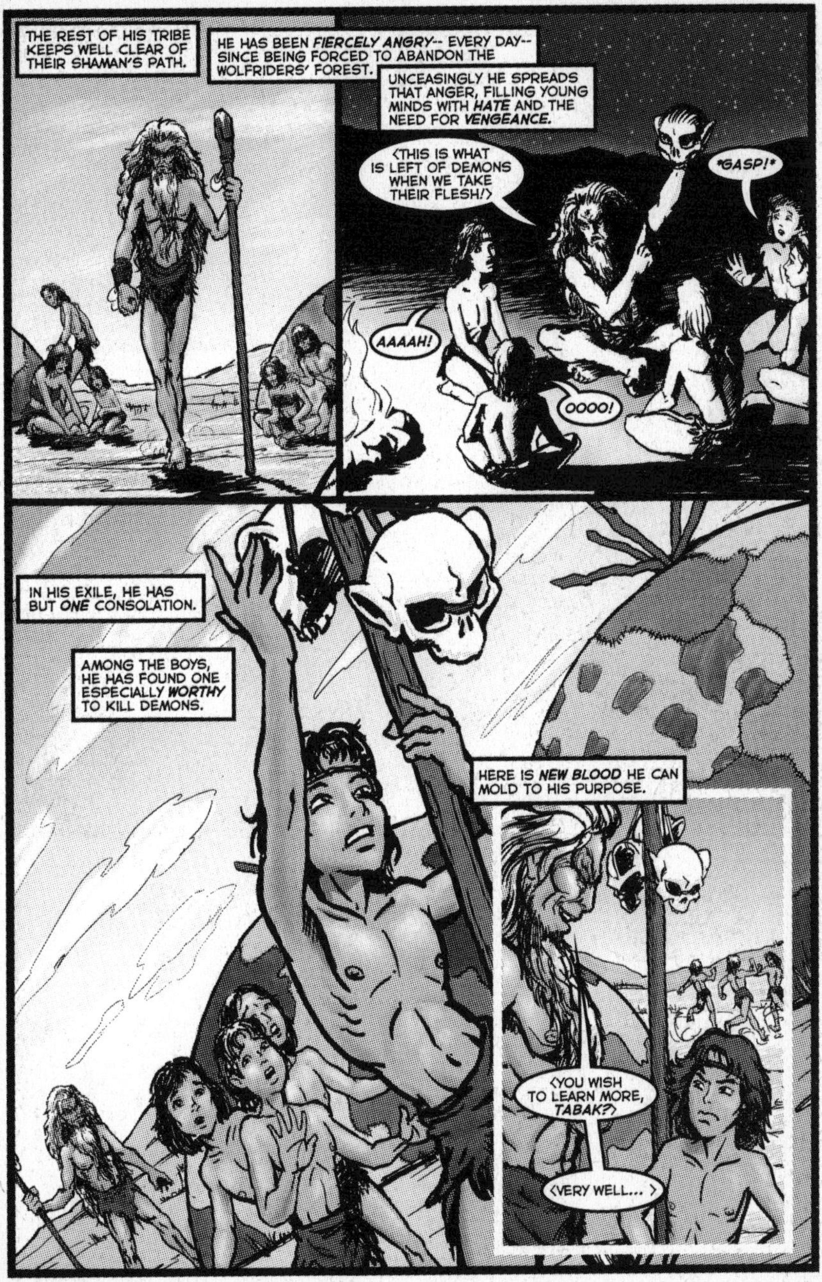
THE REST OF HIS TRIBE KEEPS WELL CLEAR OF THEIR SHAMAN'S PATH.
HE HAS BEEN FIERCELY ANGRY-- EVERY DAY-- SINCE BEING FORCED TO ABANDON THE WOLFRIDERS' FOREST.
UNCEASINGLY HE SPREADS THAT ANGER, FILLING YOUNG MINDS WITH HATE AND THE NEED FOR VENGEANCE.
<THIS IS WHAT IS LEFT OF DEMONS WHEN WE TAKE THEIR FLESH!>
GASP!
AAAAH!
OOOO!
IN HIS EXILE, HE HAS BUT ONE CONSOLATION.
AMONG THE BOYS, HE HAS FOUND ONE ESPECIALLY WORTHY TO KILL DEMONS.
HERE IS NEW BLOOD HE CAN MOLD TO HIS PURPOSE.
<YOU WISH TO LEARN MORE, TABAK?>
<VERY WELL... >

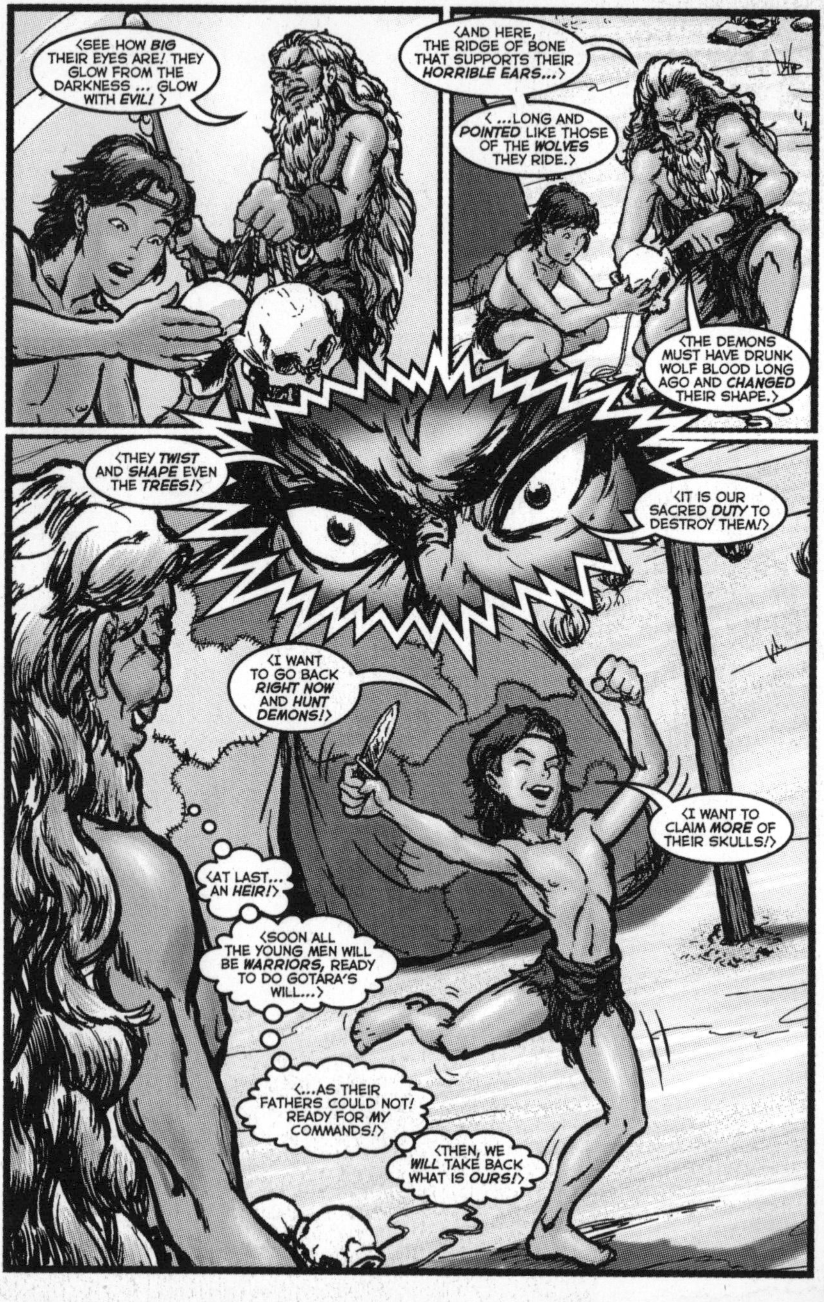
<SEE HOW BIG THEIR EYES ARE! THEY GLOW FROM THE DARKNESS ... GLOW WITH EVIL! >
<AND HERE, THE RIDGE OF BONE THAT SUPPORTS THEIR HORRIBLE EARS...>
< ...LONG AND POINTED LIKE THOSE OF THE WOLVES THEY RIDE.>
<THE DEMONS MUST HAVE DRUNK WOLF BLOOD LONG AGO AND CHANGED THEIR SHAPE.>
<THEY TWIST AND SHAPE EVEN THE TREES!>
<IT IS OUR SACRED DUTY TO DESTROY THEM!>
<I WANT TO GO BACK RIGHT NOW AND HUNT DEMONS!>
<I WANT TO CLAIM MORE OF THEIR SKULLS!>
<AT LAST... AN HEIR!>
<SOON ALL THE YOUNG MEN WILL BE WARRIORS, READY TO DO GOTARA'S WILL...>
<...AS THEIR FATHERS COULD NOT! READY FOR MY COMMANDS!>
<THEN, WE WILL TAKE BACK WHAT IS OURS!>

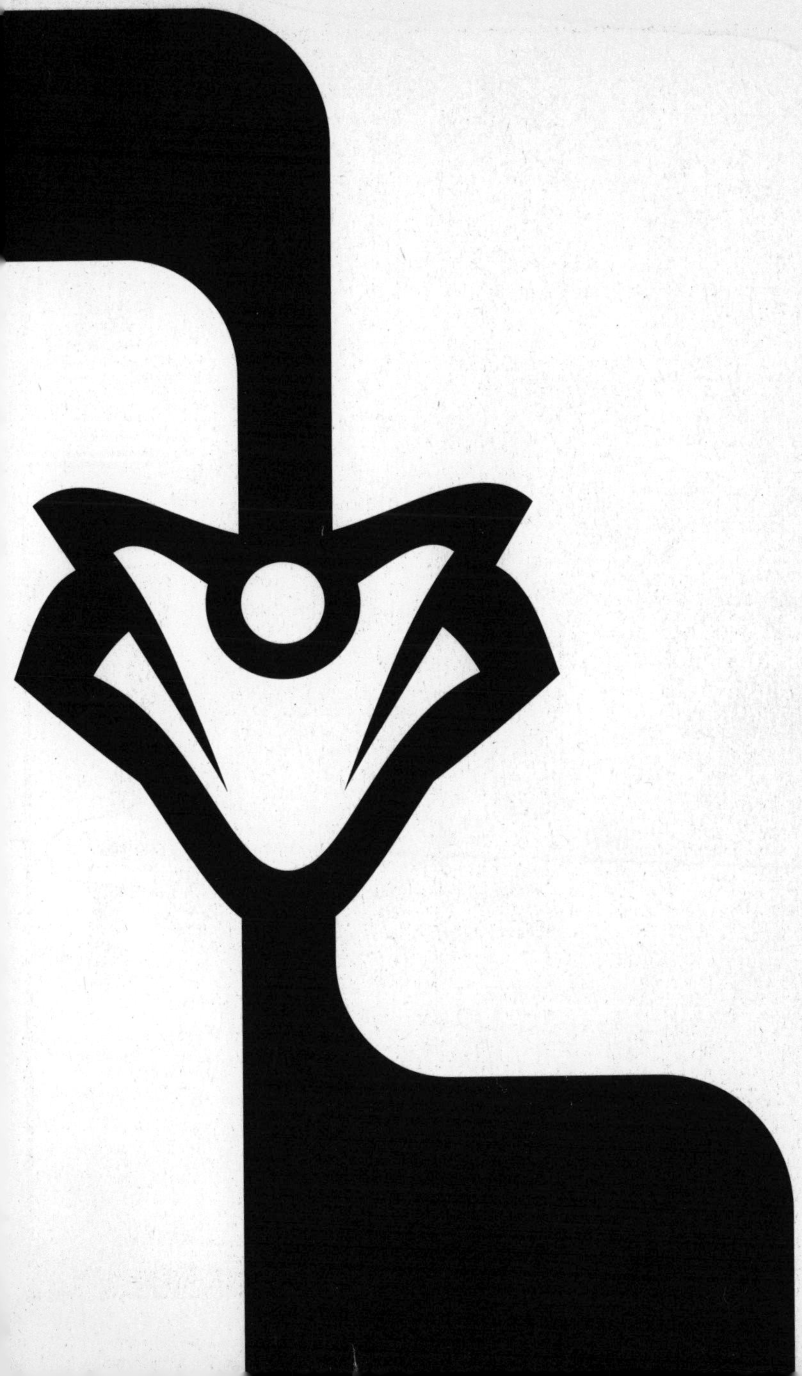

IN VOLUME

2

BEARCLAW
LAYS HIS LIFE
ON THE LINE
TO END THE
HUMANS'
THREAT TO
THE HOLT!

CUTTER'S
HONOR IS
TESTED AS
HE ENDURES
A YEAR'S
CONFINEMENT
WITH THE TROLLS!

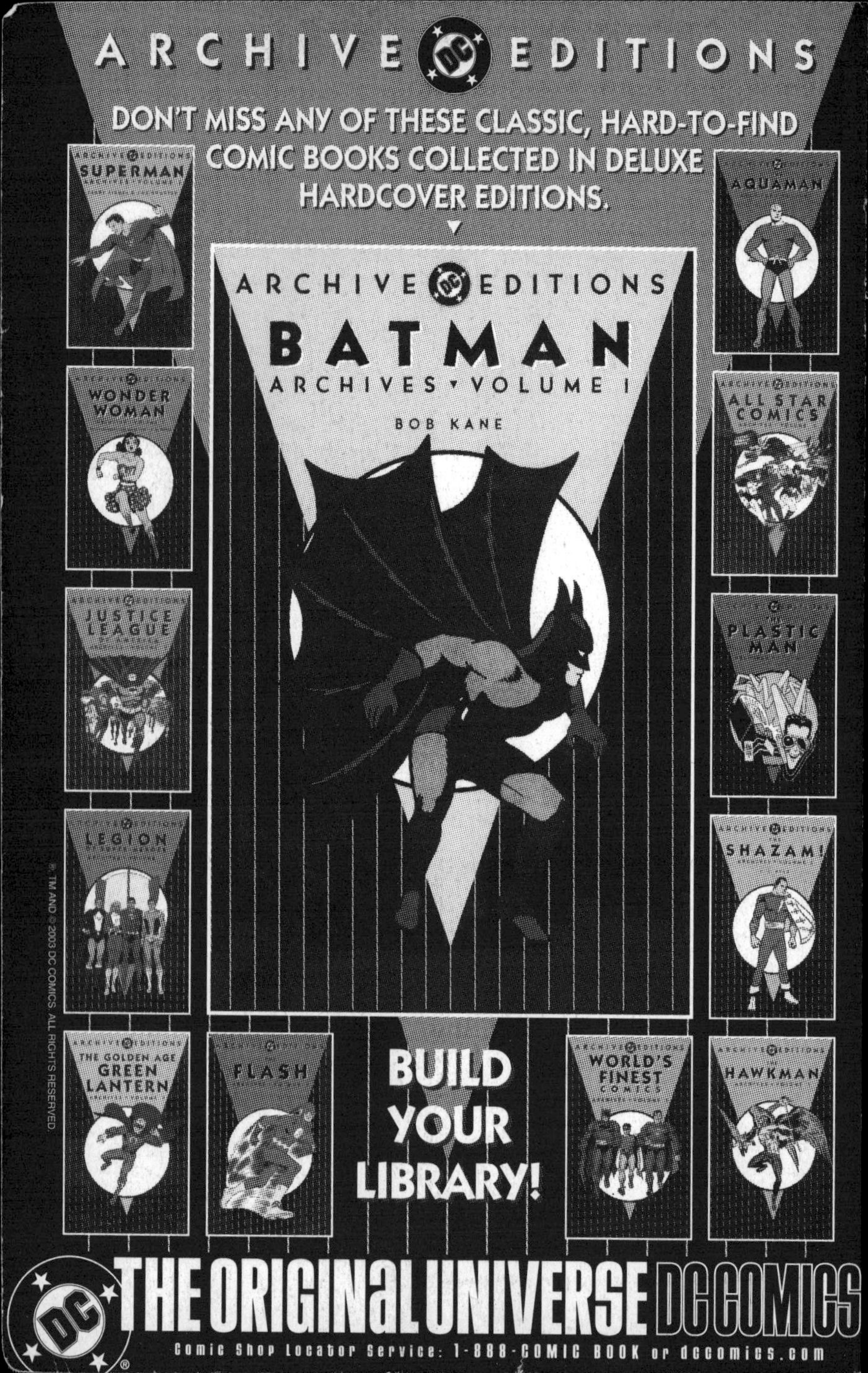
ARCHIVE DC EDITIONS
DON'T MISS ANY OF THESE CLASSIC, HARD-TO-FIND COMIC BOOKS COLLECTED IN DELUXE HARDCOVER EDITIONS.
SUPERMAN
WONDER WOMAN
JUSTICE LEAGUE
LEGION
AQUAMAN
ALL STAR COMICS
PLASTIC MAN
SHAZAM!
ARCHIVE EDITIONS
BATMAN
ARCHIVES • VOLUME 1
BOB KANE
THE GOLDEN AGE GREEN LANTERN
FLASH
BUILD YOUR LIBRARY!
WORLD'S FINEST COMICS
HAWKMAN
®, TM AND © 2003 DC COMICS. ALL RIGHTS RESERVED.
THE ORIGINAL UNIVERSE DC COMICS
Comic Shop Locator Service: 1-888-COMIC BOOK or dccomics.com